Barriers to Full Employment

Papers from a conference sponsored by the Labour Market Policy Section of the International Institute of Management of the Wissenschafts-zentrum of Berlin

Edited by
J. A. KREGEL
Professor of Economics
The Johns Hopkins University, Bologna Center, Italy

EGON MATZNER
Professor of Public Economics
Technical University of Vienna
Director, The Labour Market Policy Section
International Institute of Management, Berlin

ALESSANDRO RONCAGLIA
Professor of Economics
University of Rome

St. Martin's Press   New York

© Wissenschaftszentrum Berlin, Internationales Institut für
Management und Verwaltung: Arbeitsmarktpolitik 1988

All rights reserved. For information, write:
Scholarly and Reference Division,
St. Martin's Press, Inc., 175 Fifth Avenue, New York, NY 10010

First published in the United States of America in 1988

Printed in Hong Kong

ISBN 0–312–01628–X

Library of Congress Cataloguing-in-Publication Data
Barriers to full employment.
Bibliography: p.
Includes index.
1. Full employment policies—Mathematical models.
2. Labor supply—Mathematical models.   3. Fiscal
policy—Mathematical models.   I. Kregel, J. A.
II. Matzner, Egon, 1938– .   III. Roncaglia,
Alessandro, 1947–
HD5701.6.B37 1988   339.5   87-28637
ISBN 0–312–01628–X

Contents

List of the Participants	vii
Introduction	1

PART I THEORETICAL BARRIERS TO FULL EMPLOYMENT

1 Wage Costs and Employment: The Sraffian View
  Alessandro Roncaglia — 9
  Comment *Johannes Schneider* — 24

2 The Theory of Demand and Supply of Labour: The Post-Keynesian View
  J. A. Kregel — 27
  Comment *R. A. Hart* — 43

3 New Information Theoretic Approaches to Labour Market Theory
  Erich Streissler — 48
  Comment *Kurt Rothschild* — 66

PART II FINANCIAL MARKETS AND FISCAL POLICY

4 Financial Markets, Investment and Employment
  Paul Davidson — 73
  Comments *Salvatore Biasco, Malcolm C. Sawyer* — 93

5 Fiscal and Monetary Policy in the Keynes–Kalecki Tradition
  Alois Guger and *Ewald Walterskirchen* — 103
  Comment *Bertil Holmlund, H.-Peter Spahn* — 133

PART III PUBLIC LABOUR MARKET POLICY

6 The Role of Manpower Policy in the Swedish Model
  Rudolf Meidner — 143
  Comment *William R. Dymond, Günther Schmid* — 162

PART IV WELFARE STATE REGULATIONS, INDUSTRIAL RELATIONS, TECHNOLOGY AND THE ENVIRONMENT

7 The Welfare State and Jobs
  Robert Delorme   177
  Comment   *Meinhard Miegel, Christopher Büchtemann and Georg Voruba*   204

8 Industrial Relations and Unemployment: The Case for Flexible Corporatism
  David Soskice   212
  Comment   *Wolfgang Streeck*   227

9 New Technologies and Employment in the 1980s: From Science and Technology to Macroeconomic Modelling
  Robert Boyer   233
  Comment   *Arndt Sorge*   269

10 Environment Problems and Employment Opportunities
   Bertram Schefold   273
   Comment   *Peter Nijkamp, Klaus Zimmermann*   288

PART V THE INTERPLAY BETWEEN ECONOMIC AND INSTITUTIONAL FACTORS

11 The Interplay Between Institutional and Material Factors
   N. Georgescu-Roegen   297
   Comment   *Fritz W. Scharpf, Michele Salvati*   327

PART VI A SUMMING UP AND CONCLUSIONS

12 New Lines of Research on the Question of Full Employment
   Josef Steindl   343

Index   351

List of the Participants

S. Biasco, University of Rome

R. A. Boyer, CEPREMAP, Paris

C. Büchtemann, International Institute of Management, Wissenschaftszentrum Berlin

P. Davidson, editor, *Journal of Post Keynesian Economics*, University of Tennessee, Knoxville, USA

R. Delorme, University of Lille and CEPREMAP, Paris

W. R. Dymond, OECD, Paris

N. Georgescu-Roegen, Vanderbilt University, Nashville, Tennessee, USA

A. Guger, Austrian Institute for Economic Research, Vienna

R. A. Hart, International Institute of Management, Wissenschaftszentrum Berlin

B. Holmlund, Stockholm

G. Klepper, Institute for World Economics, Kiel

J. A. Kregel, Johns Hopkins University, Bologna Center, Italy

E. Matzner, Technical University of Vienna, Director Labour Market Policy, International Institute of Managment, Wissenschaftszentrum Berlin

R. Meidner, Centre for Working Life, Stockholm

M. Miegel, Institute of Economic and Social Policy, Bonn

P. Nijkamp, Free University of Amsterdam

A. Roncaglia, University of Rome

K. W. Rothschild, University of Linz and Austrian Institute for Economic Research, Vienna

M. Salvati, University of Milan

M. C. Sawyer, University of York, UK

List of the Participants

F. W. Scharpf, International Institute of Management, Wissenschaftszentrum Berlin

B. Schefold, University of Frankfurt on Main

G. Schmid, Free University of Berlin and International Institute of Management, Wissenschaftszentrum Berlin

J. Schneider, University of Regensburg

A. Sorge, International Institute of Management, Wissenschaftszentrum Berlin

D. Soskice, University College, Oxford

H.-P. Spahn, Free University of Berlin, and International Institute of Management, Wissenschaftszentrum Berlin

J. Steindl, University of Vienna and Austrian Institute for Economic Research

W. Streeck, International Institute of Management, Wissenschaftszentrum Berlin

E. Streissler, University of Vienna

G. Voruba, International Institute of Management, Wissenschaftszentrum Berlin

E. Walterskirchen, Austrian Institute for Economic Research, Vienna

K. Zimmermann, University of the Federal Armed Services, Hamburg and International Institute for Environmental Policy, Wissenschaftszentrum Berlin

Introduction

By the middle of the 1980s the world's industrialised economies were entering their second decade of stagnant growth and persistent mass unemployment. Indeed, in some countries unemployment was still on the increase. Only the extended depression in Europe which occurred during the Great Slump of the inter-war period provides a parallel to contemporary experience. Neither neo-conservative policies, which eventually replaced traditional Keynesian remedies, nor attempts to redefine the measure of the number seeking employment, have succeeded in halting the inexorable increase in the unemployment statistics. Given the duration and extensiveness of the phenomenon, the stigma of failure to deal with unemployment has touched governments of all political extractions from conservative to liberal to social-democratic. Experience of the past decade has so dampened politicians' and economists' beliefs in their ability to deal with the problem that the emphasis of policy now seems to be on ways to adapt to conditions of massive unemployment on a long-term basis, rather than a concerted search for permanent remedies for the phenomenon. The 'post-industrial' society seems to have become a euphemism for a society which is no longer able to provide work for all those seeking gainful employment.

The contemporary experience thus suggests that new perspectives and points of view on the unemployment problem are required. It was to this end that a group of social scientists met in Berlin in October of 1985 under the auspices of the International Institute of Management's Labour Market Policy section. This book, the outcome of those discussions, seeks to make a small contribution to initiating new lines of thinking by identifying and discussing the various factors which act to impede higher levels of employment in industrialised countries. Although the contributors have concentrated on economic aspects, their analysis points up the central role played by political, sociological and institutional factors in the existing barriers to full employment, and thus in any proposals for new ways to achieve full employment.

To give order to the discussions, however, the book starts by questioning the analytical framework which is implicitly adopted by most economists and politicians in thinking about the problem of unemployment. The first and most important barrier to new views about the problem of employment may indeed be constituted by theoretical barriers, by the implicit use of theories which limit or even eliminate alternative lines of investigation. Since the shortcomings of theories are best seen when criticised from the point of view of a competing theory, Part I, dealing with the 'Theoretical Barriers' to full employment presents three alternative approaches to the conception of the demand and supply of labour. Alessandro Roncaglia writes from the perspective of the criticism of the traditional theory of value, based on the work of Piero Sraffa, suggesting how it may be employed to provide a framework for the positive analysis of the problem of employment. On the other hand, J. A. Kregel looks back to some basic propositions of Keynes' analysis of employment which have become neglected in recent times. He bases his alternative on the writings of Keynes and the post-Keynesians, in particular Sidney Weintraub. Erich Streissler critically surveys the most modern of the attempts by traditional theory to deal more directly with the problem of unemployment in order to determine whether or not they present true alternatives to standard policy prescriptions.

Part I thus seeks not only to provide criticism of the existing theoretical schemes used to analyse employment problems, but also to suggest alternative frameworks. The papers presented suggest that useful insight into the construction of alternatives is to be found in a reconsideration of the works of Classical economists such as Smith, and modern economists such as Keynes, Kalecki and Schumpeter. In addition, a number of the technical tools which have emerged from the Walrasian and Marshallian traditions (e.g. linear programming or the notion of elasticity) may be of use if they are removed from the implicit theoretical presumptions that unemployment could not permanently exist, and are reinterpreted with respect to the real world in which we live. As Streissler, and his discussant, Kurt Rothschild, demonstrate, some new insights can even be harvested from the modern attempts of traditional theorists, but they are most fruitfully applied only by removing them from the neo-classical framework. On the other hand, J. Schneider's comment on Roncaglia's paper represents the traditional position that theory could not present a barrier, at least not general equilibrium theory, which he presents as all encompassing and without limits in terms of the problems that it can solve. R. Hart's comment on Kregel's presentation of the post-Keynesian position accepts the validity of the fallacy of composition, and thus the necessity of an explanation of the aggregate level of activity, but none the less makes a plea for the importance of purely microeconomic analysis of the labour market. These various positions well represent the difficulty the existence of theoretical barriers presents to new approaches to full employment.

Since any policy proposal rests implicitly or explicitly on some basic theoretical propositions concerning the behaviour of the variables that it seeks to influence, policies must be judged not only in terms of results, but also in terms of theoretical coherence. Thus the majority of the policies that have been applied in the 1970s and 1980s have not only failed in application, they demonstrate serious theoretical insufficiencies. This does not, however, imply that the correct course would be simply to return to the policies applied in the 1950s and 1960s, the so-called 'Golden Age' of fine-tuning demand management. These policies, irrespective of how successful they may have been, left a legacy which paved the way for the resurgence of restrictive policy in the monetarist counter-revolution. Even more importantly, the economic system has undergone substantial change since that period, with the fall of the Bretton Woods-based international monetary system, the political and economic effects of the oil shock, the emergence of environmental issues, and the initiation of a new epoch of technological change.

One of the areas which has been most changed since the 1950s is the monetary and financial system. Part II seeks to emphasise the importance of monetary and fiscal factors, but from the point of view of the international linkages between financial markets and the inter-relationships between fiscal and monetary actions. Paul Davidson outlines the ways in which financial factors may hinder the full employment goal, stressing that a correct understanding of the operation of financial markets will be a necessary prerequisite to any discussion of policy. While in basic agreement with Davidson's account, in his discussion Salvatore Biasco calls attention to the need to recognise the importance of differences in the institutional structures in different countries. Malcolm Sawyer, on the other hand, questions the ability of government to carry out the tasks which will be required even when the proper understanding of financial markets has been achieved.

The experiences of Austro-Keynesianism dominates Alois Guger and Ewald Walterskirchen's assessment of the theory and practical operation of fiscal and monetary policy in support of the objective of full employment. H.-P. Spahn extends this assessment to the wider international context of monetary and financial policy, while B. Holmlund draws attention to statistical studies which seem to suggest that the Austrian performance is unique.

The role of government is not limited to the use of the traditional macroeconomic variables, but is often a direct participant in the labour market. In Part III Rudolf Meidner deals with the experience of one country which consciously uses its presence in the labour market as a policy to combat unemployment: Sweden. Although the discussion of both W. R. Dymond and G. Schmid expressed appreciation for the way Swedish policy had coped with employment problems in the past, a certain scepticism was expressed about its usefulness as a guide for new approaches in current conditions.

Part IV seeks to assess two interrelated factors which characterised the 1950s and 1960s, with Robert Delorme dealing with the relation between the rise of the European Welfare State and employment, and David Soskice the impact of industrial relations. The impact of technology has been an ever-present culprit in periods of prolonged unemployment: Robert Boyer seeks to find the balance of its contribution, while Bertram Schefold raises the problem of the impact of technology on the environment and the relation between the defence of the environment and the defence of employment. As might have been expected this section produced discussion by Büchtemann and Voruba and Miegel of the appropriate definition of the Welfare State, while Streeck emphasised the necessity of recognising the importance of the expression of political will in the decisions to expand the scope of State provision in the economy. A. Sorge drew attention to the relation between changes in total output and changes in output per man and the importance of policies to assure that the former at least kept up with the latter. K. Zimmerman singled out one of the possible future 'styles' or scenarios presented by Schefold and criticised it as limiting the individual initiative necessary for the operation of a Capitalist economy, while Nijkamp referred to the extensive Dutch experience in the area of the analysis of environmental problems.

One of the fundamental aspects of evaluating past economic policy in order to formulate better and more applicable policies is the recognition of the way that policy itself brings about changes in the economy which it attempts to influence. Professor Georgescu-Roegen provides a view of the interplay of economic policy and institutional factors in the search for the barrier to full employment. F. W. Scharpf and M. Salvati deal with particular issues from this wide-ranging paper which represents, as Salvati suggests, a lifetime of reflection on this contested topic. These comments bring together the role of political, sociological and institutional factors which had been evoked in the discussions of the earlier papers.

The outcome of this discussion is that reconstruction of a new policy approach must thus take full account of the changes in social and political conditions as well as working out a more solid theoretical foundation. This is why sound theorising must also be done with reference to the practical and actual, with direct relevance to what is happening in the real world. Thus the point of view adopted here is that it would be inappropriate to think of two distinct and separate levels of analysis, one theoretical and abstract, the other applied and practical; rather there are any number of different levels, all of which contribute to an adequate comprehension of economic phenomena.

It would be impractical to give a summary of all the various factors; Josef Steindl provides a personal assessment, based on a lifetime of experience no less rich than Georgescu-Roegen's, of the most important issues to emerge from the papers and the discussions. The outcome suggests that the problem is much more multi-faceted than has often been recognised and that each of the various facets may require different analytical tools and the aid of diverse disciplines. This later point perhaps deserves further stress. While economic analysis must be seen as a necessary condition for any explanation of unemployment, and thus for any policy proposals to eliminate it, economic analysis cannot be been as a sufficient condition to this result. What is required in addition is the consideration of political, social, institutional and technological elements. This suggests the need for interdisciplinary enquiries, a number of which are evoked in the papers included here. The book none the less concentrates on the economic aspects in the hope that it can aid in the formulation of perspectives from which economists can fruitfully contribute to interdisciplinary research projects designed to investigate the problems of employment in the 1980s. Indeed, the purpose of the Conference was to generate such proposals for investigation by the Labour Market Policy section of the Institute.

Part I
Theoretical Barriers to Full Employment

Part I
Theoretical Barriers to Full Employment

1 Wage Costs and Employment: the Sraffian View

Alessandro Roncaglia*

INTRODUCTION

Few would contest 'the lack of scientific agreement on the causes of mass unemployment and on the effectiveness of conventional employment and labour market policy'. (IIM/LMP, 1984). The theoretical debate thus acquires immediate practical relevance, since 'the contradictions between scientific analyses correspond to the controversy about which economic strategies would be suitable for eliminating high unemployment'.

In considering some aspects of this debate from a Sraffian point of view, we will proceed as follows. Section 2 considers the traditional views of market economies as ensuring an optimal utilisation of productive resources, including labour; and the analytical foundation of these views, the inverse wage-employment relationship. Section 3 recalls the Sraffian criticism of such a relationship. Section 4 shows that the traditional inverse relationship between real wages and employment cannot find a 'modern' rehabilitation in the full-cost pricing behaviour of oligopolistic firms. Section 5 discusses the shift in the research programme of economic science proposed by Sraffa, implying a different (i.e. Classical) perspective for the analysis of employment. On this basis, section 6 discusses the relationship between 'Keynesian' and 'Classical' unemployment; and finally section 7 discusses, in this perspective, the complexity of the wage–employment relationship.

---

*Thanks for useful comments and suggestions on a previous draft (without implication) are due to M. Corsi, J. Kregel, G. Rodano, P. Sylos Labini, M. Tonveronachi.

THE TRADITIONAL VIEWS AND THE INVERSE WAGE-EMPLOYMENT RELATIONSHIP

The theoretical clash referred to above is a complex one, since there are many contending approaches. However some simplificatory grouping of different theories is possible. In fact, a large majority of 'mainstream' theories – neo-classical synthesis or 'bastard' Keynesianism, New Classical Macroeconomics or Monetarism – rely on a common basis, namely the idea rooted in the century-old marginalist tradition that market equilibrium is determined by the forces of supply and demand, for labour as for any other commodity. Within this group of theories, differences mainly concern the strength of market mechanisms in pushing the economy to full employment equilibrium.[1]

Thus many mainstream economists recommend active fiscal and/or monetary policies in order to overcome real-world frictions and rigidities or reinforce the equilibrium tendency of the market. For instance, the liquidity trap or downward money-wage rate rigidity are both classified as market imperfections which hinder the automatic tendency towards full employment equilibrium. Other economists defend a laissez-faire attitude by finding additional ways (such as the Pigou effect) to strengthen the market mechanisms which push the economy to its full-employment equilibrium position. Analogously, short-run cyclical fluctuations in income and employment attributed to monetary disturbances are easily reconciled with a long-run equilibrium determined by 'real' factors alone. More recently, the so-called New Classical School utilises the rational expectations assumption to suggest that any deviations from 'natural' values (i.e. full employment) must be temporary and can only be caused by unforeseen policy decisions or supply shocks.

In fact, underlying a wide spectrum of policy attitudes, from interventionism to liberalism, all theories stemming from the marginalist tradition display a basic common belief, according to which the long-run employment equilibrium is determined by the intersection of the schedule of labour supply (which is in general a non-negative function of the wage rate) with the schedule representing the demand for labour, derived from the principle of profit maximisation applied to the production function. The postulate of decreasing marginal productivity, applied to labour as to any other factor of production, implies that the demand for labour be a negative function of the wage rate. This is a necessary condition for the stability of full employment equilibrium under competitive conditions. Now, it is precisely this basic presupposition of the marginalist tradition that both Sraffa and Keynes chose to attack, though in different ways.

I will not consider here the hotly debated issue (see, for instance, the papers in Kregel, 1983) concerning the relative relevance of the criticisms levelled by Keynes and by Sraffa against the traditional marginalist belief in a supply-and-demand mechanism for the determination of employment levels, implying an inverse relationship between real wage rates and employment. In short, let me recall that Keynes stresses the role of uncertainty in monetary production economies by opposing his notion of effective demand, based on the interdependence of the demand for labour and the demand for output based on entrepreneurs' expectations, to the traditional notion of the schedule of demand for labour based on the postulate of decreasing marginal productivity of labour which is independent of aggregate expenditure; and by opposing his notion of the rate of interest based on liquidity preference to the traditional notion of the rate of interest as the 'price' of capital as a 'factor of production', namely a price which in equilibrium was assumed to ensure the balancing of supply for, and demand of, loanable funds.[2] As we will better see in the next section, Sraffa in turn paves the way for a crucial logical criticism of a theorem which is central to the marginalist tradition: the theorem according to which a fall in real wage rates provoked by an excess supply of labour reduces the capital–labour ratio sufficiently to provide employment for the unemployed with a given amount of capital. Both Sraffa and Keynes thus highlight the need to substitute employment theories stemming from the marginalist tradition with a new approach, different in its basic theoretical underpinnings from the traditional one, and open to recognising the fact that unemployment may turn out to be a persistent feature of market economies.

THE SRAFFIAN CRITIQUE OF THE INVERSE WAGE-EMPLOYMENT RELATIONSHIP

The capital theory debates stemming from Sraffa's 1960 book, *Production of Commodities by Means of Commodities*, centre on the traditional marginalist conception of the economy, according to which society is endowed with given amounts of the basic productive resources (which may be reduced to the trinity: labour, land and capital), and according to which a competitive market economy is capable of ensuring the full utilisation of the scarce resources. The market mechanisms mainly consist in changes in the 'prices' of productive resources (namely, in the case of capital and labour, changes in wage rates and interest rates), such as to ensure in all markets – including the markets for productive resources – the equality between supply and demand, and thus full employment in the case of labour.

The critiques stemming from Sraffa's analysis directly concern the traditional notion of capital as a scarce factor of production, and the corresponding notion of the interest rate as the price for the use of this scarce factor of production (price in the traditional marginalist meaning of index of scarcity for the commodity being considered).

Sraffa's analysis points to the fact that the term 'capital' does not refer to a specific commodity, but to the value of a set of different commodities which are utilised as means of production and which are themselves produced. The value of capital can thus change, either because of changes in the quantities of the various commodities used as means of production, or because of changes in their prices. Sraffa shows that a change in the interest rate (in Sraffa's own terms, in the rate of profits), barring some awkward exceptions, provokes changes in the relative prices of the various commodities, so that the value of capital changes as well, in a way which is not liable to simple and univocal laws. It is possible, for instance, that when the profit rate rises, the 'quantity of capital' utilised in the economy rises as well (while the physical quantities of the various means of production remain unchanged): which is the exact opposite of what should happen in the traditional marginalist theory which predicts that an increase in the price of any commodity should provoke a fall in the demand for it. Even more importantly, it is also possible that a fall in the real wage-rate (and a rise in the rate of profits), affects the relative prices of the various means of production in such a way that the utilisation of production techniques employing more machines and less labour becomes more profitable. Again, this is exactly the opposite of what one expects in traditional marginalist theories where a fall in real wage-rates caused by unemployment should provoke a shift from the use of 'capital' to the use of labour.

These phenomena were already recognised by some authors within the marginalist tradition, but their relevance and their implications were not fully recognised until after Sraffa's contribution and the capital theory debates of the 1960s.[3] The possibility of such phenomena shows that the traditional market mechanisms ensuring an automatic tendency to full employment (namely the downward pressure of a fall in real wages induced by unemployment on the capital–labour ratio) are without theoretical foundations.[4]

FULL COST PRICING AND THE WAGE-EMPLOYMENT RELATIONSHIP

In this section we will consider an attempt to rehabilitate the inverse relationship between real wage-rates and employment by reference to firms' pricing behaviour.[5]

The archetype of this approach may be found in Modigliani's (1963) reference to 'modern' oligopoly theories of the firm in which price-leaders set their prices by 'marking-up' direct costs. In these theories, the difference between prices and direct costs is determined by the ratio of direct to indirect costs, and by the barriers to entry (due to technological discontinuities, or to market segmentation inside each industry) which allow existing firms to enjoy profitability higher than that prevailing in competitive sectors. As Modigliani and Padoa-Schioppa (1977, p. 9) stress, if the mark-up of money prices over labour costs is assumed to be an increasing function of quantity produced, then 'modern' oligopoly theory parallels the traditional marginalist approach, providing us once again with an inverse relationship between real wage rates and employment.

If (long-run) productivity is considered as exogenously given, constant direct labour costs in money terms imply given money wage-rates. Thus, if real wages (the ratio of money wages, implicit in labour costs, to money prices) fall when employment rises, this must be due to the increase in the mark-up and hence in the ratio of money prices to direct costs.

The idea that the mark-up is an increasing function of the quantity produced is a 'modern' transfiguration (made necessary by the recognition of oligopolistic conditions) of the traditional marginalist notion of U-shaped cost curves, implying decreasing returns when the quantity produced by the firm or the industry rises above a certain level. This idea is supported by reference to the pressure of demand on money prices; but such an explanation, which is an obvious outcome of traditional marginalist logic, has not been confirmed by the extensive empirical investigation which it has generated.[6]

Contrary to what Modigliani suggests, however, this fact should not be considered a surprise within modern oligopoly theory.[7] Let us briefly consider this point.

Changes in quantity produced, in conditions of exogenously given productivity implicit in the existing productive structure (plant and machinery), correspond either to changes in the actual degree of capacity utilisation around the 'normal' one, or to changes in the 'normal' degree of capacity utilisation. In neither case is there any reason to suppose that the mark-up should be an increasing function of the quantity produced.

In the first case of variations in output around the 'normal' degree of capacity utilisation there is no reason for price-leaders to vary the ratio of money prices to direct money costs of their products, because this ratio depends on exogenous elements such as technology determining the ratio of indirect to direct costs and the barriers to entry. Further, widespread overmanning in modern industrial firms suggests that short-run changes in the actual degree of capacity utilisation imply changes in labour productivity. In other words, when the quantity produced is larger than that corresponding to the 'normal' degree of capacity utilisation, labour costs per unit of product are likely to be lower than 'normal' costs, i.e. those corresponding to 'normal' utilisation of plant and machinery. If prices are fixed on the basis of 'normal' costs, an unchanged mark-up when the degree of capacity utilisation is higher than 'normal' produces a higher profit margin per unit of output. Thus, an increase in the quantity produced should, if anything, provoke a downward, and not an upward, pressure on the mark-up and, as a consequence, leave room for higher, not lower, real wage-rates.

In the second case of a change in the 'normal' degree of capacity utilisation there is an important factor pushing the mark-up in the opposite direction to the quantity produced, namely changes in unit fixed costs. Increases in the quantity produced with an unchanged productive capacity imply a reduction in unit fixed costs, which allows a reduction in the mark-up without reduction in unit profit margins net of the depreciation allowance.

In both cases, the reasons usually adduced for maintaining that unit costs move in the same direction as the quantity produced, namely, the need to put into use less efficient machinery and less efficient workers, the higher costs of overtime, and the like, when the degree of capacity utilisation increases over its 'normal' level, generally appear to be much less strong than the countervailing pressures exerted by elements such as overmanning and changes in unit fixed costs.

Thus oligopolistic pricing behaviour does not provide a 'modern microfoundation' to support the presupposition of an inverse relationship between real wage rate and employment.[8]

THE SRAFFIAN SHIFT IN THE RESEARCH PROGRAMME

We are thus left with the task of reconstructing an alternative to mainstream theories of employment which is not based on a demand function for labour implying an inverse relationship between real wage-rates and employment. Here I will limit myself to some brief considerations of the contribution which Sraffa's analysis may provide to this task of reconstruction, without prejudice to Keynes' well-known and much debated contributions, such as the notion of effective demand.

There are two different ways of utilising Sraffa's analysis in building a new theory of employment levels: (i) 'building over' Sraffa's price equations, with a *direct* utilisation of Sraffa's (1960) analysis; and (ii) following Sraffa's general lead towards a reconstruction of Classical political economy, thus relying only indirectly on his specifically analytic contribution.

The second way is, in our opinion, the most fruitful one[9] for the *positive* analysis of employment (as distinct from the *negative* side of Sraffa's contribution, providing – side by side with Keynes – a destructive criticism of traditional marginalist positions). This is due to the fact that Sraffa (not only through his 1960 book, but also with his edition of Ricardo's *Works and Correspondence*) provides the background for a drastic shift in the 'research programme' of economic science: away from the dominant marginalist approach, towards the so-called surplus approach rooted in the Classical tradition.

I have dealt elsewhere at length (Roncaglia, 1978) with the nature of, and the reasons for, this shift. Here let me summarise briefly, with a drastic simplification, the main characteristics of the marginalist tradition which Sraffa criticises and of the Classical tradition which Sraffa re-proposes.

Sraffa (1960, p. 93) points to the 'striking contrast' between the Classical 'picture of the system of production and consumption as a circular process', and the marginalist 'view ... of a one-way avenue that leads from "Factors of production" to "Consumption goods"'. Here Sraffa hints at a difference in the basic conception of the economy, which is reflected in a basic difference concerning the choice of the data and the variables to be explained in the area of value theory, which is commonly regarded as the foundation for other aspects of economic analysis. On the one side, Classical economists do not commonly consider as an analytical necessity the simultaneous determination of relative prices, relative activity levels and income distribution. On the other side, marginalist economists search for equilibrium prices and quantities stemming from the confrontation of initial resource endowments (which in some models – mainly the so-called temporary equilibrium models – include produced means of production side by side with primary inputs) and economic agents' preferences (generally mediated not only through exchange, but also through production).

From this we can derive a relevant difference concerning the way in which the analysis of employment is to be conducted. Contrary to the traditional marginalist approach, Classical analysis does not aim at identifying an 'equilibrium' level for output, and hence for employment, for any given set of conditions. Rather, Classical analysis assumes as given the level reached by employment (and unemployment) at some moment in time, and then looks at how and why these variables move over time. This implies rejection of both the traditional notion of equilibrium, as the balancing of the forces of supply and demand, and Hahn's (1973, p. 25) more general definition that 'an economy is in equilibrium when it generates messages which do not cause agents to change the theories which they hold or the policies which they pursue', which requires that agents do not 'learn' and that their objectives do not change.

Following the Classical approach, we can then consider changes in employment (and unemployment) levels as determined by a number of factors, the most important of which are (i) technical progress, which reduces the amount of labour required for obtaining a given amount of output, generating so-called technological unemployment;[10] and (ii) effective demand, expressing entrepreneurs' decisions on whether, and how much, to increase or decrease activity levels.

According to Keynes's own vision (Keynes, 1931), technical change constitutes in the long run the main menace to the attainment and maintenance of satisfactory employment levels. This notwithstanding, technical change should be stimulated rather than hindered by economic policy measures, because of its decisive role for economic progress. Thus employment policy necessarily involves support of effective demand: active state intervention in the economy is required because of the need to ensure continuous growth of effective demand, if technical progress is to generate increased welfare rather than increased unemployment.

While these two elements – technical change and effective demand – directly determine the employment path, unemployment also depends on labour supply, namely the demographic elements determining the size of population and its change, and the social factors determining the share of active population, i.e. the size of the labour force.

ON THE RELATIONSHIP BETWEEN KEYNESIAN AND CLASSICAL UNEMPLOYMENT

The approach hinted at above allows for a connection between the so-called 'Keynesian' and 'Classical' explanations of unemployment. As traditionally defined (by marginalist economists such as Malinvaud and Hahn), 'Keynesian' unemployment corresponds to the fact that involuntarily unemployed workers co-exist with unused productive capacity, so that a decision by entrepreneurs to increase production would increase both employment and the degree of capacity utilisation.[11] Classical unemployment, on the other hand, is due to the fact that the available productive capacity is insufficient to accommodate the available labour force. We should recall, in this respect, that Classical economists concede but a limited role to capital–labour substitution: at any moment in time, productive capacity is embodied in plants and machinery corresponding to past technological developments, and to the historical path followed by accumulation. 'Malleability of capital' cannot be relied upon, within the Classical approach, to provide the flexibility in the capital–labour ratio required for any supply of labour to be fully accommodated by a given capital stock: neo-classical 'comparative statics' does not capture the main forces at work in economic processes, as commonly depicted from a Classical vantage point.[12]

The link connecting 'Keynesian' and Classical unemployment consists in this: the first creates the conditions in which the second appears. As we have just noted, 'Keynesian' unemployment is accompanied by under-utilisation of the available productive capacity. Confronted with such a situation, entrepreneurs will not need to expand productive capacity whenever they decide to increase production, at least up to a certain point. Gradually existing plants and machinery deteriorate; and when entrepreneurs are confronted with persistent under-utilisation of productive capacity, they will even avoid replacing old machines and equipment going out of use. Gradually entrepreneurs are able to restore an 'acceptable' degree of capacity utilisation (which, under oligopolistic conditions, does not necessarily correspond to full utilisation), through a reduction in existing productive capacity. Substitutions of old with new machines incorporating technical progress may strengthen this process, through which 'Keynesian' unemployment is transformed into Classical unemployment.

This conception of unemployment calls forth a change in perspective for economic policy. Traditionally the remedies for Classical unemployment are seen as distinct from the remedies for 'Keynesian' unemployment: the latter requiring stimuli to demand, in order to induce a higher utilisation of existing productive capacity, the former requiring stimuli to savings in order to free resources for accumulation and enlargement of available productive capacity. However, in the light of what has just been said this policy dichotomy appears as radically misleading, for if stimulating savings reduces demand (as generally happens), resources freed for expanding productive capacity are unlikely to be utilised for that purpose.[13] The most likely outcome is a short-run fall in production levels and capacity utilisation. After a while, as noted above, this reinforces rather than combats Classical unemployment. On the contrary, a 'Keynesian' stimulus to demand, even if not completely composed of increased (public) investments, aims directly at an increase in the degree of capacity utilisation which stimulates investments and thus acts, indirectly, as a remedy for Classical unemployment as well.

WAGE COSTS AND EMPLOYMENT: A MULTI-SIDED RELATIONSHIP

When the problem of unemployment is approached in the way described in the previous section, wage costs play a strikingly different role from that played in the traditional approach. This final section is devoted to sketching this difference.

The fundamental position of the inverse relationship between real wages and employment in the traditional approach has already been referred to in the opening sections of this paper. Keynes's direct criticism of the marginalist tradition, incorporated in the 'neo-classical synthesis', consists of recalling that unemployment directly affects money wages, which in turn can affect money prices, so that real wages do not necessarily move in the same direction – and certainly not by the same magnitude – as money wages. Moreover, changes in money wages (and in expectations of the future course of money wages) provoke changes in effective demand, and this element may dominate any 'substitution' effect working through changes in the capital–labour ratio induced by changes in the relative prices of the two 'factors of production', capital and labour. Thus, while not necessarily denying the mechanisms on which traditional marginalist analysis relied for maintaining an automatic tendency to full employment in competitive economies, Keynes proposes a radical change in the line of enquiry for the employment issue. Sraffa, by providing the elements for a direct logical critique of the main marginalist mechanism (capital–labour substitution), strengthens the Keynesian suggestion for a new perspective in the analysis of employment; moreover, through his re-proposal of the Classical approach, Sraffa provides a possible connection between so-called Classical and Keynesian unemployment.

Changes in wage costs thus have a dual impact.[14] On the one hand, increases in wage costs may reduce profitability, and hence the stimulus to investment (and the ease with which investment is financed by firms from internal sources, which are generally preferred to external ones). Through this chain, increases in wage costs negatively affect production and employment. On the other side, wages constitute a major component of final demand. Thus if wages do not grow *pari passu* with technical progress, insufficient growth in final demand opens the way to 'technological unemployment'. The relationship, central to traditional theory, connecting unemployment to real wages, is thus substituted neither by a different functional relationship connecting the two variables, nor by a nihilist analytical indeterminacy, but by a complex set of relationships expressing countervailing effects of wages on employment, acting through different chains of direct cause-and-effect relations.[15] Thus the net effects of changes in wage costs on employment levels turn out to depend on the various links of cause and effect in the different chains summarily depicted above, so that the road is open to recognising a wider role to a variety of elements – among which institutional factors are prominent – shaping the wage–employment nexus, and calling for a larger flexibility in wage and employment policies, which cannot be directly deduced from basic economic principles by logic alone.[16]

Notes

1. Modern general equilibrium theory (cf., for example, Hahn, 1982) admits the possibility of multiple equilibria, and the possibility of underemployment equilibria, or of unstable equilibria. However, even when admitted, these cases have been often played down (as 'curiosa') by marginalist economists, especially prior to the capital theory debates of the 1960s, stemming from Sraffa's contribution. Yet, statements referring to 'the' Walrasian full employment equilibrium still abound in the literature (see, for example, Friedman, 1970, or the rational expectations models of the New Classical Macroeconomics. (The shift to the 'natural rate of unemployment' notion does not imply a change in the basic theoretical structure.)

    In fact, when Hahn criticises Friedman and New Classical Macroeconomists for their appeal to general equilibrium theory as the basis for the uniqueness of full employment equilibrium, he is, so to say, affected by the spirit of the Cambridge debates, joining forces with the critical tradition stemming from Sraffa's analysis, In this respect, it should be noted that, unlike Sraffa, Hahn does not accompany his critiques with the proposal of a positive approach for the analysis of concrete policy issues, alternative to the marginalist one.
2. On the opposition of liquidity preference to loanable funds theories, cf. Kregel, 1984.
3. For a detailed account of these debates, cf. Harcourt, 1972. For a specific discussion of employment theories from this viewpoint, cf. Garegnani, 1978–9.
4. It should be stressed, in this respect, that the same reasoning applies to any attempt at maintaining that market mechanisms ensure an automatic tendency to some 'natural rate of unemployment'.
5. This criticism was developed in Roncaglia, Tonveronachi, 1978.
6. Cf., for example, Sylos Labini, 1984, especially pp. 188–9; Coutts, Godley, Nordhaus, 1978; and the writings quoted in these volumes and in Roncaglia, Tonveronachi, 1978, p. 15. References to the inconclusive debate in the 1930s over the influence of demand on prices under imperfect competition are also provided in Roncaglia, Tonveronachi, 1978, p. 13.
7. In agreement with Modigliani, the main reference in this respect is Sylos Labini, 1962.
8. The traditional Marshallian 'microfoundations', which are implicitly employed by Modigliani, namely U-shaped cost curves, were the object of devastating criticisms made by Sraffa more than fifty years ago, cf. Sraffa, 1925.

    It may be interesting to recall that Marshall's belief in an inverse relationship between real wages and employment was accepted by Keynes in the *General Theory* (Keynes, 1936, p. 10), mainly due to Kahn's influence; but subsequently, under the influence of Dunlop, 1938, Tarshis, 1938, 1939, and Kalecki, 1938, Keynes, 1939 recognised the likelihood of a positive relationship between real wages and employment, stressing that such a relationship reinforced his interventionist policy attitude based on his theory of effective demand.

For recent empirical analyses of the employment–real wage relationship, see Geary and Kennan, 1982, Bils, 1985.

9. Following the first way, Vicarelli, 1974 and Arena, 1984 propose 'real-monetary' models, which incorporate Sraffa-type price equations side by side with Keynesian-type equations depicting the functioning of the money markets, investment and consumption decisions. Vicarelli, 1974 stresses the relevance of the production structure in determining the outcome on employment of movements in endogenous variables. Arena, 1984 stresses the compatibility between the Classical and Keynesian conceptualisation of the functioning of a market economy. On analogous lines, Pasinetti's important contributions (Pasinetti, 1965 and 1981, combining Sraffa-type price equations with Engel curves expressing changes over time in the demand for final outputs, and with differential technical progress), provide a set of conditions required for continuous full employment, in an economic system subject to exogenous changes in technology and in the structure of consumers' demand. However none of these models pretend to provide an explanation of the factors determining the path actually followed by employment over time.

10. 'Technological unemployment' and its reabsorption figure prominently in the debates among Classical economists – as, for instance, in the debate following Ricardo's change of mind in the third edition (1821) of the *Principles*, with the new chapter 'On Machinery' opposing the up-to-then prevailing 'compensation doctrine', according to which economic growth stimulated by technical progress automatically ensures, after a while, reabsorption of technological unemployment. For a survey of this debate see Berg, 1980.

11. This interpretation, which is the dominant one, connects the Keynesian analysis of unemployment to cyclical fluctuations. Here we do not tackle the issue of its correctness; but see Tonveronachi, 1983.

12. See, for example, the debate on machinery and the 'compensation doctrine' referred to in Note 10; and among modern economists Sylos Labini, 1984. In this connection we may note that the relevance of Classical unemployment for underdeveloped countries may be attributed to the sudden availability of modern technology transferable from developed countries. Underdeveloped countries are thus confronted with a potential technical progress depressing the demand for labour as soon as it is actually introduced. The available capital endowment is insufficient for realising full employment only if we refer – as we must do, because of worldwide competition – to the best-available techniques, namely those prevailing in developed countries.

13. At least this is true for the private sector of the economy. Direct State intervention through public investments, however, is precisely one of the main policy tools proposed by Keynes, who even uses the catchword 'socialisation of investments'.

14. This is stressed by Sylos Labini in a number of writings. See, for example, Sylos Labini, 1984.

15. Other chains of cause-and-effect relationships can be considered as well.

For instance: wage costs influence product prices and hence foreign competitiveness, and hence in turn imports and exports; these may affect both internal activity levels (and hence employment), and the exchange rate (with a feedback effect on internal prices and real wages). The analysis of possible chains implies a dynamic analysis of the economy under consideration, which should take into account its specific characteristics, since these (as synthesised in lags, values of parameters, etc.) determine the prevalence of the one or the other among the possible effects.

16. A single example: according to the marginalist tradition, incomes policy can only be used as a remedy to unemployment if it is framed in such a way as to provoke a reduction in real wage costs. On the contrary, a Classical–Keynesian analysis would rather stress the reduction in social tensions and uncertainty associated with a 'social pact' involving a parallel reduction in the growth rates of both money wages and money prices.

References

Arena, R. (1984) 'Réflexions sur la compatibilité des approches ricardienne et keynésienne du fonctionnement de l'activité économique', *Economie Appliquée*, 35 n. 3.

Berg, M. (1980) *The Machinery Question and the Making of Political Economy, 1815–1848* (Cambridge: Cambridge University Press).

Bils, M. J. (1985) 'Real Wages over the Business Cycle: Evidence from Panel Data', *Journal of Political Economy*, 93 n. 4.

Coutts, K., Godley, W., Nordhaus, W. (1978) *Industrial Pricing in the British Manufacturing Industries* (Cambridge: Cambridge University Press).

Dunlop, J. (1938) 'The Movement of Real and Money Wage Rates', *Economic Journal*, Sept.

Friedman, M. (1970) 'A Theoretical Framework for Monetary Analysis', *Journal of Political Economy*, March.

Garegnani, P. (1978) 'Notes on Consumption, Investment and Effective Demand', *Cambridge Journal of Economics*, vol. II, pp. 335–53 and vol. III, pp. 63–82.

Geary, P. T., Kennan, J. (1982) 'The Employment-Real Wage Relationship: an International Study, *Journal of Political Economy*, vol. 93, n. 4.

Hahn, F. (1973) *On the Notion of Equilibrium in Economics* (Cambridge: Cambridge University Press).

Hahn, F. (1982) *Money and Inflation* (Oxford: Blackwell).

Harcourt, G. C. (1972) *Some Cambridge Controversies in the Theory of Capital* (Cambridge: Cambridge University Press).

International Institute of Management (IIM/LMP 1984), *Research Program for 1985–89*, mimeo, Berlin.

Kalecki, M. (1938) 'The Determinants of Distribution of the National Income', *Econometrica*, April.

Keynes, J. M. (1931) 'Economic Possibilities for our Grandchildren', in *Essays in Persuasion* (London: Macmillan).

Keynes, J. M. (1936) *The General Theory of Employment, Interest and Money* (London: Macmillan).
Keynes, J. M. (1939) 'Relative Movements of Real Wages and Output', *Economic Journal*, March.
Kregel, J. (ed.) (1983) *Distribution, Effective Demand and International Economic Relations* (London: Macmillan).
Kregel, J. (1984) 'Constraints on Output and Employment', *Journal of Post Keynesian Economics*, vol. VIII, n. 2.
Modigliani, F. (1963) 'The Monetary Mechanism and its Interaction with Real Phenomena', *Review of Economics and Statistics*, Suppl., February.
Modigliani, F. and Padoa-Schioppa, T. (1977) 'La politica economica in una economia con salari indicizzati al 100 o più', *Moneta e credito*, n. 117.
Pasinetti, L. (1965) 'A New Theoretical Approach to the Problems of Economic Growth', *Pontificiae Academiae Scientiarum Scripta Varia* (Amsterdam: North Holland).
Pasinetti, L. (1981) *Structural Change and Economic Growth* (Cambridge: Cambridge University Press).
Ricardo, D. (1951–5) *Works and Correspondence*, ed. by P. Sraffa, in 10 vols. (Cambridge: Cambridge University Press).
Roncaglia, A. (1978) *Sraffa and the Theory of Prices* (New York: Wiley).
Roncaglia, A. and Tonveronachi, M. (1978) 'Commenti a un recente studio di Modigliani e Padoa-Schioppa', *Moneta e credito*, n. 121.
Sraffa, P. (1925) 'Sulle relazioni tra costo e quantità prodotta', *Annali di economia*, II.
Sraffa, P. (1960) *Production of Commodities by means of Commodities* (Cambridge: Cambridge University Press).
Sylos, Labini P. (1962) *Oligopoly and Technical Progress* (Cambridge, Mass: Harvard University Press).
Sylos, Labini P. (1984) *The Forces of Economic Growth and Decline* (Cambridge, Mass.: MIT Press).
Tarshis, L. (1938) 'Real Wages in the United States and Great Britain', *Canadian Journal of Economics*, August.
Tarshis, L. (1939) 'Changes in Real and Money Wages', *Economic Journal*, March.
Tonveronachi, M. (1983) *J. M. Keynes. Dall'instabilità ciclica all'equilibrio di sottoccupazione* (Firenze: La Nuova Italia Scientifica).
Vicarelli, F. (1984) 'Introduzione' and 'Disoccupazione e prezzi relativi: un tentativo di reinterpretazione di Keynes', in Vicarelli, F. (ed.), *La controversia keynesiana* (Bologna: Il Mulino).

COMMENT

Johannes Schneider

When the views of the critic and the criticised greatly diverge, it is no doubt difficult to achieve a well-balanced evaluation even when space and time are adequate; it is no doubt impossible when the latter prerequisites are entirely lacking. Positive value-judgements are obscured and I should apologise for the overemphasis on the negative.

I will thus focus my criticism on the two main theses of Roncaglia's paper.

Thesis 1 The market clearing theory of traditional economics is obsolete because the claim of the existence of an inverse relation between wage rate and employment does not hold true.

Thesis 2 Neo-Ricardian criticism of traditional theory suggests a shift in the economic 'Weltbild', away from the marginalism of neoclassical theory toward the surplus approach of Classical theory.

Roncaglia attempts to provide a two-fold argument for the basis of Thesis 1. On the one hand he claims that in the case of competition the idea of a market-clearing wage mechanism is already refuted by Sraffa's work. On the other hand, in the case of monopolistic structures, Roncaglia tries to convince us that wage and employment levels rise simultaneously, thus excluding the action of automatic adjustment mechanisms. A detailed treatment of the latter statements would draw us into the immense field of industrial economics and thus exceed the limits of this discussion. Nevertheless it should be mentioned that a number of economists trace unemployment to monopolistic factors, e.g. Hart, 1982 and Weitzman, 1982. None of them, however, would deny the customary constellation of the labour market. On the contrary, they attempt to explain fixed nominal or real wages, according to their respective approach.

The competitive part of the argument can serve as a good example. Here Sraffa's original criticism should be recalled. Among other things he demonstrated the possibility of the re-switching phenomenon, thereby showing that an inverse relationship between capital-labour-ratio and wage-interest-ratio posited by neo-classical theory did not hold true in models with heterogenous capital goods. This criticism has been widely accepted and has even been confirmed by the theory of general equilibrium. These statements refer to the level of capital-labour-ratio in their dependence on varying wage-interest situations – in other words, statements which only apply to certain conditions of wage and interest rates. This has to be clearly distinguished from the problem of market clearing. In Sraffa's theory, the occurrence or non-occurrence of the re-switching phenomenon depends upon the available technology. In the general equilibrium model, preferences and endowments also play a role, since the non-substitution theorem does not hold, and thus cost-minimising technology is not seen as independent from final demand. In the neo-Ricardian model, the problem of market clearing is also dependent upon the elasticity of labour demand in respect to wage rates and their variability. Sensibly, it cannot be assumed that labour demand is inelastic since even in the case of fixed technology the overall demand is characterised by price elasticity. In this case, however, a theory of unemployment, even in the neo-Ricardian model, must provide an explanation for fixed wages. This is the same problem found in the general equilibrium theory.

This leads us to the question of which of the two approaches is preferable. Bliss, 1975, and Hahn, 1982, have both argued extensively that neo-Ricardian theory, including Sraffa, does not contain a logical criticism of the general equilibrium theory, since it is merely a specialised version of the latter. Nevertheless one might prefer the surplus approach of Classical theory to the marginalism of the neo-classics. However, in my view, the antithetical pairs are wrongly chosen. It is not a matter of marginalism vs. Classic theory, but rather of general equilibrium theory vs. neo-Ricardianism. Here use of the term 'general equilibrium' is meant in the wide sense of the word, and also includes the non-Walrasian theories. It comprises all theories based on rational action and price formation in markets (even monopolised ones). My interpretation of the neo-Ricardian theory is that it consists of a modern version of the cost of production theory, a theory of factor payments which is not specified and a theory of quantity-systems which does not allow comparison of the substitution effect of a wage rise and the resultant consumption effect on labour demand. Marginalism only arose because the treatment of a number of problems, such as optimisation, proof of existence, stability discussion, etc., was relatively simple in the case of continuously differentiable functions. Understandably the corresponding assumptions have been made. But modern mathematical economics seems to have shown that such assumptions were by no means essential and may be relaxed. What remains are basic principles.

But let us return to the question in hand. From the standpoint of the history of economic theory, all criticism of the general equilibrium theory – whether ideologically motivated or not – has resulted from so-called 'anomalies' of neo-classical theory. Unemployment, above all when involuntary, cash-balances, share markets and numerous problems connected with informational deficiencies and the formation of expectations appeared to be inexplicable in the framework of neo-classical equilibrium theory – even in its modern form, the Walrasian model formulated by Arrow and Debreu. In the meantime, however, it has become clear that the only obstacle to an explanation of such problems in the framework of equilibrium theory was the idealisation of the Walrasian version of the theory. More generalised and realistic theoretical assumptions could lead to a solution of all the deficiencies of the theory. Naturally there will be some puzzles left to solve, but it appears to me that this theory is capable of providing explanations for everything that is the case and everything that could be the case.

How greatly limited, by comparison, the neo-Ricardian theory is. Money and other financial assets are given no consideration at all; the same is true of such factors as uncertainty, information and expectations. The portfolio theory is degraded to the so-called Cambridge equation. Logically, financial markets are not even discussed. All of this stands in strong contradiction to the importance attributed to these phenomena in economic life. To sum up the balance of the preceding, somewhat restricted discussion, in a mildly polemical way the theory may well belong in every book on the history of economic thought – as an appendix to the chapter on Ricardo, as a modern reconstruction of his theory of value.

References

Bliss, C. J. (1975) *Capital Theory and the Distribution of Income* (Amsterdam: North Holland).

Hahn, F. (1982) 'The Neoricardians', *Cambridge Journal of Economics*, 6.

Hart, O. D. (1982) 'A Model of Imperfect Competition with Keynesian Features', *Quarterly Journal of Economics*, 36.

Weitzman, M. L. (1982) 'Increasing Returns and the Foundations of Unemployment Theory', *Economic Journal*, 92.

2 The Theory of Demand and Supply of Labour – The Post-Keynesian View

J. A. Kregel

'Employment is not a function of real wages in the sense that a given degree of employment requires a determinate level of real wages, irrespective of how the employment is brought about.' (JMK, XIII, p. 180)

The problem of the relation of wages to employment is certainly as old, and as widely debated, as the relation between money and prices proposed in the Quantity Theory of money. It is significant that Keynes broke with both positions (which he considered as being analytically equivalent) in his *Treatise on Money*. The quotation given above, which is still a fair representation of the post-Keynesian position, dates from a September 1930 memo for the Economists Advisory Council which Keynes prepared just after completion of work on the book.

Keynes' position in the *General Theory* is basically unchanged, but Keynes believed his new method of analysing the problem highlighted his departure from the traditional positions: 'the consequences of a change in money-wages are complicated. A reduction in money-wages is quite capable in certain circumstances of affording a stimulus to output as the classical theory supposes. My difference from this theory is primarily a difference of analysis.' (JMK, VII, p. 257) Keynes based his criticism of classical theory on its failure to notice that it provided no explanation of the determinants of the level of demand for output as a whole. This basic criticism also applied to the classical relation of wages to employment:

> whilst no one would wish to deny the proposition that a reduction in money-wages *accompanied by the same aggregate demand as*

before will be associated with an increase in employment, the precise question at issue is whether the reduction in money-wages will or will not be accompanied by the same aggregate effective demand as before measured in money, or, at any rate, by an aggregate effective demand which is not reduced in full proportion to the reduction in money-wages (ibid., pp. 259–60).

A theoretical framework which provided no explanation of the level of output and employment as a whole was ill-suited to the analysis of the effect of a change in wages on these magnitudes. Thus Keynes' emphasis on the difference in his analysis from the traditional theory.

This difference in analysis can perhaps be seen by reference to the argument, often advanced in times of economic downturn, that wages are 'too high'. Being a relative concept, wages must be 'too high' with respect to something. In traditional theory there is an equilibrium wage which produces market-clearing equilibrium in the labour market. The existence of unemployment, in excess of what should be expected from frictional causes, then indicates that wages are too high relative to that equilibrium wage. This is also often expressed as the money wage exceeding the value of the marginal product of labour.

Since the argument that wages are too high relates to money wage costs relative to output prices, there is also an implicit assumption that changes in money-wages towards equilibrium levels will be reflected in like movements in real wages since money-wages must fall relative to prices, decreasing real wages as well. This implies that changes in money wages are independent of the determination prices. Such independence is usually explained by the proposition that the level of money prices is determined by the quantity of money, or by the independence of the average revenue curve from the firm's level of output in conditions of perfect competition (i.e. that the level of demand facing the individual firm is independent of its output). But, as Keynes points out, it is illegitimate 'to extend by analogy ... conclusions in respect of a particular industry to industry as a whole'. Classical theory, he charged, 'is wholly unable to answer the question what effect on employment a reduction in money wages will have' (JMK, VII, p. 260). The absence of an explanation of the determinants of the demand for output as a whole thus calls into question the implicit assumption of Classical theory that changes in money wages will bring about equivalent movements in real wages. The relation of money to prices and of money to real wages are thus linked in supporting the Classical view of the relation between real wages and employment. Keynes' rejection of the Quantity Theory thus also placed in doubt the answer to the question of whether wages are too high by reference to the equilibrium real wage determined by market-clearing equilibrium in the labour market. Keynes was thus led to question the functional relation between real wages and employment, and to call attention to the method by which *changes in real wages* were brought about in practice. For example, if money and real wages are inversely related then the existence of unemployment suggests that money wages are too low. But, such questions can only be treated in a framework which analyses the relation between wages and demand which Keynes attempted in his theory of 'effective demand'.[1]

As he had already noted in the 1930 memo, 'Real wages seem to me to come about as a by-product of the remedies which we adopt to restore equilibrium' (JMK, XIII, p. 180), they cannot be acted on either directly or indirectly via changes in money-wage rates. Real wages are viewed as being determined by the operation of the economy as a whole, not by the participants in the labour market.

Keynes' response to the question of whether wages are 'too high' could not then refer to the equilibrium level of *real* wages, but instead to the effects of an *increase* in *money* wages on those factors which determine the level of employment, i.e., with reference to effective demand. Rather than referring to the elasticity of demand for labour in response to a change in money wages for a particular industry and then extending this analysis to the economy as a whole, Keynes sets about producing an elasticity of employment consistent with an endogenous determination of the level of demand. The purpose of this paper will be to attempt to sketch Keynes' alternative method of analysis. In doing so we shall draw heavily on the path-breaking work of Sidney Weintraub (e.g. Weintraub, 1956, 1957, 1958), one of the few economists who recognised that Keynes' theory made the concept of an industry demand for labour curve based on a given level of demand inappropriate as the micro-foundation of the demand for labour curve for the economy as a whole. When aggregate demand is endogenously determined the aggregate demand for labour curve cannot be based on the aggregation of the individual industry demand for labour curves based on the equilibrium relations between wages and marginal value productivity of labour for they depend on the level of aggregate demand. Weintraub instead proposes what might be called a 'macro-foundation' for the microeconomic demand for labour curve (cf. Kregel, 1985, for a more extensive summary of Weintraub's position).

Traditional micro theory analyses economic behaviour on the assumption that the level of income is given exogenously of the behaviour of the variables under examination. This is what is usually called partial equilibrium. Such an assumption is easily justified if the system is always producing its full employment output. If it is not, it requires analyses of the way agents' decisions affect the overall income constraint. This problem is especially important in the analysis of wages which appear as both the major cost of production and the major source of the demand for output. Consider an extreme case, in which wages are reduced in one industry producing, say, yachts, which are not purchased by its own labour force. Demand for yachts will fall, but by less than the reduction in the wage bill and by an amount which depends on the pattern of consumption spending and technology. Prices thus fall by less than wages per unit of output (corrected for the increase in costs due to diminishing returns). The value of marginal yacht output per worker thus exceeds the money wage and entrepreneurs will seek to expand output by hiring more labour. An increase in employment thus follows on a reduction in both money and real wages. But, if the fall in wages extends to other industries, or if workers and capitalists buy the products of the industries in which they are engaged, both of which will be true of the aggregate economy, then demand and prices may fall by just the amount of the reduction in wages and the two sides of the effect of wages, on costs and on expenditures, may just cancel out.

It is at this point that traditional analysis introduces the real balance effect with outside money to keep demand from falling in step with costs. But, if contracts are fixed in terms of money, or if all money is inside or credit money, the losses of debtors will exceed or just offset the gains of creditors. The same would be true of other real and financial assets. Expenditure could be kept from falling by the full extent of the reduction in wages only by means of wealth illusion in which the owners of non-labour assets presume their incomes to be unaffected, i.e. exactly the same assumption concerning demand that Keynes rejected. The problem is then to find a way of representing the macroeconomic effect on the income constraint of each microeconomic decision.

To achieve this Weintraub developed a unique concept that he called the 'demand-outlay curve'. Consider the supply curve of an industry, i, given by s_i in Figure 2.1. P_1 is the supply price necessary to convince producers in the industry to hire labour sufficient to produce an amount of output equal to Q_{1s}. Given the level of overall incomes

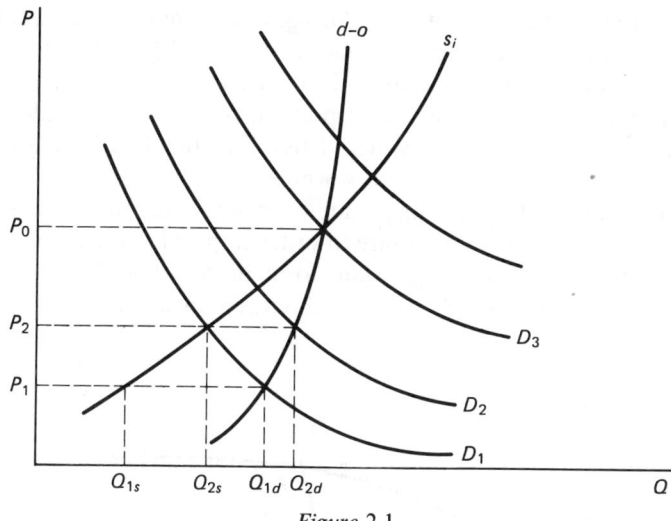

Figure 2.1

generated by that level of output and at that price, desired consumer outlays on the product of the industry as represented by the Marshallian demand curve D_1 turn out to be Q_{1d}, greater than Q_{1s}. At a higher level of expected price and output, P_2 and Q_{2s} yields a higher level of income and a D_2 curve showing desired consumer outlay of Q_{2d}. Equilibrium output occurs at the point where desired consumer outlay purchases output produced at the expected price, P_0 and $Q_s = Q_d$. The curve linking all the desired consumer outlay points, Q_d, is the demand outlay ($d-o$) curve and represents the impact on own demand of changes in output in the industry.

Since there is an amount of industry employment implicit in each point on the demand outlay curve and since PQ_d represent aggregate desired expenditure sums, the $d-o$ curves can be used to construct an aggregate demand curve relating aggregate desired money expenditure for the industry to amounts of employment in the industry. Neither prices, nor the level of income, are presumed given in the construction of these curves which thus satisfy the desired requirement of representing the behaviour of decisionmakers under conditions of an endogenously determined level of income.

These industry aggregate demand curves can also be aggregated, given the appropriate weights determined by the proportion of each industry in total output, to produce an aggregate demand curve, D, relating expected proceeds to the level of the employment for the economy as a whole in Figure 2.2. An aggregate supply curve, Z, can be similarly constructed from the s_i curves, linking PQ_s and N for each industry and aggregating across industries with the same weights. The intersection of the two curves represents what Keynes called the 'point of effective demand' which determined the aggregate level of employment for the economy as a whole.

The Z curve relates the aggregate of the expected proceeds which each entrepreneur would require in order to provide the amounts of employment which find aggregate form in N, while D relates the aggregate of the proceeds which each entrepreneur in each industry

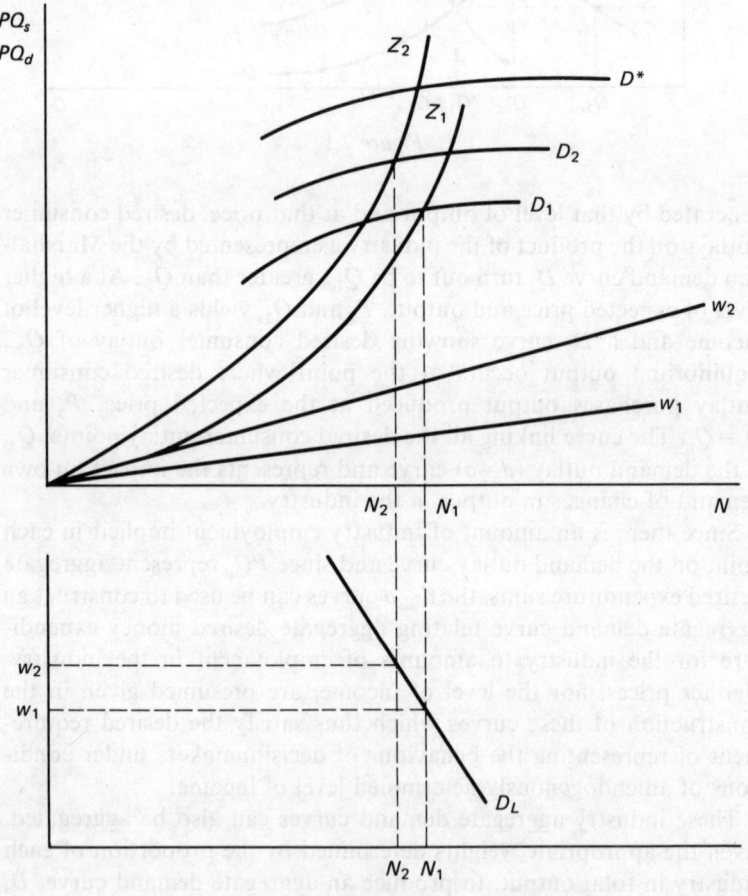

Figure 2.2

would expect given his decision to offer employment, the aggregate quantity of which is given by N. The equilibrium level of employment is then given by the point of effective demand at which the expected receipts required for that volume of employment are equal to the receipts that are in fact anticipated. Given technology this level of N represents a level of output, Q, corresponding to the collection of various outputs included within $PQ_s = PQ_d$. There is thus a PQ combination imbedded in each point on the aggregate supply curve, and one such combination consistent with the point of effective demand.

Thus, by answering the question of the determination of the level of output and employment as a whole the level of overall, and industry by industry, employment emerges as a by-product. Any analysis of the demand for labour within this framework must then be consistent with the aggregate analysis; indeed, it must be built from it. For example, we could go back to each industry d–o in curve and hypothesise an increase in money wages. We should then have to determine the impact on the supply curve and on the demand-outlay curve. While the former is relatively straightforward, the latter will require knowledge of how it effects the demand for the outputs of the other industries, i.e. on the point of effective demand. Thus the analysis must start with the impact on Z and D. In Figure 2.2 an increase in wages from w_1 to w_2 will shift Z_1 and D_1 upwards to Z_2 and D_2. If the two curves are shifted in the same proportion there is no impact on the aggregate level of employment. A demand for labour curve drawn up to link various levels of the money-wage and the level of employment would then be vertical. If labour is not the sole cost of production and these other costs are not affected by the changes in wages, or are affected less than in proportion, then Z will rise by less than D and the level of employment will be lower when money-wages are higher. The demand for labour curve would then have the more traditional negative slope such as D_L in Figure 2.2. On the other hand, if there are increasing returns, the demand for labour curve would have a positive slope as higher wages increase the level of employment. Kregel (1979) discusses reasons why the fact that the Z curve contains money costs makes this an unlikely case, even in the presence of increasing returns in real terms. The slope of the demand for labour curve will then depend on the impact of the change in the money wage on consumption and investment decisions relative to the impact on aggregate supply, that is, on the effect on the distribution of income and the level of investment which point up the importance of these macrofoundations of the demand for labour. Thus, in his discussion of money-wages in ch. 19 of the *General Theory* Keynes undertakes a step by step analysis of the effect of changes in money wages on the determinants of investment, i.e. the marginal efficiency of capital and the rate of interest, and on the propensity of consume, the three independent variables determining D and on the conditions of production and costs determining Z.

Before turning to these issues, two points should be noted. First, the level of employment is here determined without any direct reference to the labour market, nor to the interaction of the supply and demand for labour. Indeed, the supply of labour, consistent with Keynes' belief that labour was not in a position to determine the real-wage at which it worked, is not even considered until the constraint of full employment. This absence of direct labour market analysis is explained by the second point, the determination of the real wage. Just as the demand for labour is endogenously determined by the influence of the aggregate variables, so is the real wage. To every point on the demand for labour curve there corresponds a point of effective demand and an implicit PQ combination. It is the part of P which reflects the consumption basket of labour which will influence the real wage. If it rises more than in proportion as money wages rise then real wages fall as money wages increase, if it rises in the same or in lesser proportion then real and money wages move together. But, as Keynes notes, this is a complex question, the answer to which is not straightforward because it depends on the aggregate adjustment process.

On the basis of this aggregate relation it would be possible to construct a supply of labour curve which would furnish the basis for a labour market analysis capable of determining the money wage. The construction of this curve is complicated (which may explain why neither Keynes nor Weintraub thought it necessary to use it) for if we reject the traditional explanation that labour suffers from money illusion, supply decisions must be based on labour's expectation of the real value of the money wage for which it is willing to work, i.e. on the prices expected to prevail for consumption goods over the contract period. One possibility is to derive this real value from the wage-price combinations implicit in each point of effective demand. For example, for a level of employment, N_1, given by the intersection of the D_1 and Z_1 curves in Figure 2.2 there is an implicit real-wage determined by the money-wage rate and price of consumer goods implicit in the point of effective demand. Just as the demand-outlay curve was derived from points on the Marshallian product demand curve which showed desired expenditures for given levels of income and money-wages for notional variations in price levels, we can derive labour-supply curves associated with each point of effective demand by notional variations in money-wages, given the level of income and prices. The supply of labour curve thus shows the desired supply of labour at the w-P combination for the associated point of effective demand as well as the supplies that would be forthcoming at higher and lower money wages, wN and P assumed to be given. In Figure 2.3, labour would like to offer N_{s1} given by labour supply curve S_1 when money wages are w_1, but as Keynes points out, labour is not in a position to determine its desired position on its labour supply curve, for actual employment will be N_{d1} given by the labour demand curve. The fact that all equilibrium $D=Z$ points lie on the demand for labour curve, rather than the supply of labour curve, simply represents the fact that it is the first Classical postulate that holds and not the second.

The desired labour supply points for each one of these labour-

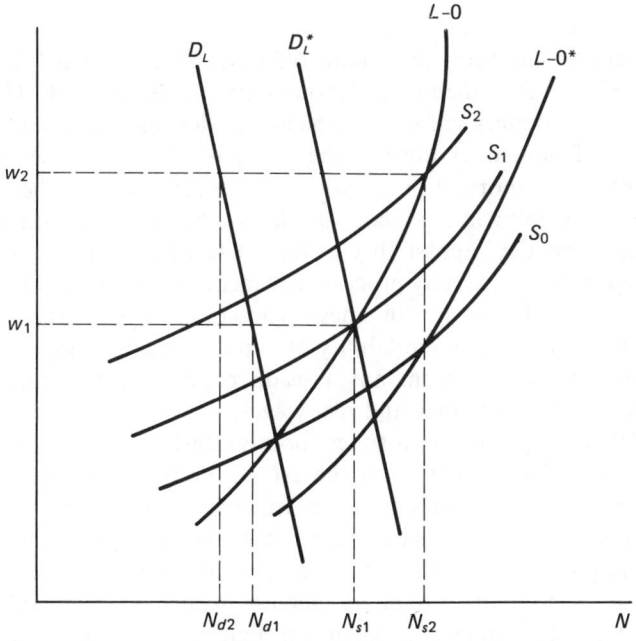

Figure 2.3

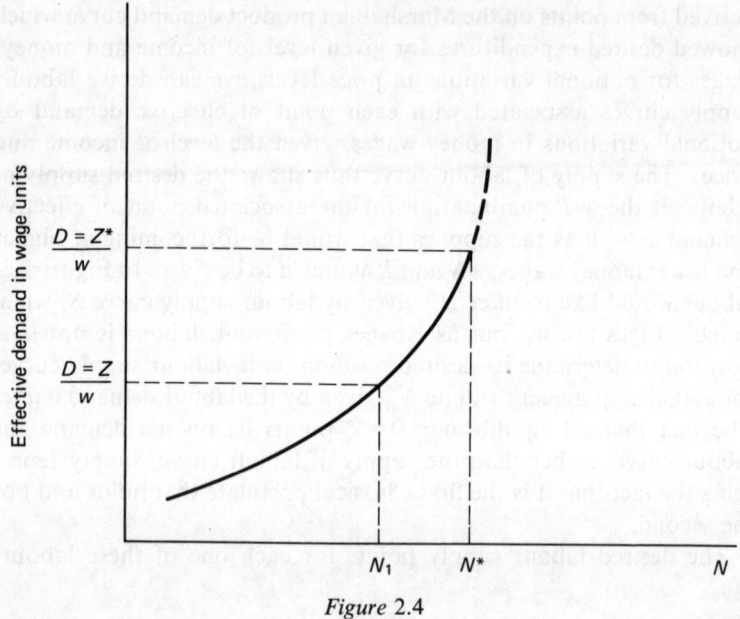

Figure 2.4

supply curves will form the labour-offer $(L-0)$ curve which can be compared to the demand for labour curve in Figure 2.3. Thus a change in w produces shifts along the labour demand curve and shifts along the labour-offer curve. The analysis as set out here thus highlights two important propositions in Keynes' analysis: the irrelevance of bargaining in the labour market to the determination of the real-wage, and the impossibility of labour to directly determine the real-wage in the bargaining process. The fact of labour bargaining for a money-wage (and its unwillingness to accept money-wage cuts) thus results more from the impossibility of stipulating a binding contract over real-wages than from any illusion concerning the difference between changes in money and real wages.

While Keynes' analysis puts these points clearly, it leaves one point unresolved. It is evident from the labour market diagram that a reduction in money-wages leads to an increase in the quantity of labour demanded and thus movement towards the intersection of the demand and labour-offer curves. It may or may not lead to a rise in real wages. On the other hand an increase in effective demand, given increasing costs, implies that when N is higher, given w, prices will be higher and real-wages will be lower. Thus, even in Keynes' alternate method of analysis lower money wages are associated with higher levels of employment; and lower real wages, given money wages, are associated with higher levels of employment. As Keynes noted,

> this conclusion was inconvenient, since it had a tendency to offset the influence of the main forces which I was discussing and made it necessary for me to introduce qualifications.[2] ... In particular, the traditional conclusion played an important part, it will be remembered, in the discussions, some ten years ago, as to the effect of expansionist policies on employment ... Prof. Pigou ... explained the observed result by the reduction in real wages covertly effected by the rise in prices which ensued on the increase in effective demand. It was held that public investment policies (and also an improvement in the trade balance through tariffs) produced their effect by deceiving so to speak, the working classes into accepting a lower real wage, effecting by this means the favourable influence on employment which, according to these economists, would have resulted from a more direct attack on real wages (e.g. by reducing money wages whilst enforcing a credit policy calculated to leave prices unchanged) (Keynes, 1939, in JMK, vii, pp. 400–1).

Of course, this potential confusion was based on the proposition of increasing costs leading to higher prices and lower real wages as demand increased with given money wages. But, statistical evidence produced by Dunlop, Tarshis and others failed to find any evidence of such an inverse relation between the level of output and real wages. Keynes thus comments that 'If the falling tendency of real wages in periods of rising demand is denied, this alternative explanation must, of course, fall to the ground.' (ibid.)[3]

But, Keynes also pointed out, this argument confused

> two different problems ... the reaction of real wages to changes in output [in] ... situations where changes in real and money wages were a reflection of changes in the level of employment caused by changes in effective demand ... [and] the case where changes in wages reflect changes in prices or in the conditions governing the wage bargain which do not correspond to, or are not primarily the result of, changes in the level of output and employment and are not caused (although they may cause) changes in effective demand. (ibid., p. 395)

The statistical evidence referred to the first problem (although Kalecki (1938) did attempt to provide evidence on the second from the Blum experiment). Although Keynes tries to treat the two questions separately, the whole point of his analysis of the second question is that it cannot be analysed independently of the first. In traditional theory it was possible to consider the impact of a change in wages on the labour market because the level of demand was assumed to be given, but Keynes argued that this was impossible because changes in money wages would have an impact on the determinants of effective demand. It was for this reason that he insisted on the importance of 'how the employment is brought about'. The traditional argument that a reduction in money wages was the same whether it occurred through a monetary expansion producing a rise in prices relative to wages (cf. Lerner, 1977) or whether it operated directly by reducing money wages (as in the reference to Pigou above), made it necessary for Keynes to argue that labour would be willing to accept the former rather than the latter type of reduction. However, these restrictions are unnecessary if the existence of increasing returns allows real wages to increase as output expands.

Accepting the prevalence of increasing returns has a number of implications. The first is that it is no longer necessary to retain Keynes' point of contact with the Classical theory as given by the first Classical postulate concerning the equality between the wage and the marginal product of labour which assured that points of effective demand would produce a real-wage employment combination equivalent to that produced by the Classical demand curve. If diminishing returns, which assure the downward slope of the classical demand for labour curve and the stability of labour-market equilibrium, no longer hold then the traditional analysis no longer applies. Keynes' analysis, as seen above, is open to a forward-rising demand for labour curve and no longer implies even the equality of the real wage and labour's marginal product.

The answer to the question of the effect of wages on employment then still depends on the effect of the changes in wages on aggregate demand, with real wages determined by the combined effect on aggregate demand and supply. It cannot be answered directly by reference to conditions in the labour market. This, as Keynes stresses, is a difference of analysis which may or may not produce different results. The difference in analysis is perhaps best represented by the closest equivalent to the traditional labour market analysis in Keynes' system: the employment function.

The employment function can be constructed from the labour-outlay curves: if we plot the level of effective demand deflated by the level of the associated wage rate relative to the associated levels of N we get a relation between effective demand and employment. Note that at each point on this curve the demand for labour equals intended labour offer. An increase in effective demand (say from D_1 to D^* in Figure 2.2) shifts both demand and supply of labour (D_L^* and $L-0^*$ in Figure 2.3) producing a new equilibrium level of employment given by N^* in Figure 2.4. Full employment is thus defined by the point where the employment function is perfectly inelastic with respect to an increase in the level of effective demand in wage units. Here we can clearly see that the question of whether wages are 'too high' must be answered by reference to the level of effective demand. As long as the curve is elastic, the level of wages cannot be considered as being 'too high' for an increase in effective demand produces an increase in employment. *On the other hand, this does not imply that an increase, any more than a decrease, in wages would bring about the increase in effective demand necessary to increase employment.* This will depend on the impact of wages on the marginal efficiency of capital, liquidity preference and the propensity to consume, an analysis that Keynes undertakes in ch. 19, of the *General Theory*. As is well known, he comes to no clear conclusion concerning the effect of wages on the propensity to consume; thus any effect must come through either the rate of interest or the efficiency of capital. When reduced to these terms the problem becomes identical to the ability of monetary policy to control the rate of interest so as to assure full employment. Here, Keynes points out that if the quantity of money is endogenously determined by the wage and price levels, then wage changes cannot affect the demand for money. If it is not endogenous, the result depends on the effect on liquidity preference.

There are two conclusions which follow. The first is that since the real wage is endogenous it cannot be a tool of policy, and that since there is no necessary link between changes in money wages and real wages, it is best to try to keep money wages constant (this is what Hicks, 1985, has called Keynes' 'labour standard'). The second is that there are conditions in which Keynes admits the possibility that a reduction in wages may increase employment, e.g. when the reduction is made relative to wages of foreign competitors measured in a common standard.

But even here Keynes emphasises the importance of the manner in which the adjustment is carried out. The point at issue in the case of an open economy is the impact of lower wages on the foreign balance, which is equivalent to the effect on investment in a closed system (the famous export-led growth propositions are based on substituting foreign demand for domestic investment). However, Keynes also notes that the reduction in wages relative to those abroad will only work if the demand for exports is sufficiently elastic and will be accompanied by a reduction in the terms of trade which will lead to the reduction in real incomes of the employed labourers and other fixed income recipients at the expense of the newly employed workers. This is the same sort of adjustment seen above associated with the rise in money wages associated with the rise in employment due to the increase in the propensity to consume as income is transferred from rentiers to wages and profits. Again, it only increases employment *if the reduction in wages is accompanied by a more than compensating increase in effective demand* (in this case from abroad). Thus, in the absence of foreign retaliation, there may be a tendency for employment to increase.

Such a result, however, depends on foreign demand increasing while domestic investment and consumption remain unchanged. As seen in the recent case of the Netherlands, where reductions in wages produced an appreciable improvement in the foreign balance, it was more than offset by the combined reduction in domestic consumption and private investment. This real world example gives a good indication of the problems associated with the policy of reducing money wages in order to reduce real wages to increase employment. The outcome will depend on the aggregate effects on overall demand. Keynes' criticism of traditional theory was that it failed to consider these aggregate demand factors and had no way to analyse them. And although he accepted that in certain conditions reductions in money wages could expand employment this possibility was conditioned on the existence of an exogenous factor (an increase in demand coming either from domestic government policy or from foreign trade or the distribution of income) to assure the required expansion in aggregate demand.[4]

In conclusion it should be stressed that Keynes' approach does not deny that under certain conditions reductions in money wages may be the best policy to increase employment. It does deny, however, any stable or predictable relation between money and real wages, or that the 'certain conditions' which are required for wage reductions to produce an increase in employment will be spontaneously produced by improving conditions of competition in the labour market or by the economy as a whole. There is simply no spontaneous tendency in a competitive capitalist economy toward full employment of labour via money wage adjustments in the labour market.[5]

Notes

1. Which had the consequence of leaving Keynesian economics with a 'Missing Theory of Money Wages'. See Weintraub, 1978/9.
2. Trevithick, 1976, attempts to formulate a labour supply curve on the basis of these 'qualifications', but the argument here suggests that it cannot take on general application within Keynes' system for the qualifications do not have general application as they only apply in conditions of diminishing returns (cf. also Kregel, 1980, p. 59, n. 7).
3. It is interesting to note that Harrod had recognised the importance of this line of argument already in the 1920s and had produced evidence of increasing returns from field studies some 10 years earlier. See the discussion in Kregel, 1985b.
4. The reader should note that all of this analysis was available in the late 1930s and widely discussed in the 1950s. None the less this has not prevented economists from persisting in employing the traditional analysis (e.g. Meltzer, 1981). For recent refutations of these ideas along similar lines cf. Davidson, 1983, 1983b.
5. Having been offered the possibility of revising the text in light of comments received I shall limit myself to this footnote, leaving the paper as it was presented. Prof. Hart is correct that I have ignored current literature dealing with wage-price rigidity. Prof. Streissler's conclusions that few of the results of this literature bear extension to the economy as a whole, which is the point that I was attempting to make, explains why. It is not possible to accept these aggregate effects and then return to a 'micro-world' in which they can be assumed away. The same argument holds for the estimates of the elasticity of substitution: they are subject to the effect of changes in wages on aggregate income about which generalisation is difficult. Here I might refer the reader to the use of the same point by Nickell and Layard (Clare Group report on 'Jobs and Pay' in Midland Bank Review, 1985) in criticism of Nigel Lawson's statement that a 1 per cent reduction in real earnings would increase the level of employment by 0.5 to 1 per cent or 'between 150 000 and 200 000 jobs'. It is attractive to be able to make such statements, but the macroeconomic aspects of labour markets do not allow them. The same point shows why the results would not change even if the level of nominal wages were initially set at the market clearing level in the diagrams, for higher nominal wages might still produce higher employment and output.

References

Davidson, P. (1983) 'The marginal product curve is not the demand curve for labor Lucas's labor supply curve is not the supply curve for labor in the real world'. *Journal of Post Keynesian Economics*, 4:1, Fall.

Davidson, P. (1983b) 'The Dubious Labor Market Analysis in Meltzer's Restatement', *Journal of Economic Literature*, 21.

Hicks, John (1985) 'Keynes and the World Economy' in *Keynes' Relevance Today* (London: Macmillan).

Kalecki, M. (1938) 'The Lessons of the Blum Experiment', *Economic Journal*, 48.

Keynes, J. M. (JMK) *The Collected Writings of John Maynard Keynes* (VII) *The General Theory of Employment, Interest, and Money* (XIII) *The General Theory and After – Part I: Preparation*.

Kregel, J. A. (1979) 'A Keynesian Approach to Inflation Theory and Policy' in *Models and Policy: Perspectives in Inflation* (ed.) D. Heathfield (London: Longman).

Kregel, J. A. (1980) 'I fondamenti Marshalliani del principio della domanda effettiva di Keynes', *Giornale degli Economisti*, March–April.

Kregel, J. A. (1985) 'Sidney Weintraub's Macro Foundations of Microeconomics and the Theory of Distribution', *Journal of Post-Keynesian Economics*, 7:4, Summer.

Kregel, J. A. (1985b) 'Harrod and Keynes: Increasing Returns, The Theory of Employment and Dynamic Economics', in *Keynes and his Contemporaries* (ed.) G. C. Harcourt (London: Macmillan).

Lerner, A. P. (1977) 'From Pre-Keynes to Post-Keynes', *Social Research*, Autumn.

Meltzer, A. H. (1981) 'Keynes's General Theory: A Different Perspective', *Journal of Economic Literature*, 19.

Trevithick, J. (1976) 'Money Wage Inflexibility and the Keynesian labour Supply Function', *Economic Journal*, 86.

Weintraub, S. (1956) 'A Macroeconomic Approach to the Theory of Wages', *American Economic Review*, 46, December.

Weintraub, S. (1957) 'The Micro-Foundations of Aggregate Demand and Supply', *Economic Journal*, 67, September.

COMMENT

R. A. Hart

The influence of the New Classical Economics on labour market research (and elsewhere) has long since peaked and it is currently sliding, at probably approaching maximum speed, downhill. The Keynesians are once again scrambling to capture the high ground. Apart from the usual cyclical changes of fashion in economics, why is this happening? The reasons would appear to be largely empirical; many of the labour market predictions of the New Classical School do not fit comfortably with a number of important stylised facts. Akerlof (1979) produces a useful summary of the empirical debate, as do Gordon (1983) and Stiglitz (1984) from somewhat different perspectives.

One particularly successful challenge to the New Classical Economics relates to unemployment. The so-called 'new view' lays particular stress on two related features of unemployment. First, workers are unemployed because an imperfect knowledge of the real wage on offer leads them to believe that they can achieve higher wages through search. This is in the spirit of the famous Sargent supply equation. Secondly, the unemployment characterised by this activity is essentially of *short-term* duration; it lasts for as long as it takes to correct misconceptions. Therefore, unemployment consists principally of persons experiencing relatively short periods out of employment rather than stocks of long-term unemployed workers. Developing measurement concepts largely initiated by Clark and Summers, 1978, a number of researchers have now firmly established that most unemployment is accounted for by unemployed workers experiencing spell lengths which can be regarded as neither short-lived nor voluntarily incurred. The observed pattern of unemployment rests much more comfortably in a world of disequilibrium with relatively sticky wages and prices and where market clearing is not necessarily attained in either the goods or the labour market. Here, unemployment is largely involuntary and the level of aggregate demand is such that output lies below the full employment level.

But even as the Keynesians contemplate hoisting their flag at the summit, they become once again liable to attack from their old enemies. Their important points of weakness are well known. The main area of vulnerability is a general lack of adequate explanation of why wages and prices fail to attain market clearing levels. In this respect, however, the fortifications are perhaps somewhat stronger than in earlier periods. A body of literature has relatively recently evolved that has sought to give much stronger theoretical support as to why wages and prices may be downwardly sticky during recessionary periods. The approaches are somewhat divergent, and in places competing, and include implicit contract models, efficient wage models (for an excellent comparison of both literatures see Stiglitz, 1984) and inventory/output-price models (e.g. Blinder, 1982). In all these approaches, the emphasis is firmly on microfoundations with the labour market playing either the central or, at least, a highly important role.

Professor Kregel's paper addresses the problem of the relationship between wages and employment within a marked Keynesian setting. Thus, from the outset, it has the advantage of belonging to the (currently) ascendant school of thought. As is well known, however, there are several distinct groups fighting under the Keynesian flag. Professor Kregel would appear to belong firmly to those who wish to adhere to the pure word of Keynes himself and then to convey it to the rest of us in the form of a careful and succinct piece of analysis. Kregel is clearly an expert in this area and I would not dare to challenge his scholarly and illuminating interpretations.

Since the paper seems to step aside from the current debate over the explanation of sticky wages and prices by emphasising 'macrofoundations' not microfoundations, I shall emphasise these two issues in my comments.

A common starting point in the microeconomics of the employment-wage relationship is to derive factor demand equations for a cost minimising individual firm that takes the level of real demand as given. If one is interested in understanding the macro relationship between employment and wages, however, it is clearly not satisfactory to aggregate individual micro units and in effect to apply the same optimising conditions to the aggregate of all firms. At the macro level, aggregate demand is clearly an endogenous variable, being a function of real labour costs. Kregel correctly emphasises this point but, in doing so, he seems to me to give far too much weight to its role within the overall model structure.

Returning to the micro world, the firm can supply its portion of aggregate output by a combination of different factor inputs as well as by variations in inventory holdings. Depending on relative factor prices and inventory costs, it can seek to minimise its total costs by employing a stock of workers, average hours per worker, capital equipment (including vintages of machines) and capacity utilisation in some optimum combination. It can also vary its inventory-stock to output-sales ratio. Moreover, the 'wage' it faces is a complex variable that reflects inputs and includes the wage rate, premium payments and bonuses, deferred fringe benefit compensation, specific human capital expenditures, etc. It also faces capital costs, depreciation and capital subsidies, inventory storage costs. In this complex, but realistic, world a change in the wage has an implication for factor allocation depending on complementarities and substitutabilities among factor components, that have potentially profound implications for the employment-wage relationship.

The essential point to note, with reference to the present paper, is that such factor and inventory substitution does not disappear at the aggregate level and, in this respect, Kregel's analysis is far from complete. Nor should the quantitative effects of factor substitution be underestimated. Hamermesh, 1985, provides an extremely detailed and wide review of macro-level econometric studies on the real wage-employment relationship that largely emphasise the factor substitution aspect of the problem. He finds that, typically, the long-run wage elasticity of employment lies between -0.2 and -0.5. At a more general level, a recent report by OECD, 1985, summarises a UK study undertaken by the Treasury. This allows for *both* factor substitution and induced changes in aggregate output. It suggests a labour demand-real wage elasticity for the whole economy within the range of -0.5 to -1.0.

On the basis of these wider considerations, it is simply not possible to agree with Kregel's contention (page 33) that, 'analysis of the demand for labour ... must then be consistent with the aggregate analysis; indeed, it must be built from it.' There is no reason to expect consistency between Kregel's aggregate findings and the aggregation of microcomponents since a large part of the explanation of what determines employment-wage elasticities is simply missing in the macro analysis we have here. This is unfortunate because Kregel does appear to be intent on accommodating 'the real world' in a general way since, for example, he goes to some pains towards the end of his paper to integrate the impact of international trade considerations within his model framework.

My second main comment on the paper refers to disequilibrium and I can be much briefer about this. In the aggregate demand and supply analysis of the labour market, the wage rate seems to be set arbitrarily above the market clearing level. Suppliers of labour have no control over this because 'labour is not in a position to determine its desired position on its labour supply curve' (page 35). This is all very well, but it seems to beg a number of fundamental questions. Why do we assume that the economy is in excess supply in the first place? How did it get there? Kregel seems somewhat vague on this point. Indeed little concern is given to what others regard as *the* critical aspect of the disequilibrium problem. As I mentioned at the beginning of my comments, there is a great deal of concern over this sort of assumption by many economists, in New Classical, Keynesian and other camps. Further, as also earlier mentioned, attempts at explanation are almost all embedded firmly in microeconomic foundations. Unfortunately it is microeconomics which Kregel wishes to avoid.

My last comment concerns the aggregate supply equation and it runs parallel to my points on the demand side. I firmly believe that such an aggregate treatment of the supply side of the labour market faces potentially onerous difficulties. At the level of the individual firm, the employer faces a labour supply that, unlike in the aggregate analysis, does have some say on determining its position on the supply curve. It may be able to work more or less overtime hours; it may have some choice between work-sharing and an inverse seniority layoff system; it may be able to supply combinations of part-time and full-time labour services and so on. Again, while Kregel's aggregate endogeneity point is well taken, the supply side of his model misses the important element of complementarity and substitution among the supply choice given changes in relative wage payments.

Notwithstanding my criticisms, this is a stimulating paper and worthy of wide attention. None the less, I believe that it is misdirected in two important respects. First, despite Kregel's well-taken point that special problems arise at the aggregate level, the overall approach adopted does not shake my belief that it is in the study of the microeconomics of the problem that the greatest possibilities for advancement lie. Secondly, and closely related, I believe that the labour market does play an essential role in understanding the relationships highlighted in the paper and to ignore it leaves us with some potentially serious misinterpretations.

References

Akerlof, G. A. (1979) 'The Case Against Conservative Macroeconomics', *Economica*, 46.

Blinder, A. S. (1982) 'Inventories and Sticky Prices: More on the Microeconomic Foundations of Macroeconomics', *American Economic Review*, 72.

Clark, K. B. and L. H. Summers (1979) 'Labour Market Dynamics and Unemployment: A Reconsideration', *Brookings Papers*, 1.

Gordon, R. J. (1983) 'A Comment on a Paper by Rosen', Carnegie-Rochester Conference Series on Public Policy, vol. 19.

Hamermesh, D. S. (1985) 'The Demand for Labor in the Long Run', in O. Ashenfelter and R. Layard (eds) *Handbook of Labour Economics* (Amsterdam: North Holland).

Organisation for Economic Co-operation and Development (1985 Sept.) *Employment Outlook* (Paris: OECD).

Stiglitz, J. E. (1984) 'Theories of Wage Rigidity', *National Bureau of Economic Research*, Working Paper No. 1442.

3 New Information Theoretic Approaches to Labour Market Theory

Erich Streissler

The last decade or so has spawned a huge amount of literature on theoretical aspects of the labour market. Most of it has to do with problems of information either in the sense that incomplete information about what is going to happen or even about what is happening to the demand and supply conditions of firms influences labour contracts; or in the sense that firms' incomplete information about their employees actual implementation of labour contracts influences employment strategies. The main strands of thought which I call information theoretic in this wide sense are the implicit or explicit contract theories of wages on the one hand, the efficiency wage literature on the other. I intend to review the salient features of these endeavours in my paper. Since surveys of various aspects of this literature abound, I shall review the most recent models from a very particular point of view: economists can no longer be accused of sidestepping the problem of unemployment in their work. In fact, in the last decade some of the most brilliant economic theoreticians in the profession have tried to explain unemployment. But in spite of much effort by the best brains, they have *not succeeded*. *There is still no genuinely economic explanation of long-term involuntary unemployment at hand.* This does not mean that we economists, *as social scientists*, cannot contribute much to the understanding of the reasons for unemployment. But we always have to fall back on psychological, sociological or institutional and political explanations of why unemployment persists. The charge can still not be refuted that from the purely economic standpoint continuing involuntary unemployment remains a puzzle which suggests a lacuna in the explanatory power of economics. Fifty years ago Keynes wrote:

> It is an outstanding characteristic of the economic system in which we live that . . . it seems capable of remaining in a chronic condition

of sub-normal activity for a considerable period without any marked tendency either towards recovery or towards complete collapse. (Keynes, 1936, p. 249)

Once more this description seems to ring true. And how did Keynes explain the phenomenon? Not as an economist: 'Since these facts of experience do not follow of logical necessity, one must suppose [!] that the environment and the psychological propensities of the modern world must be [!] of such a character as to produce these results' (ibid., p. 250). After a further ten years of intensive research we cannot advance much beyond such an intellectually defeatist statement.

What we have learned in recent years is to show with ease why wages in the short run will neither correspond to the marginal product of labour, nor to the opportunity cost of work for the labourer. In fact, we now have dozens of reasons for this. But that does not bring us nearer to an explanation of involuntary unemployment. With quite a few special assumptions, plausible only in particular circumstances, we can explain why employment will fluctuate more than it would in a Walrasian spot market. But this helps little, as a Walrasian spot market is an unreal measuring rod and, what is more, employment fluctuation is not the most difficult thing to explain. It is not at all easy for a modern economist to explain how involuntary employment arises, or, to put it in other words, to explain the firing of workers. Some older explanations appear to me to be more convincing than some of the newer ones. To my mind, the most suggestive recent work is the efficiency wage literature which – in basically taking a page out of Marx and reformulating it in neo-classical language – for the first time in orthodox economic literature gives an explanation for a level of perpetual unemployment; though unfortunately under the most plausible assumptions this level should fluctuate countercyclically, being lower in recession and higher in the boom. The efficient wage theory shows that under certain conditions unemployment is necessary to the working of any economic system. But it cannot show that the conditions for its necessity are themselves necessary. Thus the explanation of continuing unemployment remains at best a partial one and is not really long run in nature, long run in the sense that it also encompasses the creation of mutually advantageous changes in institutions. The real problem to be explained appears to me the situation typical now for many European countries for more than a decade: a continuing high level of unemployment which follows a kind of step function: unemployment rising in every recession (a thing not difficult to explain), remaining virtually constant during the ensuing recovery, and during the next recession rising once again from the new higher level. This to me appears to be the stylised fact impossible to explain in purely economic terms. Or worse still, how can one as an economist explain rising unemployment during moderate economic growth? How can one explain, without reference to an outside *deus ex machina*, the rationale behind the type of forecast not infrequently made that a sustained rate of growth of x percent for a certain country will entail a rise in its unemployment rate to y percent within the next z years? It is this question of the possibility of formulating an explanation for a continuing high level of unemployment, or even a rising level without unexpected business downturns, the explanation of constant or rising unemployment within a stable and foreseeable economic environment, which this paper tries to address.

What we wish to explain is, of course, only *involuntary* unemployment. Explanations of why voluntary unemployment can arise are all too easy to think up and are a dozen to every ounce of the economist's logic. And though there certainly is some voluntary unemployment covered within the measured unemployment rates, empirical research seems to suggest that it is not the major part. Therefore we must define clearly what is meant here by involuntary unemployment. I take it the standard definition of involuntary unemployment is still more or less that of Keynes: 'Men are involuntarily unemployed if, in the event of a small rise in the price of wage-goods relatively to the money-wage, both the aggregate supply of labour willing to work for the current money-wage and the aggregate demand for it at that wage would be greater than the existing volume of employment' (Keynes, 1936, p. 15). Today we are somewhat more concerned with specifying explicitly the exact qualification and ability of workers. A man can then be said to be involuntarily unemployed if other men of equal qualification and ability are employed in a similar type of job at a wage marginally higher than the one he would be willing to accept.

Note that this definition implies that a qualified university lecturer out of work, who is offered a job as a dishwasher and does not accept it, is involuntarily unemployed in spite of declining this job. On the other hand, I would consider myself voluntarily unemployed if, when out of work, I am offered an equivalently paid position in a ministry or as a manager in a large corporation and decline this position. Qualified for administrative staff work just as much as for teaching or basic research, I must not decline such a similar position, if I do not wish to be counted as voluntarily unemployed. The frequent cases, however, where someone does not accept an inferior position because he is under the *illusion* that he is fully qualified and able to fill a certain position but actually is not, must be classed as voluntary unemployment. Coming from a country with a breakdown in confidence in its politicians, I have to stress this point. Since at least every other Austrian thinks himself at least as able and qualified as the majority of Members of Parliament, and at least every tenth Austrian believes himself superior to many Cabinet Ministers, hardly any Austrian could ever be voluntarily unemployed if we accept the indubitable fact that not everyone will immediately enter Parliament or be named to the cabinet the moment he loses his present employment.

I now turn to the question of why it is so difficult for economists, while preserving their basically economic paradigm, to explain long-term involuntary unemployment. The task has been made so difficult by the intellectual power of Adam Smith. I take it the basic economic paradigm, a paradigm common to all variants of economic thought, whether they are classical, neo-classical, Marxist or Keynesian, is that men purposely try to avoid waste, or, as it is usually put today, that they try to exploit all mutually advantageous gains from trade. It is this basic economic paradigm that was first fully exploited by Adam Smith and applied by him in order to show that the 'simple and obvious system of natural liberty' by itself and without any need of political intervention would lead to full employment. Full employment results from the obvious inclinations of men. Smith's argument is very forceful and I shall summarise it briefly. First he shows that in the aggregate, demand will always equal supply in goods markets, i.e. he created Say's Law of Markets, named after one of the authors who popularised his work. Smith not only created Say's Law, he proved it in a way extremely difficult to fault:

> That portion of his revenue which a rich man anually spends, is in most cases consumed by idle guests, and menial servants, who leave nothing behind them in return for their consumption. That portion which he annually saves, *as for the sake of the profit it is immediately employed as capital*, is consumed in the same manner, and nearly in the same time too, but by a different set of people, by labourers, manufacturers and artificers, who reproduce with a profit the value of their annual consumption. (Smith, 1776, p. 18)

Thus, either the saver or the agent to whom he entrusts his saving, e.g. the bank, will see to it that all savings are invested in real terms in order to earn profit. Anything else would entail wastefully foregoing possible income. Note that this argument is completely impervious e.g. to Marx's snide remarks that it is absurd to assume a perpetual coincidence between income and expenditure for every period. Smith would answer that, on the contrary, for the economy as a whole it is absurd to assume that people would not at least strive for such a coincidence because otherwise they would be acting wastefully. Neither does Smith assume well-functioning credit-markets in constant equilibrium or an equalisation of saving and investment via the rate of interest. His argument only requires *some* 'profit' for investment, i.e. a strictly positive nominal rate of interest, a very weak assumption indeed. The consequence of Smith's argument for the goods market is that there must always be gainful opportunities for employment of labour. Since demand for commodities will approximately equal their supply in the aggregate, one can assume that normally demand will not diverge too far from supply in most markets. A similar argument can be made for the labour market. It probably appeared so obvious to Smith that he did not make it explicit; but it is implicit in his reasoning. Any potential employee who has to work for his living will take a low wage job in preference to no job at all; and at low wages it becomes advantageous for employers to hire additional men. It is fully in the spirit of Adam Smith to argue that as long as human institutions are subject to economic choices types of contracts which impede such mutually advantageous trades will be replaced by other types of contract that do not impede them; and that if certain institutions make such trades impossible, one will try to overthrow them or at least seek ways to circumvent them.

Now of course I do not wish to rediscover Say's Law of Markets for you, or create the impression that I do not know that Keynes finally succeeded in faulting it 160 years after its enunciation with his idea of speculative demand. But Keynes' argument is the sole argument that has been made against it; and it is not a long-run argument. More importantly Keynes' counter-argument does not extend to Smith's corresponding reasoning concerning the *labour market*.

Curiously, though Keynes is the apostle of the short run, his charge against Smith's reasoning is basically that it is *too* short-run! Smith's idea that it would be irrational not to invest (directly or indirectly) savings because of the lost profit applies only to current, one-period profit. In the absence of perfect futures markets, if there is a likelihood of a capital loss in excess of the anticipated short-term profit on the invested funds, there will be no reason why real demand will just equal factor supply. Consequently labour can become involuntarily unemployed because of demand deficiency caused by pessimistic expectations about future capital values. In effect Keynes employs a two-period model to contrast with Smith's one-period model: Profit in the first period is counterbalanced by likely capital losses in the second. But as a mere two-period model the argument still remains a slightly longer-term short-run model. It cannot explain continuous, long-term involuntary unemployment.

Let us dwell briefly upon the fact that contrary to what some superficial readers of Keynes seem to think, Keynes does *not* explain *long-term* unemployment. His argument is mainly expectational: high interest rates or a low marginal efficiency of capital, *relative to normal levels*, cause a downturn in production and employment. One cannot apply his exposition to a situation where there is an unchanging state of expectations adjusted to a continuing low rate of growth. His 'employment function' is a labour demand function derived from a medium-run Marshallian demand function for goods. But such a function depends upon a given stock of plant and equipment, to say nothing of the given state of technical knowledge and given institutions. For long-run supply one would have to assume that with long-run unemployment more and more labour-intensive methods of production would come into use and more and more labour intensive commodities would be produced, so that even with a given real wage for any type of employed labour the employment function would shift towards a higher use of labour per unit of average output. Although Keynes suggests that in the short-run workers will fear that downward wage adjustments will entail only a relative worsening of their position relative to other workers (an argument which does not hold water when *all* wages are seen to drift downward) he does not explain why in states of continuous long run unemployment the real wage will not drift downward. Yet his 'employment function' is parametrised on a given 'wage unit'. Once more, even in a strictly Keynesian analysis, we cannot assume that unemployment would persist after five or ten years (though, it is true, Keynes presented arguments why a return to full employment would be slow). Keynes' unemployment equilibrium is a medium-run market equilibrium, explicitly abstracting from change in the typical Marshallian long-run factors and aducing only short-run reasons for downward nominal wages inflexibility.

Keynes' argument that expected capital losses may cause aggregate demand in the goods market to fall short of aggregate supply at given prices and that this has repercussions on the labour market thus only holds in the short-run. But even this does not weaken Adam Smith's idea that there will be strong tendencies for the labour market to clear of its own accord. According to the basic economic paradigm there are strong market-clearing forces in *every* market; for otherwise there would be waste in this market. This is, of course, particularly true for markets for perishable commodities; but labour, as everyone knows, is exactly the prototypical perishable commodity: foregone labour is lost forever. In fact, labour is *perishable* in a *double* sense: not only does the involuntarily unemployed worker lose the income for his labour during the time of unemployment, his human capital deteriorates the longer he stays out of employment. His capacity to work is also perishable. Unemployed workers both unlearn useful knowledge and after some time their work habits and possibly even character traits and health deteriorate. Thus the Keynesian 'speculative motive' works in reverse in the case of the labour market: for fear of capital losses in their human capital the unemployed should try to make new labour contracts *more* rapidly than they otherwise would. The buyers in the labour market, on the other hand, do not gain from the sellers' capital loss because their loss is not simply temporary: they have really become 'worse buys'. Thus a 'speculative motive' in the labour market should rather reinforce any tendency for unemployment to vanish.

The normal operation of the Keynesian 'speculative motive' to impede labour market clearing would be produced if workers suffer serious capital losses by being 'locked in' to a disadvantageous labour contract. If one contracts to work during an extended period at a lower wage than one might alternatively get, this lowers one's lifetime income. This is, of course, a well-known reason for assiduous search for a good job. But as a long-run argument for withholding labour this argument does not really hold water, or only under exceptional and therefore presumably rare additional conditions, and anyway it could not explain persistent involuntary unemployment. One condition necessary for a bad contract to impede employment would be that it cannot be revoked when a better employment opportunity arises. Since the right of workers to quit in order to take up a better job is virtually unlimited in modern industrial market economies, this condition is not realistic. In these conditions, it is better for a worker to take a bad job temporarily until a better job turns up than to stay unemployed till the good job arises. A second condition would be that potential employers always think a worker only as good as his last pay and only offer him jobs commensurate with his last pay. As is well-known, this is not infrequently the case with managers. In this case one should not take a low-paid job with one employer because this worsens the chance to get a better paid one. But again, this is not really a long-run argument. Presumably employers have some ability to evaluate the quality of their employees independently of what they have been paid previously. If previous pay is of some importance for future pay, and one has taken a badly-paid job because no other was available, one is presumably only locked-in to this bad pay until one has proved one's worth to the new employer. In the long run, taking a badly paid job temporarily does not matter. Finally, there could be transaction costs of taking any job, good or bad; above all high removal costs. The normal transaction cost (for instance, of moving) is, however, a once-over lump sum. It therefore fades in importance with the passage of time. Transaction costs are, admittedly, very important but short-run, arguments for the persistence of unemployment. I conclude: the basic Keynesian idea that one has to take into account possible next period capital losses as well as present period advantages in order to judge whether trade is advantageous in general works in the *opposite* direction in the labour market than in non-perishable goods markets: it reinforces the reasons for trade instead of weakening them.

I close this section on the difficulty of explaining long-term unemployment within the basic economic paradigm by returning once more to one of Adam Smith's ideas of why labour markets have a particular tendency to clear. This is the idea of the invisible hand, which is mentioned in the *Wealth of Nations* only once, and put forward precisely to show the tendency towards full employment in a free market economy. Now Adam Smith's real argument of the invisible hand is regrettably little known among economists and not at all a metaphysical concept, as many think, but a sharp and down-to-earth argument. Adam Smith first assumes very plausibly that entrepreneurs are risk averse and therefore prefer, for a given average profitability, less risky ways of production. He then says that labour intensive methods of production are less risky methods of production. This is certainly true if capital costs are fixed and labour costs adjustable to the level of production which is optimal for a given level of demand. It is also true from the point of view of the lender, e.g. a bank, who only finances fixed capital. Risk for the lender is smaller if the percentage of total costs financed via credit is small, i.e. if all capital or a fixed percentage of capital is credit financed in the case where production is more labour intensive. Thus by the lucky coincidence that labour intensive ways of production are *ceteris paribus* also less risky, risk averse investors tend to increase the amount of labour employed per unit of production. This lucky coincidence Smith calls the 'invisible hand' which leads to the social good of highest possible employment. He says of the typically risk averse entrepreneur: 'He intends only his own security ... and he is in this, as in many other cases, led by an invisible hand to promote an end which was no part of his intention' (Smith, 1776, IV, ii, 9). The end, which is immaterial to the single entrepreneur, is, of course, full employment. The argument stripped of its generalising overtones is still valid. We can safely assume that in extended periods of low growth the demand for large-scale, capital-intensive enterprises declines. With continuing high saving levels in affluent societies, the banks are therefore forced to look for new outlets for their loans. As new firms in general cannot offer much collateral, the banks will ration their new customers. This will work in the direction of production which is on the average more labour intensive. As time goes on it therefore becomes, not less, but more difficult for the economist to explain long-run involuntary unemployment.

I shall now turn to a brief review of the literature on labour contracts, usually called the 'implicit contract' theory, though whether labour contracts are implicit or explicit is really immaterial for the central questions at hand. This literature started out from the vague notion that full wage flexibility in the sense of period by period auction labour markets is a necessary and sufficient condition for involuntary unemployment to be non-existent; though, in fact, it is at best a necessary and not a sufficient condition; and not even a necessary condition for certain types of inter-temporal behaviour of an inventory type implying that labour supply is perfectly elastic at a given wage. Therefore a large body of literature tried to find more or less new and more or less good reasons for sticky real wages and thus of deviations of wages from marginal labour productivity for any one period. Then authors tended to *suggest* that what they had found contributed to an explanation of the volume of unemployment without actually proving it. A typical case in question is the seminal article on implicit labour contracts by Baily (1974), where the author actually says: 'I have avoided the question whether or not one can say that wage stickiness has caused or exacerbated unemployment ... I do not know the answer ... My feeling [!] is that [it does]' (ibid., p. 50).

According to Baily's central idea firms are less likely to be risk averse than workers because they have easier access to capital and because they are larger financial units relative to their workers in the sense of a greater likelihood of a compensation of risks in their financial inflows and outflows. Thus it is profitable for the firms, and utility increasing for workers taking a new job, to write in effect two contracts at the same time: a labour contract and an *insurance contract*, stating that as long as the worker is employed his wage will vary less than demand varies over time. If the firm is fully risk neutral, workers will be fully covered by this insurance, i.e. they will receive a non-varying, *constant* wage. The provision of this wage insurance by the firm, and not by an outside insurer or a trade-union, is cheaper because the firm has a pay-office anyway and the cost of administering payment to the workforce is further reduced by paying a constant wage. Baily stresses: 'Risk-reducing policies are the cheapest and hence most profitable way of attracting any given workforce' (Baily, 1974, p. 37).

Once one realises that insuring workers against inter-temporal income fluctuations basically implies writing *two* contracts at the date of employment, a labour contract and an insurance contract, one also realises that this idea cannot explain additional unemployment and particularly not involuntary unemployment. In essence the second contract, the insurance contract, just smoothes foreseeable wage variations over time, given the first contract. And why should it influence the first contract, or rather the decision of when to employ a worker and when not to? Why should it therefore change employment conditions? In fact, Baily's main theorem says just that; it runs: 'If you consider any [employment] strategy with a stochastic wage path, there is always another that yields higher profits, for a given expected utility' (ibid., p. 44). It is thus just wage smoothing that is profitable, not a different pattern of hiring and firing. What *is* explained, however, as the other seminal article by Azariadis (1975) points out, is that *if* there is employment variation, 'reductions in employment appear as layoffs rather than voluntary withdrawals of labour services'. We seem to get an explanation of *involuntary* cyclical unemployment. But as Baily goes on to show (in a side issue of his paper) if the costs of mobility between firms are high for firms and/or workers, i.e. high relative to the variation in demand the firm faces, then firms will insure workers against both wage fluctuation and against unemployment and will tend to hoard labour under adverse demand conditions. So while Baily implicitly started out to give reasons for cyclical unemployment, he comes out with the statement that under plausible conditions there will be little employment variation. This is reinforced by Azariadis (1975) who comes out with the not too surprising statement that firms will find it profitable to lay off their workers if these do not mind too much! He provides an interesting, but not very astonishing, characterisation of the *structure* of unemployment, but not of its size: 'Layoffs should be more frequent in industries with relatively volatile ... or relatively inelastic ... demand schedules' (Azariadis, 1975, p. 1194).

Quite a few other papers have tried to show under what conditions firms will insure workers, not only against income variation, but simultaneously against employment variation as well. Some of these models have suggested that it will only be profitable to insure certain workers against employment fluctuation. For instance, the internal career models suggest that it will be profitable for workers always to stay with one firm if they can thus rise to higher and higher pay levels; and profitable for firms to promise such a chance of promotion to the workers, whom it also promises to keep till retirement, because the firm can then initially pay workers much below their marginal product and also less than their marginal products over their working lives. The firm may also employ other – unskilled – workers to whom it does not promise careers and whom it hires and fires at will. Such models of a dual labour market have again been misunderstood to provide explanations of the volume of cyclical unemployment. But they cannot serve as such. They just explain *what type* of worker will be unemployed, not what will be the total number of unemployed on average.

Apart from risk-shifting there are quite a few other avenues for arguing that optimal labour contracts will provide for relatively rigid wages over time. Particularly appealing seems to me is the idea of Klein (1984) that 'labour (and most other inputs) are purchased by explicit and implicit long-term contracts rather than in spot markets because of the presence of firm specific investments' (p. 332). In other words, fixed capital, be it owned by the worker or by the firm, is also conducive to fixed wages. Another recent ingenious contribution by Johnson (1985) uses the argument long used for the advantages if suppliers of brand products impose a fixed price on their retailers: this economises on consumers' search costs for the best price. Johnson points out that if all firms pay the same price for the same kind of job this means that only the unemployed have to search and then only for the first job they get, not for the best paid job since all jobs are paid equally. These ideas are interesting, but they cannot really contribute to our economic understanding of unemployment. They have been mentioned only to show that the initial idea of insurance of workers against income fluctuations by firms is not essential for the conclusions on employment generated from it.

No contract theory can explain involuntary unemployment ex-ante: i.e. unemployment at the time the contract is made. Some varieties can explain unemployment ex-post. A particularly ingenious sustained attempt to do so has been made in numerous articles by Oliver Hart. He assumes an insurance model for workers' incomes against inter-temporal fluctuations. But now the firms are risk-averse too so that workers are not fully insured against adverse demand conditions: they are paid less when demand for their product is low than when it is high. Then Hart introduces a situation of asymmetric information between workers and the firm: Only the firm knows the real state of demand for its product. The poorly informed workers are faced with a problem of moral hazard: Possibly the firm only tells them that demand is very low in order to pay them a lower wage and thereby to increase profits? In order to demonstrate convincingly to the workers that times are really bad and to justify a reduction of wages, firms therefore have simultaneously to lay off workers. Unemployment decisions are thus necessary to make workers accept lower wages.

This is an interesting argument to explain lay-offs. But it was shown to have its weaknesses. Under the usual optimising set-up of labour contract models, in which it is assumed that leisure is a normal good whose demand rises with higher income, workers must be assumed to contract for an amount of labour at an average wage at which the utility of income just outweighs the utility of leisure foregone. Some models then seem to suggest that at the lower than average wage in bad times the utility of workers' leisure is higher than the utility from income so that exactly in bad times workers would prefer to be unemployed. At the depth of a depression workers still in employment are therefore involuntarily overemployed while by a corresponding argument it is precisely in the boom that they are involuntarily unemployed. This only proves that a sufficiently ingenious economic model can plausibly derive even the most absurd practical conclusions – or that we are all wrong in what we think we observe.

The asymmetric information version of the insurance or risk-shifting labour contract model as an explanation of macroeconomic unemployment suffers from a further weakness that Hart himself has pointed out in a recent unpublished paper with Holmstrom. It is because workers are badly informed about the actual state of demand in the market that some of them have to be laid off in order to persuade the others to take a wage cut. But if demand in general is low in the economy and this causes lay-offs by some firms, e.g. because many more firms go bankrupt than usual, then the other firms do not have to fire workers in order to persuade their own workers to take a wage cut. Workers are well informed about a general fall in demand because they can easily see the general condition of unemployment it creates. Thus, the idea of an asymmetric information between firms and workers is a microeconomic one not generalisable to economy-wide demand conditions.

And even in as far as some conclusions can be derived from contract models as to reasons for involuntary lay-offs, no real conclusion about involuntary unemployment levels can be made from them. The models explain at best why someone *becomes* unemployed. Levels of unemployment can only be derived from this if we know why people then *stay* unemployed. Why do they not bid down wages in firms not bound by implicit or explicit contracts? Why are no new firms started to capitalise on unemployed labour and its presumably low wage demands? Why do the unemployed workers not set up as self-employed labour?

I now turn to a second kind of argument which purports to explain the level of unemployment; and at least in its intent the *long-run* level of *involuntary* unemployment and not only its cyclical variations. This is the efficiency wage literature.

The efficiency wage model assumes that labour contracts cannot exactly specify what is actually to be done by the worker; and even if the contract could do so it is impossible to control every moment of the worker's actual performance. The desired quality of the labour service therefore has to be achieved in an indirect way: by high wages. What the firm is interested in is buying most cheaply not just labour hours but an efficiency unit of labour. Efficiency of labour or the effort put into labour quality rises with higher wages. We can find a point where the wage paid per efficiency unit of labour becomes a minimum and the firm therefore achieves the highest return for its money: viz. where the schedule of effort of the worker or the quality of his labour service in efficiency units is of unitary elasticity relative to the (real) wage (Yellen, 1984). Thus basically the argument of a monopsonistic buyer faced with an upward sloping supply schedule of effort or labour quality is used; in other words, the common argument of the price rising per effective unit bought. The firm optimally buys labour at a level where the real wage offered equals its marginal product paying due regard to the (positive) dependence of effort on wage. Thus, on the labour demand side the neo-classical optimality condition holds, as Keynes had assumed. Not so, however, on the labour supply side, as Keynes again had postulated. Involuntary unemployment exists because workers would be willing to work at a lower wage than those that are employed. But, given the necessity to pay all workers the same wage (a decisive condition!), more workers are not taken on because hiring them at a lower wage and thus lowering correspondingly wages for all, thus exert a negative external effect on the quantity of labour effort supplied, which makes it suboptimal to take them on. We can thus say that wages have to stay above the market clearing level in order to create optimal labour effort; or, alternatively, unemployment is necessary to create a sufficiently high loss for workers in case they are fired to keep them on their toes and to make them supply the requisite amount of effort. The wage of those employed has to be high relative to the monetary and non-monetary advantages of the state of being unemployed; or the penalty of unemployment has to be high in order to make workers supply average effort without constant control. The level of unemployment plays a socially useful role and has to be continually above zero in order to induce sufficient effort. Reminiscences of Marx's 'reserve army of labour' immediately come to mind. Furthermore, real wages are once more sticky because marginal productivity depends on them. If there are stochastic supply shocks or microeconomic demand shocks, employment and production vary, not the real wage. We have thus explained cyclical variation in involuntary unemployment as well as a groundswell of long-term unemployment.

There are numerous subvarieties of the efficiency wage argument. In the simplest model, due to Shapiro and Stiglitz (1984), 'workers can decide whether to work or to shirk', i.e. whether to work or to do nothing at all. 'Workers who shirk have some chance of getting caught, with the penalty of being fired' (Yellen, 1984, p. 201). If the penalty is sufficiently high, i.e. the real wage sufficiently above the opportunity value of unemployment or alternatively, of wages in other employments, only an optimal number of workers, possibly zero, will laze and thus the average amount of work done by workers will be high. One can make this model more sophisticated and less individualistic, if one assumes, as Miyazaki (1984) does, that the firm bases the workers' remuneration on the average performance in each work group, which creates an incentive, but that each worker does not wish to work harder than the average performance in his work group. In this case effort increases with the wage (or vice versa), it decreases with the average group effort and it also decreases with group size, as it is easier to assume a free rider position in a large group. Firms therefore have to stay small and intimate in order to create sufficient incentives for effort – this attempt to remain small causes involuntary unemployment. One can also use the well-known argument (Malcolmson, 1981) that higher wages attract better quality workers and that performance in efficiency units depends on the quality or ability of workers. If workers more or less know their ability and the able demand higher wages, low wages are not worth it because of the adverse selection effect on worker quality. Note once more that this argument crucially depends on the need to pay all workers, in this case good and bad workers, exactly the same wage. The last version to be mentioned does not suffer from this fault. We can just assume that there are high transaction costs to labour turnover for the firm and high set up costs for creating new firms (Salop, 1979). A plausible transaction cost is that of training a new worker. Firms therefore try to optimise labour turnover. Higher than market clearing wages reduce quits and thus save training costs. A level of involuntary unemployment, whose social function is to eliminate excessive labour turnover, is once more explained.

Thus the efficiency wage model seems at last to have provided reasons both for a long-term level of involuntary unemployment and for its cyclical variation by using only the economic paradigm of individual optimising behaviour. But has it really?

Note first that with the shirking model directly, and with other varieties of the efficiency wage model indirectly, the arguments explaining the cyclical variation of unemployment and the necessity for its long-run non-zero level are not necessarily incompatible.

If unemployment rises cyclically, for instance if some firms go bankrupt, work effort levels and labour productivity in other firms should rise, as they actually do. But then surviving firms should decrease real wages, and this they possibly also do; and hire more workers, and this they do not. Unemployment should have a tendency to stay close to the 'natural' level explained by the efficiency wage model. It is therefore not quite true, as the survey by Yellen claims, that efficiency wage models 'provide a new, consistent, and plausible microfoundation for a Keynesian model of the cycle' (Yellen, 1984, p. 205). Actually, in many European countries we have witnessed a rise to new levels of unemployment in each recession and a level of unemployment then remaining at the once achieved higher level afterwards; and this is unexplained by the efficiency wage theory.

There are some arguments in recent literature concerning why it is difficult to regain full employment once it has been lost. C. Schultze (1985) has recently used the familiar argument that it is difficult for firms to distinguish between a transitory and a permanent worsening of demand conditions and this makes them hesitate to adjust prices downward in conditions of low demand with further negative effects on sales and employment. But this is only a medium-run argument. The same is true of Neary and Stiglitz (1983), who argue that the expectation of being rationed in the future in the goods market (for firms) and in the labour market (for workers) causes adaptive behaviour already in the present which increases existing quantity constraints. Particularly workers who fear unemployment save more, thus reducing demand and actual employment levels. Howitt (1985) has argued that it is more costly to sell in thinner markets so that a decline in demand induces a strong decline in supply. I quote: 'Transaction costs and the externality of thin markets might account for persistently high rates of unemployment' (ibid., p. 97). The difficulty is only that this again does not account for *persistent* unemployment: factor prices just have to fall more than otherwise.

Returning to the efficiency wage theory as an explanation of really long-run involuntary unemployment we come up with further difficulties, many of which are pointed out very clearly in the excellent short survey article by Yellen (1984). Why do not other types of labour contracts arise which are Pareto-superior to unemployment? Why do firms, for instance, not impose a penalty on workers caught shirking in the shirking model, a penalty payable to the *firm*, and thus increasing its profits while the penalty of unemployment profits no one? Why do not workers in the training cost-reduction of labour turnover model pay the firm for training or post a bond for leaving prematurely as they, in fact, do in many ways in many countries and have done so in even more ways throughout history? Why are firms not able to pay the better workers more in the adverse selection model as, in fact, they again frequently do? Why, finally, are they not able to pay different wages to workers hired at different times, why are they not able to contract with every worker individually at an individual wage? Why are there no other incentives to ensure effort? All this is not explained.

And even if we have explained all that away one has to recognise that the basically stationary framework of the efficiency wage model assumes that the number of firms are fixed or at most that the structure of supply over branches of industry has to remain constant and that there is only one optimal organisation of firm in each industry. Adam Smith would have laughed such an argument out of court and would immediately have asked: Why do not new types of organisations of firms arise? Why do firms not start in other branches of production, e.g. in services? Why, finally, do the unemployed not become self-employed?

There is no explanation why these structural changes to eliminate long-run involuntary unemployment do not occur if one stays within the economic paradigm. Evidently there seem to be very different socio-cultural abilities in different societies to find new types of employment once one has lost a job. Evidently long-run unemployment is much exacerbated by declining industries where the workers have to find totally different occupations. Evidently difficulties of forming new enterprises differ much from society to society; and most evidently the costs of unemployment are very different in different societies. But all this only means that while long-run unemployment may be involuntary from the point of view of the worker, it is voluntary from the point of view of the choices of society itself.

References

Azariadis, C. (1975) 'Implicit Contracts and Unemployment Equilibria', *Journal of Political Economy*, 83.
Baily, M. N. (1974) 'Wages and Employment under Uncertain Demand', *Review of Economic Studies*, 41.
Hart, O. and Holmstrom, B. (1985) 'The Theory of Contracts', mimeo., Fifth World Conference of the Econometric Society, Boston.
Howitt, P. (1985) 'Transaction Costs in the Theory of Unemployment', *American Economic Review*, 125.
Johnson, W. R. (1985) 'The Social Efficiency of Fixed Wages', *Quarterly Journal of Economics*, 100.
Keynes, J. M. (1936) *The General Theory of Employment, Interest, and Money* (London: Macmillan).

Klein, B. (1984) 'Contract Costs and Administered Prices: An Economic Theory of Rigid Wages', *American Economic Review*, 124.

Malcolmson, J. (1981) 'Unemployment and the Efficiency Wage Hypothesis', *Economic Journal*, 91.

Miyazaki, H. (1984) 'Work Norms and Involuntary Unemployment', *Quarterly Journal of Economics*, 99.

Neary, J. P. and Stiglitz, J. E. (1983) 'Toward a Reconstruction of Keynesian Economics: Expectations and Constrained Equilibria', *Quarterly Journal of Economics*, 98.

Salop, S. (1979) 'A Model of the Natural Rate of Unemployment', *American Economic Review*, 119.

Schultze, Ch. L. (1985) 'Microeconomic Efficiency and Nominal Wage Stickiness', *American Economic Review*, 125.

Shapiro, C. and Stiglitz, J. E. (1984) 'Equilibrium Unemployment as a Worker Discipline Device', *American Economic Review*, 124.

Smith, A. (1776) *An Inquiry into the Nature and Causes of the Wealth of Nations* (London: Oxford University Press, 1976).

Yellen, J. L. (1984) 'Efficiency Wage Models of Unemployment', *American Economic Review*, 124.

COMMENT

Kurt Rothschild

Professor Streissler has written an interesting paper and has managed to pack a lot of material and problems into a very short space. There are many entry points for a discussion. I shall raise just a few of them as they came to mind; I do not pretend that they are the most important ones.

Streissler throws up some difficulties because contrary to the title of the paper, which promises only some information on information aspects in labour market theory, he really extends his approach to the wider problem of whether economic theory has succeeded in providing a '*genuinely economic* explanation of long-term involuntary unemployment', a question which he answers in the negative. Now quite apart from the question whether one agrees with Streissler's negative results or not, the difficulty with regard to his second problem – an *economic* explanation of involuntary unemployment – arises from the fact that he restricts his analysis to recent contract and efficiency approaches to wage and employment problems. This is probably too narrow a choice for this very wide question.

Contract theories in particular, but also to some extent efficiency approaches, are attempts to explain the existence of *rigid wages* in the face of changing conditions and non-cleared markets. In so far as we regard rigid wages as the sole (or main) cause of unemployment these theories could indeed be regarded as the decisive (new) contributions to unemployment analysis. If, however, we allow for other mechanisms leading to long-term unemployment, then the search for satisfactory explanations must go beyond the theories which are so well reviewed in Streissler's paper.

This seems particularly justified in view of the fact that Keynes – whose idea of 'involuntary' unemployment is at stake – was at pains to point out that wage flexibility might *not* be the key to employment creation. It is true that this refers to money wages, while Streissler – with Adam Smith – refers to real wages; but money wages are what is fixed and kept rigid in contract and efficiency theories. So more hope for an explanation of involuntary unemployment may lie in other directions, not least in those of disequilibrium economics and quantity rationing. Here a word might be added on Adam Smith's position. I doubt whether Streissler is correct in taking the modern neo-classical economist's difficulties with involuntary unemployment right back to

Adam Smith's ideas of market clearing and the invisible hand. Smith could rely on the invisible hand and Say's Law because he envisaged a natural inclination to barter and truck *and* to look for one's best advantage. This leads quite easily to market-clearing prices in goods markets where people get rid of goods they do not want and then stop producing them. Smith probably did not think that this 'model' could be easily applied to the labour market. In ch. 8 of his *Wealth of Nations* we find a multitude of explanatory approaches to wage formation (subsistence costs, bargaining, economic growth, wage fund) which shows that he was aware of the *peculiarities* and the longer-term character of labour market phenomena. This is, by the way, also characteristic of the modern theories discussed by Streissler which – *in this respect* – are in fact more in tune with Adam Smith than with the simple Walrasian tatonnnement models. On the whole I would think that Smith's writings on labour do not lead in any direct way to questions of unemployment, its level and its duration.

I am also not quite sure how far Streissler is correct in saying that Keynes does not 'explain' long-term unemployment. It is, of course, true that the *General Theory* as a whole concentrates on the short and medium period and this implies that unemployment, too, is discussed in this framework. But an important message of the Keynesian approach is certainly that once a certain disturbance has lasted for some time there are actual and expectational tendencies (bankruptcies, lack of demand, pessmism, etc.) which hamper a return to 'normalcy'. The long run can then be seen as a continuation of short runs which have a tendency towards perpetuation. This concept may not be a satisfactory explanation – it certainly needs further support – but it provides an *attempt* to explain persistent unemployment.

Let me now turn to the second part of Streissler's paper in which he gives a lucid and concise account of contract and efficiency wage approaches seen from the angle of unemployment. Here he presents a very useful survey of the new ideas and all I shall and can do is to add some minor remarks on a few points. As I stressed before, the contract theories were mainly concerned with explaining rigid wages and only *then* some authors tried to link these observations to unemployment. Streissler is a bit hard on these theories when he complains (on p. 56) that they 'tended to *suggest* that what they had found contributed to the theory of unemployment without actually proving it'. Is that not asking too much? Could one not say in the same vein that the orthodox theory 'tends to suggest that what it has found contributed to the theory of *full* employment without actually proving it"? If proof means strict tautological reasoning then, of course, attempts to bring in new factors will rarely succeed; but they may well *contribute* to our insights.

In some places (e.g. on p. 58) Streissler complains that the existence and structure of unemployment is explained, but not its *size* ('the total number')! Do we really expect to obtain quantitative information at this level of theoretical abstraction?

As far as the dual labour market is concerned (p. 58) I wonder whether an additional point could not be considered. If there are qualified people in the firm who are safeguarded, as far as wages *and* employment is concerned, by implicit contracts while less qualified secondary workers are 'left in the cold' then – *assuming fixed proportions* between primary and secondary work – the higher rigid wages of the *secure* workers may cause involuntary unemployment among secondary workers which cannot be overcome by their willingness to accept lower wages.

The seeming paradox (on p. 59) that one could speak of involuntary *over*employment in recessions because with lower wages workers should demand more leisure and those still employed could thus be classified as 'involuntary employed' is easily removed when we take into account one very special feature of the labour market: the fixed working hours. People might well prefer to work a *little* bit less when wages are lower, but they do not want to be laid off altogether. So there is only involuntary *un*employment.

The efficiency wage model with its many possible variations is interesting because it introduces considerable uncertainty into the traditional wage analysis. The wage level is no longer 'explained' by marginal productivity which can be seen and modelled in different ways. The effects of wage changes on employment and unemployment can now follow different paths. As Streissler shows there is no clear message as far as unemployment goes.

One plausible argument which Streissler mentions needs some modification. Wages, it is said, may not only be kept above the market clearing level to elicit greater effort, but also in order to create the unemployment which will 'keep the workers on their toes and make them supply the requisite amount of effort'. Now I am not denying that the idea of having some unemployment in order to keep up discipline is quite popular among some employers. But this works only if there is *general* unemployment. A single firm cannot contribute to it. This is not a question of microeconomics but belongs to the analysis of union policy-making and lobbying.

In the final section Streissler asks a number of pertinent questions with regard to the forces which cause unemployment in the models which he discussed. Why are there certain decisive constraints? Why do all workers have to get the same wage, why can there not be better forms of effort evaluation, why do unemployed persons not become self-employed, and, and, and . . . ? All these questions could give rise to important and long discussions. I cannot enter into such discussions now. But I want to point out that these very relevant questions show very clearly that a *full* answer to the problem of involuntary and long-run unemployment can probably not be found without introducing psychological and sociological considerations which lie outside the traditional field of narrow economic theorising.

At the beginning of his paper Streissler says that economists *as social scientists* can contribute significantly to the understanding of the reasons for unemployment. 'But,' he adds rather sadly, 'we always have *to fall back* [my italics] on psychological, sociological or institutional and political explanations of why unemployment persists . . . From the purely economic standpoint continuing involuntary unemployment remains a puzzle'. Why, I may ask, should we try to explain a phenomenon which is not 'purely economic' in the narrow sense of a scientific discipline exactly and exclusively in terms of that discipline? Why not 'fall back' on further information?

Part II
Financial Markets and Fiscal Policy

4 Financial Markets, Investment and Employment

Paul Davidson

The concept of a financial market is limited, in the following analysis, to any market where easily resaleable debt and/or equity securities of business firms and governments are traded.[1] Financial markets, therefore, always encompass well-organised, continuous and orderly spot markets.

LIQUIDITY AND THE ROLE OF SPOT FINANCIAL MARKETS

Well-organised markets for financial assets are essential to the development of liquidity properties for any asset other than money. For an agent to possess liquidity one must have the ability to meet one's contractual obligations when they come due, i.e., to be liquid means that an agent has available, or can readily obtain, the means of contractual settlement. In order to provide *liquidity*, therefore, any asset other than money must be readily resaleable in a well-organised, continuous spot market in order to obtain the means of contractual settlement. (Money which, by definition, is *the* means of contractual settlement, possesses the highest degree of liquidity possible.)

A real world requirement for the existence of any well-organised spot market is a *market maker*, i.e., an institution willing, and able, to act as the buyer and/or seller of last resort in the market.

A fully liquid asset, is any durable whose resale market is dominated by a market maker who (i) stands ready to buy or sell any quantity of the asset being traded *at a fixed announced nominal price*, and (ii) has virtually unlimited resources to maintain this market price. Fully liquid assets, therefore, can be converted into the medium of contractual settlement at the option of the holder. In modern bank-money economies, this implies that all fully liquid assets are those whose value in terms of domestic money is guaranteed via a market-maker institution which is either a division or an agent of the Central Bank.

A *liquid asset* is a durable traded in a well-organised, continuous resale market in which the market maker is expected to intervene only to maintain 'orderliness' in the spot market, whenever price movements become, in the judgement of the market maker acting under the rules of the particular organised market, too volatile to be justified by the circumstances. In liquid asset spot markets, it is expected that, in normal times, the price will change by small increments over time; most of the transactions will involve bull and bear individuals, with very few transactions involving the market maker. The latter will be required by the rules to intervene to slow price changes only when one side of the market (either the bulls or the bears) tend to dry up – with the result of disorderly, discontinuous large changes in spot market prices in the absence of deliberate market-maker actions. The existence of market makers in liquid asset financial markets permits most market participants to expect that they can liquidate their holdings easily whenever they desire. Most financial markets trade in liquid, rather than fully liquid, assets.

Finally, an *illiquid asset* is any durable whose spot market is poorly organised, disorderly, and/or even notional. Most real capital goods are illiquid assets. Some debt (e.g., most consumer and some business bank loans) as well as some small business equity certificates are essentially illiquid assets.

FINANCE, FUNDING AND NEW INVESTMENT

Financial markets play two important roles in the economy. First, via the 'new issue' segment of the financial market, money is transferred from economic agents who currently possess some wealth in the form of the medium of contractual payment to others who desire to 'fund' investment in costly, long-lived, illiquid assets. The concept of *funding* involves the selling of new issues of long-term debt and/or equity securities by buyers who use these 'funds' to immediately pay the producers of illiquid fixed capital goods for delivery – thereby permitting investors to take a position in real illiquid assets (cf. Davidson, 1982, pp. 36–7). Since fixed capital goods are not expected to generate sufficient quasi-rents to pay for themselves in the current period, buyers must fund the purchase price over a long period.

If entrepreneurs, who desire to establish profitable positions in costly illiquid real fixed capital, could not be assured of obtaining funding at acceptable costs via the new issue market by underwriting institutions, then these investors would not be willing to contractually commit themselves by ordering forward the new capital goods upon which the growth of the economy depends. The underwriting commitment for future funding permits entrepreneurial investors to contractually commit themselves today for the future (date of delivery) purchase of capital goods.

The producers of capital goods, armed with these forward contractual purchase orders, can then borrow finance from their bankers. These short-term bank loans permit capital goods producers to build up their working capital which when completed are the finished capital goods sold to investors who use their funding proceeds to meet their purchase obligations. The resulting sales receipts of the capital goods producers are used to pay off their working capital loans – and become a revolving fund available from the banks to finance the production of new working capital.

FINANCE AND LIQUIDITY

The second function of financial markets – and the most important one in modern economies – involves the spot market segment. Spot financial markets that deal in 'second-hand' assets provide various degrees of liquidity havens for those wealth owners who, facing an uncertain future, currently do not want to commit all their current claims on resources either (i) to purchase currently produced consumer goods, or (ii) to contractually order specific future produceable consumer goods at a specified future date, or (iii) to the current purchase of illiquid assets which can be expected to generate a specific dated future time-stream of purchasing power via quasi-rents. The development of well-organised resale spot markets, by providing liquidity for the second-hand assets which are actively traded in such markets, make the initial sale of these securities in the new issue market more attractive to wealth owners, facing an uncertain future, who are looking for freedom to delay decisions on the current commitment of resource claims.

Organised resale securities markets represent the continuous conflict of expectations of bulls and bears about the spot prices in the uncertain (not statistically predictable) future; they are speculative markets. 'A speculative market is *inherently restless*' as any *'con-*

stancy of ... price is contrary to the expectation on which it depends' (Shackle, 1972, pp. 200–1). Spot prices of liquid assets must be 'inherently restless' over time – or else there would not be groups of bulls and bears to continuously enter the market and provide the liquidity upon which the market depends.

Since second-hand liquid assets are essentially perfectly substitutable assets for new issues, the current resale spot price equals the cost of current funding. Since the funding requirement is related to the supply price of new capital, which, in turn, includes the cost of borrowing from the banks to finance working capital loans by producers (cf. Davidson, 1972, Chapters 11–13), therefore, the costs of funding, liquidity, and short-term bank loans for financing production flows are inevitably interrelated.

WHY DO FINANCIAL MARKET SPOT PRICES CHANGE OVER TIME?

There are two fundamentally incompatible explanations regarding the observed price movements which occur in well-organised, spot markets for second-hand liquid financial assets, namely [a] the psychological account and [b] the rational expectations narrative.

The foremost exponent of the first view was Keynes who argued that the spot bond price i.e.,

> the rate of interest is a highly psychological phenomenon ... It might be more accurate, perhaps, to say that the rate of interest is a highly conventional, rather than a highly psychological, phenomenon. For its actual value is largely governed by the prevailing view as to what it is expected to be. (Keynes, 1936, pp. 203–4)

The rational expectations (hereafter ratex) approach, on the other hand, implies that all financial markets are 'efficient'. Ratex assumes [a] that relevant information regarding future events is currently available to all; and [b] that the expectations of all agents, based on the available information, are either homogeneous or else dispersions of expectations about the mean expectation do not affect future trends via false trades, bankruptcies, etc. Efficient market theorists assume that the spot price of second-hand equity financial assets is the present value (using a stable real discount factor) of optimally forecasted future real dividends over the life of the securities. In a complete general equilibrium framework, these future real dividends are determined by the marginal physical productivity of capital.

The efficient market theory implies that in the absence of government interference, regulation, and discretionary monetary policy, the economy will, in the long run, achieve the state of bliss of full employment and a rate of economic growth that is limited only by technical progress and the growth in the labour force. Using a parade of sophisticated tools, the ratex approach justifies the old classical homilies, that *informed* agents acting in their own best interests will, in the absence of discretionary government actions, reach a state of full employment.

In Keynes' alternative model of a monetary production economy, there need not currently exist any information or market signals about future events because the future may *not* exist, even in a probabilistic sense. Accordingly, current expectations are anchored only by conventions. The Keynesian psychological view of financial markets implies, therefore, that if expectations are unsecured, financial market prices can either fluctuate violently or temporarily pause at any value, thereby affecting the liquidity of the economy and interest rates and consequently the rate of investment, employment, and economic growth. Accordingly, there is an active role for government in promoting sticky expectations regarding spot financial market prices, via a discretionary monetary and exchange rate policy, at levels which are compatible with full employment and rapid economic growth.

The efficient markets approach has driven the psychological approach from economic discussions, despite the mounting empirical evidence, of both a short-run and long-run nature, which is incompatible with the efficient market thesis. Shiller, for example, has examined the long-run relationship between real stock prices and real dividends in the United States from 1889 to 1981 and has concluded that 'the volatility of stock market price indexes appears to be too high to accord with the efficient market model given the observed variability of aggregate dividends' (Shiller, 1984, p. 3).

Recent very short-run analysis, showing increasing financial spot price volatility, is also incompatible with an efficient market view. For example, *The Economist* (1985, p. 74) indicated that during the first few months of 1985 the daily exchange rate volatility of the D-Mark and sterling 'have often swung 2–3 per cent a day against the dollar. Not so the yen (because of Bank of Japan intervention) . . . In terms of daily movements, European currencies have become more volatile this year than 1980–84 (see table).'

Table 4.1 Daily volatility* of dollar exchange rates, percentage changes

	1980–84 average	1985 to date
D-Mark	0.7	0.9
Sterling	0.6	1.1
Yen	0.7	0.5

*Standard deviation of % change.

Source: The Economist, 18 May, 1985.

Since there has been no obvious increase in either random shocks or the amount of daily information flows regarding the future in the first 4 months of 1985 vis-à-vis the past four years, the data in Table 4.1 appear to be inconsistent with the efficient market hypothesis! This observed increase in European currency fluctuations is compatible with unanchored expectations in the absence of any government intervention conventions; while the daily stickiness in the Japanese exchange rate can be associated with expectations secured on the active role of the Bank of Japan.

With the decline in prestige of the Keynesian psychological explanation and the ascendancy of the ratex view of financial market prices in both academic and governmental policy discussions, there has been, not coincidentally, a similar decline in the successful growth and employment in the developed countries and a return to the slower pace of international expansion, and the higher rates of unemployment associated with pre-Keynesian years when the philosophy of free market optimisation dominated our economic thinking and policies. Until we get our theories of financial markets 'right', we will not be able to re-establish the economic policies and progress associated with the earlier post-Keynesia, post-Second World War period.

TIME AND STRUCTURAL STABILITY

A fundamental axiom of the ratex market approach is that the future structure of the economic system is already determined in the current period, at least in a stochastic sense. Under this view, human beings can only discover the economic future, they cannot create it.

Technically this implies that all future economic events are the result of an already operating ergodic stochastic process. In an ergodic stochastic process, the probability function which governed the occurrence of past events is the same as the probability distribution which determines today's outcomes and it is also the same as the probability function out of which the future events will be drawn (see Davidson, 1982–3). The economic universe is presumed to be in a state of statistical control over time (Davidson, 1972, 1980). Thus the efficient financial market theory is a modern hi-tech analogue of the classical theory of determinism – with *the economic future being merely a stochastic reflection of the past*; actual future events determined, despite Einstein's warning to the contrary, by Nature's throw of the dice!

By contrast, in non-ergodic circumstances, statistical time averages calculated over a single time series realisation will not approach the space (fixed point of time) average calculated from a universe of realisations with a probability of unity as the realisations approach infinity. In other words, in a non-ergodic environment, the statistical probability distribution based on past observations is not relevant for determining the probabilities of either current or future outcomes.

For ratex theorists, the study of economics is similar to astronomy – a non-experimental, but empirical science, where the governing 'scientific laws' are *timeless* and hence the economic world is presumed to be ergodic. Ratex 'scientific' economists are searching for economic laws similar to the ahistorical laws that make up Newtonian physics. But as Hicks has noted (picking up a theme developed by Keynes and more explicitly by Shackle):

> experimental science in its very nature, is out of historical time; it has to be irrelevant, for the significance of an experiment, at what *date* it is made, or repeated (Hicks, 1979, p. 3).

Non-experimental natural sciences such as astronomy rely on the laws developed in the experimental sciences such as physics. Hence astronomical predictions are based on ergodic 'laws' which are assumed to be invariant with respect to calendar time. Thus for Hicks, economics is not like astronomy; in economics one cannot suppose that past evidence is sufficient for drawing inferences about the future (cf. Shackle, 1972).

For economic decisions, calendar time and history (not just age) are essential aspects of future outcomes, i.e., observations (results) are not necessarily independent of the date that crucial decisions are carried out. The economic situation may be non-ergodic. Econometrically established past 'real' relationships cannot be automatically presumed to hold in the future. The economic future can never be fully determined, even in a stochastic sense. Accordingly, sensible economic agents know that there are always some future events which cannot be captured in the existing information about the past and the present.

TIME AND CRUCIAL DECISIONS

Marshall, in his *Principles* (1890, p. vii) noted that the 'element of time is the centre of the chief difficulty of almost every economic problem'. And Shackle has added '[t]ime and logic are alien to each other. The one entails ignorance, the other pre-supposes a sufficient axiom system, a system embracing everything relevant. The void of future, but relevant, time destroys the possibility of logic.' (Shackle, 1972, p. 254).

Shackle has identified the concept of *crucialness* in economic affairs. 'Crucialness is the real and important source of uniqueness in any occasion of choosing' (Shackle, 1955, p. 63). A crucial decision occurs when the person 'concerned cannot exclude from his mind the possibility that the very act of performing the experiment may destroy forever the circumstances in which it is performed' (Shackle, 1955, p. 6). Consequently, crucial economic decision making, by definition, assures a non-ergodic situation so that the economic variables which impinge upon the decison makers' environment are not ahistorical. Crucial decisions create a new future. In such circumstances, rational expectations are not relevant and our choice between alternatives depends upon 'our innate urge to activity which makes the wheels go round' (Keynes, 1936, p. 163) versus our inborn needs for safety.

Many economists strongly resist the implication of Shackle's conceptualisation of crucialness in economic affairs and Keynes's emphasis (1936, ch. 12) on (non-ergodic) uncertainty dominating financial markets. Samuelson, for example, has insisted that the condition of ergodicity and the timelessness of economic models are fundamental requirements of scientific economic analysis. Samuelson notes that in neo-classical theory there is

> an interesting assumption ... I shall call it the ergodic hypothesis ... technically speaking we theorists hoped not to introduce *hysteresis* phenomena into our model, as the Bible does when it

says 'We pass this way only once' and in so saying, takes the subject out of the realm of science into the realm of genuine history. (Samuelson, 1968, pp. 184–5)

To Samuelson, the economics discipline is unscientific if its practioners believe that economic agents by their own crucial actions can create the future and, therefore, the economic process depends on the history of who 'passed this way only once'. If agents can create the economic future, then, according to Samuelson, economics becomes a humanistic, historical study, which by inference, make economists second-class citizens in the scientific community.[2] Neither Samuelson nor ratex proponents want such second class citizenship.

Even the strongest advocates of ratex, however, reluctantly admit that sometimes it is impossible to draw statistical inferences about future outcomes based on existing evidence. In so doing, they are implicitly conceding the possibility of Shackle's crucial decision-making activities impinging on future human outcomes in a non-ergodic world. For example, Lucas and Sargent state:

> we observe an agent, or a collection of agents, behaving through time; we wish to use these observations to infer how this behaviour *would have* differed had the agent's environment been altered in some specified way. Stated so generally, it is clear that some inferences of this type will be impossible to draw. (How would one's life have been different had one married someone else?) The belief in the possibility of a nonexperimental empirical economics, is, however, equivalent to the belief that inferences of this kind can be made, in *some* circumstances. (Lucas and Sargent, 1981, p. xii)

Lucas and Sargent provide no criteria to indicate when these '*some* circumstances' prevail in the economy. Indeed they tend to imply that in most circumstances non-crucial decision making pertains. But if such mundane decisions as the choice of spouse are, in Lucas' and Sargent's view, so crucial that despite the vast historical record on the outcomes of past marriages it is impossible to draw any statistical inference, then what about crucial funding decisions wedding entrepreneurs to specific illiquid investment projects or production processes, or consumers to big-ticket expenditures? Are not these economic choices *crucial* to the future outcome of most economic events? And do not these impact on, and interact with, spot financial market prices?

Accordingly, a significant difference between most leading mainstream neo-classical economists (e.g., Lucas, Sargent, Samuelson) and Keynes and many post-Keynesians is whether they believe that crucialness in a non-ergodic context is a salient characteristic of the economic decision-making process under study.

Ratex theorists explicitly presume that currently there exists sufficient information about future probability functions so that no matter what decision is made, cruciality is not involved. As the aforementioned quote from Samuelson indicates, Neo-classical Synthesis Keynesians had already implicitly accepted this ergodic presumption. For Keynes, and post-Keynesians, on the other hand, the economic future does not currently exist and hence there are no market signals that future agents can provide today's decision-makers. *The future does not possess an informational shadow that it can cast today.*

> We should not conclude from this that everything depends on waves of irrational psychology. On the contrary, the state of long term expectation is often steady, and, even when it is not, the other factors exert compensating effects. We are merely reminding ourselves that human decisions affecting the future, whether personal or political or economic, cannot depend on strict mathematical expectation, since the basis for making such calculations does not exist (Keynes, 1936, pp. 162–3).

For Keynes, financial expectations cannot be rationally based on an ergodic economic process. To anchor financial expectations over time therefore, required conventions which encourage the belief in stability plus deliberate policy actions to offset wild fluctuations in private sector psychology, if such swings should occur. There is thus a vast philosophical difference between those who profess a ratex view and those who hold a post-Keynesian position. For the latter, as Hicks (1979, p. 39) declared, there are 'no constants in economics' determined by 'real' forces independent of human control and actions.

> It is just that economics is in time, in a way that the natural sciences are not. All economic data are dated; so that inductive evidence can never do more than establish a relation which appears to hold within a period to which the data refer. If a relation has held ... over (say) the last fifty years ... we can not even reasonably guess it

will continue to hold for the next fifty years. In the sciences such guesses are reasonable; in economics they are not. Economics... is on the edge of science and on the edge of history. (Hicks, 1979, p. 38)

In a recent paper, Solow (1985, p. 330) argues that 'the end product of economic analysis [should be]... a collection of models contingent on society's circumstances – on the historical context'. Solow believes, therefore, that mainstream scientific economists have been misled by following the 'best and the brightest in the profession [who] proceed as if economics is the physics of society... [where t]here is a single universally valid model of the world' (ibid., p. 330). Thus, at least some of the leaders of orthodox economic theory have, at last, recognised the non-ergodic nature of economic science. With the apparent conversion of J. R. Hicks and R. M. Solow to the non-ergodic view of economics, can the rest of mainstream economists be far behind?

ARE ECONOMIC AGENTS IN FINANCIAL MARKETS ROBOTS?

A Robot World

General equilibrium theory, especially in its ratex version, attempts to develop a theory of choice which models 'a *robot* decision maker' (Lucas and Sargent, 1981, p. xiii, italics added).

If, however, the mainstream view of a stable (real? monetary?) long-term rate of interest disturbed only by random shocks were applicable, then the robot rational agents would 'know' that it would never pay to speculate against the market by holding any specific security for a period of time less than the agents optimising inter-temporal consumption decision. Since the robots would recognise that the market is the most efficient forecaster of the future, they would decide that, in the long run, all bull and/or bear speculation against the average market opinion must prove fruitless. (With the existence of transactions costs, speculation against the market must, in the long run, be costly to the speculators.) Consequently, rational expectation robot decision makers would deprive the market of any intermediate bull–bear transactions, thereby stripping bonds of the liquidity that they provide real-world bondholders who may not wish to hold bonds to maturity. Accordingly, the neo-classical assumption of a long-run parametric (real) interest rate in an ergodic world is logically incompatible with a real world bond market where bondholders desire liquidity to protect themselves from unforeseen and unforeseeable events and therefore require the continuous action of the bulls to provide the liquidity for the market.

In a world of rational expectations with inter-temporal gross substitution of consumer goods by optimising robot households[3] and the existence of contingency contracts, if bonds for all maturity dates exist, every specific bond would be sold only once, in the new issues market, to robot agents whose inter-temporal consumption plan called for the expected consumption of that portion of their wealth at that bond's future maturity date.

A Human World

Post-Keynesians, on the other hand, argue for an analysis of an economic system where decision makers have choice and free will; where humans – not robots – create the future via their crucial decisions. In such a world, the spot market is a battleground for conflicting and changing expectations which may not be resolved except via death or other grave wounds.

This view of continual conflict is most clearly discerned in the battle between the bulls and the bears in financial markets. The price of liquid assets in spot markets where activity is continuous, involves the *momentary* balancing of differing expectations about future spot prices of the traded securities. Since only one spot price will exist at any moment currently or at any specified future time, the expectations of at least half of the market participants (either the bulls or the bears) will be disappointed at each point of time.

In the real world, the continuous gyrations of spot security prices are not considered by the bull and bear players as merely random movements around a parametised long-period price. These short-run price movements are, in a significant sense, 'expected' by the market 'player' participants for these movements represent potential profit-making opportunities if they can buy at a lower price than they sell. The only relevant consideration for profit-seeking spot market players is the next period's expected return (R):

$$R = P_{t+1} - P_t - T$$

where P_{t+1} is the next period's expected spot price (including accrued interest earnings), P_t is the current market price and T is the transactions cost of buying and selling. If $T=0$, then it is only the difference between the next moment's price and the current price which is important; with $T>0$, the expected difference in price (including accrued interest) must exceed transactions costs for an agent to act bullishly on his expectations. As long as transactions costs are relatively low; the long-run expected return over the life of the asset is irrelevant for market players. Only if transactions costs were inordinately high, would the purchase of a security become 'permanent and indissoluble, like marriage, except by reason of death or other grave cause' (Keynes, 1936, p. 161) and only then would the long-run expected return be relevant as the liquidity characteristics of the asset vanished.

Hence those who 'play' the real world financial markets for profit are never concerned with the long-run price. As long as there is the potential for short-run price movements which exceed transaction costs, market players searching for profit opportunities need concentrate and speculate solely on these expected short-run price movements.

Times series data of spot financial prices are merely the stringing together of momentary, hourly, daily, etc., historical price observations in speculative markets which primarily reflect the actions of those who are attempting to outguess average opinion. No wonder that despite the billions of man-hours of computations spent searching these statistical realisations for systematic repetitive patterns to be used as the basis for forecasting future spot financial prices, no one has ever succeeded.[4] These spot price movements reflect the non-ergodic ebb and flow of speculative expectations. These expectations regarding future spot prices are anchored in the convention that liquid asset market prices are supposed to be in continual flux, while extreme (disorderly) movements are limited by market-maker actions.

LIQUID ASSET PRICES AND THE MARGINAL PRODUCTIVITY OF CAPITAL

Shiller's aforementioned study (1984) is compatible with Keynes' psychological view of spot financial price movements. One implication of this approach is that, even in the long run, time series of spot prices of liquid assets do *not* reflect a technologically determined marginal productivity of capital (cf. Keynes, 1936, ch. 16).

The lack of any such link to the real productivity of capital is especially obvious once it is recognised that resale markets for many pre-existing durables, other than liquid debt and equity securities, exist in the real world. In the absence of a 'market-maker' institution which fixes market prices by acting as the buyer and/or seller of last resort at announced prices (as opposed to a market-maker who merely limits disorderly price movements), spot prices of all pre-existing durables (not only securities) which are capable of being stored and resold on well-organised, continuous markets must be inherently restless.

These other resale markets also provide liquidity and an outlet for the same inherently restless speculation found in spot markets for financial assets. Unlike debt and equity securities whose present value is often linked to a technically determined real marginal productivity of capital by neo-classical economists, resaleable durables such as gold, old postage stamps, old masters and other collectibles cannot conceivably have any future marginal productivity 'real earnings' streams associated with their possession. Nevertheless, the spot market price movements of these durables are carefully followed by many wealth holders; with movement in spot prices readily reported in various publications. Wealth owners believe that 'other' resaleable liquid durables, such as used postage stamps, are important liquid substitutes for the speculative financial assets in their portfolios.

The mere existence of spot speculative markets for liquid 'collectibles' where there cannot be any conceivable relationship between these assets and the 'real' marginal productivity of capital should be sufficient to cast doubt on the general equilibrium foundations of the efficient market hypothesis which is ultimately based on a concept of a long-run real return on capital parameter determined by 'real productivity'.

Though the organisation of these various speculative 'collectibles' markets differ in detail, all have some institutional market-maker which acts to limit volatility in spot prices and thereby encourage both speculative activities of market players and the liquidity properties of the underlying asset. The market demand and supply of all such durables could not be safely assumed to be sticky over time without the specific rules for 'market-maker' institutions which operate to limit spot price movements.

Any durable goods markets without institutional market makers involve resale difficulties which severely limit the potential liquidity of the durables involved; hence such durables cannot be important objects of speculation. It is the conventional belief in the rules under which market-maker institutions operate in specific markets, and not stochastic determinacy, which more or less anchor expectations regarding the future spot prices of both financial assets and resaleable collectibles. These anchors are as frail as the ability of those in charge to enforce the market-making rules and practices under any circumstances. Ultimately, therefore, it is the liquidity position of the market-maker institution which assures its ability to make the market. This, in turn (as is liquidity in general), is tied to the monetary policy of the Central Bank.

POLICY IMPLICATIONS

The policy implications of this non-ergodic view of speculative spot security markets, in a world where money contracts are used to organise production activities (Davidson, 1982) and hence the ability to meet contractual commitments (liquidity) is essential, is startlingly different from the ratex approach. In the latter there is no role for discretionary interest rate policy, while in the former, *an essential aspect of providing for the stability of the non-ergodic macroeconomic system is a Monetary Authority whose activities, either directly, or indirectly via other institutional market-makers, limit the otherwise inherently restless and potentially disorderly movements in the prices of financial assets and hence interest rates.*

The Monetary Authority and, by extension, the banking system must act as a balancing factor–leaning against the potential buffeting winds of irrational psychology. By operating either directly or via financial intermediaries on the spot market for liquid assets, and, by laying down the rules of the financial game either by law or custom, the Monetary Authority via the banking system can affect not only the spot prices and volume of securities available for the public to hold, but also the cost and availability of working capital loans necessary to finance production flows in a system organised via money contracts.

Since interest rates (spot prices of financial assets) are an important determinant of aggregate employment and output, a full employment goal will *require* a Monetary Authority who will undertake a deliberate, discretionary policy of creating expectations of sticky financial prices – limiting financial spot price movements to a narrow band around that level which is necessary to provide sufficient liquidity to encourage a full employment level of effective demand. The judgement as to what is the proper level of interest rates and liquidity, which may vary over time as unforeseen and unforeseeable circumstances change, is too important an economic factor to be left to the non-probabilistic vagaries of an unfettered speculative financial market. Although, in a non-ergodic world, it is impossible to assure that a Monetary Authority will not make any errors of judgement, at least, it can be hoped for that an enlightened Authority, endowed with proper tools can act (i) to create an environment where private sector swings in liquidity preference are small, and (ii) to alleviate any shortage of liquidity if it develops.

Ultimately, the power of the Monetary Authority depends on the viability (acceptability) of the Monetary System. This viability, in a non-ergodic world, depends on the conventional belief in the stability of the money-efficiency wage (i.e., the money wage rate divided by labour productivity) and, more generally, the money costs of production of goods. In the absence of some deliberate form of incomes policy, if the efficiency wage increases rapidly, then the Monetary Authority is likely to be 'the only game in town' to protect the viability of the Monetary System from the ravages of inflation by instituting a policy of explicitly constraining liquidity to create unemployment and thereby reduce the upward pressure on efficiency wages and other monetary costs of production. In carrying out such an anti-inflation policy, the Monetary Authority is creating a shortage of liquidity rather than alleviating it. The result will be unemployment, underutilised capacity, and unnecessary and undesirable economic deprivation.

Neo-classical economic theories such as ratex, on the other hand, assume invariant relationships over time, while postulating that in the absence of short-run random shocks to the system, the prices of financial assets and therefore interest rates will settle down to an unchanging, long-run value based on the real productivity of capital (and/or real time preference). In the long run, therefore, there is no need for any discretionary monetary policy. Despite the ubiquitous lip service paid in the ratex literature to the view that expectations drive the economic system, it logically follows from their ergodic assumption that in ratex economics 'real' phenomena of productivity and time preference drive the economic system – at least in the long run (when we shall all be dead!).

SHOULD EXPECTATIONS BE ENDOGENOUSLY RATIONAL?

For those economist 'scientists' who ultimately believe in an ergodic economic system, expectations about the future can never be autonomous – for such expectations would admit an indeterminateness in the argument and an openness in the system so that past quantitative measures of economic affairs need not be an adequate probabilistic guide to future events.

For post-Keynesians, on the other hand, the economic system is open-ended – the economic future is to be created by human actions. Keynes' emphasis on 'animal spirits' driving investment decisions requires an autonomous role for expectations. Keynes' response to those who wish to make expectations a well developed endogenous quantitative variable was 'As soon as one is dealing with the influence of expectations one is, in the nature of things, outside the realm of the formally exact' (Keynes, 1973, p. 2). For Keynes, the difference between a static and dynamic economic analysis 'is not the economy under observation which is moving in the one case and stationary in the other, but our expectations of the future environment which are shifting in the one case and stationary in the other' (Keynes, 1973, p. 511). Problems in the real world can be analysed only when on average 'our previous expectations are liable to disappointment and expectations concerning the future affect what we do today' (Keynes, 1936, pp. 393–4).

It is only in a world of potential disappointment regarding future events – our world – that the 'peculiar properties of money as a link between the present and the future must enter into our calculations' (Keynes, 1936, p. 294). It is only in the real world that money is not neutral and hence speculative activities on financial markets have real effects on output, employment, and growth in both the short and long run!

UNEMPLOYMENT, EXPECTATIONS AND THE NEUTRALITY OF MONEY

In the ratex theory, markets clear at every point of time. Logically consistency requires, therefore, the absence of involuntary unemployment – even in the short run. When faced by empirical evidence, however, ratex theorists will admit that labour resources are often, in the real world, unemployed – but not involuntarily so. Short-run changes in 'voluntary' unemployment occurs, in ratex models, when agents make a mistake by confusing an observed change in their nominal selling price (assumed to be due to an absolute price level increase without any change in relative prices) for a change in the relative price of their output *vis-à-vis* all other products. As Lucas and Sargent state:

> under certain conditions, agents tend temporarily to mistake a general increase in all absolute prices as an increase in the relative price of the good they are selling, leading them to increase their supply of that good over what they have previously planned. Since on the average everyone is making the same mistake, aggregate output rises above what it would have been ... Symmetrically, aggregate output decreases whenever the aggregate price level turns out to be lower than agents had expected. (Lucas and Sargent, 1979, p. 307)

This ratex explanation of variations in observed unemployment over the business cycle, involves a sophisticated variant of the money illusion argument, i.e., erroneous (temporary) market responses are made in response to fluctuations in nominal values rather than (real) relative prices. For a theory which is based on the neutrality of money assumption, it is surprising that ratex can only explain the recurring real world changes in observed unemployment rates over the business cycle as due to continuous erroneous money illusion which causes money to be non-neutral.

Since the business cycle and observed variations in unemployment are persistent real world phenomena, then the ratex theorists should be required to reply to the following obvious questions: (i) Since there is a long historical record of business cycles, why does not the processing of the past evidence lead sellers to form rational expectations that tell them that it is erroneous to interpret inflationary rises in the absolute price level as changes in their product prices relative to others? In other words, why does history indicate that people continue to suffer from recurrent money illusion? and (ii) If, in the real world, money illusions and the non-neutrality of money persists, what is the relevance of a theory of rational expectations which assumes the continuous neutrality of money for its equilibrium results?

In a post-Keynesian monetary production economy, on the other hand, an uncertain, non-ergodic future means that money is always non-neutral, in either the long run or the short run (Keynes, 1973, pp. 411–12). Thus right from the very beginning, unemployment is not just an errant event in a 'rational' world; rather it is a fundamental potential outcome of any laissez-faire economy where uncertainty and liquidity aspects are important and money and financial markets are non-neutral.

Notes

1. Thus any transactions in illiquid real or financial assets (defined below) are not included. This does not mean that purchases of basically illiquid assets are not affected by financial market conditions.
2. Yet in their political activities in working for the election of specific candidates for public office, these same self-proclaimed economic 'scientists' would probably not accept the implication of their ahistorical creed, namely that, *in the long run*, it makes no difference whether a Ronald Reagan or a Mrs Thatcher *vis-à-vis* a Walter Mondale or a Neil Kinnock is elected leader of the nation. For if the economic world is ergodic and ahistoric, the long-run economic outcomes are determined by technical conditions and is as independent of the decisions of political leaders as are the eclipses of the sun!
3. Indeed, Danziger *et al.* (1982–83) have shown the facts regarding consumption spending by the elderly are incompatible with the notion of inter-temporal gross substitution in consumption plans. Instead the facts are compatible with consumer behaviour under non-ergodic uncertainty.
4. Instant riches awaits anyone who can identify a systematic pattern.

References

Clower, R. W. (1969) *Monetary Theory* (Middlesex: Penguin).
Danziger, S., Van der Gaag, J., Smolensky, E., Taussig, M. (1982-3) 'The Life Cycle Hypotheses and the Consumption Behavior of the Elderly', *Journal of Post Keynesian Economics*, 5.
Davidson, P. (1967) 'A Keynesian View of Patinkin's Theory of Employment', *Economic Journal*, 77.
—— (1972) *Money and The Real World* (London: Macmillan).
—— (1980) 'Post Keynesian Economics: Solving The Crisis In Economic Theory', *The Public Interest*, 1980; reprinted in *The Crisis In Economic Theory*, edited by I. Kristol and D. Bell (New York: Basic Books).
—— (1982) *International Money and The Real World* (London: Macmillan).
—— (1982-3) 'Rational Expectations: A Fallacious Foundation for Crucial Decision Making', *Journal of Post Keynesian Economics*, 5.
Hicks, J. R. (1979) *Causality in Economics* (New York: Basic Books).

Keynes, J. M. (1973) *The Collected Writings of John Maynard Keynes, 14* (ed.) D. Moggridge (London: Macmillan).

—— (1936) *The General Theory of Employment, Interest, and Money* (London: Macmillan).

Lucas, R. E. and Sargent, T. J. (1979) 'After Keynesian Macroeconomics' *Federal Reserve Bank of Minneapolis Quarterly Review*, 3; reprinted in Lucas and Sargent (1981). All page references are to reprinted version.

—— (1981) *Rational Expectations and Econometric Practice* (Minneapolis: University of Minnesota Press).

Marshall, A. (1890) *Principles of Economics*, 1st ed (London: Macmillan).

Samuelson, P. A. (1968) 'What Classical and Neoclassical Monetary Theory Really Was', *Canadian Journal Of Economics*, 1. (Reprinted in Clower, 1969. All page references are to the reprinted version.)

Shackle, G. L. S. (1972) *Epistemics and Economics* (Cambridge: Cambridge University Press).

—— (1955) *Uncertainty in Economics* (Cambridge: Cambridge University Press).

—— (1980) 'Imagination, Unknowledge, and Choice' *Greek Economic Review*, 2.

Shiller, R. J. (1984) 'Financial Markets and Macroeconomic Fluctuations' (mimeo).

Solow, R. M. (1985) 'Economic History and Economics' *American Economic Review Papers and Proceedings*, 75.

The Economist, 295, No. 7394, May 18–24, 1985.

COMMENT

Salvatore Biasco

I will comment on Paul Davidson's paper first in terms of what it contains, and second in terms of what it does not contain.

According to Davidson, theories can be distinguished by the way in which they conceive the future and they treat time. Rational expectations, which relies on a mechanistic conception of economic processes and on the idea of efficient markets, considers the economic system to be inherently stable. In the Keynesian approach, on the other hand, stability can only be induced by the behaviour of economic authorities and by monetary and institutional arrangements. This seems to me the core of Davidson's analytical reasoning from which he draws some policy implications which will be discussed later.

As far as the analytical propositions are concerned, there is no real basis for disagreement. I do not fully agree, however, with the form and emphasis of some of these propositions.

My first objection is terminological, but not entirely. I do not think that it is correct to call the Keynesian theory a psychological theory. This expression might give rise to the idea that on the one hand there is a theory of rationality, which is anyway a theory of information, and that on the other hand there is a theory, if not actually of irrationality, of the indefinite; a theory based on the psychic and everchanging mood of the operators. I prefer the expression 'theory of conventionality' which better reflects the Keynesian idea that there are no quantitatively defined, unique connections between variables. In other words the range of values that a variable can assume (in the market where it is determined) in relation to values taken on by other variables (in their markets) is wide, both ex-ante and ex-post.

The relationships which can be established are only of a qualitative nature and are useful to focus on the forces at work and to distinguish the causes and the effects.

I would like to stress that these qualitative relationships also concern the relationships between the signals that operators select from the processes at work and the way in which these signals orient their choice of future action. As regards expectations, the nature of these relationships is an issue which Keynesians must face even if they consider these relationships changeable and conditioned by particular circumstances. Thus I cannot be satisfied by an analysis that appears to reject links between market signals and decisions, simply because this is the starting point of the rational expectations hypothesis.

Sometimes Davidson is too extreme and he implies that expectations – and here is the importance of terminology – are in some way only connected to the psychology of operators; and therefore they simply cannot be explained. If we follow this position there is no room for further theory and we are confined to the only conclusion (which is perfectly correct, but partial) that markets are inherently unstable and restless. (I would suggest, for example, that the expression 'autonomous expectations'—autonomous from what?—should be avoided.)

I entirely share Davidson's intentions and analytical focus: there is nothing in the economy that can be understood as the fundamentals upon which the operators can unanimously anchor their expectations.

However we must not be led into an a priori rejection of the possibility that financial decisions are made according to subjective conceptions of the behaviour of markets (represented through economic models), or of interrelationships of variables in the economy, or of anticipation of the behaviour and reactions of the authorities. Sometimes these beliefs can be very widespread, as for example when policy actions can only be in one direction and can be anticipated by a large section of the market. It must be said, however, that neither the entity nor the moment in time of the authorities' intervention (or of a discontinuous succession of interventions) can be anticipated. In general, the signals are always incomplete and they are deciphered in a different way by different operators. Nothing in the past can constitute objective probability for a future event.

Professor Davidson's criticism of rational expectations is conclusive when he emphasises the fact that economic processes are non-ergodic. On the other hand, his criticism is less well taken when he states that it is crucial to rational expectations to assume that financial assets are kept to maturity.

It is one thing to assume that exchange of assets in financial markets cannot be contemplated in the rational expectations approach and quite another thing to state that, if such exchange does take place, it has no influence on the path followed by exchange rates, interest rates, or stock prices, when adjustments are generated by exogeneous or unanticipated shocks. The second is the case of rational expectation theory. The crucial assumption of rational expectations is that adjustment always takes place in conditions of continuous stock equilibrium.

The equilibrium value of asset prices is at any moment fully recognised by all the operators, it is instantaneously reached and it is maintained along the whole (mechanical) path followed by financial variables up to the final equilibrium value. It is perfectly conceivable that prices are formed without any actual transactions, but it is irrelevant to the rational expectations approach whether exchange of financial assets takes place or not at portfolio equilibrium prices.

The force of Davidson's criticism may also be blunted by followers of rational expectations with the assumption that rational expectations are myopic. The problem for them is that they must also assume that 'myopic' expectations are 'perfect'.

Continuously-maintained stock equilibrium is a very strong assumption. This marks the fundamental difference between rational expectations and what I have called the 'conventional' approach. I totally agree with Tobin (1982, p. 125) when he states that:

> The major alternatives to models of financial and asset markets that assume rational expectations and efficient use of information are models that assume slow adjustment periods and disequilibrium. Disequilibrium need not mean that markets are failing to clear, though it may take that form. It may be simply that portfolio investors are off their desired portfolios.

I will try in what follows to connect Tobin's idea with what Davidson states in his paper.

I would say that there are two sides to the explanation of changes in spot prices over time in financial markets (or, in general, in organised markets). The first side concerns the reason why some financial variables follow a one directional movement for a period of time and then reverse themselves so as to give way to a cycle. The other side concerns volatility of values of the same variables over the cycle. For example both the reasons why the dollar tendentially depreciated against the mark from 1977 to 1980 and appreciated from 1981 to 1984 must be explained as well as its pronounced variability from day to day.

The conception of expectations discussed above concerns the first side of the problem. Davidson is much more interested in the second side. Neither can be treated separately.

(a) If it is true that uncertainty gives way to volatility, then volatility in its turn increases uncertainty. Even when there is relative agreement in the interpretation of market signals, volatility and strong contrasts always exist in expectations. Volatility is one of the reasons why portfolio adjustment takes place gradually. Obviously it is not the only reason: information, costs and inertia work to delay the adjustment.

(b) Graduality in portfolio adjustment does not have a stabilising effect on the financial market: it can be the cause of excessive movements in prices if the adjustments only concern flows, if a large share of market adjustment goes in the same direction, or if speculators taking opposite positions are lacking or slow to act.

(c) In these circumstances, explosive events are likely. Signals given out by these markets can lead to irreversible decisions elsewhere, or to institutional changes in the same markets, or to reactions of the authorities.

(d) In this context of fragile and uncertain expectations stock adjustment can take a long time leaving 'portfolio investors off their desired portfolios'. In the meantime the situation can evolve in a completely different direction and provoke an adjustment of a completely different character, which is superimposed on the first, while the first has not yet been concluded.

In rational expectations, the distinction between short-term variability and longer-term cycles of financial variables is not worth making. This is because at any given moment the market is in stock equilibrium and therefore expresses full knowledge of the tendencies and the adjustment path, for the information set available at that moment. Any variation is the product of a change in exogenous data. An inversion of tendency can be the product of a shock which takes place in the opposite direction of the one that preceded it.

A conventionalist approach never presumes that the financial market is in a stock equilibrium but, beyond that, it is characterised by the focus it places on facts which develop endogenously during the economic process and which are liable to change the features, and often invert the direction, of the process itself. These facts also include the change in authorities behaviour. Dynamic adjustment occurs in historical time and can never take the form of gravitation towards long-run equilibrium.

We can now refer back to the sequence of points (a) to (d) discussed above to relate them to events in the foreign exchange market and the dollar–mark exchange rate. We can also refer to Davidson's table.

Rational expectations economists would think that any change in the exchange rate comes from an adjustment to a shock and even when they deem that the adjustment path is not straight towards a new situation of equilibrium (as in the case of overshooting) they would consider that the operators cannot mistake the long-term (mechanical) dynamics and the values towards which it converges. This presupposes that the background conditions are independent of the path the exchange rate follows. The economy whose currency is appreciating (sometimes with bandwagon phenomena), such as Germany in 1977–80, is put under pressure to adapt its productive structure in a way which allows it to tolerate a stronger exchange rate; moreover it exhibits a low inflation rate which tends to become structural, because a prolonged period of low inflation influences the behaviour of private and public operators even when the currency is no longer appreciating. Between jumps in one direction and another the upward movement of the exchange rate is supported and accelerated by signals sent out by these structural changes. This cannot but provoke reactions by the authorities, which in their turn dampen (extrapolative) expectations. Moreover, it can also provoke endogenous phenomena which sooner or later invert expectations.

There are periods in which signals, especially for operators adopting a monetarist point of view are contradictory.

Policies aimed at stabilising depreciating (appreciating) exchange rates succeed in correcting the current account imbalance (since the effects of relative changes in demand have dominated in the real world over the effects of changes in relative competitivity). While the current account becomes positive (negative), the pre-existing inflation differentials are not immediately corrected; nor are differentials in money supply growth (because of the endogeneity of money). Even differentials in monetary and real interest rates are not immediately corrected (because of the differentials in inflation rates). The memory of the past also plays a role in blurring operators decisions, as convictions on the status of long run strength or weakness for any currency are slow to recede, even when the background conditions change radically. The range of expectations is at its widest and the difficulties in detecting the future trend produces maximum volatility in exchange rates, as in 1980 and 1985. The time horizon of speculators becomes ever shorter.

When the inversion of the situation becomes a general conviction (usually with a delay), the currency which had previously been weak – for instance the dollar from 1981 onwards – is pushed up by the same mechanism of extrapolative expectations which pulled it down at the beginning of the cycle. In this scheme volatility emerges as a by-product of exaggeration of currency changes, of signals sent out by changes in production structure, by endogenous developments that sooner or later convince the market that an inversion of trend might come to the fore.

None of the points which I have brought up seem to be in contrast with the core of Davidson's affirmations, which I entirely share: the future is uncertain (not in a probabilistic sense), financial markets are restless, and processes are non-ergodic.

From these conclusions Davidson seems to proceed in the following way: (a) volatility in financial markets reduces the propensity to invest, (b) the monetary authority must try and stabilise markets and at the same time provide sufficient liquidity to encourage a full employment level of effective demand.

As far as the first part of Davidson's argument is concerned I have nothing to add save two minor observations: (i) I would have avoided reference to a strict connection between the decline in growth in the developed countries in the last decade and the volatility in financial markets, because it may be taken as an oversimplification. (ii) I would have placed more emphasis on the volatility of foreign exchange markets than on the volatility in other financial markets because it is the market with major effects on other markets. Variability connected to the cyclical behaviour of exchange rates has stimulated changes in production structure during the re-evaluation period which have proved irreversible during the devaluation period. Variability connected to volatility of short-term spot prices for currencies has deprived changes in relative prices in goods markets (both across and within countries) of their information content, and in this way it has worked as a barrier to entry.

The second of Davidson's propositions seems to me to be easier to state than to implement. I would have liked Professor Davidson to have gone more deeply into the issue of policy implications, instead of dealing with it in such a provocative way.

We live in open economies with huge public deficits, sometimes they are inflation-prone, they are modelled and governed by concrete institutions. How can Davidson's affirmations be made compatible with current conditions? By administrative means and controls? I would not reject such proposals out of hand, but I would have liked some discussion of the consequences. Such discussion would have to start by recognising that the Italian financial system is different from both the German and the Anglo-Saxon systems.

The use of discretionary powers for liquidity and interest rate management is important, but it may not be sufficient. Given that the critical approach to macroeconomics starts its analysis from the existence of concrete institutions, the problem of the appropriate financial structure to favour employment and accumulation must be faced.

It will have to consider the relationship between banks and firms, the desirable degree of competition and segmentation in financial markets, intermediation and disintermediation. We need greater insights into these matters in order to know how to make financial institutions a propellant to stable and strong accumulation.

Reference

Tobin, J. (1982) 'The State of Exchange Rate Theory: Some Skeptical Observations', in R. Cooper, P. Kenen, J. Braga de Macedo and J. van Ypersele (eds) *The International Monetary System Under Flexible Exchange Rates* (Cambridge, Mass: Ballinger).

Malcolm C. Sawyer

My comments focus on those aspects of Paul Davidson's paper with which I do not agree completely. Much of the paper is a critique of the so-called 'new classical macroeconomics' associated with authors such as Lucas and Sargent. Before discussing this critique, I would like to ask whether, in late 1985, any critique of the new classical macroeconomics, at least in its rational expectations, market clearing, no involuntary unemployment version, is necessary. I find that when teaching new classical macroeconomics to graduate students, I have great difficulty in convincing students that any sensible person could seriously adhere to such views. The evidence of 30 million or more unemployed in the OECD area has surely been a major factor in empirically discrediting the new classical macroeconomics. It is impossible to attribute prolonged periods of high levels of unemployment to misperceptions about real wages. The interviews with new macroeconomists reported by Klamer[1] indicate their difficulties in explaining persistent unemployment.

The first major comment I have to make relates to Davidson's discussion of ergodic and non-ergodic processes. The idea of an ergodic process arises from consideration of a Markov process, where the probability of the system moving from one state (say S_i) to another (say S_j) in one period is independent of the time period considered and of the previous history of the system. Let us label that probability P_{ij}. The system is then considered to be ergodic if the transition probabilities are such that the system can effectively be in a stochastic equilibrium. There are several ways in which a system could be said to be non-ergodic, if by that we merely mean that the system is not ergodic (whereas the technical definition would be a Markov process which did not have the property of being ergodic). I am not sure in what sense Davidson is using the term non-ergodic – I suspect that a number of different senses are being used. I think it may be useful to distinguish four ways in which a system can be non-ergodic.

These four ways can be typified as follows. First, it is conceivable that an individual is uncertain (i.e. does not know and cannot estimate the relevant P_{ij}'s), yet the process itself could be ergodic. This would link with one of the criticisms of rational expectations when applied to the real world, namely that at the beginning of a new era the relevant probabilities and properties of an economic system will not be known to individuals since there is no relevant previous knowledge from which the relevant probabilities could be estimated. Even so, the probabilities themselves could be dictating how the system moves over time. In this view, there is no scope for decison making on the part of the individual, a point to which we return below.

The second possibility is that the probabilities change over time and/or are not independent of previous events (i.e. it is not a Markov process). This may involve uncertainty (if the change of probabilities cannot be accurately forecast) and history matters.

Thirdly, the system may be non-ergodic in the technical sense of not being capable of generating a stochastic equilibrium outcome, which indicates that to say a system is ergodic involves assumptions on the relationship between the transition probabilities. In that sense, Davidson's comment (p. 79) that 'in a non-ergodic environment, the statistical distribution based on past observations is not relevant for determining the probabilities of either current or future outcomes' would not be correct. Previous transition probabilities would still hold, and in that way the probability of future outcomes, given the current situation, can be estimated.

The fourth way is for the system to evolve in a deterministic manner but with movements between different states, i.e. the $P_{ij}s$ take values of 0 or 1. A self-perpetuating trade cycle could fall into that category. For example, suppose the economic cycle follows a sine curve pattern. Its previous movements are a good guide to future movements, and from its current position and rate of change its position at any time in the future can be exactly forecast.

Underlying this discussion and much else in Davidson's paper, there are ideas concerning the relationship between individuals and the over-all system, and the importance or otherwise of individual decision-making. In his paper, Davidson appears to adopt a position of stressing the importance of individual decisions, following authors such as Shackle (perhaps one could say adopting an Austrian position), particularly those decisions of a non-routine type, and playing down the role of external constraints on individuals. In contrast, the new classical position can be seen as a combination of 'robot' decision making with largely routine decisions and a world in which individuals do not influence outcomes, since outcomes are determined by some mysterious market forces. But those market forces are supposedly based on individual decisons. If an economy is in some sense in a repetitive equilibrium then there are, of course, no new decisions to be made since the world repeats itself. Indeed, if the world were ergodic, then individuals would be thrown around by the wheel of fortune as described by the transition probabilities. Individuals may believe that they make important decisions (at least important to themselves), but this appears to have no impact on the operation of the economy. It is paradoxical that whilst Davidson stresses the role of individual decison making, there are many post-Keynesians, Marxists and others who emphasise the notion that there are aggregate level relationships which have no micro counterparts *and* the way in which the system bears down on the individuals in their decision making (notably the forces of competition). In contrast, the supply-siders (at least those of a neo-classical orientation, though not those of a more Austrian persuasion) emphasise the role of individual decision making but then place individuals in a framework where those decisions have no effect on the operation of the economy.

One outcome of the onslaught of the supply-siders has been a general questioning of the ability of governments to perform the sort of tasks which Davidson seeks to assign to governments. For example he advocates that authorities act 'rationally' when the market is not acting 'rationally', i.e. to know better than the market, with 'the monetary authorities ... act[ing] as a balancing force – leaning against the potential buffeting winds of irrational psychology'. There are likely to be times when governments are swept along by a similar irrational psychology, for fashions and moods influence governments as well as markets. More seriously, we have to address the question of whether governments are able to operate in the way in which Davidson would like, particularly in financial markets. This includes the question of whether governments have sufficient knowledge and desire to do so. But of relevance in financial markets is the question of whether governments now have the power and resources to move against the market. For example, in 1980-1 could the British government have held down the sterling exchange rate even if it had wanted to do so? The trends of the past fifteen years in the determination of exchange and interest rates would appear to be in the direction of increased power for the markets and diminished power for the authorities. The break-down of the Bretton Woods system is illustrative of this trend. Similarly, there must be a question-mark against the ability in any relevant sense of governments to control the money supply.

In conclusion, I would like to half-agree with Davidson when he writes that 'until we get our theories of financial markets right, we will not be able to re-establish the economic policies and progress associated with the earlier post-Keynesian, post Second World War period'. It is only half-agreement in that I would argue that getting the theories of financial markets 'right' would be a major intellectual advance, which would help illuminate the constraints on a return to full employment. But in many respects the capitalist world was able to have full employment before without having developed the 'right' theories of financial markets. Indeed, much of the conventional Keynesian macroeconomics ignored financial markets or treated them in a cavalier manner (e.g. assumed exogenous money supply, willingness of financial markets to finance government deficits). This neglect of the financial markets in some respects opened up the way for later trouble. The assumption of exogenous money which could be controlled by the government (as represented in the IS-LM approach) could easily be taken over by the monetarists. Neglect of the financing requirement for a government deficit weakened the position of Keynesian policy and theory, when as in the mid-seventies government deficits on a large scale became necessary for the maintenance of employment levels. Unfortunately when we get the theories of financial markets 'right', we may well realise that the constraints which those markets pose for reflationary policies are such that the prospects for recovery are rather slim.

Note

1. Klamer, A. *The New Classical Macro-economics* (Brighton: Wheatsheaf, 1984).

5 Fiscal and Monetary Policy in the Keynes–Kalecki Tradition
Alois Guger and Ewald Walterskirchen*

INTRODUCTION

The co-existence of rising inflation, unemployment rates and budget deficits has discredited fiscal policy in the last decade. Keynesian economics, the dominant mode of thought in economic policy and economic analysis, has been depreciated and the old orthodoxy has gained ground again.

After the war, Keynesian demand management policies were adopted and, though there may be some disagreement about their active role, there can be no doubt that budgetary policies played a key part in avoiding a major set-back for more than twenty years. On the one hand, in most countries the widespread belief that governments will and can counteract cyclical fluctuations by fiscal action strengthened business confidence and thus acted in itself stabilising upon the economic development (Baily, 1978; Bisphan and Boltho, 1982). On the other hand, the universal growth of public expenditures led to overall expansionary pressure and the build-up of the welfare state increased the built-in stability of the system substantially. Though the degree of active commitment to demand management between countries varied – the UK, Sweden, Norway, and possibly Austria were much more committed to intervention than Germany and Switzerland, thus causing divergent rates of inflation and disequilibrium in the balances of payments which forced some governments repeatedly to restrictive actions – unemployment rates declined and the rates of growth reached unprecedented levels.

Since the late 1960s circumstances have changed radically. In the

*Helpful comments by Professor J. Stendl are gratefully acknowledged.

face of cost-determined inflationary pressures, i.e. rising wages and raw material prices, the demand-side instruments of the orthodox Keynesians were doomed to failure. Restrictive fiscal and monetary measures lowered inflation, but only after long delays and with substantial declines in output and employment. Keynesian theory and policy making lost ground in these years. In many countries confidence in demand management policies has been shaken and restrictive monetary policy has revived. It turned out that the Keynesians were right in warning that full employment could not be maintained by relying on demand management strategies alone. In 1943 J. Robinson warned that unemployment in a capitalist economy had the function of preserving the value of money, and M. Kalecki pointed out that

> Full employment capitalism will have . . . to develop new social and political institutions which will reflect the increased power of the working class. (Kalecki 1943)[1]

In 1944, when the British Government incurred the responsibility for a 'high and stable level of employment' (in the Employment White Paper) Cambridge and Oxford economists gave a comprehensive account to the problems a policy of maintaining long-term full employment would have to face in a capitalist system. They envisaged the need for direct controls because the pursuit of such a policy would be constrained by trade imbalances and inflationary pressures.

In the first part of this paper our point of departure is Keynes's attitude to the policies applied, after the war, under the auspices of 'Keynesian conventional wisdom'. We are going to refer to Keynes himself and the scepticism of his fellow economists in Cambridge concerning the long-run outcome of the demand management strategies of the 'Bastard Keynesians' based on a failure to recognise the limits to such a policy arising from inflationary pressures and trade deficits. Here we are concerned to look at the place of fiscal and monetary policy in Keynes' thinking and his policy recommendations for the post-war years. We shall learn that in Keynes' thinking fiscal policy did not occupy as central a position as it did in the conventional Keynesian models and in policy-making in the 1950s and 1960s. Keynes' policy advice turns out to be much less straightforward than Lerner's concept of 'functional finance' might lead one to believe.

The second part of the paper is based on Kalecki's views on post-war employment policy. First, we deal with the problems which, growing out of the era of high employment in the 1960s, led to major policy reorientations in many countries in the 1970s. Then we consider the consequences of these restrictive policies for both the employment and budgetary situation in the last decade, as well as for possible future fiscal actions. In a final part we shall give a summary of the barriers that we foresee to full employment fiscal strategies in the near future and to remedies of which we consider necessary to make further application of fiscal policies more efficient.

KEYNES ON FISCAL POLICY AND POST-WAR STABILISATION

In considering Keynes' views on fiscal policy we should not forget that Keynes was first and foremost a monetary economist. He always attached utmost importance to money; yet after the war in a number of countries Keynesianism has come to be considered as identical with fiscalism, that Keynes' theory implied that nothing could be done with monetary policy. Employment policy would have to rely on government's budget alone.

KEYNES ON MONETARY POLICY

Keynes' theory is 'A Monetary Theory of Production', as he himself reminds us (Keynes, 1933, JMK, xiii; Leijonhufvud, 1968; Davidson, 1972; Minsky, 1975), explaining the need for government intervention to mitigate business fluctuations and prevent mass unemployment. In his *General Theory of Employment, Interest, and Money* (1936, JMK, vii) he analysed the important role that money and interest play in determining output and employment in a capitalist economy. The central conclusion was that monetary policy has to play the primary part in keeping the economy on a stable growth path, though it is not sufficient to prevent unemployment and depression. Thus, monetary policy has to be supported by budgetary actions.

Keynes' views on the goals and instruments of economic policy gradually, sometimes suddenly, changed under the weight of events and with the evolution of his theoretical thinking (Moggridge and Howson, 1974). In 1932, when Britain was in a slump, Keynes pointed out that

> a reduction of the long-term rate of interest to a low level is

probably the most necessary of all measures if we are to escape from the slump and secure a lasting revival of enterprise. (JMK, XXI, p. 114)

Monetary policy aiming at the long-run rate of interest was Keynes' primary concern from the *Treatise* up to well after the *General Theory*. Late in 1934, when Keynes was completing his *General Theory*, he pointed out in a letter: 'my main argument centres round the rate of interest' (JMK, XXI, p. 346). However, in the *General Theory* (JMK, VII, p. 164) itself he also expressed his scepticism about the possibilities for monetary policy alone to counterbalance fluctuations in the marginal efficiency of capital by influencing the rate of interest. He rather held the State responsible for organising investment more directly. But in 1937, a peak year, when he was dealing with the upper turning-point of the cycle he insisted on cheap money:

> it is a fatal mistake to use a high rate of interest as a means of damping down the boom ... the long-term rate of interest must be kept continuously as near as possible to what we believe to be the long-term optimum. It is not suitable to be used as a short-period weapon. (JMK, XXI, p. 389)

Contrary to many economists in the 1930s and 1940s Keynes always held the view that low interest rates play an important part in determining the volume of investment. But, by the time he was writing his *General Theory* he began to lose confidence in purely monetary policies for influencing interest rates.

KEYNES ON FISCAL POLICY

In 1943 Keynes wrote to a reader of his *General Theory*:

> It is not quite correct that I attach primary importance to the rate of interest ... I should regard state intervention to encourage investment as probably a more important factor than low rates of interest taken in isolation. (JMK, XXVII, p. 350)

Looking at the, now published, written evidence of Keynes' involvement in the activities referring to post-war employment policies it is possible to see that Keynes' position on fiscal action was more complex than its simplified representation by the 'Bastard Keynesians' and in Lerner's concept of 'functional finance'.

In the discussions of post-war employment policies Keynes drew a sharp distinction between stimulating investment or consumption, and laid much more stress on the prevention of a slump than on its cure. Hence, as J. Kregel (1985) has recently shown by reference to documentary evidence, Keynes put great emphasis on long-term planning of government actions.

Linked to the primary importance of the stabilisation of investment in the long run was the necessity of both a low and stable level of interest rates and a 'Public Capital Budget', i.e. a long-term investment programme, whose principal purpose was to 'balance and stabilise the Investment Budget for the national economy as a whole' (1945, JMK, XXVII, p. 409).

The idea was to counterbalance prospective fluctuations in private investment by capital expenditures of public and semi-public bodies in order to stabilise aggregate demand and maintain full employment. Having perceived a 'somewhat comprehensive socialisation of investment' as the 'only means of securing an approximation to full employment' (JMK, VII, p. 378) in his *General Theory*, later in 1943, he thought it would be necessary for authorities to carry out a long-term investment programme covering two-thirds to three-quarters of total investment if the range of business fluctuations were to be reduced (JMK, XXVII, pp. 353, 322).

Anticyclical budgetary actions would be accomplished by changes in the Capital Budget, which was to be balanced in the long run; yet 'in the last resort ... if the machinery of capital budgeting had broken down ... and the volume of planned investment fails to produce equilibrium, the lack of balance would be met by unbalancing ... the current budget' (1943, JMK, XXVII, p. 352).

Keynes opposed short-term variations in consumption because 'people established standards of life' (JMK, XXVII, p. 319) and would be very upset to be forced to vary them constantly up and down. He therefore concentrated on a long-term programme of capital formation to foster full employment and long-term growth to improve the standards of life in the long run.[2]

Having made reference to Keynes' support of long-term public investment programmes and his scepticism as regards stimulating consumption by public action, we would warn against putting too much stress on this point, since the whole discussion in these years referred to a particular situation in a certain time period,[3] a limitation clearly indicated by Keynes himself.

KEYNES' VISION OF POST-WAR DEVELOPMENT

In 'The Long-term Problem of Full Employment' (written in 1943 but not published before 1980, JMK, XXVII, p. 320) Keynes had envisaged three phases of post-war development:

1. For the first five years after the war – the transition period – the inducement to investment would be higher than the desired ('indicated') level of savings. To prevent inflation he thought of limiting investment by suitable controls and of limiting consumption by some kind of rationing.[4]
2. For the next five to twenty years, Keynes foresaw a second phase in which the 'urgent level of necessary investment is no longer higher than the indicated level of savings' (JMK, XXVII, p. 321). The discussions of post-war employment policy of the Economic Section of the War Cabinet in these years were first and foremost related to this second period. The primary problem was to ensure a high level of employment by preventing business fluctuations and to foster the growth of welfare by encouraging 'less urgent, but nevertheless useful, investment'. I think we can quite safely say that these circumstances correspond to the 1950s and 1960s, when by fostering private investment and economic growth the universal growth of public expenditures could be easily financed.
3. After twenty years of large scale investment, the economy would ease into a third phase in which 'we shall be faced, if not with saturation of investment, at any rate with increasing difficulties in finding satisfactory outlets for new investment' (JMK, XXVII, p. 360); the desired level of saving would exceed the demand for useful investment.

This perspective of stagnation was taken up by A. Hansen in the USA. In 1943 Keynes drew these conclusions for this period:

> we shall then have to start on very important social changes, aimed at the discouragement of saving and a redistribution of the national wealth and a tax system which encourages consumption and discourages saving ... and to absorb some part of the unwanted surplus by increased leisure, more holidays (which are a wonderful way of getting rid of money) and shorter hours. (JMK, XXVII, pp. 360, 323)

While Keynes definitely preferred stimulating investment in the second period, he laid primary importance to 'securing the right long-period trend in the propensity to consume' (JMK, XXVII, p. 326) for this later period.

At this point we may refer to one of the rare hints at fiscal policy in the *General Theory*: the support of fiscal action to promote a more equal distribution of income and wealth by 'income taxes especially when they discriminate against "unearned" income. Taxes on capital-profits, death-duties and the like' being as relevant as the rate of interest to increase the propensity to consume (JMK, VII, pp. 94–5). While Keynes expected a more or less balanced budgetary performance across cycles in the second period, he envisaged no escape from deficit budgeting (JMK, XXVII, pp. 353, 356) for the third phase:

> I should expect for a long time to come that the government debt or government-guaranteed debt would be continually increasing in grand total. (JMK, XXVII, p. 278)

While Keynes had never dwelled upon the question of how the transition from the second to the third period would come about, theoretical explanations of saturation in investment demand have been put forward in the 'stagnation thesis' of A. Hansen and R. Harrod and in J. Steindl's 'maturity theorem'.

While A. Hansen's and R. Harrod's explanations relied on exogenous factors, i.e. population growth, technical innovations, etc., J. Steindl's (1952) theory is based on endogenous factors inherent in the development of capitalism. According to Steindl's theory the transition of the market structure away from competition to oligopoly, accompanied by an increase in the profit-margins, leads to excess capacity and, thus, to depressing effects on investment decisions.

The consequences of these 'vanishing investment opportunities' (Schumpeter) on the stability and the development of the economy were expressed by R. Harrod's (1939) 'fundamental equation':

(1) $g = s/c$

where s stands for the desired savings-income ratio,
c for marginal capital-income ratio and
g is the 'warranted' rate of growth.

As is well known, this 'warranted' rate of growth is that rate of expansion which is consistent with people's desire to save and the planned investment of firms. Thus, g can be seen as the equilibrium rate of growth implying that the increase of effective demand is equal to the increment of capacity; hence leaving capacity utilisation constant.

As Harrod pointed out, this 'fundamental equation' brings two major problems of the cyclical nature of economic development to the fore. On the one hand, this 'warranted' rate of growth is unstable, it sets a rigid pace for equilibrium growth; so that any deviation leads to a cumulative upward or downward process. On the other hand, g, determined by savings behaviour and technology, has to be considered as fairly rigid and unable to counterbalance variations in the actual rate of growth.

Thus the 'warranted' rate of growth sets the pace and the actual rate of expansion has to keep up with it if the slump is to be avoided. The tradition of Keynes and Kalecki as expressed by Steindl's 'maturity theorem' and Harrod's 'fundamental equation' leads to the following conclusions:

1. a secular tendency to stagnation; i.e. in a maturing economy capital accumulation will tend to falter while the propensity to save is more likely to increase with rising income, thus driving up g;[5]
2. if the economy's saving ratio had been adapted to a high rate of growth any exogenous factor, such as rising raw materials prices or restrictive policy actions, pushing down the actual rate of expansion, will cause cumulative downward pressures.

In the post-war period this stagnative perspective has been substantially weakened by a considerable increase in the demand for public goods and the rapid extension of international trade. We shall take account of these factors by introducing the budget deficit–income ratio and the trade balance–income ratio into Harrod's 'fundamental equation:

Letting b = budget deficit-income ratio = $(G - T)/Y$
$\quad\quad\quad a$ = trade balance, i.e. net export to income ratio = $(X - M)/Y$
we can derive an extended form of Harrod's 'equation'[6]

(2) $g = (s - b - a)/c$

This extended Harrod equation takes takes account of budget deficits and net foreign demand.

At the beginning of the 1960s, in the USA Kennedy's tax reductions to weaken 'fiscal drag' and later on the Vietnam War neutralised the overall stagnative tendency by increasing the actual rate of growth and lowering the 'warranted' rate. While a large trade deficit weakened this expansive fiscal effect for the USA it fostered growth in the rest of the world by increasing the actual rate of growth and lowering the 'warranted' rate.

In the 1970s sharply rising raw material prices leading to large trade deficits in the industrialised world pushed the economy into a slump by lowering the actual rate of growth and at the same time increasing g. But these restrictive effects were partly neutralised by enlarging budget deficits. While after the first oil crisis this relief from the fiscal side had been quite considerable, it was much weaker after the last oil price rise in late 1979.

The economic development of the last decade, in this line of reasoning, can be examined in more detail by a flow of funds analysis (Mooslechner and Nowotny, 1980; Steindl, 1982, Walterskirchen, 1984). Simple algebraic manipulations of the extended Harrod equation (2) (cf. note 6) lead us to the well-known saving-investment identity for an open system that can be seen as the lending-borrowing identity of the flow of funds analysis.

(3) $S - I = (G - T) + (X - M)$

By distinguishing between households and firms we can write[7]

(4) $Sh - Ih = (Iu - Su) + (G - T) + (X - M)$

where Sh and Su stand for household and business saving and Ih and Iu for household investment in dwelling houses and business investment, respectively.

From identity (4) it follows that net lending of private households has to find its outlet either in borrowing by firms, by the public sector, or by the foreign sector. A fall in business net borrowing (e.g. by a fall in investment demand) leads either, through a decline in income and employment (automatic stabilisers) to smaller household net lending, higher budget deficits, and higher net foreign demand, or it is neutralised by discretionary measures through an increase in public expenditures or lower taxes. In Table 5.1 data are presented to illustrate the financial interplay of these sectors. Net lending or net borrowing is expressed in percentage of GDP.

While households are typical net lenders the business sector is generally a net borrower. Household saving amounts to 10–25 per cent (Table 5.2) of disposable household income and household net lending between 5 and 10 per cent of GDP (Table 5.1).

Table 5.1 Financial balances by sectors

Surplus/deficit in % of GDP

	1973	1974	1975	1976	1977	1978	1979	1980	1981	1982	1983	1984[2]
USA												
Households	2.8	4.0	4.7	2.7	1.2	1.2	1.3	2.6	3.3	3.4	1.6	1.4
Enterprises	−2.9	−3.3	0.7	−0.2	−1.0	−2.0	−2.0	−1.2	−2.3	0.1	0.1	−1.0
Public Sector	0.6	−0.3	−4.2	−2.1	−0.9	0.2	0.6	−1.2	−0.9	−3.8	−3.9	−3.7
Foreign Sector[1]	−0.5	−0.3	−1.2	−0.3	0.7	0.7	0.1	−0.2	−0.1	0.3	2.2	3.3
Japan												
Households	8.0	9.9	9.6	10.7	9.9	9.7	8.5	7.8	10.3	11.9	12.6	12.8
Enterprises	−8.7	−11.2	−6.9	−6.2	−4.6	−2.4	−4.6	−4.4	−5.9	−7.1	−7.2	−7.7
Public Sector	0.7	0.4	−2.8	−3.8	−3.8	−5.5	−4.8	−4.5	−4.0	−4.1	−3.4	−2.5
Foreign Sector[1]	0.0	1.0	0.1	−0.7	−1.5	−1.7	0.9	1.1	−0.5	−0.7	−2.0	−2.6
Germany												
Households	7.9	8.6	9.4	7.8	7.0	6.7	7.0	7.3	7.9	7.5	6.5	5.9
Enterprises	−7.8	−4.7	−2.7	−3.6	−3.9	−2.8	−5.2	−6.3	−5.3	−3.5	−2.5	−2.9
Public Sector	1.2	−1.4	−5.7	−3.4	−2.4	−2.5	−2.7	−3.1	−3.9	−3.5	−3.1	−2.1
Foreign Sector[1]	−1.3	−2.6	−1.0	−0.8	−0.7	−1.3	0.9	2.1	1.2	−0.5	−0.8	−0.8
France												
Households	3.5	3.7	5.7	3.8	4.3	5.2	3.8	3.2	4.5	4.5	4.3	4.7
Enterprises	−4.6	−6.8	−3.6	−5.0	−4.2	−2.8	−2.8	−4.9	−4.1	−4.9	−1.7	−0.5
Public Sector	0.9	0.6	−2.2	−0.5	−0.8	−1.9	−1.1	0.3	−1.9	−2.6	−3.4	−3.8
Foreign Sector[1]	0.2	2.4	0.1	1.6	0.8	−0.5	0.1	1.4	1.4	3.0	0.7	−0.4

United Kingdom										
Households	4.0	5.1	5.4	4.8	3.8	4.9	5.2	7.2	5.6	3.8	3.6	3.2
Enterprises	−2.7	−5.3	−2.3	−0.6	−0.8	0.0	−2.3	−2.3	−0.2	0.3	−0.5	−0.3
Public Sector	−2.7	−3.8	−4.6	−4.9	−3.2	−4.2	−3.2	−3.5	−2.8	−2.0	−2.7	−2.3
Foreign Sector[1]	1.4	4.0	1.4	0.7	0.2	−0.7	0.3	−1.4	−2.6	−2.0	−0.4	−0.6
Italy												
Households	11.9	12.1	17.5	13.7	14.2	15.1	14.2	9.7	12.2	11.6	11.7	12.2
Enterprises	−6.7	−9.8	−6.1	−6.2	−5.1	−3.0	−3.0	−4.1	−2.8	−1.3	0.7	0.6
Public Sector	−7.0	−7.0	−11.7	−9.0	−8.0	−9.7	−9.5	−8.0	−11.7	−11.9	−12.0	−12.5
Foreign Sector[1]	1.8	4.7	0.3	1.5	−1.1	−2.4	−1.7	2.4	2.3	1.6	−0.4	−0.3
Austria												
Households	4.7	4.8	6.2	6.6	5.0	7.1	7.2	6.1	4.8	5.3	4.4	5.0
Enterprises	−6.3	−7.0	−3.8	−5.1	−6.3	−5.1	−5.7	−7.1	−5.3	−1.2	−0.9	−3.4
Public Sector	1.3	1.3	−2.5	−3.7	−2.4	−2.8	−2.4	−1.7	−1.6	−3.1	−3.4	−2.4
Foreign Sector[1]	0.3	1.0	0.1	2.3	3.6	0.7	1.0	2.7	2.0	−1.1	−0.3	0.8

Source: OECD (1983b), WIFO.

[1] The Balance of the Foreign Sector corresponds to the current account with a negative sign (M − X).
[2] Preliminary.

Table 5.2 Savings ratios

	1960	1965	1970	1975	1980	1982[1]
			in % of disposable income[2]			
USA	11.3	12.3	13.2	14.1	11.8	13.0
Canada	9.4	11.3	10.9	15.3	14.6	17.0
Japan	—	—	22.3	26.6	25.0	25.0
United Kingdom	7.0	8.7	8.7	11.2	15.2	12.0
France	15.2	16.2	16.7	18.6	14.1	15.0
Italy	—	—	22.5	26.5	23.0	24.0
Germany[3]	8.6	12.2	13.8	15.1	12.8	13.5
Austria[3]	—	7.7	11.9	9.9	11.0	10.1

Source: OECD (1983a).

[1] Preliminary.
[2] Including small enterprises.
[3] Level not comparable with other countries.

The household savings ratios indicate, on the one hand, with rising income in real terms an increasing trend and, on the other hand, an anti-cyclical behaviour.

Let us consider the implications of the increasing trend of saving: The data of Table 5.2 indicate a generally increasing trend in the saving ratios for the period of rising real incomes (1960–75); since 1975, however, real household incomes have stagnated.

Household savings have to be absorbed by borrowing from the business sector, the public, and the foreign sector. Though there were considerable differences between the various countries for the 1960s and early 1970s (Steindl, 1982) the data for all OECD countries taken together indicate a broad accordance between business borrowings and household net lending in this period. Thus the net borrowings of the public and the foreign sector amounted to just 0.3 per cent of GDP, respectively (OECD, 1985, Tables 6.7 and 6.15).

But, since the first oil crisis the situation has considerably changed. While the borrowing of the business sector has been strongly reduced by the low level of investment demand and trade balances have often been in deficit, public sector borrowing has increased strongly (Table 5.1). For all OECD countries together, public sector borrowings amounted to 2.3 per cent of GDP in the period 1974–79 and 3.5 per cent for 1980–83.

Coming back to the perspective of vanishing investment opportunities we have to conclude that constant or even rising household savings will lead to a rising trend in budget deficits (Matzner, 1978).

We turn to the implications of anti-cyclical saving behaviour. While, according to the conventional view, household saving ratios fall in a recession because people try to maintain their standards of life when incomes fall, in the recessions of 1974/75 and 1981/83 saving ratios increased (Table 5.1). People postponed spending for consumer durables and dwelling-house expenditures. Thus, the decline in business borrowing, i.e. the fall in investment demand, has been enforced by a lower propensity to consume in the recession after the first oil crisis. Since 1979 this development has been reinforced by an enormous increase in interest rates.

The economic development of the 1970s has taught us, on the one hand, that an increasing trend of budget deficits can only be prevented if fiscal policy is able to stimulate private investment and to increase the consumption–income ratio by redistributing income and, on the other hand, that to reduce public deficits by restrictive measures will be doomed to fail if private investment or foreign demand, i.e. by passing on the burden to the trading partners, cannot be stimulated at the same time.

KALECKI'S THREE WAYS TO FULL EMPLOYMENT AND THE POST-WAR EMPLOYMENT EXPERIENCE

While Keynes was more of a pragmatic thinker, finding the right answer to ever-changing actual questions of economic policy, always considering whether the implications of theory are acceptable to the politicians, Michal Kalecki's thinking was more abstract and uncompromising, a clear-cut analysis in its essentials and implications.

Characterising unemployment as a consequence of demand-deficiency Kalecki (1944) offers three ways to full employment: deficit spending, stimulating private investment and income redistribution.

Deficit spending would be labelled today as typically Keynesian policy. Kalecki did not only think of bond-financed public investment, but also of subsidies for mass consumption (e.g. family allowances). He suggested that public expenditure should be financed as long as possible by higher income taxes, and after that by government bonds.

Stimulating private investment by income tax reductions or low interest rates has only a temporary effect and must be repeated since the higher capacity created reduces the degree of utilisation and thus eventually tends to depress investment again. Apart from problems of over-capacity, there may arise a conflict with income redistribution. Kalecki was very sceptical concerning this second way to full employment, he rather preferred deficit spending and income redistribution.

Income redistribution from high to low income classes is intended to raise the propensity to consume. This is a way of stimulating demand without running into budget deficits. But one must be careful not to impede investment by income redistribution. We see that Keynes and Kalecki were very much in accordance concerning employment policy. Perhaps Keynes put more stress on monetary policy, Kalecki on income redistribution.

What was the relevance of these ideas in the past decades and what is it now?

Public expenditures have been rather widely used for decades – especially in war times when the effect was most evident (Second World War, Korean and Vietnam wars, etc.). Since the majority of countries pursued an expansive strategy, budget deficits did not lead to balance-of-payments problems in the period before 1970. Keynes argued that if a budget deficit results there is something wrong. With a successful demand management no budget deficit arises. Matthews (1968) was wrong when he concluded from balanced budgets that Keynesian policies had not been adopted. The general attitude towards growth and public expenditure was the crucial point. The self-financing of government expenditure worked quite well. Demand management was used alternately in Britain as a Stop/Go strategy and no one doubted that demand could be influenced by State intervention. It was too evident.

Stimulating private investment has also been extensively used in recent decades (depreciation allowances, interest subsidies, etc.) and has produced a tendency to falling taxes on profits. It may have been overdone in some countries (with respect to income redistribution) in the last decade when it was seen as a supply-side strategy. Yet, this could not prevent a marked decline of the share of investment in most industrialised countries since the early seventies. Industrial policy, much stressed by J. Steindl to counteract long-run underinvestment, was adopted only by Japan but with great success. In Western Europe, depreciation allowances and subsidies to declining firms in general favoured the wrong structure (capital-intensive processes versus research- and employment-intensive innovation).

Income redistribution (from saving to consuming groups) was in general not consciously used as an instrument of employment policy, it was regarded as an instrument of social policy. On the contrary, savings were still promoted in most countries.

During the last decade as a consequence of the monetarist revolution all the three ways to full employment remained under-utilised, even after unemployment had risen dramatically. Discretionary fiscal measures were restrictive in most countries to stop the rise in budget deficits brought about by recession and increasing interest payments. Private investment was impeded by extremely high real interest rates, and income distribution was shifted to the wealthy by high interest rates, high unemployment of the poor and welfare cuts.

FUNDAMENTAL QUESTIONS OF EMPLOYMENT POLICY

All the fundamental questions of employment policy that the critics are raising today have already been discussed by Keynes, Kalecki and the Oxford and Cambridge groups in the 1930s and 1940s, namely inflation, balance of payments, crowding out and interest payments.

Inflation

The Keynesians wanted to stop deficit spending once full capacity was reached. Otherwise this would necessarily lead to inflation. They not only saw the problem of demand-deficiency, but also saw the process of inflation caused by excess demand for raw materials. monopolisation and rising money wages at full employment. Keynes proposed buffer stocks to stabilise raw material prices (JMK, xxvii, Part I). (Kaldor, 1983, has recently taken up this idea.) Some others proposed a central board for wage negotiations to counteract inflationary tendencies from the wage side.

The prediction that full employment would lead to inflation proved right. But no major country had pursued an incomes policy to keep real wages in line with productivity growth, and there were no buffer stocks to stabilise raw material prices, as Keynes had suggested.

Inflation certainly turned out to be the crucial obstacle to employment policy in the 1970s. Most governments adopted a tight monetary policy (partly after the first oil shock and generally after the second one) and deliberately accepted an enormous rise in unemployment to stop inflation.

At the same time, Keynesian policies have been rejected as inflationary and ineffective. However, the latest business upswing in the United States gives another illustration that deficit spending does not necessarily lead to inflation as many critics argue. The crucial points are full capacity, full employment and bottlenecks of raw materials.

We must see this shift in priorities from employment to price stability in a broader socio-economic context as Kalecki (1943) had done in his famous article on the political business cycle. They have called for stability of prices and consolidation of the budget, but they have meant more stability of the social structure and of the existing distribution of income and wealth, after the rapid social changes that the period of full employment has brought about.

Where did this policy lead to? The inflation rate was reduced, but only after some time and at the very high cost of mass unemployment and high interest rates. The goal of reducing budget deficits, however, could not be achieved since tight monetary policies increased budget deficits in two ways: they caused cyclical deficits by aggravating recession and they dramatically increased interest payments for government debt by high interest rates.

The redistributional effects of tight policy are evident: high interest rates favour the creditor and hurt the debtor. That means in general that it favours the old at the cost of the new. Young developing countries are typically high debtors, the same is true for young households and new firms. So it turns out that tight monetary policy is a 'conservative' policy in its strictest sense: conserving the old, obstructing progress.

Interest Payments for Government Debt

The problems of high interest rates were clearly seen by Keynes. He advocated very low interest rates even in the boom. In 1937 he warned: 'We must fear high interest rates like hell-fire.'

The problems of high interest payments for government debt, however, were not seen fully in the 1930s and 1940s, partly because it was not expected then that the Keynesian policy of low interest would be given up so soon to be replaced (in the 1980s) by its very opposite. Kalecki and the Oxford group were fully prepared to accept long-run budget deficits up to the long-run growth rate of GDP to be financed by a small capital tax. Capital controls were advocated to stop capital outflows. In Abba Lerner's proposal of 'functional finance', government debt did not matter at all, no matter how high it might be.

Domestic public borrowing is considered to be just an internal transfer, a distributional problem.

In fact, interest payments are now a major impediment for employment policy. While the rise in inflation rates in the early 1970s was the starting point for the radical change in economic policies, rising interest payments for government debt are now the main reason for not envisaging expansive fiscal policies, even after inflation rates have dropped.

The rapid growth in interest payments is certainly the consequence of high real interest rates and persistent large deficits. Interest payments have nearly no expansionary effect (because they are usually saved) and their redistributional effect runs in the wrong direction from the point of view of employment policy.

Let us consider the performance of the OECD countries in this respect (Table 5.3). In the OECD countries general government net borrowing rose between 1970 and 1985 by 3.9 percentage points of GDP. Cyclical effects raised the budget deficits by nearly 2 percentage points of GDP (according to OECD calculations) so that structural deficits rose by about 2 percentage points. This is totally attributable to higher interest payments. Interest payments for public debt rose by 3.3 percentage points of GDP. Even if we assume that the government can recover about $\frac{1}{3}$ of these interest incomes this implies that governments actually pursued a restrictive fiscal policy (in terms of discretionary measures).

Table 5.3 Effect of business cycle and interest payments on general government budget balances

	OECD countries		
	1970	1985	1970–85
	% of GDP		Change
Budget balance	+0.2	−3.7	−3.9
Cyclical effect	−0.3	−2.1	−1.8
Structural budget	+0.5	−1.6	−2.1
Interest payments			
for government debt	1.9	5.2	+3.3
'NET' interest payments[1]	1.3	3.5	+2.2

Source: OECD and WIFO calculations.

[1] Under the assumption that roughly one third of interest payments will be recovered by various taxes.

Tight monetary policies can thus be held responsible for both high interest payments and high cyclical deficits. And we may conclude that tight monetary policy after a decade or so has also forced fiscal policy to subordinate itself to the restrictive course of policy. This was, of course, intended. To quote an international monetary institution: since fighting against inflation has the highest priority the main task of fiscal policy is to support the restrictive stance of monetary policy. (The same was also intended for wage policy – to tighten one's belt.)

The experiment with tight monetary policies, however, came to an abrupt end in the United States when a change in monetary policy was enforced by the world debt crisis that was itself produced by the tight policies. US monetarism was in fact abandoned in August 1982 when Mexico's inability to pay threatened the world banking system. To save US banks from bankruptcy the Federal Reserve had to loosen the belt. But all European monetary authorities and many economists still have their eyes fixed on the money supply.

Balance of Payments

Keynesians paid great attention to the balance-of-payments implications of employment policies. They considered it to be crucial, approaching it, as they did, from the British point of view.

The current account actually turned out to be a major problem for employment policies, but as long as most countries were following expansionary policies it was not the crucial one. Apart from Stop/Go Policies induced by the balance of payments no major troubles turned up. Rising imports were met by rising exports.

But in the seventies when international trade further increased (tariffs were removed or reduced in the European Community) and many countries started a restrictive policy, trade deficits more and more became an obstacle to the practical implementation of employment policies. With rising import quotas and fast increasing interest payments the multiplier became lower and lower.

In France expansive fiscal policies in the early 1980s were dramatically reversed as France gained less from them than the neighbour countries (Germany). The United States, with its low import quota, could afford to play the locomotive role for a couple of years, but at the end a high trade deficit stopped the US business upswing.

Certainly the locomotive role produces current account and budget deficits in the country adopting it. On the other hand, its trading partners experience export-led growth, followed by a recovery of investment.

In Germany it is often argued that expansionary fiscal measures will have no lasting effect. This argument seems to be linked to the observation that all the problems stay with the expanding country, all the advantages with the 'free-rider'. This, of course, reduces the willingness of a country to play the locomotive role on its own. Germany and Japan now strictly reject the idea that they should do something to aid international expansion.

Crowding Out

The view that budget deficits would crowd out investment is so widely held nowadays that it can be called commonplace. The crowding-out argument builds upon the well-known fact that the financial balances of the economic sectors must add up to zero. Many economists (Feldstein, OECD, IMF, etc.) interpret this tautology in the following way: the budget deficit is absorbing too great a part of domestic savings (in the US about two thirds). Limiting private investment to the remaining savings raises interest rates exorbitantly. (Although it is occasionally admitted that capital inflow might finance additional investment.)

Keynes' argument against crowding-out was that public credit demand would have no different effect than the credit demand of large enterprises. If, however, every credit demand had crowded out some other then business upswing could never occur. An accommodating monetary policy must be taken for granted. In the case of restrictive monetary policies, interest rates rise when credit demand increases no matter where they may come from (private or public).

A majority of economists expected the large deficits in the USA to paralyse investment (and keep interest rates and dollar high). They were on the wrong track. On the contrary, deficit spending and expansive monetary policy have led to higher capacity utilisation, higher profits and higher investment. This is even admitted in a journal of an economic research institute in Hamburg (HWWA) that is certainly not suspected of being Keynesian.

Steindl (1982) has shown that the explanation for the high budget deficits since 1974 lies in another direction: The long-run worldwide decline in investment – reflecting restrictive economic policies and the structural troubles of oligopolistic industries—has caused high budget deficits through the operation of automatic stabilisers. If this decline in investment had not been matched by budget deficits an even greater demand deficiency would have resulted. (The rapid decline of GDP in Switzerland in 1975 where there were hardly any automatic stabilisers existing is a good illustration.

Steindl added that it would not be possible to reduce budget deficits worldwide by restrictive policies since tax revenue would be cut by the fall in incomes which would be the more drastic since durable consumers expenditure and instalment credits would fall abruptly and after a time investment of the business sector would decline. Only those countries which restrict their internal demand more than their trading partners could consolidate their budgets.

That's exactly what has happened (Table 5.4). Tightening of monetary policy has increased the financial surplus of the private sector by restricting spending on durables including housing and investment. The budget was consolidated mainly in three countries during the last years: Germany, Japan and Belgium. In all these countries the reduction in budget deficits was made possible because it was completely matched by a higher current account surplus. This implies, however, that other countries (USA) had to be prepared to accept higher current account and budget deficits.

Another argument against employment policy was that budget deficits could no longer be financed. The financial identity of lending and borrowing of the various sectors makes clear why there are in general no difficulties in financing public deficits since there must always be a corresponding private sector surplus unless a trade deficit occurs. (In which case the country is dependent on foreign credits.)

We would now like to follow the different paths of employment policies in various countries. The traditional Keynesian way to stimulate growth by discretionary fiscal actions predominant in the 1960s has been adopted by only a few countries. The more typical way was to reduce growth by discretionary fiscal actions with the aim of

Table 5.4   Budget consolidation via trade balance

	Budget	Current Account
	% of GDP change 1981–85	
Germany	+2.3	+2.9
Belgium	+3.8	+3.8
Japan	+2.6	+2.8

Source: OECD.

long-run budget consolidation. But many countries tried to keep unemployment low (despite a poor employment situation) by increasing public employment or by reducing the supply of labour.

Step 1: Budget and growth in various countries

There is undoubtedly a positive correlation between expansive fiscal measures (measured in terms of discretionary actions) and economic growth. The effect of fiscal policy is most clearly seen in the United States in recent years. But domestic demand was also increased in France in the early 1980s when an expansionary policy was pursued.

Fiscal policy has certainly influenced growth, but it was in some cases not the main factor (crude oil in Norway, industrial policy and rising market shares in Japan, etc.).

On the other hand, those countries which restrained demand more than others experienced lower growth rates (Switzerland in the 1970s, Germany in the first half of the 1980s.) The effect of fiscal policy on growth can be illustrated by a comparison of developments in Germany and Austria (Table 5.5): in every year in which fiscal policy was more expansive in Austria than in Germany the growth of GDP was higher in Austria; in every year in which fiscal policy was more restrictive in Austria GDP growth was also lower.

But it must be admitted that increasing cyclically-adjusted deficits did not lead to higher growth rates in every case. There were quite a few countries with large deficits where the increase in the budget deficit was only due to higher interest payments (Italy, Belgium and others see Table 5.6). In this case the rising deficit had nearly no

Table 5.5 Fiscal policy and GDP-growth in Germany and Austria

	Growth differential Austria/Germany	Change in structural budget (% of GDP)		
		Austria	Germany	Austria/Germany
1981	−0.1	+1.4	+0.3	+1.1
1982	+2.1	−0.7	+1.4	−2.1
1983	+1.1	−0.6	+1.2	−1.8
1984	−0.6	+0.8	+0.4	+0.4
1985	+0.5	−0.1	+0.5	−0.6
1981–85 (p.a.)	+0.6	+0.2	+0.8	−0.6

Source: OECD and Austrian Institute for Economic Research calculations.

Table 5.6 Budget deficits and interest payments

	Budget deficits 1980 % of GDP	Budget deficits 1985 % of GDP	Interest payments 1980 % of GDP	Interest payments 1985 % of GDP
Italy	−8.0	−13.1	6.3	10.1
Belgium	−8.6	−10.3	6.1	10.1
Netherlands	−4.0	−5.6	3.7	6.5
Sweden	−3.7	−3.0	4.2	8.0
Denmark	−3.3	−3.0	3.9	9.8

Source: OECD.

expansive effect. On the contrary, it led to restrictive measures affecting final demand.

Step 2: Growth and employment

A fairly close positive relationship between economic growth and employment can be demonstrated in an international cross-section analysis. In those countries where economic growth is higher employment also grows faster. The same is true for lower growth and employment. But there are two exceptions to this correlation: the USA and Canada, and the Nordic countries. For Northern America the reason seems to be the high employment growth in the low-wage service sector. In the Nordic countries it was the effect of the welfare state. It can be shown that employment in the public sector increased at a fast pace (Table 5.7). They can afford to have no unemployment (not caring too much about economic growth). This seems to be a short-run alternative, for in the long run it is limited by the level of taxation (Sweden). In a welfare state not only public expenditures for employment, but also the costs of automatic stabilisers are high. On the other hand, in Germany the federal budget was consolidated largely by restrictions of public employment and unemployment benefits.

Many economists nowadays try again to explain low employment growth in Western Europe by too-high real wage increases and relatively too-low interest rates (compared with the US). If this neoclassical hypothesis of factor substitution was true investment quotas should have increased in Western Europe compared to the US during the 1970s. Just the contrary was true.

In addition, there is no evidence in an international cross-section analysis (1979–84) for any relationship between increases in real

Table 5.7 General government share in employment

	1970 %	1982
Sweden	20.6	31.8
Denmark	16.8	31.1
Norway	16.4	22.9
Finland	11.8	19.5
Belgium	13.9	19.5
Austria	13.7	19.2
USA	18.1	16.7
France	13.4	16.1
Germany	11.2	15.6
Italy	11.8	15.3

Source: OECD.

wages and employment. (See Figure 5.1 which shows that the relationship between real wages and employment is ambiguous. A reduction in real wages may certainly lead to an increase in employment by improving international competitiveness (similar to a devaluation). But this cannot be followed by all countries simultaneously.

Normally there is a positive relationship between real wages and employment (in time-series analysis) that is induced by changes in demand: an increase in effective demand raises real wages and employment. A trade-off between real wages and employment may occur in response to supply shocks. A rapid increase of the population in the working age can increase (low-wage) employment and reduce the average level of real wages. (This was an important reason for high employment growth in the USA in the last decade.)

Those countries which tried to stimulate employment by real wage cuts (to be measured by the real wage gap) did not succeed. The idea that excessively high real wages are the major impediment to full employment has gained wide credence in Western Germany and the United Kingdom. In both countries real wages are rising in line with productivity (terms-of-trade adjusted), while in most other countries they have risen faster over the last ten years (Table 5.8). At the same time, the reduction of employment in Germany and the United Kingdom was even greater than would have been expected from their low rates of economic growth (see Figure 5.2).

Figure 5.1 Real wages and employment (increase in per cent)

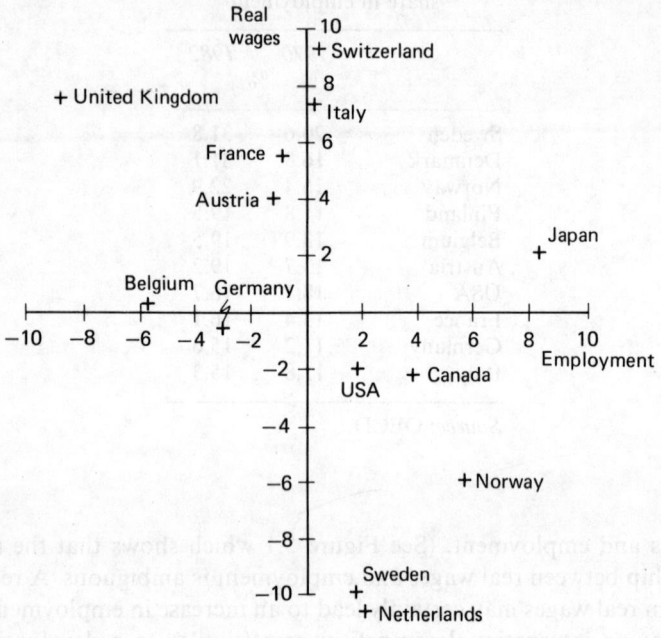

Table 5.8 Real wage gap and employment

	Real compensation per head	Productivity corrected for terms of trade 1972–82	Real Wage gap	Employment gap
France	+39.8	+25.6	+11.4	+6.5
Italy	+25.8	+14.1	+9.9	+13.0
Canada	+10.4	+1.6	+8.6	+28.5
Japan	+34.9	+24.6	+8.1	+18.3
Austria	+30.1	+22.4	+6.3	+10.1
USA	+3.9	+1.1	+2.6	+21.6
United Kingdom	+23.5	+21.6	+1.0	−4.0
Germany	+23.4	+25.1	−1.4	−1.1

Source: OECD, *Economic Outlook*, December 1982, Austrian Institute for Economic Research calculations.

[1] Index of real compensation per head divided by the index of productivity corrected for terms of trade.

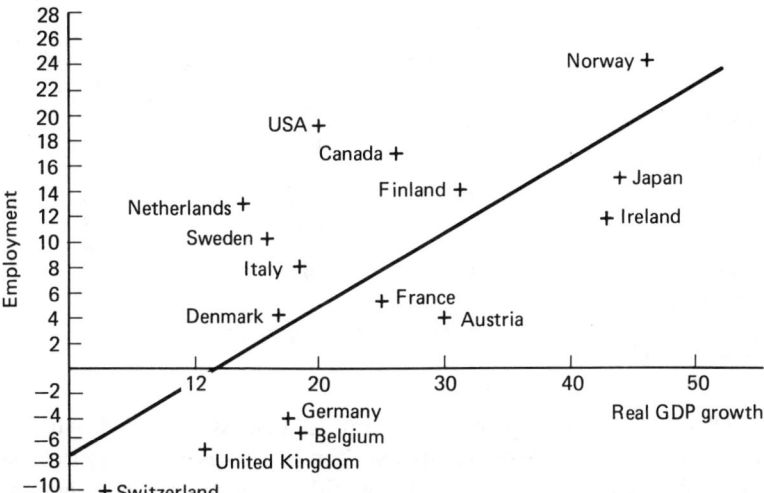

Figure 5.2 Growth and employment 1973–83

Step 3: Employment–unemployment

In the 1970s the rising labour force was an important factor for increasing unemployment. Higher investment would have been necessary to employ this rising labour supply, but investment was faltering. The share of government in investment was reduced (see Table 5.9) despite the needs for environmental protection, energy saving, etc. We should not forget that many countries tried to keep unemployment low despite the poor employment situation. The standard way was to reduce the labour supply of foreign workers, older workers and women.

The Swiss way to low unemployment (and low budget deficits) was a restrictive economic policy leading to low growth rates and a very poor employment situation. This was combined with a massive reduction of foreign workers and female employment that kept unemployment low.

The Austrian way to low unemployment was an expansive economic policy leading to relatively high growth rates. Employment in Austria did not rise faster than would have been expected from the higher growth rates (despite labour hoarding in the nationalised industries, reduction of working hours, etc.). Unemployment was additionally kept low by a reduction of foreign workers and by early retirement (a very costly way).

Table 5.9 General government share in investment

	1970	1982	Change 1970–1982
	(% of gross fixed investment)		(percentage points)
Japan	12.6	19.8	+7.2
Finland	12.8	14.2	+1.4
Italy	10.7	10.1	−0.6
Austria	18.0	16.5	−1.5
France	13.9	12.0	−1.9
Germany	17.3	13.9	−3.4
USA	14.4	9.2	−5.2
United Kingdom	15.5	9.4	−6.1

Source: OECD.

This seems the appropriate point to discuss so-called Austro-Keynesianism. Austro-Keynesianism can be seen as a strategy to keep unemployment low in a hostile world. It is mainly a policy of stimulating growth without risking inflation. The main elements are: (i) An expansive fiscal policy – given the constraints of the current account and interest payments. The most important instruments are investment promotion (a supply-side element), interest subsidies, public investment (construction), subsidies to firms suffering from recession, etc. (ii) A high exchange rate policy to counteract inflation (backed by an incomes policy). There are no monetary targets in Austria, but a constant relation of the Schilling to the D-Mark implies a constraint on interest rate policy to prevent capital outflows. (iii) Social partnership is an instrument of stabilisation policy (Wage and Price Committees). A voluntary wage and price discipline is preferred to an austerity policy. (iv) Nationalised industries are a stabilising element, accounting for about one fourth of Austrian industry. There are, however, great structural problems in the steel industry so that this 'socialisation of investment' does not help very much in long term structural policy. In the traditional concept of Austro-Keynesianism industrial policy does not play the role that it should play. Long-term planning is neglected.

CONCLUSIONS AND REMEDIES

Current policy is saddled with an overhang of three enormous problems:

1. a large public debt and a large developing countries debt;
2. a large supply of surplus of labour, due partly to the inability to absorb the increasing labour supply in the 1970s;
3. an inappropriate industrial structure (heavy industries and mass production).

The main barrier to employment policy today is the high interest payment for public debt and the lack of international co-ordination of economic policies.

As a legacy of a decade of monetarism budget deficits are so high in many countries that high and uncontrollable interest payments do not leave much room for manoeuvre in fiscal policy. Actually, a shift in employment policy from fiscal stimulus to *monetary policy* (lower interest rates) and income redistribution appears to be necessary. First the morass produced by monetarism has to be overcome, then there will be more room for manoeuvre in fiscal policy. Lower interest rates for consumer credits and mortgages would stimulate demand and hence investment. Lower interest rates would also reduce budget deficits directly since a substantial part of public debt is financed by bank credits with flexible rates. Higher demand induced by a more expansive monetary policy would also reduce the cyclical part of the budget deficit. With a reduction of budget deficits by these two ways no further discretionary measures to reduce deficits would be necessary.

At the moment an expansive *fiscal policy* is in fact only feasible in those countries where deficits (as a percentage of GDP) are relatively low (below the medium-term growth rate). Among the large countries this is in Japan, Germany and maybe the United Kingdom. But these countries prefer to live as 'free-riders', restricting internal demand (by real wage cuts and tight policies) more than their trading partners to produce large foreign trade surpluses. The continuous threat of protectionism in the US may well be a weapon to remove these beggar-my-neighbour policies.

Stimulating private investment as a means of employment policy has been largely misdirected from a structural point of view (favouring basic industries). Taxes on profits have been reduced at the cost of higher taxes for the employed. Industrial policy oriented towards employment-intensive research and development may well be an important instrument to stimulate investment and innovation.

Wage policy is too restrictive in most countries. This would have been advisable in the inflationary period of the early 1970s, but with the current low inflation rates and rising profits there is more room for expansion. The actual investment recovery in Western Europe is bound to end soon if there is no concomitant rise in the wage bill and in consumer demand.

Income redistribution from higher to lower income groups (respectively from saving to consuming groups) is an important support for employment especially in a period of high budget deficits. Higher indirect taxes on luxuries, reduction of income tax exemptions and deductions and redistribution by public expenditure would raise the propensity to consume and hence growth and investment without adding to budget deficits. Stopping savings promotion would also be appropriate.

The legacy of monetarism is an extremely high share of interest incomes in national income. Since it is a main task of economic policy in an industrial society to encourage entrepreneurial spirits and to discourage rentier attitudes higher taxes on interest returns are highly recommended. International co-ordination of such taxation and of other economic strategies is, however, advisable to prevent capital outflow. The problem is that the level of economic integration is much higher than the willingness of governments to co-operate. The economies of the industrial countries have become highly interrelated which has made them dependent on each other and, mainly, on the largest economic powers and financial centres. This interdependence limits the possibilities of an autonomous economic policy drastically. At the same time the large countries have become less prepared to co-operate with the aim of seeking rational solutions to the problems of employment.

Notes

1. Studies based on the interaction between the economic development and institutional constraints in various countries reveal considerable differences in the economic performance of industrial countries according to their institutional structures (Scharpf, 1981, Blaas and Guger 1985).
2. Keynes only accepted J. Meade's proposal to produce anti-cyclical effects by varying the contributions of employers and employees to the social security funds after prolonged discussion; he opposed variations of income tax rates.
3. Since Keynes' time the share of consumer durables in consumption expenditures has more than doubled; today between 10 and 15 per cent of consumer spending is on durables.
4. Kalecki estimated more than 6 years for the UK and Steindl about 2 years for the USA (see Worswick, 1985).

5. This tendency is enforced by the accumulation of 'unwanted amortisation funds' as Keynes (1936, p. 99f) had already envisaged. Harrod, 1970; Bhaduri, 1972; Steindl, 1979, have taken up this point.
6. Using the usual textbook symbols we can write

(2a) $dY/Y = ((S-(G-T)-(X-M))/Y)/(dK/dY)$

(2b) $(dK/dY)(dY/Y) = (S-(G-T)-(X-M))/Y$

(2c) $I = S-(G-T)-(X-M)$

7. We have to keep in mind that (2) is an equilibrium condition determined by ex ante factors, while (3) and (4) are ex post identities.

References

Baily, Martin N. (1978) 'Stabilization policy and private economic behavior', *Brookings Papers of Economic Activity*, 1.

Bhaduri, Amit (1972) 'Unwanted amortisation funds', *Economic Journal*, 82, March.

Blaas, Wolfgang and Guger, Alois (1985) 'Arbeitsbeziehungen und makroökonomische Stabilität im internationalen Vergleich', in Peter Gerlich, Edgar Grande and Wolfgang C. Müller (eds) *Sozialpartnerschaft in der Krise*, (Wien: Bohlau).

Bispham, John and Boltho, Andrea (1982) 'Demand Management', in Andrea Boltho (ed.) *The European Economy. Growth & Crisis* (Oxford: Oxford University Press).

Davidson, Paul (1972) *Money and the Real World* (London: Macmillan).

Guger, Alois (1983) 'Sparen, Beschäftigung und Wachstum – ein Beitrag zur Diskussion um die Zinsertragssteuer', *Der öffentliche Sektor*, 3.

Harrod, Roy (1939) 'An essay in dynamic theory', *Economic Journal*, 49, March.

Harrod, Roy (1970) 'Replacements, net investment, amortisation funds', *Economic Journal*, 80, March.

Kaldor, Nicholas (1983) 'The role of commodity prices in economic recovery', *Lloyds Bank Review*, July.

Kalecki, Michal (1943) 'Political aspects of full employment', *Political Quarterly*.

Kalecki, Michael (1944) 'Three ways to full employment', in: *The Economics of Full Employment*, (ed.) The Oxford University Institute of Statistics (Oxford: Blackwell).

Keynes, J. M. (JMK) *The Collected Writings of John Maynard Keynes* (ed.) Austin Robinson and Donald Moggridge for The Royal Economic Society, 1971–83, vols I–XXIX

Kregel, J. A. (1985) 'Budget deficits, stabilisation policy and liquidity preference: Keynes's post-war policy proposals', in Fausto Vicarelli (ed.) *Keynes's Relevance Today* (London: Macmillan).

Leijonhufvud, Axel (1968) *On Keynesian Economics and the Economics of Keynes* (Oxford University Press).
Matthews, R. C. O. (1968) 'Why has Britain had full employment since the war?' *Economic Journal*, 78, September.
Matzner, Egon (1978) *Wohlfahrtsstaat und Wirtschaftskrise* (Reinbek, Hamburg: Rowohlt).
Minsky, Hyman (1975) *John Maynard Keynes* (London: Macmillan).
Moggridge, Donald E. and Howson, Susan (1974) 'Keynes on monetary policy 1910–1946', *Oxford Economic Papers*, 26, July.
Mooslechner, Peter and Nowotny, Ewald (1980) *Gesamtwirtschaftliche Finanzierung und öffentliche Verschuldung* (Wien: Sparkassenverlag).
OECD (1983a) 'Alternative measures of saving', *Economic Outlook*, Occasional Studies, June.
OECD (1983b) 'Public sector deficits: problems and policy implication', Occasional Studies, June.
OECD (1983c) *Economic Outlook*, December.
OECD (1985) *Historical Statistics* 1960–83, Paris.
Robinson, Joan (1943) 'Planning full employment'. *The Times*, 23 January, reprinted in Joan Robinson *Collected Economic Papers*, vol. 1 (Oxford: Blackwell, 1951).
Scharpf, Fritz W. (1981) 'The political economy of inflation and unemployment in Western Europe: An Outline', WZB-Diskussionspapier IIM/LMP 81–21 Berlin.
Steindl, Josef (1952) *Maturity and Stagnation in American Capitalism* (Oxford: Blackwell).
Steindl, Josef (1979) 'Stagnation theory and stagnation policy', *Cambridge Journal of Economics*, 3.
Steindl, Josef (1982) 'The role of household saving in the modern economy'. *Banca Nationale del Lavoro, Quarterly Review*, No. 140, March.
Walterskirchen, Ewald (1984) 'Budgetdefizite und private Überschüsse', *Monatsberichte des Instituts für Wirtschaftsforschung*, 1.
Worswick, David (1985) 'Jobs for all?', *Economic Journal*, 95, March.

COMMENT

Bertil Holmlund

I would like to draw attention to some empirical evidence on the relationship between real wages and employment. The authors argue that 'normally there is a positive relationship between real wages and employment'. A number of econometric studies have provided a different message. Several recent investigations indicate that real wages matter a great deal for labour demand, and the typical relationship is negative, as conventional neo-classical theory predicts. A few examples:

1. Bruno and Sachs (1985) find in their book on world-wide stagflation that the real product wage in manufacturing has a strong and significant negative effect in 8 out of the 9 OECD economies they study. The average real wage elasticity is estimated to around -0.5 in the short run and about -1.0 in the long run.
2. Newell and Symons (1985) study 16 OECD economies, and the real wage shows up with a negative sign in 13 out of the 16 employment functions; the long-run elasticity of labour demand is estimated at around -0.9.
3. Symons (1985) estimates a labour demand function for British manufacturing and concludes as a 'striking implication for policy' that 'measures of demand (output, money, government spending) do not have a significant influence on manufacturing employment, controlling for the effects of relative prices'. The real wage is found to have a powerful but a slow-acting negative effect on the demand for labour.
4. Layard and Symons (1985) explore the determinants of manufacturing employment in 6 major OECD economies. Their main result is that the level of employment is determined by relative prices (real wages and real material prices), whereas measures of aggregate demand appear unimportant.

The issue regarding the relationship between employment and real wages is, of course, by no means settled. But recent studies have brought confirmatory evidence in favour of the neo-classical labour demand function. There are, presumably, other empirical investigations with results fundamentally different from those quoted above. It is unfortunate that the authors offer no guide to a curious reader on this point.

Of course, a neo-classical labour demand relationship does not rule out Keynesian-type policies. It may still be possible to increase employment by expansionary policies, but the employment effect will in this case arise as a result of lower real wages induced by a demand expansion.

References

Bruno, M. and Sachs, J. (1985) *Economics of Worldwide Stagflation* (Oxford: Basil Blackwell).
Newell, A. and Symons, J. (1985) 'Wages and Employment in the OECD Countries'. London School of Economics, Centre for Labour Economics, Discussion Paper No. 219.
Symons, J. (1985) 'Relative Prices and the Demand for Labour in British Manufacturing', *Economica*, February.
Symons, J. and Layard, R. (1984) 'Neoclassical Demand for Labour Functions for Six Major Economies', *Economic Journal*, December.

H.-Peter Spahn

There are several points in the paper by Guger and Walterskirchen which could be called into question. To begin with, the victory of Keynesianism after the Second World War has not been so straightforward as both authors seem to believe. At least in Germany, there was no Keynesian demand management until the 1960s. Rather, fiscal policy acted to dampen demand in order to make way for the coincidence of strong investment *and* a current account surplus. But I will confine myself to three problems: (1) redistribution in favour of consumption, (2) possibilities for fiscal and monetary policies in a worldwide monetary economy, and (3) fiscal policy and the fear of inflation.

1. As for the first issue, it may be helpful to support effective demand by using tax policies which redistribute income from profit- to wage-earners, thus strengthening the demand for consumption goods. If there are idle resources and if investment behaviour is not affected, such an attempt might work. Though output and employment could be increased, it may be doubtful whether such a policy will lead to a lower profit share in the end. Because income distribution in itself is, to a large extent, determined by demand factors, it cannot be

ruled out that firms will be able to pass the tax burden on to final buyers. Therefore, the profit share may not change after all, or even rise (Steindl, 1979). Supporting demand, on the one hand, and trying to reduce profits, on the other, seem to be two strategies which are not in general compatible.

These inter-relations are sometimes overlooked, especially in Germany, where some left-wing Keynesians often argue that 'unused' profits should be directed to people with higher spending propensities in order to 'use' these profits for demand. But, of course, profits or, generally speaking, savings can never be 'spent away'. They are always nothing but the *result* of private and public expenditures. A situation in which the profit share or the average savings ratio exceeds the relation of investment to income does not, therefore, indicate the possibility of 'turning profits or savings into demand'. Rather, it indicates an *existing* budget deficit or a current account surplus, and an increase in expenditure will not eliminate the 'excess' savings or profits, but reconstitute them.

It may be added that, according to a flow-of-funds analysis, it is not quite correct, and misleading, to speak of the 'absorption' of private savings by public deficits. Being a flow, savings are never 'absorbed' but always 'produced' (Kregel, 1984–5). A smaller deficit, other things being equal, must lead to a *reduction* of the volume of savings and profits. Speaking of absorption, instead, gives credence to some neoclassical economists who argue that savings could be 'more than absorbed' by public borrowing. This crude hypothesis, sometimes put forward in the crowding-out discussion, is definitely wrong with respect to monetary *flows*; on the other hand, deficit spending cannot avoid an interest effect because of the changing structure of the *stock* of assets which agents have to hold.

2. Apart from this, Guger and Walterskirchen argue that in any case fiscal policy could not be used for employment purposes because of the size of the outstanding public debt in many countries. Instead, they favour 'easy money' coupled with incomes policies. The analysis seems to be based on the idea that monetarism is the true villain of the piece that has been playing for the past decade now, with the shift to the goal of price stability explained in terms of a Kaleckian political business cycle.

However, there must be more than just political obstacles to full employment. The rise of monetarism should be assessed against the background of a period of worldwide inflation and fluctuating exchange rates which forced international wealth-owners to choose between different financial assets denominated in different currencies. Particularly in an international monetary economy, 'money matters', but some national currencies may rapidly lose their property of being money for the purposes of wealth-owners, if 'confidence' vanishes due to economic developments and policies which they consider 'unsound'.

Therefore, it has been market mechanisms which have led national governments to adopt tight monetary policies (which in turn put constraints on fiscal policy) in order to avoid severe problems brought about by capital outflows and depreciating exchange rates. In times when money-holders are upset by the fear of inflation, it is no surprise that easy money policies are condemned to fail if agents, rightly or wrongly, deduce the future rate of inflation from the expected or announced rate of money growth. It is unlikely that incomes policies could provide counteracting tendencies if monetary policy is considered to be ultimately inflationary. The German experience with incomes policies show that they cannot guarantee price stability; rather, one needs the confidence in price stability to make incomes policies work. But then one may ask what incomes policies are good for in the first place.

Of course, if there are losers in the competition between currencies driven by the liquidity preferences of wealth-owners, there must also be winners. In the 1970s, while the dollar was declining, preferences shifted in favour of the Swiss franc and the German mark. These currencies were revalued and domestic interest rates fell. But Germany only partly used the widening room for fiscal policy, though the market would have accepted a larger supply of public bonds. By contrast, the United States did so, when the change in the monetary regime in late 1979 brought renewed confidence in the dollar. Besides their relatively high liquidity, dollar assets offered outstanding interest rates, and both aspects are of considerable importance in a period of stagnation when returns from real assets are uncertain and low.

American economic policy took advantage of the liquidity preferences of wealth-owners by letting the capital inflow finance a domestic expansion. In the aggregate, fiscal policy outweighed the negative impact of the strong dollar on domestic industries and, hence, on employment. 'Supply-side economics' have turned out to be a rather clever medium-term strategy of Keynesian demand policy. This is now widely acknowledged and it is not at all certain that the long-run costs will prove it to have been a losing strategy (Sachs, 1985).

It has become commonplace to criticise the American budget deficit for the 'absorption' of worldwide savings. On the other hand, foreign countries must be aware of the necessity to compensate external with internal demand if the American deficit is to be reduced in the next few years. Guger and Walterskirchen are right to call for an expansional fiscal policy pursued, at least, by those countries which can afford it, especially Japan, and Germany who is now running a 'structural' budget surplus. This would reduce the American deficit problems and, at the same time, redirect some capital flows towards those countries in response to interest rate signals (Blanchard/Dornbusch, 1984), provided that there is no fear of inflation.

3. In spite of the American example, which did *not* lead to a speed-up in the rate of inflation, fiscal policy seems to be out of fashion regarding the goal of full employment. Even in a situation of economic crisis, accompanied by idle resources, it is sometimes assumed that the income and profit generating effects of deficit spending are outweighed by the deterioration of long-run expectations stemming from the anticipated rise of interest rates, taxes, wages and prices. Things are held to be worse in a 'stagnation equilibrium' in which excess productive capacity has been eliminated. The economy is thought to be suffering from a (physical) supply constraint, which results from the preceding slowdown of the rate of investment (Streissler, 1983). When there is no problem of stabilising the economy in the short run, therefore, most of the medium-term strategies for fiscal policy nowadays are centred around a balanced budget trying to improve the *structure* of public revenue and expenditure. Of course, that would be an appropriate policy in the case of full employment. But in a stagnation equilibrium with high unemployment it is said that fiscal demand policies could not help in the least because of the high degree of capacity utilisation, i.e. because of the fear of inflation.

But such an argument does not seem to be well founded. In a situation of unemployment the real wage is *above* the supply curve and *on* the demand curve, expressing the supposed supply constraints with respect to capital equipment. This can be labelled 'classical' unemployment, though it is exactly the problem Keynes dealt with. The strategy of a real wage reduction 'ex ante', then, may fail because of the well known problem that prices fall in line with wages. Instead, Keynes took for granted that there would be a real wage reduction 'ex post', as a *consequence* of a rise in demand, if prices increase due to supply constraints and nominal wages rest unchanged. Note that it is not necessary to have an absolute fall in real wages if one allows for productivity growth.

Why should labour *not* accept such a relative loss in the distribution of income in favour of a rise in the level of employment? It all depends on our belief concerning the position and stability of the supply curve of labour. If we think of supply exceeding demand at the initial real wage, no problems should arise. On the other hand, those who stress the inflation barrier to full employment have to argue that the response to an increase in prices will be a rise in nominal wages (which is the starting point of a *process* of inflation). But to assume that is to assume that labour is *on* its supply curve, rather than above it. In other words, one has to assume full employment.

Apart from structural bottlenecks in the heterogeneous labour market and the problem of wasted skills of the unemployed, there can be a difference between a *supposed* supply curve based on individual preferences and an *effective* supply curve which shows the market behaviour of unions. It has to be admitted that unions do not necessarily try to represent the preferences of the whole working class, especially not of those who are out of work. Accordingly, there can be a market equilibrium with respect to the effective supply curve, just because the notional supply of the unemployed is excluded from the process of bargaining. But given the widespread risk for the employed labour force of becoming unemployed, the effective supply curve should not be far off the notional curve. This means that the present problem of unemployment cannot be reduced to a problem of representation of interests inside the working class.

Though it is possible that the supply curve will change its shape and position over time, it is hard to see why it should do so at the very 'moment' of fiscal demand policy, so turning unemployment into a full-employment equilibrium and setting the pace for inflation. It is true that fiscal policy contributed to inflation in the early 1970s, especially in Germany, but it should be noted that this was a period of full employment. The modern prejudice against fiscal policy seems to rely on the 'new classical' idea of a permanent full-employment equilibrium which, of course, is far from the facts.

In Germany, the main response to the problem of unemployment has been an attempt to lower real wages *without* increasing demand by fiscal policy. Labour in fact did accept a decrease in the wage share, even though – as could be expected – this did not improve employment figures substantially. To the extent that the real wage has fallen off the marginal productivity curve, we face a situation of 'pure' Keynesian unemployment. Then supply constraints to full employment showing up in rising prices are not important at all. But as it is always difficult, if not impossible, to find out empirically whether the real wage today is on or below the marginal productivity curve, one may concede that fiscal demand cannot draw on idle resources. However, it is not convincing to argue that some rise in the price level will lead to a process of inflation, simply because labour is not fully employed.

To conclude, the problem of a stagnation equilibrium connected with mass unemployment is that firms have adjusted their expectations and capital equipment to a lower level of effective demand. The alternatives for economic policy then are, firstly, to accept high unemployment hoping that it will 'die out' or, secondly, to use financial resources for labour market policies to 'store' labour and keep it prepared for employment in some unknown, distant future or, thirdly, to try to push by fiscal demand expansion the economy into a *disequilibrium* again, hoping that firms will react to positive quasirents by changing their expectations concerning capital stock decisions.

For the latter strategy to work, it is essential that, firstly, a higher expected rate of profit is not offset by a rise in the rate of interests. If necessary, investors could be subsidised in order to compensate for interest costs. Secondly, firms should be made aware that fiscal demand is not just like a short-lived passion. It should be made clear that the government is pursuing a 'great national goal' which provides the economy with a lot of work. Historically, it was the construction of railways and homes which was connected with strong demand effects. In the years ahead, the task could be to solve the huge environmental problems. Apart from direct fiscal demand in accordance with that aim, putting environmental impositions on production processes will depreciate the capital *stock* thus creating additional demand for capital goods equipped with 'soft' technology, whereas in Germany impositions mainly on *new* equipment have the opposite effect of raising the value of existing plants and, therefore, of impeding investment in more costly capital goods. Policies to improve the allocation *and* employment of resources could thus be combined mitigating, in the long run, the conflicts between the environment and the goal of full employment (Binswanger *et al.*, 1983).

References

Binswanger, H. C. et al. (1983) *Arbeit ohne Umweltzerstörung* (Frankfurt: Fischer).
Blanchard, O. and Dornbusch, R. (1984) 'US Deficits, the Dollar and Europe', *Banca Nazionale del Lavoro, Quarterly Review*, 37.
Kregel, J. A. (1984–5) 'Constraints on the Expansion of Output and Employment: Real or Monetary?' *Journal of Post Keynesian Economics*, 7.
Sachs, J. D. (1985) 'The Dollar and the Policy Mix: 1985', *Brookings Papers on Economic Activity*.
Steindl, J. (1979) 'Stagnation Theory and Stagnation Policy', *Cambridge Journal of Economics*, 3.
Streissler, E. (1983) 'Stagnation – Analyse und Therapie', in G. Bombach et al. (eds), *Makroökonomik heute – Gemeinsamkeiten und Gegensätze* (Tübingen: Mohr).

Part III
Public Labour Market Policy

6 The Role of Manpower Policy in the Swedish Model

Rudolf Meidner

Sweden has a unique position amongst the Western European nations with respect both to the high priority which the country gives to full employment as a political goal, and the central role of manpower policy in Swedish economic and welfare policy. The highly ambitious goal is clearly reflected in the results which have been achieved: the labour force participation rate is exceptionally high (especially for women), open unemployment has been kept far below the average of OECD member countries even during years of economic crisis, the volume of manpower programmes is unparalleled in the western world, if measured either as share of the national budget or as proportion of the total labour force.

This is not the place for an analysis of why the full employment goal is widely accepted in Swedish society or of the fact that it was not even questioned by the non-socialist governments in the period 1976–82. The hypothesis that the union movement with the highest degree of unionisation in the world and the Social Democratic party, which has dominated the Swedish political scene since the 1930s, have played a decisive role in the historical process is a very plausible one. The full employment policy can, then, be interpreted as the very essence of the Swedish welfare model, imprinted by the labour movement's ideology and a necessary presupposition for the egalitarian and labour reforms of the post-war period.

Instead, the paper will focus on the role which manpower policy has played in contributing to the realisation of the full employment goal. Swedish politics had to solve the precarious task of defending full employment in a small country which is highly dependent on international markets and is heavily affected by the performance of most western countries which, since the mid-1970s, have been willing to pay for low inflation by tolerating high unemployment.

It is obvious that the task of meeting the full employment commitment is mainly the responsibility of general economic policy and that manpower policy only has a supporting and complementary role. A discussion of different alternatives for economic policy lies outside the framework of this paper. However, a Social Democratic government has to choose a 'third way' between the neo-liberalists' suggestions to cut taxes, reduce real wages and hollow out welfare reforms, and an expansive policy in a Keynesian spirit which must result in budget deficits, inflation and imbalance in foreign payments.

The strategy of the third way means a balance between contractive and expansive policies by supporting exports through repeated currency devaluations, by stimulating, by counteracting wage increases which exceed productivity improvements, and by pursuing an active and selective policy for the support of viable firms.

Such a policy needs as a complement a comprehensive and well-equipped manpower policy. Economic policy and manpower policy are closely linked to each other: the scope of an anti-inflationary economic policy is widened to the extent that manpower policy is capable of improving the functioning of the labour market and attacking, in a selective way, weak points in the economy.

In fact, the problem to be solved is the old and well known dilemma between unemployment and inflation which, nearly forty years ago, resulted in the proposal put forward by the Swedish unions (LO) and known as the Rehn model to combine a restrictive fiscal policy and a selective manpower policy, thereby assigning to the latter a strategic role in stabilisation policy.[1] The essence of the model is not to find an optimal point on the Phillips curve, i.e. to accept a firm trade-off between unemployment and wages (prices), but to move the curve towards the origin. The fact that it has moved in the wrong direction does not necessarily prove that the model was wrong. An explanation can be found in the international inflation after the oil shock.[2] Another explanation is the simple fact that the model has been used inappropriately.[3]

The Rehn model was a product of the expansive, overheated post-war economy, characterised by scarcity of resources, especially labour, and offered an alternative to the counter-productive regulated economy with prices, wages and investments controlled by the government.

One may question whether the same model is applicable to the present situation which is so totally different and characterised by weak expansion, surplus of labour and cost inflation. I suggest that fiscal and monetary restrictions are still necessary in order to work against increasing costs, losses of competitiveness and mounting budget deficits. The need for anti-inflationary and selective manpower measures, consequently, remains and may even be stronger than before. The model which was originally constructed in an expanding economy is also fully applicable in a stagnating economy.

But manpower policy has now, in addition to its earlier role of stabilising the economy, a role in the resolution of structural problems. It must facilitate the relocation of labour between various industries, firms, skills and regions. Adjustment is not only required from the individual's perspective, but is a condition *sine qua non* for economic growth. A well-equipped manpower policy, together with an active policy for industrial development, is a far better alternative than large subsidies to companies and branches which have lost their viability.

There is a further strong motive for an active manpower policy, which is connected with the wage policy of solidarity and its consequences for employment. A wage structure which is unrelated to the profitability of the firms and oriented towards the notion of 'fair wage relations' eliminates the role of wage differentials as stimulus for labour market mobility. The possibility that firms and, in some cases, whole industries unable to pay 'fair wages', lose their competitiveness and are squeezed out from the market, cannot be excluded.

It is then the task of labour market policy to facilitate the transfer of labour to expansive parts of the economy using the traditional means such as retraining, education for higher qualifications, mobility grants, etc. Not even in a stagnating economy is there a total absence of areas with demand for labour, but their identification is of course much more difficult than in a growing economy.

Let me summarise the main motives for a comprehensive manpower policy:

1. the first and most important motive is the traditional one: *alleviating the search process*, matching applicants with job opportunities. But the Swedish manpower policy has objectives which go far beyond this and give it a key role in the Swedish model, namely
2. the *stabilisation-oriented motive* which follows from the model's demand for fiscal and monetary restrictiveness even in periods of economic slack,
3. *the structural motive* which requires that manpower policy puts great emphasis on growth promoting measures, and finally

4. the motive *to complement the wage policy of solidarity* with manpower policy measures.

Briefly let me present some background data regarding the Swedish labour market and its recent development (see Table 6.1).

A larger part of the population in the active ages than in any other country is gainfully employed: 85.6 per cent of all males and 78.2 per cent of all females (1984). The total number employed – full-time or part-time – has since 1970 increased by 400 000 up to 4.4 millions. The increase has occurred exclusively in the public sector where at present 31 per cent of the labour force are employed, a figure which gives Sweden a high international position. Registered unemployment is amongst the lowest in Western Europe and has not exceeded 3½ per cent, even in the most critical years after the oil shock.

Registered unemployment gives, however, no complete picture of the size of categories which are not absorbed by the 'regular' market. Figure 6.1 makes it clear that the proportion of the labour force which is covered by manpower programmes since the beginning of the 1970s has exceeded registered unemployment. Both open unemployment and the volume of manpower policy measures have increased during the period. In 1984 3 per cent of the labour force were openly

Table 6.1 Number of persons in the labour force, unemployed and participating in different manpower programmes, 1970–84

	1970	1980	Changes 1970–80	1984	Changes 1980–84
1. Number of persons in the productive ages (thousands)	5162	5210	+48	5287	+77
2. Number of persons in the labour force (thousands)	3913	4318	+405	4391	+73
3. (2) as percentage of (1)	75.8	82.9	—	83.9	—
4. Number of unemployed (thousands)	59	86	+27	136	+50
5. (4) as percentage of (2)	1.5	2.0	—	3.1	—
6. Proportion of persons participating in manpower programmes	1.9	2.9	—	4.1	—
7. (5)+(6)	3.4	4.9	—	7.2	—

Source: Labour Market Board and National Central Bureau of Statistics.

Figure 6.1 Registered unemployment (as percentage of labour force), registered unemployment and persons covered by manpower policy measures, 1970–84

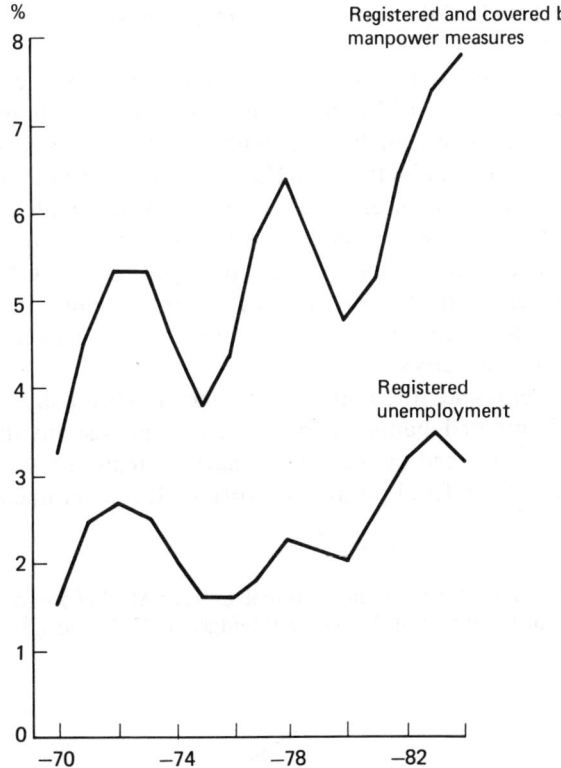

Source: Labour Market Board and National Central Bureau of Statistics.

unemployed and as many as 4 per cent covered by manpower policy measures.

However, it would be misleading to add these figures to the number of registered unemployed to get the volume of 'real' total unemployment, comparable to the average figures of unemployment in the OECD area. The core of Swedish manpower programmes is retraining, rehabilitation and productive work which should not be placed on an equal footing with unproductive idleness. But the figure reflects, without any doubt, the increasing difficulties in the Swedish labour market.

The Swedish manpower policy has been capable of keeping registered unemployment on a low level only by accessing great resources which constitute an increasing part of the national product (at present 3 per cent) and of the national budget (at present 7 per cent). See Figure 6.2.

No evaluation study exists which definitively shows whether the results justify the input of such immense resources. It is doubtful whether a cost-benefit analysis of manpower policy as a whole can be carried out in a meaningful way. The result depends to a high degree on the measures which are used. A policy which confines itself to compensating the unemployed in cash for lost income gives obviously the poorest returns to society. To use 2 per cent of GNP to pay unemployment benefits to 4 per cent of the labour force may be socially justified, but for the national economy it means a heavy loss of productive resources.

Sweden represents the opposite extreme. Traditionally the 'work-line' has dominated manpower policy, i.e. the philosophy that people who are not absorbed by the regular market – temporarily or permanently – must be offered productive work by the government or must

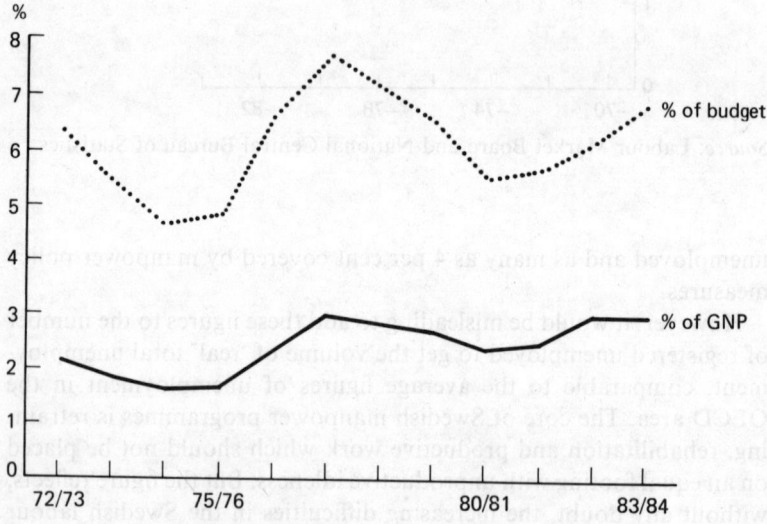

Figure 6.2 Expenditure of the National Labour Market Board (AMS) as percentage of GNP and of the national budget. 1972/73–1983/84

Source: Labour Market Board.

be given opportunities to undergo retraining, labour market education or rehabilitation. During many years 90 per cent of total expenditures for manpower programmes has been used for such 'active' measures which are productive in the sense that production losses are limited, skills can be kept alive and new human capital can be created. While it is difficult to measure the benefits for the individual who has access to productive work or training instead of receiving unemployment benefits, a large number of studies do indicate that the negative effects of unemployment are considerable.[4] The fact that financial compensation has increased from 10 per cent to 30 per cent of the LMB budget in 1984 is in Sweden considered a clear deviation from the traditional line and a failure of Swedish manpower policy.

The size and development of the most important manpower programmes for the period 1960–84 are illustrated in Table 6.2. Manpower programmes expanded rapidly up until the mid 1970s with large fluctuations in the number of persons in relief work and labour market training, but with a steady growth of support measures for disabled groups which today make up nearly half of the total number of people covered by manpower programmes.

The number of persons who received mobility grants has been noticeably stable. This measure, which was designated to become an essential part of the new manpower policy, has, as a consequence of its nature as a non-recurrent expense to subsidise moving expenses, played a very marginal role.

It can be seen from Table 6.2 that manpower programmes during the crisis of the early 1980s by means of training, education, job opportunities or wage subsidies, covered between 3 and 4 per cent of the Swedish labour force.

What was new with the 'New manpower policy' which was launched by the LO in the beginning of the 1950s was not only its integration into general economic politics and the multiplicity of its purposes but the emphasis on the supply-side measures such as labour market education, retraining, rehabilitation and mobility assistance. This focus was natural if one bears in mind that at that time a demand surplus existed in the Swedish economy, which forced the labour market policy to adjust supply to demand in an economy in a state of heavy expansion. The demand-side measures could concentrate on relief work for handicapped groups and economically weak regions.

Table 6.2 Number of persons in different manpower programmes, thousands, 1960–84

	(1) Labour market training	(2) In-plant training	(3) Relief work	(4) Sheltered work	(5) Work training	(6) Employed with wage subsidies	(7) Total 1–6	(8) As % of labour force	(9) Mobility grants
1960	6	—	6	2	—	2	16	0.4	—
1963	11	1	11	—	6	—	29	0.8	—
1970	29	4	15	11	2	10	72	1.9	24
1975	27	8	17	16	3	23	94	2.3	19
1980	44	2	24	22	3	29	124	2.9	23
1981	32	3	25	23	4	32	119	2.8	21
1982	35	4	43	23	5	34	144	3.4	20
1983	38	5	59	25	5	36	168	3.9	22
1984	41	2	75[1]	26	5	37	186	4.1	31

Source: Labour Market Board and National Central Bureau of Statistics.

[1] Including 31 public youth jobs.

This picture has changed considerably since the beginning of the 1980s when decreasing demand forced manpower policy to create new jobs (see Figure 6.3). At the same time financial compensation to the unemployed increased heavily whilst the share of expenditures for employment service remained at 10 per cent of total expenditures for manpower programmes. Measures to which earlier high priority had been given such as labour market training and employment service now received only one fourth of the Labour Market Board's budget.

This change can be interpreted in two different ways: either general economic policy had pressed manpower policy to take over too high a responsibility for unemployment, or the functioning of the labour market had deteriorated, which made it necessary to strengthen manpower policy, especially measures of a job-creating nature.

A combination of both these factors may be the most adequate way to explain what has really happened in Sweden. Again we have to remember that the original model was built on the condition that the expansive parts of the economy were able to swallow the surplus of labour which arose in the non-competitive sections. Manpower policy could concentrate on facilitating this adjustment process by emphasising the supply-side measures. When the structural problems became more accentuated in the mid 1970s, as industrial expansion

Figure 6.3 The development of supply oriented and demand oriented manpower measures, 1970–84 (%)

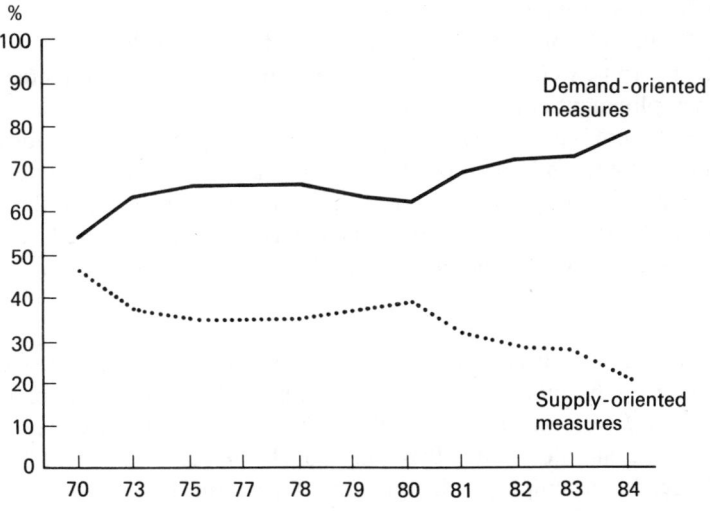

Source: Labour Market Board.

weakened, and at the same time, the expansion of the public sector was impeded by budget restrictions, manpower programmes became the last resort in the arsenal of measures in defence of full employment.

The situation had been aggravated further by the fact that in the beginning of the 1980s the government pursued a rather pro-cyclical fiscal policy, i.e. a contractive one in years with unsatisfactory demand and unused production capacities. The labour market programmes were, consequently, given tasks which exceeded their normal competence.

Also tendencies of a more structural character contributed to the imbalance in the labour market. On the *supply side* the inflow of women into the labour market continued and the proportion of age groups with high labour force participation rates increased. More important are the factors on the *demand side*. Manufacturing industry lost more than one tenth of its labour force since the beginning of the 1970s and a further decrease seems to be a realistic forecast for the future. The public sector has in the period 1970–84 absorbed the whole growth of the Swedish labour force or 400 000 persons, but this expansion has been dampened in recent years, mainly for financial reasons.[5] The exceptional growth rate of more than 6 per cent in the 1970s has decreased to only 2 per cent in the 1980s. Also in the private service sector recent figures indicate the expansion has come to a standstill. The large changes in the Swedish labour force between different sectors are illustrated in Table 6.3.

It must be concluded that the ability of the Swedish labour market to absorb new entrants is deteriorating and that the risk of increasing unemployment is a serious one.

But there is also a second explanation of the growing difficulties for employment and manpower policies which seems to be relevant, namely the obvious malfunctioning of the labour market. In the next section some of the factors which may have contributed to this development will be briefly discussed.

First, we can observe clearly the signals which indicate that *labour mobility* – the most important precondition for a good labour market – is *decreasing*. Labour mobility has been statistically measured since the middle of the 1960s. In 1966 13 per cent of all employees changed their employer, in 1983 only 8 per cent did so.

Another way to observe the changing pattern of labour mobility is

Table 6.3 The Swedish labour force, distributed by branches of economy, 1970–84

	thousands					Distribution in percent	
	1970	1980	1970–80	1984	1980–84	1970	1984
Agriculture and forestry	311	237	−74	217	−20	8.1	5.1
Manufacturing industry	1106	1077	−29	1007	−70	28.7	23.7
Construction	362	287	−75	260	−27	9.4	6.1
Private services	1315	1393	+78	1447	+54	34.1	34.0
Public services	760	1238	+478	1324	+86	19.7	31.1
Thereof: women in public services	539	922	+383	1000	+78	—	—
Total	3854	4232	+378	4255	+23	100.0	100.0

Source: Labour Market Board and National Central Bureau of Statistics.

to study migration across county borders. The number of interprovincial migrants has fallen from 200 000 in the beginning of the 1970s to 150 000 in 1984. On the other hand, commuting across municipality borders has increased. This can be considered a partial substitute for geographic mobility.

Various explanations can be given for the decrease in labour mobility. An easy explanation is that, given an individual's propensity to move, lower demand for labour reduces the number of opportunities for mobility. Another hypothesis, favoured by many economists, asserts that the equalisation of the wage structure and high marginal taxes have reduced the incentives for job changes and geographic mobility. Research seems to give some support to this hypothesis.[6] This does not imply that the wage policy of solidarity has to be abandoned. There are still strong arguments for a wage structure which is not closely related to the profitability of firms and branches.

Secondly, the severe economic crisis of the 1970s has given rise to comprehensive structural changes in Swedish manufacturing industries, mainly in basic industries as steel and shipyards, resulting in a number of closures. Many studies have proven that the re-employment of redundant labour is extremely difficult, especially in one-industry towns. For certain categories, mainly the older workforce, the result is frequently lengthy unemployment.[7]

Thirdly, open registered unemployment has increased primarily by a larger inflow of unemployment but to some extent the *prolonged spell of unemployment* has added to it. Since the beginning of the 1970s the average duration of unemployment has doubled and now amounts to 23 weeks. For the age group 55–64 years the corresponding figure is as high as 42 weeks. There is a clear connection between the duration of unemployment and the probability of getting a new job.[8]

The employment service has to make strong efforts to offer new jobs to the long-term unemployed who run the risk of losing their skills, and are often considered less attractive candidates by potential employers. There is also clear evidence that the long-term unemployed are more than other employees affected by new periods of unemployment.

Lastly, in the discussion of Swedish manpower policy there is finally the consideration of the continuously increasing ambitions of the full employment goal. 'Jobs for everybody' is not only the title of a governmental commission report[9] but also the prime motto of Swedish economic policy. This implies that categories of labour with often low work capacity must be integrated into the labour market which requires more intensive placement endeavours and a number of expensive manpower policy measures.

Critics of the high and increasing level of 'artificial' employment, in addition to regular employment, easily disregard the fact that a major part of this increase includes disabled workers who earlier did not appear as labour supply. In 1970 persons in sheltered workshops and rehabilitation centres amounted to less than one fourth of all who were covered by manpower programmes. Today the corresponding figure is near 50 per cent. Further, disabled workers account for an increasing share of all persons in labour market training and in public relief work.

The efficiency of manpower policy is highly dependent on continuous evaluation of different programmes and on subsequent integration of the results in the development of new and better methods. The Labour Market Board frequently initiates follow-up studies. However, the responsibility for evaluation research rests with a special group of experts (EFA) which is placed under the Ministry of Labour. The group has the task of initiating evaluation studies which, as a rule, are carried out by various university institutions.

Such evaluation studies can be designed along two main lines: either to analyse the real effects of a measure or to examine its implementation and the degree to which the object has been realised.

The first group of studies is the most relevant one from the viewpoint of decision makers, but at the same time methodologically difficult. Real cost/benefit studies require either controlled experiments or access to longitudinal registers of high quality. Very rarely are these conditions fulfilled. Consequently, we must mostly be satisfied with primitive 'ante/ex post' studies which do not allow reliable conclusions as to the effects of the examined measures.

Most of the evaluation studies which have been undertaken for the last two decades are described in the three main reports which EFA has published.[10] The following brief list summarises some of the more important results.

Labour market training The Labour Market Board's current follow-up studies indicate that approximately 70 per cent of the trainees get jobs six months after they have completed their course. Given that only the unemployed are eligible for such training the result can be considered satisfactory. Without access to control groups of non-trainees it is, however, difficult to fully interpret the results. Studies from the early 1970s comparing placement figures for trainees and control groups of non-trainees have shown that while labour market training leads to improved job opportunities and financial gains for the trainees; the effects for the economy as a whole are more uncertain.[11]

Preliminary results from an EFA project in process, based on a longitudinal register, suggest that the income effects of labour market training are considerable.

Mobility grants It seems that the opposite is true for measures intended to support geographic mobility. A study of persons who at the end of the 1960s migrated from a few districts in Northern Sweden showed after some years of observation only small if any economic gain compared to a corresponding group of non-migrants, because of high moving costs and, to some degree, the Swedish system of taxes and transfer payments. By the same reason the mobility gains for the economy as a whole were relatively low.

Relief work Surprisingly enough, real cost-benefit studies of this important measure which makes use of a large part of the total expenditures for manpower policy have not been undertaken in Sweden. Any 'crowding out' effect of public relief work as it has been discussed in some US studies, consequently, cannot be clearly proven for Sweden. One study, concerning relief work in the period 1964–77, indicates, however, that relief work of investment nature seems to displace other public employment, whilst public work in the area of health care causes net employment effects.[12]

Youth Teams A special scheme which enjoined the Swedish municipalities to offer unemployed persons in the ages 18–19 years four hours' employment a day with the wage costs subsidised by the national government was introduced in the beginning of 1984. The measure has already been the subject of an evaluation study.[13] The very tentative conclusion is that the participants have been less eager to search for new jobs and that their transition to the regular labour market has been delayed. A deeper analysis of this policy which has contributed quite a lot to keeping registered unemployment in Sweden low is required.

Measures for disabled Several studies of sheltered work shops indicate that the net social benefits have decreased over time. The explanation could be that the composition of persons in sheltered work has changed.[14] It must also be remembered that conventional cost/benefit studies of sheltered work do not include the alternative costs for care of disabled persons outside the sheltered workshops. Another presumption is that the disabled prefer early retirement to work. If these presumptions are changed and a purely economic analysis is completed by a 'social balance sheet' the result can be expected to be more positive.

Employment subsidies EFA has initiated two studies of marginal employment subsidies. Training benefits given to companies in the process of laying-off part of their workforce (1977) have been calculated to result in net employment effects of at most 40 per cent (the possible crowding-out effect not included).

A study of an allowance amounting to 12 000 Swedish Kroner intended to stimulate the earlier recruitment of labour (1978-9) indicated that the firms considered the allowance insufficient and that the effects therefore were marginal. Investigations made by the Labour Market Board seem to confirm these results: The LMB estimates the net effect of the recruitment allowance for 1978-9 to be 15 to 30 per cent. The corresponding figure for 1981-2 was as low as 17 per cent. In a more detailed study of marginal wage subsidies given without stipulations the firms' windfall profits were estimated to exceed 90 per cent of the subsidies.[15]

It must be emphasised that all the studies mentioned here concern temporary wage subsidies. It is possible that more permanent subsidies and schemes which focus employment expansion incentives on marginal decisions would lead to more encouraging results.[16]

Intensified employment service This central and classic instrument of all manpower policy has only to a very small extent become the subject of labour market research. However, in the mid 1970s a small study of intensified employment service for long-term unemployed was carried out in the Swedish city of Eskilstuna. By spending $7\frac{1}{2}$ hours for each client (instead of normally $1\frac{1}{2}$ hours) the employment office accomplished significantly better results regarding placement, wages and productivity in the new job. In spite of the small size of the study the researcher draws the conclusion that intensified employment service at a low cost can bring about very positive employment and income effects.

What lessons can be learned from the many years of experience and extensive evaluation of manpower for the *future development of labour market policy*? As we have seen in the preceding section the research results are not clear-cut, but give some indications. The employment service seems to be the component of the manpower policy's arsenal where marginal improvements can be expected to bring about considerable effects. Secondly, supply oriented measures, principally labour market training facilities and mobility allowances, give the highest returns. Apparently, the net effects of demand oriented measures, 'job creation' such as relief work of different categories, are more limited.

It is evident that the development has gone in the opposite, i.e. in the wrong direction. The employment service holds a constantly low share of the LMB budget (less than 10 per cent). The number of trainees in labour market education has stagnated and the training facilities are not fully used. It seems that the attractiveness of labour market training has lessened. Mobility allowances are a marginal part of the LMB budget accounting for only one per cent of total expenditures. The expansion of Swedish labour market policy has occurred mainly within the area of demand promoting measures. The impact of supply oriented measures has further declined as a consequence of the rise in cash compensation to the intolerable figure of 30 per cent of the LMB budget. Earlier in this paper it is presumed that Swedish manpower policy will face great difficulties in the next years. Since the beginning of the 1970s Sweden has entered each recessionary phase with a gradually higher rate of unemployment and with an increasing part of the labour force under the umbrella of manpower programmes (cf. Table 6.4).

Table 6.4 Unemployment and manpower training

Last year of boom period	Registered unemployment (per cent)	Share of labour force in LMB	Total share of persons outside regular labour market
1970	1.5	1.8	3.3
1975	1.6	2.3	3.9
1980	2.0	2.9	4.9
1985*	3.0	3.5	6.5

*Estimated by Labour Market Board.

The task for the remainder of the 1980s is to reduce the already high registered unemployment and to decrease the large volume of manpower policy measures, to create balance between labour supply which for structural reasons is expected to increase and labour demand which threatens to stagnate and, finally, to combat the next recession which is approaching.

Obviously, these immense tasks cannot be solved by manpower policy alone. The basis is a 'policy for balanced growth' where an active policy for industrial development must play a more central role than earlier in Sweden. The problems of shortening work hours should not even in Sweden be put under taboo albeit Sweden tries to find other solutions than general reductions of work hours.[17]

However, manpower policy is confronted with such severe problems that *a change of strategy* seems necessary. Recent guide-lines put forward by the Labour Market Board (August 1985) give an indication of the tenor of this change.

According to this programme a more important role should be given to the employment service and resources should concentrate on shortening the duration of job vacancies and eliminating bottle-necks in manufacturing industry where the scarcity of highly skilled labour has become a serious problem.

It follows that greater emphasis must be given to the supply oriented measures. Mobility allowances which cover only part of the real costs for the migrants should be increased considerably and not be available only for unemployed persons. Labour market training must be reinforced and be better adapted to the needs of private industry. Wage subsidies must cover longer periods and be used to stimulate employment without exacerbating inflation. The focus on 'work' must regain its dominant position in Swedish manpower policy and financial compensation to the unemployed be relegated to a policy of last resort.

By restructuring the policy in this way special emphasis can be given to the weaker groups in the labour market, the young and disabled. There are very strong reasons to eliminate youth employment and Sweden's low youth unemployment in the ages below 20 years shows that the problem is manageable. There are also strong reasons from a welfare point of view to further expand the sheltered work system. Even in a programme which is clearly growth-oriented the interests of the weakest groups must be protected.

The changed strategy is not 'new' but implies a return to ideas which were developed more than thirty years ago. The emphasis on supply oriented measures does not indicate an adjustment to neo-liberal 'supply economics' but can be characterised as a natural part of the Swedish model for a selective and flexible policy. The 'new' manpower policy programme is, in fact, in better congruence with the philosophy of the 1961 and 1966 LO reports[16] than the manpower policy which has been practised in Sweden in recent years.

Notes

1. *Trade unions and full employment*, A report submitted to the 1951 LO Congress, Stockholm, 1952. See also R. Turvey (ed.), *Wages policy under full employment* (London, 1952).
2. An econometric study which has been undertaken by the Swedish Ministry of Finance shows that a given rate of unemployment corresponds to a gradually higher rate of inflation. An unemployment rate of 2 per cent corresponded during the 1960s to 3 per cent inflation, in the 1970s to 9 per cent inflation and in the beginning of the 1980s to 13 per cent inflation (*Long-Term Report LU 84*, Ministry of Finance, Stockholm, 1984). The study indicates that the Swedish Phillips curve behaves in an almost Friedmanian way, a development which of course is quite contrary to the intentions of the Swedish government but which is heavily affected by international influences.
3. L. Erixon, 'What is wrong with the Swedish Model? An analysis of its effects and changed conditions, 1974–85', The Swedish Institute for Social Research (Stockholm, 1985).
4. There exists a comprehensive literature concerning the social and individual effects of unemployment. Among the earliest studies should be mentioned the classic works of Marie Jahoda, *Die Arbeitslosen von Marienthal* (Leipzig, 1933) and E. W. Bakke, *Citizen without work* (New Haven, 1940). For more recent studies which show similar results cfr. M. Frese-G. Mohr, 'Die psychopathologischen Folgen des Entzugs von Arbeit', in Frase-Greif-Semmer (eds), *Industrielle Psychopathologie* (Bern, 1978).
5. It is a widely held opinion, both amongst Swedes and foreign observers, that the public sector's expansion has been the result of a deliberate and planned employment policy, with the intention to compensate for lost jobs in private industry. This interpretation is erroneous. *Ex post* it is easy to point to the fact that the public expansion has facilitated the task of keeping employment high, especially amongst women, but the rapid expansion of public services is the result of a number of dramatic social reforms which created a corresponding demand for labour. There is no evidence that the main impetus for these reforms was to create new jobs.
6. B. Holmlund, *Labor mobility* (Stockholm, 1984).
7. P. Mossfeldt, *Sista skiftet* (The last shift). A report on close-down research in Sweden during twenty years (Stockholm, 1983). See also P. A. Edin, *Individuella sysselsättningskonsekvenser av ned läggningar* (Individual consequences of close-downs for employment) Working Paper nr 119, Swedish School of Economics (Helsinki, 1984).

8. L. Heikensten, 'Studies in structural change and labour market adjustment' (Stockholm School of Economics, 1984).
9. *Arbete åt alla* (Jobs for everybody), Report from the governmental Employment Commission (Stockholm, 1975). The commission's final report *Sysselsättningspolitik för arbete åt alla* (Employment policy for jobs for everybody) was published in 1979.
10. *Att utvärdera arbetsmarknadspolitik* (The evaluation of labour market policy), Stockholm, 1974; *Arbetsmarknadspolitik i förändring* (Labour market policy in transition), Stockholm, 1978 (English summary is available) and *Arbetsmarknadspolitik under omprövning* (Labour market policy under reconsideration), Stockholm, 1984 (English summary is available).
11. Åke Dahlberg, 'Arbetsmarknadsutbildning – verkningar för den enskilde och samhället' (Labour market training – effects for the individual and the national economy), Umeå, 1972.
12. E. Gramlich-B. Ysander, 'Relief work and grant displacement in Sweden', in G. Eliasson (ed.), *Studies in labour market behavior: Sweden and the United States*, Stockholm, 1981.
13. B. Winander, 'Ungdomslagens inverkan på utslussningen av ungdomar' (The effects of youth teams on the placement of youth in regular jobs), SINOVA, 1984, mim.
14. E. Wadenejö, 'Disability policy in Sweden', in R. Haveman-V. Halberstadt-R. Burkhauser, *Public policy toward disabled workers* (Ithaca, 1984).
15. V. Vlachos, *Temporära lönesubventioner* (Temporary wage subsidies), Lund Economic Studies, 1985 (with English summary).
16 R. Haveman, 'The potential of targeted marginal employment subsidies', in *Marginal employment subsidies* (OECD, Paris, 1982).
17. The Swedish Ministry of Labour has initiated a study of the effects of shorter working hours on employment during the period 1963-83. The report has quite recently been published and gives no support to the hypothesis that shortening of work time affects employment in the private sector of the economy whilst some effects have been observed in the public sector. See Ynove Åberg, Produktionens och sysselsättningens bestämningsfaktorer i svensk ekonomi (The determining factors for production and employment in the Swedish economy), Ministry of Labour, Stockholm, 1985 (mim). An English translation is forthcoming.
18. T. L. Johnston (ed.), *Economic expansion and structural change*, A report submitted to the 1961 LO Congress, and S. D. Andeman (ed.), *Trade unions and technological change*, A report submitted to the 1966 LO Congress, London, 1967.

COMMENT

W. R. Dymond*

It is relatively easy to criticise a model and to criticise the application of the model as a determinant of the economic and employment performance of a country. It is even easier when the country in question and the objectives of the model have highly ambitious goals such as full employment at less than 2 per cent, low inflation, a highly developed welfare state and high economic growth.

I should first however, like to start out on a positive rather than a critical note. The Rehn/Meidner model (I shall call it this because Meidner has been excessively modest in dubbing it the Rehn model) has been extremely influential in the development of labour market policies and set the conceptual framework for the development of manpower policies in the developed OECD economies in the 1960s and early 1970s. This process was effectively guided by Gosta Rehn who served as Director of the Manpower and Social Affairs of OECD over this period.

The model, however, was never fully applied in any country, not even fully in Sweden and primarily served to identify particular measures that could be applied to bring a better balance to the labour market. No country other than Sweden succeeded in using it to stabilise employment levels and reduce unemployment markedly during the troughs of cyclical swings, primarily because of the lags in government decision making on counter cyclical expenditure programmes. Further the anti-inflationary and selective fiscal policy aspects of the model to prevent inflationary overheating was either little understood or was not considered relevant to the economic context in which most countries found themselves.

This being said, I shall devote myself to a somewhat cursory examination of the relevance of the model and its performance in the context of developments in the Swedish economy and labour market. This task is incidentally facilitated by Meidner's assertion: 'The model which was originally constructed in an expanding economy is also fully applicable in a stagnating economy' (page 145). If this were true it would be the only important economic theory which has survived intact from the ravages of the two oil shocks, slow growth, double digit inflation (until recently), continuing high unemployment, an

---

*The text does not engage the responsibility of the OECD.

accelerating pace of structural change and growing international interdependence.

The model in the context of general economic policy is designed to play 'a supporting and complementary role' to the achievement of the full employment commitment. While I think it can be safely argued, as Meidner does, that the model played this role up until the mid 1970s it was still relatively marginal as an instrument in the achievement of this objective. Most OECD countries also had relatively low unemployment and in Sweden's case it was largely achieved by a substantial growth in public employment from 19.7 per cent in 1970 to 31.1 per cent of total employment in 1984 (see Meidner Table 6.3). The growth of output and employment in the private sector was heavily dependent on exports which in the late 1970s were heavily fuelled by successive devaluations of the Swedish currency (five since 1976). The role of the policy was largely to remove people during cyclical down turns from open unemployment as is revealed by Meidner's Table 6.1. This is not to suggest that the stabilisation of open unemployment over these years at the level of 2 per cent or less is a mean achievement. The cost of course, was in terms of higher inflation rates and losses of competitivity subsequently overcome by currency devaluations. In the later years, it contributed to heavy budget deficits and in earlier years to high marginal tax rates. I would not, however, be prepared to argue that the benefits in terms of low unemployment have not been worth the price, *provided* that the methods used do not lead in the longer term to a reduced growth rate and a reduction in the growth of real income per capita.

Meidner assigns a key role for the model in moving the Phillips-curve towards the origin. It is on this criterion, given the Swedish reality of labour market performance, that the application of the model has had its most noticeable failure. Meidner asserts that this failure has not proved the model to be wrong, but attributes it to international inflation and the inappropriate application of the model by the authorities. I do not find this defence particularly credible as an open economy like Sweden's has to be able to absorb the periodic shocks which lead to inflationary and pressures and any economic model has to be capable of application, at least part of the time, by political policy makers. The Phillips-curve over the period 1962 to 1984 has certainly moved a very long way from its 1962–70 position (cf. Meidner, note 2, p. 160). A comment on the Phillips-curve deterioration is made in the May 1985 OECD *Economic Survey of Sweden* in the following terms:

The price of this internationally outstanding (unemployment) performance was a steady deterioration of the Phillips-curve relationship, i.e. a ratcheting up of inflation. The attainment of such a full employment goal would require a significant effort to reduce the rigidities in the labour market in terms of both impediments to mobility (vocational as well as geographic) and insufficient wage flexibility. Otherwise the attainment of price stability would be threatened. Moreover, the commitment (to full employment) severely constrains macro policies in the case of external or exogenous shocks such as shifts in the terms of trade, in aggregate productivity or in domestic cost levels, a feature not unrelated to the deteriorating macroeconomic performance in the past.

Behind the substantial outward movement of the Phillips-curve over this period, lies a deterioration in the operation of the Swedish labour market which was not overcome even by the selective measures which were so vigorously applied by the Swedish labour market authorities in accordance with the model. This deterioration may be indicative of the direction which changes should take in the future orientation of Swedish labour market policy. Over the period, there was a steady increase in the number of persons in manpower programmes as revealed by Table 6.2 of the Meidner paper. However, as Figure 6.3 reveals, the supply oriented measures had declined in their weight, while the demand oriented measures had increased. It can be argued that if flexibility of the labour market, and the efficiency of allocation increased and pressure points in the demand for labour met, that a greater weight on supply measures is more appropriate. Meidner hints at the desirability of this in the conclusions of his paper. Over this period, as shown by the OECD *Economic Survey* of Sweden, May 1985, there has been a lack of skilled workers in some sectors (the share of companies in business tendency surveys reporting the lack of skilled labour has varied cyclically from 10 per cent at the troughs to more than 80 per cent at the peaks) and in recent years, a rise in the excess demand for technically qualified staff. These developments have been accompanied by a decline in some indicators of mobility such as quit rates, job mobility and migration which have all displayed a downward trend up to 1983. For example, job mobility measured by the rate of job changes in per cent of total employment fell from an average of 11 per cent at the beginning of the 1970s to about 8 per cent in the early 1980s. While these developments clearly reflect lower levels of employment growth prevailing in the 1980s, they also reflect significant structural changes. For example, the number of two-earner households has affected the frequency of location changes which has declined.

Labour market measures, in particular the employment service have played a role in improving the allocation process and the number of weeks it takes to fill a job in the employment service has steadily decreased from 8 in 1974 to 3 in 1984. The question can be raised however, as to whether active labour market interventions particularly on the supply side can substitute for less wage flexibility as the result of 'solidaristic' wage policy which is indicated by the differential wages of the highest and lowest paid blue-collar workers which has diminished from 30 per cent in the late 1960s to less than 15 per cent in 1982. At the same time the correlation between pay structures of branches of industry and productivity increases has persistently weakened through the 1970s (OECD *Economic Survey* of Sweden, May 1981) which would suggest a deterioration in the allocative functioning of the labour market. Unemployment in various sub-sectors of the market has co-existed with shortages of labour which has meant that the risk of inflationary bottlenecks during recoveries has significantly increased.

A thorough evaluation of the application of Swedish labour market policy needs to look at the effectiveness of those measures which removes people from open unemployment and places them in training, public works and wage subsidy programmes. Meidner in his paper has provided useful information on the evaluative studies of various elements of the policy, which provide us with some basis for such an assessment. I must say, however, it is somewhat surprising that relatively speaking there are so few such assessments in view of the magnitude of public resources devoted to labour market measures in Sweden.

As is usually the case, the results of the measures when assessed in terms of their objectives presents an extremely mixed picture which is usual for most countries and which on the basis of the evaluations suggests that if policy has a more fundamental objective than simply removing people from unemployment rather than paying them unemployment benefits, that is to secure permanent employment for them, then results are heavily dependent on the extent of growth of new jobs in the labour market. As Meidner himself points out, actions to create jobs through relief work are limited. With respect to interventions which are a significant part of Rehn's later development of the model, that is to stimulate employment and check inflation through marginal employment subsidies in the private sector, research findings suggest that such actions are severely constrained by the macro-economic context as a way of increasing general employment and suffer from both substantial substitution and windfall profit effects. Targetted employment subsidies, which are not discussed by Meidner, have in recent years in some countries proved much more effective in redistributing employment opportunities between various groups of the unemployed rather than as a means of stimulating overall net employment growth which fundamentally depends on the growth of demand as determined by fiscal and monetary policy.

A major point on the employment side of the model was that job creation programmes should be 'selective'. This was not so difficult in the 1950s and 1960s when the employment programmes were almost exclusively construction works in winter and sheltered works for the handicapped. Since then, the programmes have been extended to many other categories of the unemployed, whose problems are often neither seasonal nor cyclical – youth, women, white-collar workers and regional employment problems are usually in the long run of a structural character and affect a wide range of occupations. Given the present size and rather permanent character of relief works it becomes increasingly difficult to ensure that local authorities do not reallocate or cut their regular budgets in regions where relief works are available and thus add little to overall employment.

In the original Rehn/Meidner model a market was cleared by supply side measures which would enable most of the unemployed to take jobs. The question now is whether this model is relevant if the demand side of the market chronically fails to provide sufficient jobs and whether Meidner's implicit suggestion that more spending on supply side measures would be sufficient to clear the market is not really credible under these circumstances. The case for more supply side measures rests much more on improving the allocative function of the labour market in order to take advantage of job growth and the terms of the model to avoid the development of inflationary pressure points.

Finally, it might be mentioned that the model did not contemplate quantitative adjustments to reduce labour supply in relation to reduced demand and that as Meidner says the focus on 'work' must retain its dominant position in Swedish manpower policy. In fact, there have been supply side adjustments in the labour market which have at least indirectly been affected by government policy. An increase in the supply of female labour with the highest female participation rate among developed countries has been accommodated by a substantial growth of part-time work, parental leave and longer vacations and while employment has gone up, there has been no equivalent increase in the number of hours worked. Early retirement pensions which were introduced in 1972 have been increasingly important as a way to reduce the participation rate for workers over 60. Swedish firms find early retirement an attractive option because the costs are borne by government and it has proved attractive to older workers because of the high income replacement rates characteristic of the scheme.

To conclude with a question. If the model is defective in certain respects, what adaptations should there be if it is to address current and foreseen labour market problems?

I would not disagree with most of the elements of the change of strategy Meidner identifies at the end of his paper, i.e. an intensified role of the employment service in reducing bottlenecks, more emphasis on supply side measures and particular attention to particular groups such as the young.

However, I believe that manpower policies should shift in a more fundamental manner away from an effort to relieve short-term disequilibrium problems on the labour market at full employment levels to a longer-run role in facilitating the adjustment of the labour market to the needs of industrial restructuring including the impact of new technologies. Clearly reaching anything like full employment in most countries, if we mean by that regular jobs in the private and public sectors, is going to depend on economic growth and all of those policies which will produce a higher growth rate on a sustained, noninflationary basis. In this policy context, labour market interventions can only play a supplementary role primarily in accordance with the Rehn/Meidner model to dampen down inflationary pressures resulting from bottlenecks.

The growing dualism of labour markets to which Meidner does not refer, is a critical problem and here I would assign a particular role to demand side measures which subsidise the private sector as well as temporary job creation, to provide better access to continuing employment to the weaker groups, such as youth, some categories of women and the long-term unemployed.

Finally, in most countries labour market efficiency and the allocation process needs to be improved. This means not only positive measures to increase mobility, better employment services and labour market training, but also modification of legislation and collective agreements which inhibit flexibility and employment growth in such areas as employment security, unemployment compensation, pension provisions and housing policies.

Günther Schmid

My comments on Rudolf Meidner's contribution are restricted to some complementary remarks from the German point of view because I cannot imagine a better description of the Swedish model. Meidner himself has drawn our attention to some critical aspects of the Swedish model, and Bill Dymond has already put his finger on the sore points. I will, therefore, try to answer the following questions:

1. Should and can labour market policy in Germany be given the same strategic role as in the Swedish model?
2. Which policy measures are most adequate with respect to the present situation and to future prospects of the labour market?
3. What are the reasons for the recent deviation of Swedish manpower policy from its 'ideal path' described in the Rehn/Meidner model, and what can we learn from it?

Before I start to answer these questions I must indicate a difference in terminology: Meidner is talking about 'Manpower Policy', whereas I use the term 'Labour Market Policy'. I do not know if Meidner has consciously chosen the term 'manpower policy', but I think this term is correct in characterising the Swedish method of intervention, in the labour market. 'Manpower Policy' refers to measures of employment creation or employment promotion that affect labour supply or labour demand in a direct way, whereas 'Labour Market Policy' also includes measures that affect supply and demand in a more indirect way in changing the functional conditions of the labour *market*. I have especially in mind regulatory measures, such as regulation of minimum wages, quotas in favour of disabled or other groups, regulation of hiring and firing, regulation of industrial relations, regulation of unemployment insurance contributions. Although the Swedish model has some elements of this type of policy, it clearly concentrates on direct measures such as training, mobility grants or public work creation.

However, we should regard regulatory measures as functional equivalents to direct changes of supply and demand, especially when we have to assume that the preconditions of Swedish manpower policy are not given in other countries. Another reason is that regulatory measures already play a larger role in other countries than in Sweden. Let me only remind you of two recent examples: the change in the social security system in Great Britain and on the 'Employment Promotion Law' in the Federal Republic of Germany.

The differentiation of social security contributions (unemployment insurance contributions included) according to income classes, introduced in Great Britain in October 1985, was clearly connected with labour market intentions: the policymakers hope for an increase in employment because they expect that the progressive rate of contributions will produce an incentive to create *and* to accept low wage jobs. The German policy makers as well intended to stimulate employment by relaxing the rules of labour contracting for a limited period: the law of 1985 allows, among other things, that employers until 1989 sign labour contracts up to a maximum period of one and a half years in cases of new recruits or in taking on young people finishing their apprenticeships. This means a considerable extension of the regular probation time (half a year) and a circumvention of the dismissal law ('de-regulation'). The intention is to ease the employer's decision to take on new employees when the market situation improves, but future returns are still highly uncertain.

I have doubts about the effectiveness of both measures: for example, why should a highly developed industrial country like Great Britain start to compete with emerging industrial countries, while for the Federal Republic I fear a large scale conversion of permanent jobs to part-time jobs with reduced rights for the workers but with little net impact on employment; deterioration of productivity potentials (waste of accumulated firm specific human capital) and of industrial relations ('social peace') may result in the long run. However, this is not germane to the present debate. I only want to draw your attention to regulatory measures that may promote or prevent desired labour market or employment effects, a subject which is not taken up in Meidner's paper.

I turn now to the first question: Should and can labour market policy in Germany be given the same or a comparable strategic role as in the Swedish model? My answer is 'Yes', with some modifications to adjust for the context of the German economy.

My conditional 'Yes' is based on three assumptions. *First*, the room for manoeuvre of expansive fiscal and monetary policy in Germany is restricted, although certainly not as much as in Sweden. Germany is less prone to external inflationary shocks than Sweden; inflation is down to a level of 2 per cent, and is still decreasing (1.8 per cent in November, 1985), but unemployment is up to a level of 9 per cent, and there is no sign of substantial relief. The danger of a wage–price spiral that played a role in the 1970s is therefore relatively small. In addition, the service sector is not as developed as in Sweden. This leaves some room for manoeuvre (at least more than presently realised) for an expansive fiscal policy to create non-inflationary jobs in the service sector and in selected industries. However, the general need for a restrictive fiscal and monetary policy also holds true for Germany.

Secondly, Germany has not developed a solidaristic wage policy to such an extent as Sweden, however, German incomes policy incorporates important elements of it. An indication of this is the increasing pressure by conservatives and neo-liberals in Germany in favour of more differentiated regional and sectoral wage contracts or even of deregulation negotiated wage contracts by allowing individuals to contract below the negotiated wage (Soltwedel, 1984, for instance). If one favours a solidaristic incomes policy, and there are many good reasons for it, the need for a complementary active labour market policy to support selective growth, and to compensate for the loss of jobs, becomes evident.

Thirdly, active labour market policy expenditures in Germany are far below the level of Sweden: during the last ten years the level of manpower policy measures in Germany was around 0.8 per cent of GDP (Gross Domestic Product), in Sweden 2 per cent. The Swedish failure traced by Meidner, to excessive responsibility for full employment given to manpower policy, is not at stake in Germany. The records of the effectiveness of manpower policy are generally good (Schmid, 1982), and in terms of net employment effects even better than in Sweden (Johannesson/Schmid, 1980). In other words: the marginal impact of additional expenditures on manpower policy measures is greater in Germany than in Sweden. It has, however, to be agreed, that the consensus about the effectiveness of manpower policies is weak (see Soltwedel, 1984, for a different opinion), and much remains to be done to develop better foundations for the evaluation of manpower policy. In addition, the institutional framework for the implementation of selective and active manpower policy in Germany differs in some important respects from Sweden which makes it reasonable to look also for regulatory alternatives to direct measures of manpower policy. I return to these points later.

Let me now turn to the second question: Which policy measures are most adequate with respect to the present situation and to future prospects of the labour market?

Meidner's answer to this question, referring to the Swedish situation, is quite clear: For the remainder of the 1980s not only the large volume of manpower policy has to be reduced, but also the structure should change in favour of supply oriented measures such as mobility grants, training (not only for the unemployed), intensive labour placement services and long-term wage subsidies to stimulate employment growth. These supply-oriented measures should be complementary, not substitutive, to an 'active policy for industrial development'.

First, I fully agree with Meidner's statement that 'the employment service seems to be the component of the manpower policy's arsenal where marginal improvements can be expected to bring about considerable effects'. This holds even more true for Germany where the placement service is not as far developed as in Sweden. Improvement of the placement service is especially needed for the hard-to-place people. Evaluation studies in Germany indicate that service-oriented measures (such as pre-training, intensive counselling of employers as well as job-seekers) are more effective than general wage subsidies to induce employers to hire these people. In a situation of weak economic growth and high unemployment, wage subsidies may only be a necessary but not a sufficient condition to improve the labour market chances for these 'hard core' unemployed (Schmid/Semlinger, 1980, Semlinger/Schmid, 1985). An additional reason for the (re-)orientation from an incentive policy toward a public service policy may be given from the point of view of implementation theory: the more effective the labour administration in filling vacancies, the higher its potential to induce employers to hire hard-to-place people.

Effective labour market services create confidence, and confidence opens the door for persuasive strategies.

Secondly, I suggest some modification with respect to Meidner's statement that the supply-oriented measures of labour market policy should only be a complement to an 'active policy for industrial development', whatever that means. My suggestion is partly related to the different context of the German economy: as I mentioned above, I see some room for manoeuvre for a further expansion of public or semi-public social services. Public work creation thus can serve as an instrument to detect latent demands in social services, and – if successful – create permanent jobs in this way. In addition, for a larger part of long-term unemployed public work creation is the only realistic short-term solution (although the second-best solution) for gainful employment.

Thirdly, the other reason for my modification is more fundamental. I see a widespread agreement for the thesis that employment growth is increasingly de-coupled from investment in manufacturing industries, this seems to be especially true for large firms, less for small and medium-sized firms which have the chance to find market niches by the strategy of flexible specialisation. However, the growth potential of this type of firm depends heavily on the availability of cheap production oriented services within or outside the firm (marketing, research, financing or counselling services). Several empirical studies – our own studies in Germany included (Alban, 1984; Hull, 1984; Albrecht/Schmid, 1985) – show a strong positive correlation between stabilisation or even increase of employment in manufacturing industries and growth in production-oriented services. My conclusion, therefore, is that labour market policy should also support (within the range of its possibilities) the development of production oriented private services within or outside small and medium-sized firms.

Fourthly, I am not sure if I do justice to the Swedish model of manpower policy in saying that it is essentially a model of employment creation in an environment of steady growth and of rapid structural change. It seems to me less suitable as a model of necessary employment-sharing (or employment-redistribution) in an environment of restricted growth and of rapid structural change. Although I would go half way with the Swedish model, I would deviate from its route when too optimistic views are taken with respect to new sectors of growth. At least for Germany, the growth potentialities in private or public services or in selected industries are far from capable of absorbing the high surplus of labour.

Labour market policy has to become more an employment-sharing type of policy than a growth supporting or growth inducing type of policy. I have, therefore, some doubts about Meidner's conclusion that 'more permanent (wage) subsidies and schemes which focus on employment expansion incentives' should be introduced. I would follow this line if permanent or long-term wage subsidies for employment creation are combined with employment-sharing elements. Such conditioned wage subsidies could take two forms: (i) wage subsidies for a general reduction of working-time in combination with a marginal employment increase (a model proposed by Scharpf and

Schettkat 1984), and (ii) reduction of non-wage labour costs for regular or shorter working time and respective increase of non-wage labour costs for overtime working through a respective differentiation of unemployment insurance or social security contributions.

In turning now to the last question: What are the reasons for the recent deviation of Swedish manpower policy from its 'ideal path' described by Rehn/Meidner? I start by offering an additional explanation to Meidner's suggestions. Besides the plausible reasons Meidner has provided (the end of employment expansion in the public sector, increasing 'malfunctions' of the labour market), the deviation from supply measures to increasing demand measures has also something to do with the size and the institutional distribution of the costs of unemployment compared with the 'opportunity costs' of manpower policy.

Whether a public agency or public authority starts an employment programme or not depends – among other things – on the relative size of costs, on the institutional distribution of these costs, *and* on the certainty about the back-flow of (fiscal) returns. In other words, the probability of starting a programme decreases (i) the more the programme costs exceed the costs of unemployment, (ii) the more programme costs and fiscal returns of the programme are institutionally fragmented and incongruent, and (iii) the greater the uncertainty of returns due to substitution, displacements or windfall effects.

My argument in simple terms is that Swedish manpower policy shifted towards the less efficient public relief work-instrument because the programme costs first are lower than the costs of unemployment (or do not much exceed these costs), secondly because the institutions that pay for the programme (in Sweden a joint venture of central government, provinces and municipalities) get back the respective share of fiscal returns, and thirdly because the back-flow of fiscal returns can be expected with great certainty. All three conditions for a high probability of launch of manpower programmes look less favourable for labour market training: the programme costs substantially exceed the costs of unemployment, the central government in Sweden and the labour market fund are paying for the programme, but the fiscal returns are partly flowing to the provinces and to the municipalities, and finally, there is high uncertainty about the returns of the programme.

The explanation I have provided for the deviation of Swedish manpower policy from the 'ideal path' is still very tentative. However, I hope to have made clear the importance of institutional 'opportunity cost considerations'. Much research remains to be done in this field of institutional incentives for labour market policy (Bruche/Reissert, 1985, 132ff.; Schmid, 1986; Wadensjö, 1985). Institutional arrangements, i.e. wrong institutional incentives, may be also a barrier to full employment.

References

Alban, Cornelia (1984) 'Existenzgründungen – Ein regionaler Vergleich unter dem Aspekt der Beschäftigungswirkungen', Discussion Paper IIM/LMP 84–22, Wissenschaftszentrum Berlin.
Albrecht, Christoph and Schmid, Günther (1985) 'Beschäftigung und Qualifikationsstruktur in Berlin 1977 bis 1983. Ein Vergleich mit 11 bundesdeutschen Ballungsregionen und 20 ausgewählten Arbeitsamtsbezirken'. Discussion Paper IIM/LMP 84-4, IIM/LMP 84-4, Wissenschaftszentrum Berlin.
Bruche, Gert and Reissert, Bernd (1985) *Die Finanzierung der Arbeitsmarktpolitik. System, Effektivität, Reformansätze* (Frankfurt a.M.: Campus).
Hull, Chris (1984) 'Job Generation among Independent West German Manufacturing Firms 1974–1980. Evidence from Four Regions', Discussion Paper IIM/LMP 84–15, Wissenschaftszenrum Berlin.
Johannesson, Jan and Schmid, Günther (1980) 'The Development of Labour Market Policy in Sweden and in Germany: Competing or Convergent Models to Combat Unemployment?', *European Journal of Political Research*, 8, No. 4.
Scharpf, Fritz and Schettkat, Ronald (1984) 'Verkürzung der Wochenarbeitszeit: Nur der Staat kann den beschäftigungspolitischen Handlungsspielraum erweitern', Discussion Paper IIM/LMP 84–5, Wissenschaftszentrum Berlin.
Schmid, Günther (1982) 'Zur Effizienz der Arbeitsmarktpolitik: Ein Plädoyer für einen Schritt zurück und zwei Schritte vor', Discussion Paper IIM/LMP 82–3, Wissenschaftszentrum Berlin.
Schmid, Günther (1986) 'Finanzierung der Arbeitsmarktpolitik: Plädoyer für einen regelgebundenen Bundeszuschuß an die Bundesanstalt für Arbeit', in Karl-Jürgen Bieback (ed.), *Perspektiven der Sozialversicherung und ihrer Finanzierung* (Frankfurt: Campus).
Schmid, Günther and Semlinger, Klaus (1980) *Instrumente gezielterarbeitsmarktpolitik: Kurzarbeit, Einarbeitungszuschüsse, Eingliederungsbeihilfen* (Königstein i.Ts.: Anton Hain).
Semlinger, Klaus and Schmid, Günther (1985) *Arbeitsmarktpolitik für Behinderte* (Basel: Birkhäuser Verlag).
Soltwedel, Rüdiger (1984) *Mehr Markt am Arbeitsmarkt* (München und Wien: Philosophia Verlag).
Wadensjö, Eskil (1985) 'The Financial Effects of Unemployment and Labour Market Policy Programs for Public Authorities in Sweden', Discussion Paper IIM/LMP 85–7, Wissenschaftszentrum Berlin.

Part IV
Welfare State Regulation, Industrial Relations Technology and the Environment

Part IV

7 The Welfare State and Jobs

Robert Delorme*

INTRODUCTION

The subject area of this paper is very large. The Welfare State has undoubtedly an impact on employment, and for more than a decade now unemployment has increasingly affected the Welfare State. I shall devote more attention to the former aspect by attempting to answer three questions. What is the impact of the Welfare State on employment? What is the nature of the unemployment problem? What are the implications for economic policy? On so varied and so large a problem I am not going to present a model. Instead I will present my thoughts on what appears to be the main issues, with the help of what I know of the existing literature as well as my own work on the role of the State. I will take the conclusions reached as given and I will not attempt here to substantiate them in any detail, adopting an 'if ... then' approach. I will argue that if one recognises the massive and lasting nature of present unemployment, in Western European countries at least, then a much wider theoretical framework than that afforded by the market clearing representation of economic life is needed. If it is assumed that such a framework holds, then it may have far reaching implications for the requirements of a successful economic policy and for the Welfare State.

The view which I will develop emphasises the macroeconomic aspect of the question and the usefulness of using a configurative setting rather than a monocausal theory. It highlights the complexity of the problem. Therefore I do not intend to propose simple and clearcut 'miraculous' means of recovering full employment through the Welfare State. My profound conviction is that no such recipe exists. I apologise for the frustration which this may cause to some readers. I will attempt to show why it is a complex question and why

*I wish to thank Terry Ward for his help with the English.

the task of eliminating barriers to full employment appears as an historically unprecedented challenge for economic policy making.

Let us accept at the outset that what is called the Welfare State may cover a number of activities and may be conceived in different ways (Albeda, 1984; Maddison, 1984; Wilson, 1983).

I tentatively define it as (i) the provision by the State of benefits, in cash or in kind, to identifiable individuals, these benefits not being given in payment for any current contribution to production and (ii) the regulatory activity of the State for the social protection of individuals. Three features are essential to the existence of the Welfare State: (a) the private enterprise basis of the economy; (b) policies aimed at full employment by sustaining demand through income maintenance, including a system of social security and a system of income redistribution; (c) a minimum degree of consensus of the social partners (employers and trade unions) on the necessary policies.

The second aspect is of special importance nowadays since it illustrates the fact that the Welfare State was created in a period in which it could be easily financed by contributions from labour (from both employees and employers to varying degrees) and, above all, could be aimed at redistribution, at supporting the unemployed rather than at job creation. Though there are many differences between countries I shall concentrate on what appear to be the common features in Western industrialised countries, especially in Europe.

EMPLOYMENT, UNEMPLOYMENT AND WELFARE STATE FACTS

Let us start by considering some important features of present employment, unemployment conditions in the Welfare State based on the figures contained in Tables 7.1–7.13.

Employment and Unemployment

Though there are differences between countries, the evolution of total employment in relation to that of the working-age population (Table 7.1) suggests that an improvement is occurring on average in most European countries compared to the situation in the years 1980 to 1983. But a steady trend increase in the unemployment rates during

Table 7.1 Total employment (1) and working age population (2)

		average annual growth rates (%)				
		1980–82	1983	1984	1985	1986
France	(1)	−0.2	−0.5	−1.0	−$\frac{3}{4}$	−$\frac{1}{2}$
	(2)	1.4	1.2	1.1		
Germany	(1)	−1.3	−1.6	−0.2	0	$\frac{1}{2}$
	(2)	1.4	1.0	0.6		
Italy	(1)	0.0	0.2	0.5	$\frac{1}{4}$	0
	(2)	1.0	1.1	0.9		
Japan	(1)	0.9	1.7	0.6	$1\frac{1}{2}$	$1\frac{1}{4}$
	(2)	0.7	1.0	1.1		
UK	(1)	−2.6	−0.8	1.0	1	$1\frac{1}{4}$
	(2)	0.6	0.7	0.4		
USA	(1)	0.1	1.3	4.1	2	$1\frac{3}{4}$
	(2)	1.1	0.9	1.1		
OECD Europe	(1)	−0.7	−0.5	−0.1	$\frac{1}{4}$	$\frac{1}{2}$
	(2)	1.3	1.2	1.0		

Sources: 1980–82 to 1984: from OECD *Employment Outlook* September 1985, Tables A and D; 1985 and 1986: estimates from OECD economic outlook June 1985, Table 12.

the 1970s was followed by an acceleration in the growth of unemployment in the first years of the present decade and the level of unemployment will remain high (Table 7.2). Two distinct groups of unemployed are of particular importance. They are the long-term unemployed (Table 7.3) and the young (Table 7.4). The situation has greatly worsened for long-term unemployment except for Japan.

Table 7.2 Unemployment rates

	(percentage of total labour force)				
	1970	1979	1984	1985*	1986*
France	2.4	5.9	9.7	$10\frac{1}{2}$	$11\frac{1}{4}$
Germany	0.8	3.2	8.6	$8\frac{1}{4}$	8
Italy	5.3	7.5	10.2	$10\frac{3}{4}$	11
Japan	1.1	2.1	2.7	$2\frac{1}{2}$	$2\frac{1}{2}$
UK	3.0	5.3	13.0	12	$11\frac{3}{4}$
USA	4.8	5.8	7.4	$7\frac{1}{4}$	$7\frac{1}{4}$
OECD Europe	2.5	5.4	10.8*	11	$11\frac{1}{4}$

Source: OECD *Employment Outlook* September 1985, Table 17.

*Estimates.

Table 7.3 Long-term unemployed as a percentage of unemployment

	1979		1984	
	6 months and more	12 months and more	6 months and more	12 months and more
France	55.1	30.3	66.5	42.3
Germany	39.9	19.9	55.1	32.7
Italy	—	35.8	—	41.9*
Japan	36.7	16.5	37.6	15.2
UK	40.0	24.8	60.2	39.8
USA	8.8	4.2	19.1	12.3

Source: OECD *Employment Outlook*, September 1985, Table H.

Table 7.4 Youth unemployment rate as a percentage of youth labour force (aged 15 to 24)

	1980	1984	1985*	1986*
France	15.0	26.1	29	31
Germany	3.9	10.1	$9\frac{3}{4}$	9
Italy	25.2	34.1	$35\frac{3}{4}$	37
Japan	3.4	4.9	$4\frac{3}{4}$	5
UK	13.9	21.8	$21\frac{1}{2}$	21
USA	13.3	13.3	$12\frac{1}{2}$	$12\frac{1}{2}$
Four European countries above	13.6	21.9	$22\frac{1}{2}$	$22\frac{3}{4}$

Source: OECD *Employment Outlook*, September 1985, Table 7.
*Estimates.

Youth unemployment also increased. Three countries (Italy, France and the United Kingdom) are in an especially bad position. All in all this supports the view that unemployment in European countries is a massive and lasting problem. Moreover one should not overlook the government's role as an employer. Government employment increased during the past decade (Table 7.5), but it has slowed down in the 1980s (Table 7.6) except in the case of France in 1982.

The Welfare State

The overall context within which social spending is currently taking

Table 7.5 Government employment* as a percentage of total employment

	1971	1980	1983
France	13.8	15.5	16.4
Germany	11.6	14.9	15.9
Italy	12.5	15.0	15.6
Japan	5.9	6.6	6.5
UK	18.8	21.0	22.0
USA	18.0	16.7	16.5
OECD Europe	13.5	16.6	17.6

Source: OECD *Historical Statistics*, 1985, Table 2.13.

*Institutional sector 'General government' as defined in the SNA.

Table 7.6 Year to year percentage changes in government employment

	1980	1981	1982	1983
France	0.7	0.8	2.1	1.4
Germany	1.5	1.7	0.6	0.3
Italy	0.2	1.9	1.1	1.5
Japan	1.3	1.1	0.6	0.6
UK	−0.6	−0.6	−1.0	−0.1
USA	2.2	−0.3	0	−0.1
OECD Europe	1.3	1.1	1.0	0.9

Source: OECD *Historical Statistics*, 1985, Table 1.13.

place is that of a general restrictive orientation of fiscal policies in Europe (Table 7.7). Social transfers were an important component of the growth of public spending in the 1970s (Tables 7.8 and 7.9). But the growth of social expenditure in relation to GDP has generally slowed down in recent years (Tables 7.10 and 7.11). The main cause of increases in social spending has been the extension of provision to a wider population (OECD, 1985a). Pensions and unemployment benefits are the most rapidly growing categories in the EEC countries. While sickness benefits and family allowances have diminished as a share of total social spending, old age pensions have levelled off and unemployment benefits increased sharply (Table 7.12).

Table 7.7 Total public expenditure as a percentage of GDP

	1970	1981	1983[1]	1983[2]	1984	1985
France	39.3	49.3	51.5	51.5	52.5	51.6
Germany	39.1	49.8	48.6	48.7	48.0	47.1
Italy	34.7	51.1	57.4	57.4	58.3	57.9
Japan	19.8	34.7	34.8			
UK	39.9	47.6	47.2	45.1	44.7	43.2
USA	32.9	35.7	38.1			

Sources: 1970, 1981, C. André and R. Delorme, 'Les évolutions des finances publiques et sociales. Comparison internationale et interprétation', CEPREMAP, December 1984, p. 24.
[1] 1983, OECD Historical statistics 1985, Table 6.5.
[2] 1983, 1984, 1985: *European Economy*, 22 November 1984.

Table 7.8 Variation of public spending and of its main components between 1970 and 1981 as a % of GDP

	Total variation	Current consumption and salaries	Social transfers	Investment	Interest payments
France	+10.0	1.7	7.3	−1.0	1.0
Germany	+10.7	4.9	4.6	−1.0	1.3
Italy	+15.4	4.1	4.8	0.4	5.6
Japan	+14.9	2.7	6.5	2.4	3.0
UK	+ 7.7	4.6	4.6	−3.9	1.2
USA	+ 2.8	−0.8	3.6	−1.1	1.7

Source: C. André and R. Delorme, *ibid*. p. 26.

Finally one should note the convergence of the structure of social expenditure across countries. But there remain important differences in the pattern of funding (general taxation vs. contributions, employers' contributions vs. employees' contributions) as Table 7.13 illustrates.

Table 7.9 Variation of the main functions of public spending as a % of GDP (1970–81)

	General administration	Education	Health	Social services	Economic services	Interest payments
Germany	1.3	1.2	2.5	4.5	−0.4	1.3
Italy	1.2	1.7	2.0	5.2	1.7	5.6
Japan	0.8	1.4	1.7	4.9	1.0	3.0
UK (1970–79)	−0.2	−0.2	0.4	4.7	−1.6	0.6
USA	−2.5	+0.2	−0.5	4.3	−1.0	1.7

Source: C. André and R. Delorme, *ibid.* pp. 147–8.

Table 7.10 Elasticity of social expenditure (including education)

| | Income elasticity* | | Decrease in the annual growth rate between 1960–75 and 1975–81 | |
| | | | Real GDP | Deflated social expenditure |
	1960–75	1975–81	(Percentage points)	
France	1.6	2.2	2.2	1.1
Germany	1.8	0.8	0.8	4.6
Italy	1.7	1.6	1.4	2.6
Japan	1.6	1.8	3.9	4.4
UK	2.2	1.8	1.6	4.1
USA	2.4	1.0	0.2	4.8

Source: OECD, Social Expenditure 1960–90, 1985, Table 2.

*Ratio of the growth rate of nominal social expenditure to the growth rate of nominal GDP.

Table 7.11 Social expenditure as a % of GDP*

	1975	1980	1981	1982	1983
France	22.9	25.9	27.4	28.5	28.8
Germany	29.8	28.5	29.4	29.4	28.9
Italy	22.6	22.8	25.3	25.8	27.3
UK	19.4	21.4	23.4	23.0	23.7
EEC (9 countries Greece not included)	24.7	25.8	27.2	27.6	28.0

Source: Eurostat SESPROS, 1, 1985.

*Education not included.

Table 7.12 Share of four functions as a % of total social expenditure for the EEC (9 countries)

	1975	1980	1983
sickness	26.7	26.0	24.1
old age	33.7	33.1	33.3
family	10.6	9.2	8.3
unemployment	4.6	5.5	8.4

Source: Eurostat SESPROS, 1, 1985.

Table 7.13   Structure of social security funding (as a % of the total)

	Employers' contributions	Employees' and other individual's contributions	Government (general taxation)	Other
1975				
France	58.2	19.2	19.4	3.2
Germany	38.6	27.8	29.0	4.6
Italy	72.9	10.5	13.4	3.2
UK	37.9	16.6	39.7	5.8
EEC-9	46.5	21.5	27.5	4.5
1983				
France	52.8	23.6	20.5	3.1
Germany	40.2	29.6	26.8	3.4
Italy	53.3	13.9	30.6	2.2
UK	31.8	15.9	43.4	8.9
EEC-9	41.8	22.5	30.6	5.1

Source: Eurostat SESPROS, 1, 1985.

THE IMPACT OF THE WELFARE STATE ON LABOUR: A PARTIAL ANALYSIS[1]

Ten types of influences can be identified.

The Effects of Old-age Pensions

Old-age pensions have much more to do with labour supply than with labour demand. The participation rates of older people in most OECD countries declined in the 1970s. But there is little evidence of any systematic link across countries between the participation rates and the transfer ratios for pension outlays (OECD, 1985b). Early retirement however has been encouraged for several years in many countries as part of employment policy. The effect of pensions on household savings has received considerable attention, yet there is no convincing demonstration of it that is significant (Kessler, 1983).

Unemployment Compensation

Unemployment compensation may induce unemployment in several ways notably through moral hazard. Among the main links are: (i) a positive relationship with the replacement ratio (net benefits received while out of work divided by net income whilst in work); (ii) an increased disincentive for unemployed workers to accept job offers (job search theory) or even to seek jobs; (iii) an induced rise in labour supply through positive effects on participation rates (especially married women and teenagers). On the other hand, unemployment insurance acts as an automatic stabiliser which has a depressing effect on unemployment by expanding demand.

The net overall effect is thus a matter of empirical analysis. The available evidence suggests that it is modest (OECD, 1985b). Moreover the situation has changed over recent years in most countries. First, replacement ratios have declined. Secondly, there has been a very large increase in long-term unemployment, which is not very responsive to unemployment compensation ratios. Other reasons must therefore be found to explain the high increase in unemployment since 1980.

Sickness Benefits

Sickness benefits may have two effects on employment. First they partially maintain the income level of individuals and thus the level of demand. Secondly, they may involve an incentive to increase absenteeism so increasing the labour costs of firms (sick workers must be replaced). But this may have a positive effect on employment since its level is higher than if the number of days of absence through sickness were lower. There are some OECD data on this. Though they should be used with caution, they show no increasing trend in the main Western countries between 1960 and 1981 except in Italy where the days of absence per worker increased in the 1970s. Moreover the outlays on sickness benefits are less than 1 per cent of GDP except in France where they are just above 1 per cent (1.1 per cent in 1960, 1.2 per cent in 1970, 1.2 per cent in 1981).

Taxation

Two of the main ways of financing social security, namely income tax and social security contributions, may have an effect on employment.

Income tax and employees' contributions may affect incentives to work and labour supply, a subject which has been much studied. Here again the empirical evidence does not provide clear results (OECD, 1985b).

The impact on labour demand in the private sector deserves more attention. A rise in direct personal taxation or in social security contributions may induce higher nominal wage claims, thus increasing the price of labour relative to that of capital and encouraging the use of more labour saving techniques. It may also affect the level of business profitability through cost-price relationships, depressing the level of investment and potential output. However the channels through which these influences operate, from an initial change in the labour cost to labour demand, is complex. The nature of the tax and the extent of tax incidence (the labour cost effect being obvious for employers' and employees' social security contributions), the cyclical position of the economy, the extent of competition and of price constraints on firms must all be taken into account. Profit margins may not be reduced if output prices rise at least as much as nominal labour costs. But these price increases may weaken the competitive position for a given exchange rate, thus reducing output and employment.

On the whole this would suggest that rising real labour costs have a negative impact on labour demand.

Crowding-Out

Considerable attention has been devoted to this matter. It is of concern here because of the potential displacement of private sector activity by the public sector as a consequence of expansionary fiscal policy introduced for demand management purposes. The question then concerns the net effect on labour demand of a possible shift from private employment to public employment. A priori this seems indeterminate since it depends in the end on the nature of the private spending foregone and the nature of the public spending generated (transfers, investment or consumption in more or less labour-intensive activities).

There are various channels through which these influences operate. The focus is usually on the effects of increases in public spending financed through higher public sector borrowing. Direct crowding-out occurs when the rise in public expenditure is offset by a decline in private sector spending. The obvious case is at full employment, though 'ultra-rationality' on the part of individuals may result in crowding-out in situations at less than full employment (for instance if people regard public consumption as a substitute for private consumption), but this latter case seems to have a limited relevance.

Crowding-out is indirect when it follows from increases in interest rates initiated by a rise in government borrowing. It thus affects investment demand and other interest-sensitive spending components. When budget deficits have an inflationary impact two conflicting effects may occur: first it may leave unchanged or even reduce real interest rates (in the sense of nominal rate of interest minus the inflation rate) thus favouring investment, secondly it may worsen international price competitiveness. Again the overall effect is indeterminate.

Another effect has received less attention, but is certainly one of the major constraints on the government's margins for manoeuvre in the present context of concern about inflation, positive real rates of interest and restrictive fiscal policies in Western Europe. It is that of past and persistent budget deficits leading to rises in levels of public debt and especially in debt interest payments. Given the recent rise in this item and its inescapable nature, it is likely to induce changes in the composition of public expenditure. Observation shows that in such a situation the first items to be lowered will be those which do not involve institutionalised pre-established commitments. Public investment is thus the main category to be affected, though from a medium-term perspective it is one for which there may be good reasons to think that it should be increased.

Empirical analysis of this issue usually relies on assessing the impact of a given fiscal stimulus when simulated on a macro-econometric model. In their review of the simulation properties of several national models, Chan-Lee and Kato (1984) detect weak crowding-out in both the short run and medium term. The results of simulating an increase in real government spending equal to 1 per cent of real GDP, for each of the major OECD countries acting in isolation, using the OECD Interlink model, are presented in OECD (1985b).

The fiscal impact is estimated on four scenarios combining two options: accommodating or non-accommodating monetary policy, fixed or floating exchange rates.[2] The results are summarised in Table 7.14.

The degree of crowding-out, measured as the arithmetic average of the differences in fiscal multipliers $(A-C)$ and $(B-D)$ over four years, is almost nil in Italy though higher in other countries.

These results therefore reinforce the case for an accommodating monetary policy if the effect of rising interest rates is to be offset.

Table 7.14 Real GDP effect after four years (differences from baseline) Canada, France, Germany, Italy, Japan, United Kingdom, USA.

Monetary policy	Exchange rate Fixed	Floating
Accommodating	*A* Fiscal multiplier with respect to GDP greater than unity for all countries except the United Kingdom, highest in Japan, USA, Germany and Italy	*B* Above one and greater than in case A especially in Japan and France
Non-accommodating	*C* Upward pressure on interest rates Positive fiscal multiplier with respect to GDP but <1 (between 0.5 and 0.7) except in Italy and Japan (Slightly above one.)	*D* Roughly same magnitude of the fiscal multiplier as in case C

Family Allowances and Housing

These categories are rather small compared to the other social expenditure programmes.

Comparisons across countries are extremely difficult because these categories include tax expenditures. Family allowances, to the extent they are high enough and help in child care, may have a negative influence on the participation rate of women since they compensate partially for the loss of income from paid work. They have remained roughly constant for many years except in France and Italy where they diminished and in Germany and Japan where they increased. Public spending on housing has also an important tax expenditure content often related to family size and household income, as well as to general housing policy. The location of housing programmes, together with their standards of quality and the levels of housing allowance (interest and tax deductions), are thus likely to play an important part in labour mobility.

Education

The impact of education expenditure and of the nature of the education system on labour supply is obvious. The figures on youth unemployment rates and the discrepancy between Germany and the other large Western European countries is striking and may be related to differences in the educational systems and in their relationship to the economic and social environment (Maurice, Sellier, Sylvestre, 1982).

The Welfare State as a Job Creator

In most countries the public education system and the public health sector, together with the social service sector, are by far the largest employers. One should thus not overlook this aspect of the Welfare State even though public recruitment has now suffered for several years from the restrictive orientation of fiscal policies. Though it may seem contrary to present opinion this aspect should not be ignored as is shown in another OECD study (*The Challenge of Unemployment*, 1982). It may take the form first of direct job creation in the public sector and second of subsidies to new jobs in the private sector.

The background of prolonged high unemployment and especially of long-term unemployment suggests that we may have to think of the role of the Welfare State in a rather modified way: as a means for creating jobs.

R. Klein (1983) has illustrated this point by showing that the extra cost of employing someone in the health or welfare services at the lowest grade – as a cleaner or as a porter – rather than maintaining the same person on social security is certainly low in England. Legal minimum wage considerations and the extent to which it is possible to have recourse to part time jobs are certainly of relevance here. Even so it suggests that social services offer scope for the creation of extra employment at a low financial cost. The traditional argument against this strategy is that it would freeze labour in jobs and thus create shortages when the economic and employment upswings come. But it is less and less relevant so long as long-term unemployment increases. It is known that it mainly affects the older and the unskilled and semi-skilled parts of the unemployed population. In present conditions the probability that they will go back to work is very low. Why then not pay more attention to the problems and opportunities of employment for these people? This would suggest developing the services concerned with the caring or preventive role of the system rather than those mainly concerned with technology or cure as in the case of health. In the latter case there is a growing feeling that hospitals are wrongly used if they house the old when these could be taken care of at home.

Finally it is worth mentioning that the growth of the Welfare State can also be seen as a means of providing work opportunities for women (Rein, 1985).

Malfunctioning Effects

Alleged malfunctioning of the Welfare State falls within our subject matter since it can result in inefficiency. As a consequence it exerts a permanent upward pressure on the growth of public spending. A higher level of funding through taxation and contributions is required for a given level of service. It therefore has the same effect on employment as described in **Taxation** above.

What is the real extent of those malfunctions? Two main areas deserve attention.

One is the productivity issue. According to popular opinion, public sector productivity is low especially in labour intensive activities such as education and health care. But considerable conceptual and measurement difficulties are involved here. One way to get some idea of its importance is to look at the relative price effect: assuming that productivity growth in public services is small or even zero, public service prices increase relative to those in the private sector, leading to the growth of public spending as a share of GDP. In a study of the public education system in France, Ch. André and I (1983) found no significant evidence of such a price effect. At most it is quite weak compared with other factors (level of service, demographic evolution, level of coverage of the population). This is confirmed by a recent OECD study (1985a).

The other aspect has to do with the criteria for the provision of welfare. There seems to be growing concern about the way the Welfare State has succeeded or failed in achieving some of its objectives and about possible reforms. As regards education and health, supply rigidities may occur as a result of the predominant role of producers in deciding what services are provided. Current reaction may thus be not so much against red tape as against the way in which consumer demands are transformed into needs which are determined by the experts. Poverty has not diminished to the extent that would have been predicted from existing income maintenance and assistance programmes.

In the case of benefits which are more or less proportional to paid employment income (sickness, unemployment, retirement), those with under-average income while at work are likely to receive insufficient benefits. Means-tested benefits would appear to be more efficient. There seems to be much room for improvement in this area through a better evaluation of programmes and of target groups, a greater role of users, more reliance on local initiatives and so on. It would thus seem possible to improve the overall satisfaction of basic needs without increasing public spending.

Regulatory Impact of the Welfare State

So much has been written on this subject that it does not require a lengthy discussion here. Both the specialised literature and international organisations (OECD, EEC) have denounced labour market rigidities as a kind of European disease. Welfare State regulations in the form of legal minimum wage, administrative rigidity, firing and hiring laws, legal length of work time, legal protection of unions and right to go on strike, organisation of work on the workplace, hygiene and workplace safety are the main targets. The theme of 'increased flexibility' of real wages and in industrial relations has been extensively discussed. We shall deal with it again in section 5 and suggest that some caution may be useful.

THE ANALYTICAL BACKGROUND: THREE REPRESENTATIONS

The question of the best theoretical framework in which to consider the present problem of unemployment has been the subject of much controversy. I base my argument on the distinction between three representations of this problem.

Market Clearing

The present economic crisis is considered under this heading as a lasting and important gap between the outcome of imperfections resulting from socio-political processes (the activities of governments and trade unions) and what would be required to reach a situation closer to the competitive equilibrium. Hence the cure advocated is maximum adjustment as fast as possible. The main policy recommendations derived from this theory are that the real wages should be reduced until an optimal share of profit in income is attained and that this should be combined with restrictive fiscal and monetary policy, a reduction in the role of the State (lowering of social expenditures) and, in the medium term, a reform of industrial relations in order to restore more competition and diminish the power of trade unions.

The Disequilibrium Approach

Keynesian theory provided a framework for viewing unemployment as the outcome of disequilibrium characterised by excess supply of labour resulting from a deficient demand for goods, the economic policy consequences of which are well known.

Later on it was demonstrated as a logical possibility that deficient demand for labour could occur simultaneously with excess demand for goods if firms found it unprofitable, or were unable to increase their production and employ more labour.

The policy implication is that demand stimulation will not affect unemployment and that actions aimed at increasing business profitability are needed.

In this vein, Malinvaud (1984) has emphasised productive capacity, capital intensity (labour requirement per unit of output) and profitability.[3] According to his analysis, changes in capacity depend mainly on the accelerator and on business profitability, changes in labour requirement depend mainly on the relative cost of labour with respect to capital.

As a consequence present disequilibria may be characterised by three features: the rate of capacity utilisation in manufacturing industry remains high compared with the unemployment level, the relative cost of labour with respect to capital is too high, profitability is too low.

An overall, if simplified, picture for Western Europe would have to distinguish what happened in the 1970s and in the early 1980s following this line of analysis. The prevailing feature of the 1970s until 1979–80 would be the high rate of substitution of capital for labour which was stimulated by the high cost of labour with respect to capital, while the rise in inflation helped to maintain business profitability. Business profitability declined a lot in the early 1980s as a consequence of the new slowdown in economic activity, the rise in interest rates and the reduction in inflation and has induced a significant slowdown in the building of new productive capacity.

Policy recommendations would thus focus on the limited impact of short-term demand management in the absence of action on prices, costs and incomes. A prices and incomes policy supported by an expansionary fiscal and monetary policy together with action to change the working of the labour market would be advocated.

The 'Régulation Approach'

What has come to be known as the 'régulation approach' is associated with the work of authors, mainly French, who use similar basic assumptions in analysing the current economic crisis and the evolution of capitalism.[4]

This theory is not limited to explaining the determinants of employment and of unemployment. It is an attempt to find a more complete representation of the characteristics of the past rapid and generalised growth and of the present crisis. Its main concern is thus with the dynamics of capitalist economies. I shall refer here to the body of theory developed by authors, mainly at CEPREMAP, with whom my work on the role of the State has become closely connected.

It is impossible to fully describe the theory here and I shall restrict myself to a few essential elements. As a first hypothesis there are two sets of invariant elements. One is the set of regularities which ensure the continuity and the macroeconomic consistency of the accumulation of capital. It is schematically based on three processes: the process of production, the way aggregate income is divided between profits and wages, and the distribution between consumption and investment. The conditions under which the consistency between these processes holds (from production to income to spending and back to production) is called a regime of accumulation.

The second set consists of institutional and structural aspects: money and financing, industrial relations and the wage relation, the State, the nature of competition, the international division of labour. The term 'régulation' is used to describe the way in which these two sets operate in a coherent way, as a steady configuration.

According to a second hypothesis these configurations vary over time. The dynamics of capitalism until now can be characterised by periods or phases of a prevailing kind of régulation which alternate with periods of major crisis in which the old régulation breaks down and is replaced by a new mode of régulation.

In this way a characteristic configuration ended with the Great Depression which thus had the nature of a major crisis. It was followed by the post-war configuration of growth ('the monopolistic' or 'Fordist' mode of régulation). There are reasons to consider that the crisis which has been developing for more than a decade now is in the nature of a major crisis, with the ending of basic features of the old configuration without any new consistent configuration having yet appeared as a possible successor to it.

As an illustration the post-Second World War 'Fordist' configuration may be sketched out in the following way:

production: mass production, high and sustained productivity growth;
income: growth of real wages, of social transfers and of profits permitted by productivity growth;
consumption/investment: mass consumption of standardised commodities, high rate of investment;

together with favourable institutional and structural conditions notably: low initial indebtedness, institutionalisation of wage rules through collective bargaining or through the State, institutionalisation of social transfers, growing world trade.

The current economic crisis may be depicted as a period of change in most of the variables entering this configuration: slowdown of productivity growth, increasing share of social expenditures, increasing labour cost relative to the cost of capital, reduced profitability, a move towards less standardised consumption, export-led growth, slowdown of world trade, international economic and monetary instability (oil shocks, fluctuations of the dollar, high level of debt).

This approach suggests that two phenomena may be of special importance for economic policy-making and the Welfare State. First the growing ratios of imports and exports with respect to GDP mean that the circular flows of production and expenditure are less and less confined to a national economy. Secondly institutionalisation of social expenditures operates not only as an automatic stabiliser but also as a source of rigidity in the face of reduced productivity and profitability (Delorme, 1984). Just as it was positively associated with economic growth in the past configuration, the way it operates makes it now appear to have a negative effect: growing wages and social transfers used to stimulate demand and productivity, now they have become adverse influences on profitability and competitiveness since they appear as the sources of growing labour costs.

But that is not to say that the problem comes from wages and social transfers alone: every one of the factors affecting the two sets of variables could also be involved. This point can be illustrated by a brief reference to the current debate on flexibility and wage restraint.

THE IMPLICATIONS FOR ECONOMIC POLICY

The Pros and Cons of Flexibility

Wage restraint and reduced rigidity of the labour market and of legal regulations are the main manifestations of flexibility, an objective which seems to have gained wide support in Western countries both in doctrinal and theoretical views and in the policies pursued.

The point I wish to make is that the policy conclusions are not so obvious. There should be more caution before giving advice to policy makers. What holds at the micro level for firms considered individually may have opposite effects at the macro level.

Does a policy of wage restraint necessarily lead to reduced unemployment? To answer this question it is necessary to show how lower wages will lead to higher profits, how higher profits will lead to more investment and how more investment will lead to more employment. This is likely to be true if it can be assumed that unemployment is purely classical and profits are used to finance productive operations rather than to reimburse loans – as may happen in a period of high indebtedness of firms and high real interest rates – or rather directed towards purely financial transactions to take advantage of their relatively high profitability. Can such a policy be beneficial if unemployment is Keynesian? Three effects have to be taken into account:

The impact on aggregate demand This will be positive if the propensity to spend from profits is higher than out of wages. The opposite is usually considered to be true and seems more likely. The depressing effect on consumption is therefore likely to be larger than the stimulating effect on investment.

The influence on capital-labour substitution A reduction of wages will lead to two opposing tendencies: a reduction of aggregate demand and an increase of labour required per unit of output. The net effect will depend on the degree of capital–labour substitutability. If, as is the case, substitutability is weak in the short run, the prevailing effect will be a reduction of demand though the effect may become positive in the medium-term.

The effect on competitiveness When competitiveness is weak and it is impossible to increase the balance of payments deficit, a policy to stimulate demand is ruled out. It can be introduced if competitiveness improves. This point is clear. It has been studied with respect to the cost of labour by Drèze and Modigliani (1981). But some caution is needed. First, price is only *one* aspect of competitiveness. And it may not be the main one. Competitiveness also depends on factors such as the quality of the products, new products, the ability to innovate in productive processes, in the organisation of production and in business management; the degree of professional qualification of employees, productivity growth in general and the capacity to set up commercial networks in foreign countries. Admittedly there is an asymmetry here: it is much less easy to improve these factors than to reduce wages. But this does not seem a convincing reason to take wages alone as the main target independently of the other factors. Secondly, it is open to question whether a systematic wage restraint policy is not just a substitute for competitive devaluation or even for protectionism. If all countries pursue simultaneously this policy then it is not possible for all of them to gain a competitive advantage and export-led growth since the exports of one country are the imports of another. Looked at in this way flexibility appears to be a strategy to gain market shares in world trade. It may be favourable for one country alone. But if it is practised simultaneously by most countries it may lead to a reduction of world demand (Boyer, 1985).

Lack of space does not allow a detailed discussion of other important aspects of flexibility such as the sensitivity of wages to the level of employment and that of the share of wages to profits.[5]

What is the empirical evidence? A tentative evaluation is set out below starting with macroeconometric models.

The simulation results of the effects of a reduction of wages in France, Germany, Italy and United Kingdom using the Eurolink model are presented in *European Economy* (November, 1984). A 5 per cent reduction of nominal wages is simulated and the results are compared with the base projection over the 1984–87 period. Several variants are studied: isolated action in each country in the absence of accommodating demand policy thereby maximising the competitive impact; the same action with demand stimulation; co-ordinated action by all countries with no stimulation of demand and the same policy with demand stimulation.

As one would expect the specifications of employment, wage and investment equations differ between the national models: investment is more dependent on profits in some, more dependent on demand in others. The results must thus be considered with caution. However a common feature to appear is the favourable impact of demand stimulation when combined with wage restraint: both seem to be required.

Another set of simulations by Wharton Econometrics[6] compares the results of five variant projections of Europe's level of output over the coming decade. They are: US dollar sharply lower: a strong negative effect; lower real wages (5 per cent cut in money wages the first year followed by rises in later years equal to those in the central forecast): a negative effect. The other variants have positive effects, the largest being achieved through international co-ordination of economic policy, followed by a cut in US budget deficit and finally by lower oil prices.

The nature of unemployment is likely to vary over time and across countries. Analysing the French case Artus *et al.* (1985) find that Keynesian unemployment prevailed from 1965 to 1967, in 1975, in 1977–8 and since 1980. Lambert *et al.* (1984), working also on the French case, stress the difficulty of differentiating between the Keynesian and the classical forms of unemployment. Sneesens (1984) infers from a comparison of the levels of potential and actual employment up to 1982 in Frace, Germany, Italy, the United Kingdom and the United Sates that non-Keynesian unemployment accounted for about 50 per cent of total unemployment in the US and a higher proportion in other countries except for Germany.

Another issue which has been the subject of abundant empirical research is that of the wage gap. The results are not as clear-cut as would be expected from the prevalent view that wages have become too high. The theoretical basis for its determination is not as clear as one would wish since it depends on fixing a norm for the share of wages in national income to be used as reference point. This may vary in response to other influences than mere wage changes such as the evolution of productivity and that of industrial prices compared to those of other sectors. Thus there is much doubt on the relevance of labour shares as good indicators of a wage problem (Blanchard *et al.*, 1985; Boyer, 1985; Le Cacheux and Szpiro, 1984).

Finally, it may be worth remembering that sometimes history has something to tell us. Remember Robbin's and Rueff's opposition to unemployment policies in the 1930s and the way unlimited flexibility worked at that time and can hardly be said to have put an end to the economic crisis. On the other hand, if we accept the 'regulation' hypothesis then post-war growth appears consistent with wage rigidities and institutionalisation of the various aspects of the wage labour relation. This is not to say that the same thing will happen again. But it shows that it was through innovations in social organisation, in new institutions and labour management, as well as in technological progress in the usual sense, that economic and social progress was associated with the evolution of Western economies. According to our hypothesis we are facing the same type of problem today.

Consequences for the Welfare State

1. Though we have made an apparent 'detour', the Welfare State is at the heart of the issue through (i) its funding (taxation and contributions: which are mainly based on paid work and seen as part of labour costs); (ii) its spending side; (iii) the rules and legal regulations relating to it in labour management and in the working of the labour market.
2. It is likely that the Keynesian, classical and frictional forms of unemployment are present to various degrees in our economies. It is necessary to consider firm and sectoral aspects as well as the macroeconomic aspects. It is uncertain whether one form would so much dominate the others as to justify one-sided policies.
3. The argument developed here suggests that actions through the Welfare State alone will have little effect or may even worsen the situation if they are not part of, or not co-ordinated with, a broader economic policy. If the 'regulation' hypothesis is taken as a general framework then such a policy would have to act simultaneously on the regime of accumulation and on the institutional and structural characteristics of the economy. What is required is a policy which would bring the economy onto a new steady path (low unemployment, acceptable growth) and which therefore needs the establishment of a new régulation.
4. Given the immensity of the task, the question arises as to how the Fordist régulation was established. Though economic policies were part of the process it would be a manifest exaggeration to consider that they were the unique cause (Delorme, André, 1983; Boyer, 1985). Fordism was not the outcome of a policy explicitly aimed at creating

such a system. It was the result of a conjunction of complementary phenomena adding up to a virtuous circular process of economic development. What has been considered as the success of Keynesian macroeconomic management would not have succeeded had not the accumulation conditions and the institutional and structural context been favourable. The French experience of 1981–2 illustrates this *a contrario*. And one should not overlook the role of the favourable initial conditions in the post-war growth (needs created by the war, a general perception of lagging behind the US, little or no internal opposition to the new policy orientation in Western countries). One should not therefore overestimate the capacity of governments to initiate large changes in the absence of a big shock.

5. The approach presented here suggests that the policy needed is of a different nature than stabilisation policy. It is not in the nature of an isolated corrective policy. A change which is as yet little perceived but fundamental may be the increased and unprecedented difficulty of economic policy making and implementation (Delorme, 1984), a difficulty which is becoming more systemic.

6. The content of the future régulation configuration, whenever it comes about is impossible to describe. It is likely to result from tensions, from opposing interests between social groups and between countries, and from technological evolution. One of the pressures on governments that is likely to persist for years to come originates from unemployment. Thus not having in mind an accurate picture of the future régulation configuration should not prevent us sketching out a policy aimed at alleviating present unemployment and creating jobs, provided it is many-sided as advocated above.

7. A policy of gradual steps through a variety of actions seems consistent with the present constraints: no one-sided strategy seems justifiable; no move, even small, seems negligible; no drastic and fundamental change seems possible because of internal obstacles and international interdependency. One would expect that the more collective negotiation between social partners and international co-ordination for a demand stimulation are developed, the greater should be the impact on output and unemployment.

Incomes policies seem inevitable. They should be complemented by internationally co-ordinated demand stimulation and an initial boost to supply (Blanchard *et al.*, 1985). This is in line with policies already proposed. But it is not enough if we take the régulation theory implications seriously. It should be accompanied by explicit industrial and employment policies, together with a reorganisation – to be negotiated – of the wage–employment relationship (Boyer, 1985).

Where is the Welfare State located in this type of policy? Our analysis in section 3 above suggests that there is room for a variety of changes which would go in the direction advocated. In countries in which employers' contributions are an important fraction of social security financing, the potential impact of reforms aimed at partially disconnecting them from paid work is high (André et al., 1985). This does not necessarily argue for a reduction of social expenditures. Reorganisation on the spending side can increase efficiency while preserving a given coverage of individual needs within the boundaries of a given level of financial resources. Stabilisation rather than reduction of social spending is possible.

To conclude, there is very little reason to think that unemployment will not last for a long time, at least in Europe, if no international co-ordination together with internal reorganisation takes place. The basic demands on the social security system in the future will be changed not only by the persistence of unemployment but also by the movement towards a free time society, demographic trends, and by changes in culture and in the conception of the family. The Welfare State which developed was based on the founding principle of the right to subsist through cash or in kind distribution in otherwise full employment societies. The current crisis makes it appear insufficient. Pressures to complement it by a new right i.e. the right to work, are likely to grow. They may end in a new stage of capitalist development and of State intervention, the one in which a Workfare State would replace the Welfare State we know. Let us hope that for it to become acceptable will not require the same type of big shock as the one which backed Beveridge's programme.

Notes

1. The analysis in this section is partial because it is carried out independently of an examination of the determinants of employment and of unemployment, a question which will be discussed in the next section.
2. Monetary policy is defined as accommodating when the money supply is adjusted in order that the demand for money can be met at existing interest rates. Non-accommodating monetary policy refers to abiding by pre-determined monetary growth targets.

3. Profitability is defined as the difference between the real profit rate earned on productive operations and the real interest rate earned on finance capital.
4. For a survey see M. de Vroey, 'A regulation approach interpretation of contemporary crisis', *Capital and Class*, Summer 1984, pp. 45–66. The term 'regulation' may be misleading. It has nothing to do with regulation by government. This is the reason why I use the French term 'régulation'. Boyer defines it as 'The way in which a system as a whole functions, the conjunction of economic mechanisms associated with a given set of social relationships, of institutional forms and structures'. The initiating contribution to this approach is by M. Aglietta, *A Theory of Capitalist Regulation: The US Experience* (New Left Books, 1979) (French edition 1976).
5. See Boyer (1985) for an extensive analysis.
6. 'Could Europe Grow Faster?', Wharton Econometrics, May 1985, reported in *The Economist*, May 11, 1985, p. 67.

References

Albeda, W. (1984) *The Future of the Welfare State* (European Centre for Work and Society, Maastricht).

Andre, C., Delorme, R. and Penot, J. P. (1985) *Protection sociale: financement, équité et équilibre à long terme* (FEN, Paris).

Artus, P., Avouri-Dovi, S. and Laroque, G. (1985) 'Estimation d'une maquette macroéconomique trimestrielle avec rationnements quantitatifs', *Annales de l'INSEE*, 57, Janvier-mars.

Blanchard, O., Dornbusch, R., Dreze, J., Giersch, H., Layard, R. and Monti, M. (1985) 'Employment and Growth in Europe: A Two-Handed Approach', CEPS Papers, 21, Brussels.

Boyer, R. (1979) 'Wage Formation in Historical Perspective: The French Experience', *Cambridge Journal of Economics*, vol. 3.

Boyer, R. (ed.) (1986) 'L'Europe entre fordisme et flexibilités', (La Découverte, Paris; forthcoming).

Chan-Lee, J. H. and Kato, H. 'Caractéristiques comparées de simulations des modèles économétriques nationaux', *Revue économique de l'OCDE*, 2, printemps 1984.

Delorme, R. and Andre, C. (1983) *L'Etat et l'économie* (Seuil, Paris).

Delorme, R. (1984) 'Compromis institutionnalisé, Etat inséré et crise de l'Etat inséré', *Critiques de l'économie politique*, 29, janvier-mars.

Dreze, J. and Modigliani, F. (1981) 'The trade-off between real wages and employment in an open economy (Belgium)', *European Economic Review*, vol. 15, 1.

European Economy (1984) 22, November.

Kessler, D. (1983) 'Les politiques sociales modifient-elles le comportement des individus? Le cas du système de retraite', *Revue d'économie politique*, 3, mai-juin.

Klein, R. (1983) 'La crise internationale des politiques sociales: dilemmes conceptuels et choix de politiques possibles', *Politiques et Management Public*, vol. 1, 3.

Lambert, J. P., Lubrano, M. and Sneessens, H. R. (1984) 'Emploi et chômage en France de 1953 à 1982: un modèle macroéconomique annuel avec rationnement', *Annales de l'INSEE*, 55/56, juillet-décembre.

Le Cacheux, J., Szpiro, D. (1984) 'Part salariale et emploi', *Observations et diagnostics économiques*, 8, juillet.

Le Dem, J. and Pisani-Ferry, J. (1984) 'Crise et politiques économiques dans les grandes économies industrielles: permances et changements', *Critiques de l'économie politique*, 29, janvier.

Maddison, A. (1984) 'Origins and Impact of the Welfare State, 1883–1983', *Banca Nazionale del Lavoro*, March.

Malinvaud, E. (1984) *Mass Unemployment* (Basil Blackwell, Oxford).

Maurice, M., Sellier, F. and Sylvestre, J. J. (1982) *Politique d'éducation et organisation industrielle en France et en Allemagne* (PUF, Paris).

OECD (1982) *The Challenge of Unemployment*.

OECD (1984) *Employment Outlook*.

OECD (1985a) *Social Expenditure 1960–1990. Problems of growth and control*. (OECD Social Policy Studies, Paris).

OECD (1985c) *Employment Outlook*.

Rein, M. (1985) 'Social Policy and Labor Markets: The Employment Role of Social Provision' OECD (1985b) See Saunders and Klaus. (mimeo, xiiith World Congress of the International Political Science Association, Paris).

Saunders, P. and Klau, F. (1985) 'The Role of the Public Sector', *OECD Economic Studies*, 4, Spring.

Sneessens, H. (1984) 'Keynesian vs Classical Unemployment in Western Economies: An Attempt at Evaluation', (mimeo, Faculté Libre de Sciences Economiques, Lille).

Wilson, T. (1983) 'The Welfare State and Stabilisation Policies in the Current Economic Situation', (mimeo, 39th Congress of the International Institute of Public Finance, Budapest, 22–26 August).

COMMENT

Meinhard Miegel

I agree wholeheartedly with Professor Delorme that isolated changes in the Welfare State would not improve the employment situation. I also share his view that a real reform of economic and social policy in western industrialised countries could improve employment levels.

Since we agree on these basic issues and since Professor Delorme has discussed the theoretical background quite extensively, I restrict my contribution to a few very practical, specific points. Basing my comments on the information already presented by the speaker, I will look at the financing, services, and legal structure of the Welfare State.

Regarding the financing, I suggest that the idea of completely or at least partially separating labour costs and welfare costs be opened for discussion. Herein lie, in my opinion, serious problems in many industrialised countries. Consistently passing on a large part of the costs of the social Welfare State to formal employment will inevitably lead to an avoidance of formal employment (at least insofar as it incurs social welfare costs). The general decline of employment thereby automatically jeopardises the financing of the Welfare State. In other words, in many countries, including the Federal Republic of Germany, the financing of the Welfare State is set up in such a way that it is relatively unproblematic when welfare benefits are least needed, but it becomes difficult when the demand for welfare benefits increases. Such a financing scheme is senseless. Only historical reasons speak in its favour, and these are now out-dated.

The problems of the current method of financing the Welfare State will thus continue to increase in the future. It is foreseeable that new forms of work will make it more and more difficult for the state to control formal employment. As a result, the possibilities for collective contributions to finance the Welfare State will shrink. In effect, citizens will find it easier to avoid paying their dues to the Welfare State. It is important to be prepared for this development.

In practical terms this means that financing the Welfare State through contributions must be reduced step by step, and replaced by a scheme of financing through taxes. This method has been used to varying degrees in different countries. The Federal Republic of Germany and other industrialised countries still have a long way to go.

As Professor Delorme has already pointedly shown, there are three areas in which financing is based entirely or partially on formal employment: pensions, health insurance, and unemployment insurance. What can be done in these areas to separate labour costs and welfare costs?

The most important area in terms of financing and social policy are pensions. In order to separate the costs of welfare from those of labour, the employer and employee contributions to state pension funds should be gradually replaced by taxes, say, over a ten-year period. After ten years the direct and indirect taxes would then have been increased by the amount that is currently being collected through contributions. This entails no financial or tax problems. Several countries have already implemented this procedure.

This would, however, produce only marginal changes in labour costs. Substantial changes would require a reduction in the benefits of the pension system. Almost no one is considering such a thing at this time. And even if one *were* to find a political majority that would be prepared to reduce pension benefits in the medium or long term, the savings would be quickly offset or overcompensated for by demographic shifts to be expected in most western industrialised countries. There is very little room to manoeuvre.

In switching the system of financing pensions from contributions to taxes, one would also have to consider that such a move would have to lead to a greater uniformity in pension benefits sooner or later. Taxes are by nature neither designed for, nor suited to, providing different levels of benefits to individuals. Taxes are paid according to each individual's tax bracket; that is, the range of payments is wide. By contrast, benefits financed by taxes are the same for all at least in principle. A pension system financed by taxes could not remain divorced from the logic of this system forever. Separation of pension costs from labour costs therefore implies uniform pension benefits.

The same is true of a shift in the method of financing unemployment insurance. This insurance could in principle also be financed through taxes, just as it constantly receives tax subsidies, at least in the Federal Republic of Germany.

The obvious advantage of using taxes to finance unemployment insurance, which would, of course, then no longer be insurance in the strict sense of the term, is that everybody would be involved in paying for unemployment. This would also be a major step in developing a system that can survive if long-term unemployment increases, a situation that cannot be precluded.

A second step, and now I turn to the reform of the benefit side of unemployment insurance, would be to improve collective support for the long-term unemployed while reducing benefits for the short-term unemployed. There is no longer any compelling reason to provide collective support for an individual from the very first day of unemployment. Whereas the problems of long-term unemployment can only be dealt with on a collective basis, the responsibility for tiding over the short-term unemployed can, and must, be shifted back to the private household. The normal private household is fully capable of bridging a four- to eight-week period of unemployment with its own means. Households that are not capable of financing themselves in this way should, as exceptions, receive public assistance, which can be significantly less than the benefits for the long-term unemployed. I am sure that this would not only reduce the size of the budget needed for the unemployed, it would also reduce the number of unemployed. It is unrealistic to believe that our present organisation of benefits for unemployment insurance does not promote short-term unemployment.

Lastly, we come to the area of health insurance. There has been a good deal of discussion as to whether this area would be better off if financed by contributions or if financed by taxes, but no convincing conclusion has yet been reached. Quite apart from this discussion, however, health costs could most probably be reduced by certain deductibles, the amount the *individual* is to pay. I know enough about the pros and cons of this debate but believe that part of the renewal of political form and content mentioned by Professor Delorme could be achieved if we would begin by calling upon a small part of private wealth to reduce the burden of the Welfare State and thereby reduce the additional wage costs, that is, labour costs. The fact that drawing on the wealth of private households to help pay for health care has become practically taboo in the Welfare State is a profound error. By not using private wealth for care and support purposes this wealth is undermined, for it loses its economic *raison d'être*.

This brings me to the second area: the services of the Welfare State. I have already mentioned some aspects of these services in conjunction with the mode of financing the Welfare State, but one basic thought remains to be added.

We are at a crossroads in the political management of the Welfare State. Professor Delorme has already pointed out the conditions under which the Welfare State began to emerge at the end of the previous century and the beginning of this one and those under which it flourished after the Second World War. In the meantime the foundations of the Welfare State as we know it today have undergone lasting changes. Many of the basic risks in life that had to be borne by the Welfare State can today be transferred back to private households for the first time since the onset of industrialisation. In my opinion, reforming the Welfare State on the basis of economic and social policies that are in tune with the age requires defining the content of that State for the next thirty years. We must answer the question as to whether the Welfare State should, and can, continue to play the same role it has played thus far. This is taken much too much for granted. I personally do not believe it, one reason being that the interaction of the labour market and the Welfare State, which certainly used to be constructive, is now anything but that.

This brings me to the organisation of the Welfare State. To me it seems important for the spectrum of Welfare State regulations to be subjected to very detailed analysis. This process, which is already well underway, will reveal that many of the so-called social welfare achievements stubbornly defended by interested parties have little to do with the nature of the Welfare State and are often only historical coincidences or national peculiarities. To mention a couple of examples from the Federal Republic of Germany, there are anachronisms such as the law regulating business hours for stores and the prohibition of baking at night. Who knows today that this ban was decreed by Emperor William II during the First World War (1915) in order to discourage Germans from buying bread in the morning. The Emperor had hoped that old bread would lower demand. The law regulating store business hours is a similar anachronism. Italians, French, and many Germans, too, do not understand why stores close their doors at noon on Saturdays. No one in France or Italy has the impression that anyone is being treated anti-socially if people are allowed to shop in the evening or on Sunday morning. Such regulations, of which there are hundreds in every country, certainly do not do much to encourage employment. It is clear, though, that the repeal of such laws requires an extraordinary amount of political capital.

Dealing with such complicated and sensitive regulations as the legislation on employment protection legislation and the continuation of wage payments in cases of illness is even more difficult. In principle almost no one will want to change these regulations, but their practical form must be reformed. I would already regard it a sign of great progress if these areas were no longer to be treated as taboo and were to be opened up for constructive discussions instead.

So much for very practical comments on the broad theoretical field that Professor Delorme has explored and that I believe leaves enough room for practical elaboration.

Christoph F. Büchtemann and Georg Vobruba

Let us begin with an attempt to clarify what we understand by the term 'Welfare State': we are not the first social scientists to face the problem of finding a conclusive definition of what has come to be called the Welfare State. The modern usage of the term evidently stands for much more than just a series of State provisions giving financial relief to those who fail to attain acceptable market incomes. Although the share of the population living on government transfers has risen continuously over the last 50 years – in 1982 this share amounted to more than 21 per cent of the population in Western Germany – the mere provision of 'welfare', i.e. non-market income compensation, describes only a fraction of the complex functions and provisions which are associated with the modern 'Welfare State'. Delorme, therefore, has given us a fairly broad definition of the Welfare State as comprising both the public provision of 'benefits in cost or in kind' and 'the regulatory activity of the state aimed at the social protection of individuals'. We should like to suggest the definition of the Welfare State be further extended: In our view the 'Welfare State' today should be defined as a specific socio-historical arrangement of the relationship between the State and its citizens. In exchange for compulsory financial contributions by the latter it implies essentially three functions:

1. the State's obligation to define and enforce general standards and rules to prevent existing economic inequalities from being used to exploit or harm those in weaker economic positions; this, of course, includes the legal institutionalisation and guarantee of the system of industrial relations;
2. the State's obligation to provide social security for the individual against social risks and hazards associated with market economies – this essentially includes the system of social security and income maintenance;
3. the State's obligation to provide the pre-requisites for the citizens'

participation in social and economic progress – this certainly includes redistributional measures and the provision of both educational and employment opportunities.

These three functions of the Welfare State do in fact constitute the essential basis of democratic consent in modern market economies.

We, therefore, do not agree with those who talk about 'the crisis of the Welfare State'. For modern democratic societies there certainly is no alternative to the Welfare State even if we are presently witnessing the transition of industrial society from one 'configuration', as Delorme has called it, to another. There is, however, growing evidence of *functional deficits* to the Welfare State in the sense of an increasing inadequacy of *its instruments and means* to meet the challenges put forward by the changing economic conditions of industrial society.

Incorporating some of the arguments put forward in Delorme's paper our remarks will focus on two issues where – in our opinion – the current functional deficits of the Welfare State in its present condition are most evident: employment and the provision of social security. However, we shall not confine our analysis to the impact of the Welfare State upon employment, as Delorme has done in his contribution, but rather shift attention to the *dynamic interrelationship* of the two which – as we shall try to show – raises a series of questions suitable for further investigation. Our prime interest is thus not so much the macroeconomic context but rather on *structural* and *distributional* aspects of both the Welfare State and the labour market. Our starting point is the *hypothesis* that with the persisting failure of modern economies to secure full employment there is a *progressive structural dissynchronisation* of the *labour market* on the one hand and of the system of *Welfare State provisions* on the other hand.

The Welfare State in its present shape rests upon *two basic assumptions: First*, as Delorme has pointed out, it rests upon the assumption of *full employment being the normal condition of the economy*; unemployment, if there is any, is merely frictional, i.e. due to technological and sectoral shifts in the economy so unemployment spells are relatively short and the overall unemployment rate very low. The *second* basic assumption is that of a particular pattern of employment being the *normal standard of labour market participation*: the *dominant* type of employment in full employment economies can be characterised in terms of uninterrupted permanent full-time employment in medium-sized and large establishments that constitute the centres of Fordist mass production. This at the same time constitutes the type of employment that the core institutions of the modern Welfare State focus on and refer to. Thus *eligibility for social security benefits* requires a more or less *stable work history* during which benefit entitlement is acquired; *replacement ratios* of social security benefits above subsistence level are based on the assumption of *full-time work*; most regulations concerning employment security and collective bargaining at shop floor level exclusively refer to *larger establishments*; and so on.

The point to be made is: *Both* basic assumptions of the present model largely reflect the conditions and dominant trends prevailing when the modern Welfare State was built in its present shape: those two prosperous post-Second World War decades of constantly high GNP growth rates, more or less permanent full employment and the progressive inclusion of the vast majority of the working population in the system of modern capitalist market employment.

Since the mid-1970s, however, both assumptions have become increasingly less applicable. After a decade of continuous large scale unemployment hopes for a return to full employment are rapidly melting away: trust in the feasibility and outcomes of conventional employment strategies as well as hopes in the absorption potential of the service sector are fading; confidence in a merely *demographic* solution of the employment problems have been largely upset. For Western Germany recent forecasts predict registered unemployment will still amount to two millions by the end of the century. At the same time the persistent deficit of regular employment opportunities along with secular trends of changing aspiration and role patterns have led to significant changes in the *structure and dynamics of the labour market*. Apart from the rising numbers of persons being forced into long-term unemployment available evidence suggests a rather strong increase in job patterns and patterns of labour force participation that more or less *deviate* from the hitherto dominant tupe of permanent full-time employment – such as marginal labour force participation, part-time work, temporary jobs, rather precarious self employment and 'informal' market activities within the realm of the shadow economy.

What follows from these tendencies with respect to the 'working' of the Welfare State? For our present purpose we should like to draw attention to two consequences:

1. As Delorme has pointed out, persisting large scale unemployment tends to upset the financial basis of the Welfare State. The financial squeeze necessarily hits social security benefits. In most countries, therefore, the financial problems of the Welfare State due to high unemployment have resulted in further restrictions of eligibility to, and cuts in, the levels of social security benefits.
2. Along with the rising numbers of *long-term unemployed*, whose 'fate' strongly *deviates* from the 'risk-philosophy' underlying most schemes of unemployment insurance, the outlined *erosion* of permanent full-time employment as the normal standard of labour market participation is associated with an *increasing social selectivity* of Welfare State provisions and a *progressive exclusion* of growing parts of the population from its benefits. Recent measures adopted to relieve the financial burdens of social security systems by tightening eligibility requirements have certainly tended to reinforce this general pattern.

Resuming our initial hypothesis we hope our comments have shown that the progressive *dissynchronisation of a Welfare State* devised for conditions of full employment and a *labour market* characterised by chronic large scale unemployment has the implication of a growing part of the population not only being *excluded from stable employment in the labour market*, but at the same time being more or less *excluded from the protection and security provided by existing Welfare State arrangements*.

With the established structures of the Welfare State *untouched*, recently adopted strategies of encouraging *'new forms of employment'*, such as support for small establishments; programmes to promote self-employment for the unemployed; and the creation and facilitation of temporary jobs, as a more or less *cheap* solution to present labour market problems certainly will cause the *social selectivity* of the Welfare State to increase still further. Suspending the Welfare State definitively cannot be a (desirable) way to lower the barriers to full employment.

8 Industrial Relations and Unemployment: The Case for Flexible Corporatism
David Soskice*

INTRODUCTION

The debate on the appropriate form of industrial relations for full employment has recently opposed centralisation (or, in one guise or another, corporatism) to decentralisation (or a market oriented system). Without doubt, the appeal of the decentralisation argument has come from the success of the American economy in the last two or three years. But, as I shall argue, this success is both transient and more due to Keynesian policies than decentralised structures; and a better picture of the effect of decentralisation can be gauged from the UK economy, where despite 13 per cent unemployment unit labour costs (ULCs) are rising at 7 per cent (against flat ULCs in Germany), training – left to the initiative of individual companies – appears to have fallen sharply, and where a current balance of payments deficit is forecast in two years' time in spite of oil revenues and earnings from overseas investments. Moreover, at least until 1980, corporatist economies out-performed less centralised economies; and many of their problems both before and since have arisen because of low aggregate demand imposed by external constraints.

It is important to remind ourselves, in the current atmosphere of fashionable cynicism about corporatism, just how successful it has been as a form of economic organisation; and how unsuccessful has been decentralisation or laisser-faire monetarism. Corporatism has also been successful as a political model: for it has shown – albeit imperfectly, but in contrast to the United States – how mass edu-

---
*I am indebted to Professors Salvati and Streeck for helpful discussion.

cation and a relatively progressive distribution of post-tax and post-benefit income can be reconciled.

But in this paper I do not want to argue that we should return to the traditional model of corporatism. For there have been two slow, broad changes which make the mid-1980s look significantly different from the mid-1960s: these are the internationalisation of economies and the combined change in technology and product structure of markets. These changes modify the traditional model in two ways: they require that national macro policy and wage determination give way to a more international approach; and they require a more flexible, but not a less involved, relation between companies and unions. These modifications must take place in such a way that the great strengths of corporatism – the effective co-ordination of complex modern economies and its political inclusiveness – are weakened as little as possible.

The increased openness of product markets has progressively limited the ability of individual countries to pursue independent demand management policies. Or rather, a large country can impose deflationary policies on its neighbours; (unless it is prepared to finance their deficits). Thus national Keynesianism no longer has the role that the traditional corporatist model assigned it. But the new situation does not invalidate the Keynesian analysis: on the contrary, it is precisely a quantity-constrained equilibrium which demands an internationally or regionally co-ordinated Keynesian response. The difficulty is political: how to persuade the slow-growing country to reflate. A more flexible, regional corporatism may have to adapt to its requirements: in the case of West Germany, its desire for low European inflation and the belief that this would be put at risk by a more rapid regional expansion must be countered by commitment to appropriate wage bargaining behaviour. Thus, in effect, regional demand co-ordination would have as its counterpart inflation co-ordination – not in a literal sense, but in the form of appropriate national rules.

Internationalisation has also taken the form of increased openness of financial markets. This reinforces the need to move towards a regional strategy: reflation in one country will be punished rapidly by the exchanges. But, even at the regional level, international capital mobility poses the problem that European interest rates will be partially fixed elsewhere. In principle, both under fixed and floating exchange rates, real interest rates will equalise; thus there is no competitive disadvantage. Real wages, however, will bear the cost of a higher required real rate of return; and this is a consideration which a more flexible corporatism would have to accept, unless regional control of capital movements was felt to be feasible.

The second slow change has been in the structure of technology and product markets. Though it can be easily exaggerated, the degree of standardisation of products has been decreasing; products have become more sophisticated; businesses probably have to react faster to changing product market conditions, in part because competition is increasingly in the form of new products: the sophistication of new machines is greater. These developments have implications for industrial relations and hence corporatism: businesses seek closer relations with key workers; new skills are demanded, and these may be more firm-specific than before; businesses will wish for more worker flexibility. None of these implications are absolute. The challenge for a more flexible corporatism is to find a middle way. If some workers do not have job security, they should be in a queue to eventually acquire it; existing manual workers should be trained up to deal with new computerised machinery, rather than hire computer programmers; training should be in part standardised so that those workers who are made redundant do not find it difficult to use their skills elsewhere; and so on. Whatever form the more flexible corporatism takes, two principles are important. First, the power of central organisations must not be significantly weakened if they are to retain their ability to exercise a sufficient degree of control over wage negotiations; this requires that the principle of comparability and solidarity remains central. And second, that the workforce should not become divided into those with permanent jobs and those who will never have had permanent jobs; if some employment is to be insecure, such workers should have access to the training which will enable them to progress to permanent employment.

CORPORATISM AND UNEMPLOYMENT

The experience of western economies in the three decades which followed the Second World War casts at least a surface doubt on the validity of the arguments summarised in the introduction. During that long period the American economy performed less well than its Western European counterparts according to most standard economic indicators. Within Western Europe, moreover, the more corporatist economies were more successful than those with less centralised institutions. Nor, between now and then, have there been fundamental changes in the structure of institutions across countries. If economies with centralised institutions were more successful over a thirty-year period than others – notably the US and notably in respect of unemployment – care must be taken over a simple ascription of unemployment to inflexibilities and of inflexibilities to centralised institutions.

There is a further reason for caution. The main direct cause of the increase in unemployment in both of the two periods of substantial rise – in 1974–5 and 1980–2 – was a reduction of aggregate demand, the result of transfers of income to low spending OPEC countries and of the deflationary policies of the major economies. And, as we shall see below, the two periods of rapid increase in employment in the US – in 1976–8 and 1983–5 – were periods of Keynesian reflationary macroeconomic policies.

It is worth reminding ourselves of these elementary points, since they can easily be forgotten in the pursuit of new explanations. But they do not prove that centralised systems of industrial relations have played no part in the rise in unemployment, or that they present no barriers to its reduction. Actual unemployment may have been caused directly by deflationary policies, but these may have been necessitated by an increase in equilibrium unemployment which may in turn have been a consequence of the structure of institutions. We will examine separately two arguments: that centralised institutions were increasingly unable, during the late 1960s and early 1970s, to deliver the moderation and flexibility consistent with a low equilibrium level of unemployment; and/or that they were insufficiently flexible in response to the external shocks to which industrialised countries were subject during the 1970s.

We are tempted in looking back at the great boom to see a golden age of corporatist industrial relations. But on detailed examination that proves mythical: centralised institutions have seldom worked perfectly, and have often appeared to participants to be on the point of collapse. Thus we need to look at performance indicators before concluding that there was an underlying failure of institutions in the immediate pre-1974 period. Without question the authority of central organisations was weakened in the late 1960s, and that affected the extent of real wage moderation. But the problems which European countries faced in the late 1960s bore more heavily on the countries with less centralised systems of industrial relations (France, UK, and Italy). An econometric test run for the years 1968–73 shows a strong inverse relation between the Okun misery index (the sum of the rates of inflation and unemployment) and an index of the degree of corporatism of the industrial relations institutions of different countries. We can also examine the specific complaint of the previous section: it is true that for Europe as a whole the rate of profit has been declining since the 1960s, and the share of the public sector has been increasing; but these trends were very slow, at least for Europe as a whole, until the mid-1970s.

It is, of course, quite possible that the equilibrium rate of unemployment rose in the early 1970s. But it is difficult to believe, either from the data or from a knowledge of the institutional changes which occurred at that period, that the increase in the rate was significant or that it heralded a break up of the system or (the most important point) that it was a phenomenon characteristic of the more corporatist economies. On the contrary, the countries which appeared least capable of managing unemployment, inflation, and profitability were those with the most *de facto* decentralised systems – the US, the UK and Italy.

An alternative argument is that the equilibrium rate of unemployment rose during the course of the 1970s and subsequently, as a consequence of the inability of the more centralised economies to cope with the series of external shocks to which they were subject. We shall argue below that a central condition for any significant reduction in unemployment is a major reflation of aggregate demand (on a world or European regional basis). Thus, in principle, we should distinguish between those shocks which were exogenous and those caused by the world recession: for if it is argued that it was an inability to cope with shocks generated by deflation, it is *prima facie* unclear why that inability should hold back the supply-side in a reflationary context. To put this point in another way, if unemployment was caused directly or indirectly by the deflation of world aggregate demand, the rise in equilibrium or structural unemployment may have been more modest than conventional wisdom supposes.

The major shock to which industrialised countries have been subject has been the world recession itself. Its impact has been to impose deflationary policies on countries with balance of payments constraints; in a perfectly competitive world, such constraints would not arise; but in the world as it is, where trade in manufacturing is dominated by oligopolistic or imperfectly competitive markets, the scope for expanding exports by increasing market share is limited; some countries have been lucky to be in more rapidly growing markets, or those with more elastic demand; but even then their success has generally been at the expense of other countries as opposed to generating an increase in world aggregate demand. A second shock has been the intensification of international competition. There is no accepted way of measuring the extent to which this has been the result of the world recession; but an important reason for the intensification has been the need of Japan to continue its export growth at a time when the overall growth of world trade was sharply curtailed; and that curtailment dates from the deflationary policies of the mid-1970s. This is not the only reason for the intensification. The advent of NICs has increased competition particularly in the production of less sophisticated goods; and their impact – via the Third World – is more important than it seems to the European eye.

A third shock has been technological change. Here different strands need disentangling. One argument is that the mass production techniques which had provided productivity growth in the 1950s and 1960s began to dry up in the 1970s. But the sharp decline in productivity growth dates from the mid-1970s and coincides with deflation; it thus fits neatly the short-run theory of Okun and the longer-term theory of Kaldor and Verdoorn, which see productivity growth as demand-determined. A quite different, indeed converse argument is that the current unemployment is the result of an acceleration of technological change, which began in the 1970s. But for that argument to be valid we should have observed an increase in the rate of productivity growth over the last decade. Moreover (as the parallel automation debate of the early 1960s should remind us) an acceleration of technological change does not imply structural unemployment even if it translates into faster productivity growth: unemployment will only rise if aggregate demand is not appropriately increased.

The final shocks have been the changes in the real price of materials, in particular that of energy. These have been positively related to the growth of aggregate demand of the industrialised countries.

Many of the changes discussed above represent the consequences of deflationary policies – the world recession itself, much of the intensification of international trade, much of the decline in productivity growth. Of course, no likely reflation will fully reverse those consequences. But it is important in assessing the second half of the 1970s to bear in mind to what extent the problems were caused by the deflation as opposed to representing an increase in structural unemployment.

In a paper of this length such an assessment will necessarily be superficial. Two conclusions can, however, be stated with some confidence. The first is that the more institutionally centralised economies performed on average well in the period between the two oil shocks, in particular in respect of unemployment, the rate of inflation and productivity growth. The second is that the less centralised economies, especially the US, performed badly in those respects; and of the only two real American successes, one, employment growth, was a consequence of Keynesian policies of expansion, and the other, in high technology, bore little relation to the system of industrial relations.

The misery-index/corporatism correlations for 1974–9 again show the strong performance of the more corporatist economies. Productivity growth is also correlated with corporatism, but less perfectly: the UK, Italy and particularly the US perform badly. So too does Sweden – a corporatist compromise; and the bad showing of the UK and Italy is linked to their corporatist experiments in 1975–7. However, output in all three countries was highly constrained by the world deflation.

The period of bad economic performance in Western Europe relates to the 1980s; and the period of bad performance relative to the US to the last three years. Before looking at why European economies performed badly, it is worth going through the reasons why the American economy has recently done so well. First, there has been a major fiscal expansion since 1982, boosted at important moments by a loose monetary policy; this massive Keynesian stimulus has led to predictably rapid GDP growth and declining unemployment. Secondly, the resulting public sector deficit was financed in part by savings from the expanding economy, in part by official credit creation, and in part by the provision of new financial instruments; thus interest rates declined from their peak in 1980–82, albeit remaining at high real and nominal levels. These rates, and high expected returns on equity investments (profits being boosted by the economic recovery), led to an inflow of foreign funds which pushed up the dollar. Thirdly, inflation remained at a low level because of the high dollar: this kept down the prices of imported materials, and put great pressure on import-competing sectors to hold down costs. Fourthly, the current balance of payments moved into deficit, but the US has been in a position to ignore such pressure for longer than other countries. A country which ignores the external deficit (unlike France) can always use a so-called 'fiscalist' expansion policy to expand against the rest of the world. It is wrong therefore to see the US success in reducing unemployment as due to a different structure as opposed to the adoption of appropriate Keynesian policies.

By contrast to the American performance between 1983 and 1985, Western Europe has had slow growth with gently rising or static unemployment, at the high level reached during the severe recession of 1980–82. This cannot be explained by the comparative behaviour of real wages: on the contrary, real labour cost growth in Europe has lagged productivity growth, at a time moreover when public sector deficits were being reduced. It is also difficult to explain it as a result of European legislation or collective bargaining agreements on redundancies. In the first place, the pace of productivity growth (faster than would have been predicted in a slow growth environment), of redundancies themselves and of the known behaviour of many large companies suggests that the barrier to dismissals has been greatly exaggerated in the last five years. Secondly, in economic terms the existence of firing costs may reduce desired employment relative to aggregate demand for a given degree of uncertainty about whether future demand will be higher or lower, but there is no reason why it should alter the relation between changes in aggregate demand and changes in employment; in fact, since a reflationary policy reduces the likelihood that aggregate demand will fall, desired employment should rise relative to aggregate demand in such a context.

Western Europe has grown slowly in the 1980s because of deflationary macro policies, pursued in the most important case by West Germany; and because of the high trade interdependence of the region most other countries have had to follow suit. Some have done so willingly, others less so. Those countries which have been able to pursue somewhat faster growth on average (Austria, Finland, Norway, and Sweden) have done so through a mixture of foreign borrowing, a good competitive performance, relatively elastic and well-placed export markets and reflationary macro policies; even so, slow growth in the region has put tight constraints on these countries. Why have the major European economies behaved as they have done? Both Italy and France have been constrained by external factors, imposed by Germany. German policy (and British) has been dictated by the desire to reduce inflation and to bring about structural adjustments, including the reduction of the size and deficit of the public sector and the rebuilding of profitability. It is an open question whether such changes were most efficaciously achieved under a high unemployment regime and outside a social contract. Without doubt the German and British governments believed that to be the case: if high unemployment made union co-operation unnecessary, then it was safe to cut public expenditure nationally and create redundancies at local level without fear of the consequences; if anything such measures further weakened the unions, at least centrally. On the other hand, other countries achieved similar results at lower levels of unemployment with at least an element of social agreement; in some cases this was because central unions recognised the increased cost of failing to provide the necessary co-operation in a world recession, while retaining enough control over their membership to deliver on their commitments.

Could Western Europe have expanded more rapidly during the last few years? No individual country could have done so (at least not without resort to protectionism). For the block as a whole however, the marginal propensity to import is relatively small, so that a co-ordinated expansion would have been feasible from a balance of payments perspective. Moreover the falling rate of regional inflation suggests that unemployment in the region as a whole was above the equilibrium rate. Nor is there evidence to suggest that expansion would have been held back by the rate of profitability; had that been true any expansion would have been inflationary, and that has not been the case.

Are we saying merely that Europe could have performed as well as the US? No: the US performance has been achieved at the cost of a rise in the real effective exchange rate of the order of 40 per cent (between 1980 and 1985). Thus inflation has been held down but at the price of massive loss of competitiveness. As the dollar falls, so American inflation will increase. Post-war experience has shown that the US is a high unemployment economy, without the institutions which might permit low unemployment to coexist with low inflation. Such has not been the case for many countries in Western Europe.

We have suggested in this section that the centralised economies of Western Europe have consistently outperformed less centralised economies to the end of the last decade; and that the more recent success of the US is a result of aggregate demand management rather than structural factors.

CONDITIONS FOR REDUCING UNEMPLOYMENT

The current rate of real GDP growth in Western Europe is about 2.5 per cent; labour productivity is growing by the same order of magnitude; the labour force is growing by about 0.5 per cent. If the growth rates of these three variables remain constant, unemployment will not fall.

One possibility would be to reduce the growth of labour productivity by reducing that of real wages. We explained above why that argument was either incorrect or counter-productive from a long-run point of view. The marginal product of labour was seldom reduced by operating below capacity; the slow-growing productivity firms were frequently non-innovative and hit by declining demand as opposed to too high real wages; and capital-intensive investment in both physical and human capital was often associated with product and process innovation needed to keep companies in markets. In any case – leaving aside the question of imports which would be unimportant from a European regional point of view – a loss of employment from the closure of a low productivity firm would be associated with a transfer of demand to other companies; and in so far as the rise in employment in those companies was insufficient because their productivity was higher, the additional demand could always be created. This does not mean that real wage moderation is unimportant; but it should be associated with a policy of moderation of real unit labour costs, i.e. increasing productivity rather than reducing it.

The second possibility would be to reduce the growth of the labour force. One should not rule out the role such a reduction could play, under circumstances in which those who accepted to withdraw from the labour force could do so without significant disadvantage to themselves or to remaining workers. But such policies are often cruel delusions, which temporarily enable governments to evade their responsibility for measures of real economic expansion.

The only way in which unemployment can be significantly and permanently reduced is via a more rapid growth rate of GDP. It is sometimes argued that this can come about without the help of central government: (i) as a result of a series of product innovations which massively boost consumer demand; (ii) as a result of supply-side cost reductions which lower inflation and hence stimulate demand. But neither channel has had a significant success. Where GDP growth has recently been fast it has either come from exports or from government. Reliance on exports in a slow-growing world economy is a beggar-my-neighbour policy: only a limited number of countries can use it with success. (This does not mean that faster growth of exports and imports together have this drawback; the problem arises when demand is boosted via a balance of trade surplus.) The only sure way in which a faster growth rate of GDP can be achieved is by government reflationary measures; moreover, in the absence of protectionist barriers, external balance will require an internationally or intra-regionally co-ordinated expansion. It was in the absence of such co-ordination that the French expansion of 1981 failed, since it took place against the background of a world recession including a particularly sharp deflation in West Germany; and why the Schmidt locomotive of 1978–9 was stopped by the US, French and UK deflations, aggravated by the second OPEC petroleum shock. The locomotive metaphor is a bad one: what is needed is co-ordinated reflation rather than one country pulling along others; if this cannot be done on a global basis, then it must be done on a European basis.

A faster growth of GDP is necessary but not sufficient. For it does not ensure that the supply-side adjusts appropriately. We now turn to the relation between supply-side adjustment and the appropriate system of industrial relations.

What type of industrial relations system can generate the flexibilities needed for supply-side adjustment? We have discussed this question so far as though our choice is unconstrained. But, of course, it is not; it is constrained in four main ways: by the existing institutions; by the structure of the economy; by employer, political and union strategies; and (we shall argue) by the rate of unemployment. How does unemployment affect institutions? With very low unemployment, it is well-known that central unions are less able to control their membership. That may also be the case with very high unemployment as at present: as it becomes less important to business to rely on central union moderation to hold down wage increases, so it may pay them to develop closer negotiating links with their workforce, in particular their core skilled workers. Thus there may be an inverted U relation between centralisation and unemployment. (This does not fully explain the increase in decentralisation, which though usually of modest dimension, can be seen in various countries; some increase has been caused by the increased openness of economies and by technological change, which have made standardised agreements more difficult to comply with overall.) The relation is important for our purposes. For it means that a demand-induced reduction in unemployment may make it very difficult to move simultaneously towards a more decentralised system of industrial relations. Moreover, if the power of unions is in general rising with the fall in unemployment, greater decentralisation would require the consent of centralised unions: their current experience does not predispose them to it.

The strength of this argument will, of course, vary from country to country. The more effectively centralised the existing system the less it makes sense to talk of moving to greater decentralisation in the context of a reflationary economy. Even in Italy or the UK, with their much lower and less effectively centralised systems than say Germany, Austria, Sweden or Norway, greater decentralisation is of doubtful institutional feasibility with falling unemployment.

More flexibility—not necessarily as described in 'Corporatism and Unemployment', above—does not, however, imply greater decentralisation. We shall argue that what is required is more flexibility within a centralised system; and that that may require more power to central institutions in some areas.

We now turn to look at the basic requirements of supply-side adjustment as they affect industrial relations. These requirements will be presented at a first pass as economic in a mechanical sense; later, it will be suggested that they form part of a more general societal programme. Given an increase in aggregate demand, what are the possible barriers to a reduction in unemployment? An 'everyman's' list is as follows:

1. Businesses do not increase output, because
   (a) it isn't profitable to do so (real wage > marginal product of labour: classical unemployment);
   (b) shortage of capacity;
   (c) shortage of skilled labour.
2. Balance of payments constraint;
   (a) inadequate growth of world demand;
   (b) lack of international competitiveness.
3. Inflationary pressures.
4. General and sectoral financing problems;
   (a) given output (e.g. constrained by 1 (b), (c) or 2 (a), (b), insufficient savings to finance investment and the public sector deficit; (i.e. aggregate demand > output);
   (b) existence of public sector deficit.

Not all of the above are important constraints. We have already noted that 1(a) should not be taken too seriously. Equally the importance attached to 4(b) is generally exaggerated as a problem independent of 4(a). This is not the place to discuss 4(b) but two points are worth noting: the rise in public debt to GDP ratios has largely been a consequence of recession, both for the usual reasons (fall in tax revenues, rise in recession-related expenditures, etc.) and because GDP growth has been so slow; second, a large proportion of public expenditure pays directly and indirectly for itself over time (health, education, infra-structure, etc.) – growing companies are encouraged to borrow in this situation, but not the public sector. Finally, of the above constraints, 3 is taken care of by 1(a), (b), 2(b) and 4(a); we shall not consider inflation directly.

Industrial relations affects the remaining constraints in three main ways, which for simplicity will be dealt with separately: via wage bargaining; training; and its role in the range of company decisions on employment, work practice and conditions, investment and new technology. In the remainder of this paper we first discuss what policies are required from centralised unions in these areas, and then whether it is reasonable to expect them.

Real Wages In relation to the constraints mentioned above, moderation is required for three separate reasons. The most important of these reasons relates to international competitiveness (c). There is some measure of agreement that relative unit labour costs, in a common currency, are the best simple measure of c. In that case c is equal to the sum of price competitiveness (cp) and the difference between world (i.e. effective) real unit labour costs and domestic real unit labour costs, measured in logs. Thus a 1 per cent fall in the real wage (w) implies a direct 1 per cent rise in c via the change in domestic real unit labour costs ($w - LP$); and a further increase because of a rise in cp, from 0 per cent with pure world pricing to 0.8 per cent with cost-plus pricing. Leave out of account here the complication caused by the type of pricing behaviour; and assume that the country starts from a position of competitiveness: then the maintenance of competitiveness requires that domestic real wage growth is equal to real wage growth abroad plus the difference between domestic and foreign labour productivity growth.

This implies that domestic output growth is equal to world (or regional) output growth. It is possible to do better without beggar-my-neighbour policies, by raising competitiveness and growth at the same time so that imports keep pace with exports; thus the net balance of trade of the rest of the area is unchanged. This requires, for a growth rate of 1 per cent above the region, that competitveness rises by the ratio of the income-elasticity of demand (assumed the same for exports and imports) to the sum of the demand competitiveness-elasticities of exports and imports; hence real wages must fall by the same amount relative to the formula at the end of the last paragraph.

The second role of real wage moderation is to ensure sufficient profitability, relative to the real cost of borrowing, to provide an adequate incentive to rebuild the capital stock; this should grow fast enough so that capacity shortages do not constrain growth at the rate consistent with external equilibrium. This is a permissive condition for investment, the main incentive coming from enhanced growth expectations.

Finally, real wage moderation may be needed to restrain consumption. This would be necessary, if there was a large public sector deficit, heavy investment financing needs and a binding output constraint. It seems unlikely that this would be an initial problem.

The central need for restraint is that of competitiveness. The achievement of this will put a significant strain on central organisations as demand is expanding. This suggests both that the role of central unions should be expanded within the company – this is returned to below – and that profit-sharing should be further investigated as a means of easing the strain. One simple idea is that profit-sharing should be the result of local bargaining. Thus national restraint with limited drift could be more readily acceptable to workforces in highly profitable companies, if they acquired shares in lieu of higher wages. Central unions could then become the nominee shareholder for their members' shares; and agreements could be reached on the proportion of shares retained in the company.

Training The UK testifies to the problem of providing an adequate stock of skilled workers in a decentralised system; and as the system has become more decentralised in the last few years, with companies released from compulsory contributions to training schemes, so the situation has become drastically worse. Decentralised training suffers from lack of standards and general training, thus hindering mobility which it is in the individual training employer's interest to do. The danger of losing skilled workers reduces the incentive to train, shortages develop and differentials widen as poaching becomes necessary.

The lack of availability of skilled workers may impose a direct constraint on growth. From the longer-term point of view, the existence of skills determines the extent to which an economy moves towards the production of more sophisticated goods. But technology does not fully determine who is to be trained; a machine tool can be programmed by a computer programmer or by an engineer trained up to do so. The micro-processor can easily be socially divisive, creating on Braverman-type lines a de-skilled working-class with repetitive jobs programmed by an educated élite. It may pay employers to move towards a dualistic structure of work. An important role of the central union seems likely to be to counter such tendencies. Well-placed workers in companies may not object to sub-contracting, part-time workers and differential access to training; it is the role of the central union to widen that access and to ensure that company training plans are sufficient.

Technology, Employment, Work Practices It goes almost without saying that unions should enable businesses to adjust according to long-run profitability considerations in an open economy. This does not, however, mean the right to fire (or hire) or impose work practices literally at will. It means there are proper procedures for both reflection and compensation in firing, so that those affected have time to plan. Hiring should not be used to frustrate union plans for retraining and upgrading existing workers. Work practices should not be imposed which require exceptionally unpleasant work. In all these ways unions or their company representatives will properly observe, and on occasion constrain, the behaviour of companies; and our experience is that businessmen do not object to such a framework in many European countries despite its absence elsewhere.

The development of technology suggests a more positive role for central unions. The large central union is well-placed to establish technology research departments. It has a better access often to the company than either a government body or a trade organisation, via its representatives or a works council. Few managements, except in large companies, have the expertise to properly assess new developments or know in which direction research and development should be commissioned. Moreover the adoption of new technology ties in intimately with the issue of training and retraining. If, or as, unions come to play a larger role in the decision-making procedures of companies, a central involvement in the two crucial, interrelated areas of skills and technology will enable them also to play a large role in the shaping of society.

COMMENT

Wolfgang Streeck

Following the seminal work of Mancur Olson (1965; 1982), it has become popular among political economists to attribute the stagnation of western economies to the 'lobbying' activities of organised interests – or, using Olson's term, of 'distributional coalitions'. While Olson's theory may be extended to business associations and to problems such as inflation, low productivity growth, etc., in present political discourse it is mostly used to convict trade unions of responsibility for unemployment. This argument has two versions, a moderate and a radical one. The moderate version is that as a result of the way in which unions, and industrial relations in general, are organised, trade unions have been led by their institutional self-interests to misinterpret the economic necessities of the 1970s and to resist adjustments in wages and industrial structure that would have made it easier to return to high employment. A more successful economic policy therefore would require changes in trade union structure – centralisation or decentralisation, a strengthening or weakening of the influence of the full-time leadership, encouragement or discouragement of comprehensive, cross-sectoral organisation and bargaining, etc., as the case may be – which, unless trade unions are willing to change voluntarily, have to be imposed on them politically. The radical version is that no matter how trade unions, and distributional coalitions in general, may be structured, the economy would be better off without them since at the end of the day, they will always reduce output and employment below what would be possible in a perfect market. The practical consequence here is what is referred to in the United States as 'de-certification' or 'de-unionisation'. My remarks will deal with this second version, although its application is not (yet) on the agenda in West Germany. To some extent, however, it is in other countries, and diffusion effects are possible. Moreover, it seems that many who today demand a re-organisation of trade unions and industrial relations really prefer the radical solution but do not want to confess to it for reasons of political expediency.

We have pointed out elsewhere (Streeck and Schmitter, 1985) that Olson himself is extremely cautious when it comes to the 'policy implications' of his theory. Contrary to what one might have expected on the basis of his earlier work (Olson, 1976), his recent book (1982) does not explore the potential of an institutional design approach aimed at the promotion of 'comprehensive' organisation. When it comes to the question of how the densely organised western (European) societies might move from their present 'rigidities' to a free (labour) market, Olson leaves the reader conspicuously to himself. All he is offered is a cryptical remark, quoted from Thomas Jefferson, that 'the tree of liberty must be refreshed from time to time with the blood of patriots and tyrants' (Olson, 1982, p. 141). Metaphorical as this quotation undoubtedly is meant to be, it quite correctly points to the intense and long-drawn social conflict that would inevitably be associated with a transition to an economy free of organised interests. Whether such conflict would be conducive to economic performance is more than doubtful.

A similar lacuna is encountered when it comes to the role of the State. Unlike Milton Friedman – and he takes him explicitly to task for this – Olson realises that a free market cannot exist under a laissez-faire state. (The same holds, of course, for comprehensive interest organisations which would fall apart without state support and facilitation. This is why they are typically associated with corporatism.) Olson argues convincingly that economic liberty requires vigilant authoritative intervention to protect it from the tendency of market participants with similar interests to combine in distributional coalitions (Olson, 1982, p. 178). However, how a modern State would have to be organised to enforce a new 'loi Le Chapellier' is not discussed, and neither is the question of whether a state that is sufficiently remote from civil society to prevent the emergence of organised interests can still be democratic. In this respect, von Hayek, in proposing to abolish general suffrage, was clearly more consistent than Olson.

Pointing to problems like these should not be misunderstood as an attempt to shift the argument from a theoretical to a moral ground. The question is not whether anybody prefers liberal–pluralist democracy over full employment or vice versa. What I am trying to argue is, rather, that – fortunately or not – such a choice does not exist. In part, this is simply because the changes in social institutions that would be necessary to wipe out the menace of distributional coalitions would have to be of a kind that would destroy important preconditions of economic performance. In western Europe at least, any attempt at implementing Olson's free market would unleash a level of political conflict compared to which the British miners strike of 1984 was idyllic.

To most economists, with their habit of treating politics as an exogenous factor or as a source of corruption of pure economic rationality, this may sound no more than an invitation to opportunistic political 'realism': to suppress an uncomfortable truth since it does not fit the prejudices of the powers that be. Yet the realities of political conflict and the realities of economics belong to the same real world. In this world, economic prosperity requires a minimum of social integration, and social conflict imposes economic costs. Moreover, conflict and integration are not independent from each other. Just as misguided attempts at political and social integration may give rise to conflict, so conflict may enhance integration. Without social integration there can be no production. But in a complex society, social integration in production is achieved through institutions that allow expression of conflicting interests over distribution. Suppression of such conflict, far from advancing integration, undermines it. Forced integration leads to more and not to less conflict. The problem of designing a functioning political economy is to domesticate interest groups and marshal conflicts for productive purposes, rather than wiping them out. This notion is central to the corporatist tradition of industrial relations, and while institutional structures may already have begun to develop beyond the corporatist model, both integration through conflict and conflict over integration will continue. Taking into account what sociologists and political scientists have learnt about the dynamics of conflict and integration, neo-liberal recipes appear remarkably simple, unitarian, and even authoritarian.

Apart from the problems of transition to, and of the role of the state in, a political economy liberated from distributional coalitions, one of the central weaknesses of the neo-liberal school seems to be that it has never turned its attention to the social conditions of cooperation between capital and labour at the point of production. Had it done so, it would have realised that far from being merely 'distributional coalitions', interest associations – and trade unions in particular – can make indispensable contributions to social order without which the economic performance of complex organisations of work is likely to be severely constrained. Conflict and disorder at work, with their negative economic consequences, can be traced, as Fox (1974) has persuasively demonstrated, to a dynamic of social and economic exchange between employer and employee that systematically undermines mutual trust. The pluralist structure of organised interests, including trade unions, is the effect, not the cause, of low trust which derives essentially from the foundation of the employment relationship in an unequal contract. A purely contractual social order of work and production is no more than an economist's utopia, and interest pluralism in industrial relations is above all a response to the glaring deficiencies of markets, especially labour markets, as mechanisms of social integration.

It is true that trade unions may just reflect and represent low trust and thereby reinforce it. But Fox (1974, p. 245 ff.), following Tannenbaum (1964), considers also the possibility that employers' contractual claim to authority may be circumscribed and thereby legitimated by individual contracts being regulated and supplemented by pre-contractual *status rights* of workers balancing the asymmetry between owners of capital and sellers of labour. Fox remains unconvinced, however, and probably rightly so as long as collective interests and status are organised in a pluralist pattern. Experience shows, however, that the situation may be different where, in the course of a *corporatist transformation of pluralist associability*, 'industrial citizenship' becomes vested in comprehensive, monopolistic trade unions with public status acting as 'private interest governments' and capable of negotiating and enforcing collective *pacts* with employers that recognise and codify mutual entitlements and obligations (Streeck and Schmitter, 1985). By thus creating a stable framework of pre-contractual conditions of individual contractual exchange in the labour market, trade unions in a corporatist industrial relations system help break the 'vicious spiral' and the self-fulfilling prophecies of low trust and thereby enhance social integration and, ultimately, production. Only through collective status and representation can workers without property rights be sure that they will get a fair share of what they produce, and only then can they develop enough confidence to contribute beyond and above their formal contractual obligations. In this sense, it is precisely because of the existence of what Olson calls 'distributional coalitions' that 'productive coalitions' between management and labour become possible.

How trade unions and the negotiation of industrial order are to be organised–for example, in a centralised or decentralised pattern–remains an important problem of institutional design and can make a crucial difference for the kind and degree of interest accommodation that is achieved, as well as for economic performance in general and unemployment in particular. In principle at least, there is a wide range of choice here, and the advantages and disadvantages of different forms of organisation and joint regulation are being widely explored presently in the light of new pressures for more 'flexibility'. On the other hand, however strong such pressures may be, some degree of national presence and political status of trade unions seems to be indispensable – both for wage restraint in expansion periods and to provide workers with a political guarantee of their industrial citizenship.

'Unionism without unions' (Garbarino, 1984) is not a convincing alternative, at least not for the foreseeable future and certainly not in continental Europe. While it is true that under favourable conditions, a relationship of trust can be established by a provident and benevolent human resource management, it is also true that legitimate industrial governance in non-unionised firms has essentially been a spin-off from the unionised sector, with firms pressured by the threat of potential unionisation to emulate and even outbid the conditions achieved by unions elsewhere. Moreover, unionism without unions, in its attempt to generate trust and involvement among workers, free-rides on the political, as distinguished from the industrial, accomplishments of trade unions – in particular, protective 'status' legislation for workers. That it remains a precarious arrangement at best is shown by the fact that in crucial areas like the adjudication of grievances, workers have been found to have more confidence in pluralist institutions in which they are genuinely and independently represented, than in unitarian ones set up and governed, however equitably, by management alone (Garbarino, 1984).

A labour market without 'distributional coalitions' means work organisation with low trust and high conflict, manifest or latent. Essentially it is an illegitimate social order. The argument here is not that an illegitimate order cannot exist, and in fact it may even exist for a long time. However, social illegitimacy of economic institutions is economically wasteful. It has always been known that a 'Taylorist' division of labour and the associated strong hierarchical control impose costs. Today, it so happens that important markets that seem to offer major opportunities for a re-vitalisation of manufacturing – markets of customised high quality goods – cannot be successfully exploited with workers who do not have enough confidence in their status to accept responsibility for an efficient workflow and high quality. If it is true that renewed industrial expansion requires the co-operation of highly skilled workers in a decentralised and functionally enriched work organisation, then a neo-liberal destruction of 'distributional coalitions' may well increase rather than reduce unemployment.

Many more arguments could be added, but I will mention only one. Just as contracts require pre-contractual institutions that compensate for their innate insufficiencies in regulating exchange in the labour market, markets in order to function require the provision of collective goods that they themselves cannot generate. In the labour market, a crucial collective good for the firms of any given sector is a sufficient supply of skills. Far from just being 'distributional coalitions', trade unions and employers' associations in West Germany jointly and collectively, in co-operation with and under the charter of the state, administer this country's highly centralised system of vocational training whose contribution to employment has often been described. This system, which is an almost ideal-typical example of a corporatist arrangement, is a major source of consensus in West German industrial relations. It is worth asking what a neo-liberal economist promising, in the name of full employment, to rid society of 'social rigidities' would propose to put in its place.

References

Fox, A. (1974) *Beyond Contract: Work, Power and Trust Relations* (London: Faber and Faber).

Garbarino, J. W. (1974) 'Unionism Without Unions: The New Industrial Relations', *Industrial Relations*, 23.

Olson, M. (1965) *The Logic of Collective Action* (Cambridge, Mass.: Harvard University Press).

Olson, M. (1976) 'The Political Economy of Comparative Growth Rates', in *US Economic Growth from 1976 to 1986: Prospects, Problems and Patterns*, Studies Prepared for the Use of the Joint Economic Committee of the Congress of the United States, vol. 2.

Olson, M. (1982) *The Rise and Decline of Nations: Economic Growth, Stagflation and Social Rigidities* (New Haven and London: Yale University Press).

Streeck, W. and Schmitter Ph. C. (1985) 'Community, Market, State – and Associations? The Prospective Contribution of Private Interest Government to Social Order', in W. Streeck and Ph. C. Schmitter (eds), *Private Interest Government: Beyond Market and State* (London: Sage).

Tannenbaum, F. (1964) *The True Society: A Philosophy of Labor* (London: Jonathan Cape).

9 New Technologies and Employment in the 1980s: From Science and Technology to Macroeconomic Modelling

Robert Boyer

The link between machinery (now called technical progress) and employment has always been a major topic in political economy, as well as modern economic analysis. Nevertheless during the 1960s, most economists – especially macroeconomists – used to regard technical progress trends as exogenously given to the economy, and neutral with respect to employment. This feature was roughly in correspondence with what was observed during this period. Since the 1970s the panorama has drastically changed: new technologies and their effects upon employment levels and structure have become a major concern for economists, in such a way that old debates are again relevant. As always, the optimists emphasise the long-run positive influences of technical change upon employment, whereas pessimists point to the large reduction in industrial employment produced by the application of labour saving innovations. In some cases, the present mass unemployment is directly related to the introduction of new technologies.

All the books, research papers, official reports or statements on this subject would fill a whole library, particularly if the literature of the last decade is included. Thus, the question is so huge and the analyses so involved, that any survey or claim to novelty is outside the scope of a short paper! Therefore, it is necessary to define precisely the focus adopted here, both from a methodological and practical point of view. As regards *methodology*, two particularities are stressed:

First, a *tentative bride between conventional macroeconomics and research on science and technology* will be outlined. These two fields of economic research are usually rigorously separated, which is detrimental to any comprehensive analysis on the topic.

Secondly, *the present situation and previous periods* in the history of capitalist economies will be compared. In fact, the question of new technologies and productive systems can only be analysed in the very long run, far longer than the usual period considered by macroeconomists and forecasters.

With respect to *content*, the present paper will apply analysis of past experience in this area to a key question raised during the 1980s: a number of recent studies carried out by CEPREMAP to identify the possible links between technical changes and the level of employment in contemporary Europe (see the various references R. Boyer and P. Petit, 1981) will be summarised and extended here.

The European economies are now facing *the major challenge of a lasting mass unemployment*: is a lag in adaptation to a new industrial revolution responsible for this unfavourable evolution? Would new technologies, if quickly implemented, promote a return to full employment? This was one of the themes of the International Institute of Management Conference held in West Berlin in October 1985.

This general framework leads to six major conclusions or hypotheses, which will be shortly summarised here and presented with more details in the following sections.

First, it will be shown that the 1970s experienced *The breakdown of the Fordist model*, i.e. a particular mode of technical progress, organisation of work and pattern of investment (section 1). Therefore, the relation between productivity and employment can no longer be analysed on the same basis as applied in the 1960s. In fact, the employment dynamic *within a given technological paradigm* appears quite different when the search of *a new one* is proposed (section 2). Economic theorists have not reached any clear-cut conclusion to this problem: selection of different hypotheses about economic organisation and mechanisms, technical progress leads to positive, neutral or negative consequences upon the employment level (section 3).

It is thus necessary to refer to a precise and historically dated *institutional and socio-economic setting*, in order to assess the likely effects of technical change (section 4). The key problem is then about *productivity increases, distribution and sectoral pattern of consumption and investment*. The notion of an *accumulation regime* is defined to link the technical and social organisation to the general characteristics of macroeconomic dynamics – intensity and regularity of growth, employment, inflation – (section 5). The central question is then: *does flexible specialisation lead to a new socio-technical regime*, to replace the Fordist regime, and to a surge in employment? As far as no definitive answer can be proposed, it seems wise to study a larger variety of technological paradigms and accumulation regimes, taking into account significant discrepancies between sectors and countries (section 6).

A final observation (section 7): *massive job creation supposes a new and coherent socio-technical system and economic 'regulation'*, according to the French meaning of this term; its implementation is a complex and (partially) open process. A short appendix proposes some areas and hypotheses for future research, especially concerning flexible specialisation.

1 THE BREAKDOWN OF THE FORDIST MODEL

In retrospect, the exceptional post-Second World War growth – at least outside the US – seems directly related to the implementation of an original technical and economic system, which excluded experiences similar to those of the inter-war period. Four major transformations explain this major change: a new stage is reached in the deepening of the division of labour between conception and production. After the Taylorist rationalisation of work and splitting up of crafts, Fordism essentially aimed at the embodiment of workers' know-how into *specialised equipment*. The assembly-line in the car-industry is the best example of this organisation: a succession of specific machines sets the rhythm of production, as well as the volume and nature of jobs (B. Coriat, 1982). Hence productivity is mainly a matter of full utilisation of production capacities, and not strictly linked to work effort as it was in the Taylor stage.

The extreme specialisation of machines and jobs leads to *a law of increasing returns*: once the production process has been designed for a specific commodity, unit costs decline with market size. So, there exists a minimum efficient scale of output so that traditional methods based on divisibility – and therefore flexibility – are usually eliminated through competition. They remain competitive only outside mass production and consumption markets. Consequently, markets have to be growing, easy to forecast and must undergo only minor fluctuations, especially during the cyclical downturn (M. Piore and C. Sabel, 1985).

But Fordism is not only a technical principle for industrial production. Basically, a whole set of social conventions and economic mechanisms provides for *the mutual adjustment of mass consumption and production*. On one side, competition between firms is based essentially upon product differentiation and marketing; thus oligopolistic pricing allows a quasi constancy in profit share with respect to value added, which benefits investment dynamism, the more so when demand is buoyant. On the other hand, Capital–Labour compromise between capital and labour produces a novel method of wage formation: to the extent workers accept technical change and Fordist methods, they receive higher wages, rising more or less in line with productivity increases. So, workers can buy most of the industrial commodities and services, previously outside the wage-earners' standards of living. In this context, wage and profit, consumption and investment, are complementary pairs rather than substitutes (R. Boyer, 1979, M. Aglietta, 1976, H. Bertrand, 1981).

Under these mechanisms, demand fits approximately with production capacities at a high growth rate, since *ex ante* consumption plus investment varies more or less in line with output, at a macro and sectoral level. Any discrepancy is interpreted as transitory, in such a manner that stockpiling rather than price wars are the usual way of adjusting demand and supply; investment is not cut as drastically as it was during the inter-war period or in the nineteenth century. Therefore, demand outgrows productivity: *employment is growing or stable, more or less in step with the labour force*. Generally, even manufacturing is creating jobs, and services for households and firms expand significantly. During this period, quasi full-employment prevails (J. P. Benassy, R. Boyer, R. M. Gelpi, 1978).

This model is more or less common to all advanced capitalist countries, with marginal differences related to the social, economic and technological history of each country. It is possible to show that macroeconomic achievements (low unemployment and inflation rates, external and budget equilibria) are strictly correlated with the degree of implementation of the Fordist model: the various European economies range from the German, French and Italian so-called 'miracles' – at least during the 1950s and 1960s – to the 'British disease' (R. Boyer (ed.), 1986). This last example emphasises some of the weaknesses of this social and technical system.

Fordism enters a crisis after the two 'oil shocks' which had remained hidden since the end of the 1960s. The factors and determinants of this breakdown are at the core of post-Second World War mode of development.

First, *productivity increases become more and more difficult to achieve as* Fordism advances. The large specialisation of machines induces frequent imbalances because it is quite difficult to keep constant proportionality through the various components of the assembly line. Correspondingly, massive investments in large-scale plants lessen labour productivity when their degree of utilisation falls. Thus, total productivity may decline, which has adverse effects upon industrial competitiveness and profit rates and sharpens conflicts over income distribution, which may induce inflationary pressure. Beyond a certain threshold, *Fordist methods become counter-productive*. This can be measured by traditional productivity indexes and confirmed by case studies in typical plants. In some instances, traditional and divisible production techniques turn out to be more efficient than modern and indivisible processes. The success of flexible specialisation is evidence of the structural limits of Fordist mechanisation (B. Coriat, 1984). Moreover, the struggles of blue-collar workers may worsen the technical barriers to increasing productivity: high turnover and absenteeism, low intensity of work effort, disruption from strikes (even local and partial), increasing costs for work control and quality requirements suggest that *the limits to Fordism are also of a social character* (T. Weisskopf et al., 1983).

Secondly, the search for increasing returns finally produces manufacturing units on a gigantic scale. On one side, national markets become too small to absorb domestic production so that firms have to sell – and ultimately to produce – at the *world level*. Thus stabilised national oligopolies are forced into competitive struggles between multinational corporations where the institutional setting is far different from the national one; the stability of Fordism does not necessarily apply on the international level. Further, the rise of large indivisibilities reduces the ability of firms to react to sharp and unexpected variations in demand and relative prices. Hence *rigidities are considered the Achilles' heel of post-Second World War technical systems*. A major part of labour is indirect, i.e. it cannot be varied with production volume, in such a way that productivity rates decline significantly during cyclical downturns, as was observed after 1973. The oligopolies experienced severe losses, and tried to offset them by marketing, and even in some cases by lowering prices. A new area for competition and flexibilisation was opened up.

Thirdly, this strengthening of competition at the world level breaks down previous mechanisms of income formation. For any country which is not a price leader, *a profit squeeze* takes place and with it a reduction in investment in those sectors producing tradeable goods. Thus the productivity problem is even more acute and managers and governments question ruling wage agreements. The implicit or explicit mechanisms indexing wages to consumer prices come under increasing criticism; simultaneously attempts are made to hold wage increases below productivity increases. Finally, *wage formation tends to be more competitive.* As unemployment surges and old industries decline, the real-wage bill and hence consumption decelerate. If previously a high-wage was generally supposed to be good for the economy, now the ideal appears to be the lowest, socially bearable, wage. In the 1980s, wage and profit, as well as consumption and investment are *perceived as contradictory, rather than complementary.* But in fact, a milder form of complementarity is still prevailing: the virtuous circle is replaced by a vicious one in which under-investment, low productivity and quasi-stagnation reinforce each other. The diffusion of the crisis to the main macroeconomic indicators is associated with a large range of pressures leading to the disintegration of the old technological and social system.

The final outcome is a major change in employment patterns. A binding external constraint prevents almost every economy from reaching full employment. The medium-term rate of growth is then lower, in greater proportion, than the decline in productivity. There is a fall in *industrial employment lasting more than a decade*, while jobs in the services are not sufficient to compensate the inflow of new workers into the labour market. In the medium and long term, two other factors reinforce this industrialisation process (at least outside the US). Rationalisation investment outruns capacity investment, particularly when real wages do not decline: the same volume of cash-flow creates fewer and fewer jobs. In the very long run, production process innovations prevail over product innovations. Hence the vicious circle is reproduced and worsened from period to period. By contrast with the 1950s and 1960s, technical change is then perceived by most people as detrimental to the level of total employment: the negative effects in old and mature industries are far larger than job creation in high-tech and sunrise industries.

Figure 9.1 The growth of demand is no longer the key determinant for productivity (medium-term trends for OECD countries)

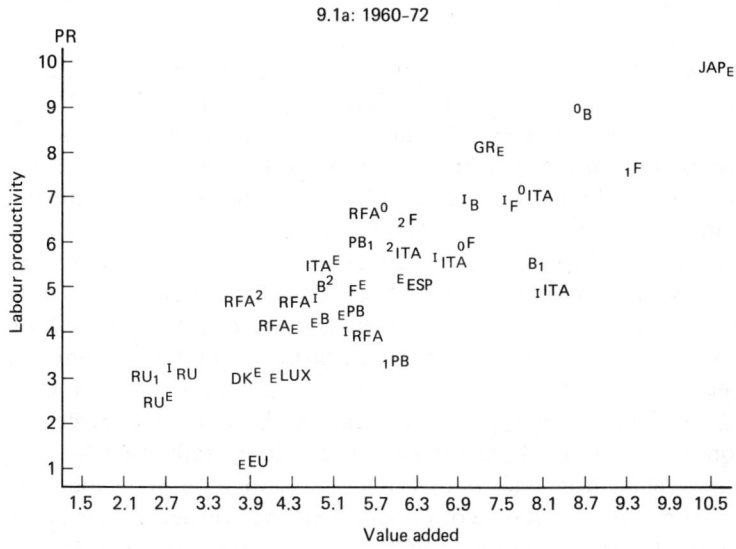

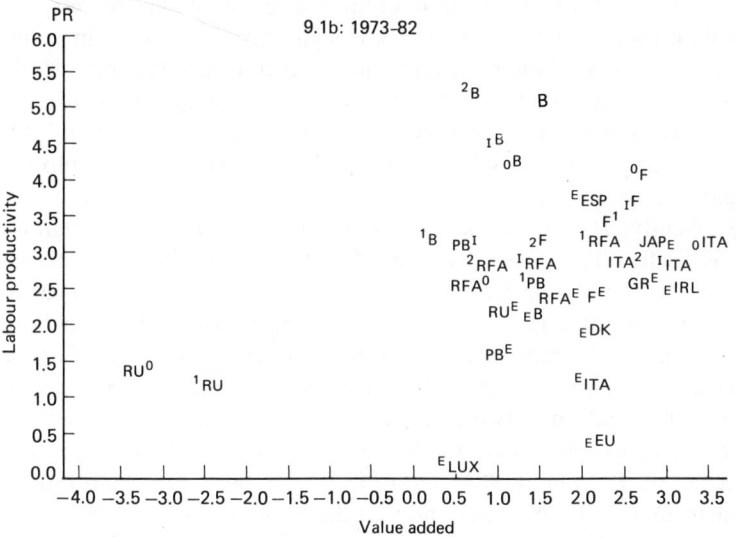

Capital letters are for the countries: JAP = JAPAN, F = FRANCE, B = BELGIUM, ITA = ITALY, GR = GREECE, RFA = GERMANY, PB = NETHERLANDS, DK = DENMARK, RU = UNITED KINGDOM, LUX=LUXEMBURG, EU=UNITED STATES, Superscripts are for the sectors, E = whole economy, I = Industry, 0 = Intermediate goods, 1 = Equipment, 2 = Consumption

2 IN THE EIGHTIES, EMPLOYMENT DETERMINED BY OTHER FACTORS THAN THOSE OF THE FORDIST SYSTEM

Now we must show that this general framework can be extended to identify the consequences of contemporary changes in technology on the level of employment. A number of statistical and econometric studies confirm that the breakdown of the post-Second World War mode of development has changed some of the key macroeconomic relations linking efficiency to employment.

The productivity slowdown is almost general. The phenomenon has been spectacular in the United States: since the announcement of the 'productivity puzzle' (Denison, 1979), many scholars have been trying to identify the reasons for the quasi-constancy in GDP per employee over the last decade and the noticeable deceleration in the growth of industrial productivity. The problem has become more acute, the more complete has been mechanisation along traditional Scientific Management principles (see various issues of Monthly Labour Review summarising Bureau of Labour Studies). The decline has often a minor relative size in other OECD countries and is posterior to 1974, i.e. after the outbreak of the international crisis. None the less, the absolute reduction in productivity is significant, especially in countries, like Japan, where GDP and industrial production clearly decelerated after the first 'oil shock'. Then, one may ask: is not this feature the outcome of the global crisis within an unchanged and still efficient technical system? Three pieces of evidence seem to imply a negative answer.

Currently, *the law of increasing returns has reduced explanatory power*. Before 1973, growth and productivity, especially for manufacturing, were highly correlated: the Kaldor–Verdoorn law seemed to be the direct consequence of the Fordist organisation of production. Whatever the direction of causality, the link cannot be denied. For the past decade, however, this relation has been much weaker, and no systematic relation between growth and productivity has emerged. These conclusions, based on R. Boyer, P. Ralle (1985) have been checked by T. Michl (1984) and other researchers, confirm a radical transformation in the functioning of the economic and technological system of OECD countries. The crisis not only reduced medium-term growth, it has also broken down the law of returns ruling under Fordism. It should be no surprise then if the relation between efficiency and employment has changed.

No *new law of returns seems to have yet emerged*. Previously, high growth industries were characterised both by rapid productivity growth and an above average rate of investment. In the 1980s these three indicators of efficiency appear to move independently without clear relationships with other macroeconomic variables (cf. Table 9.1). Of course, the evidence is partial and not very robust. Nevertheless, it does suggest that the relative position of sectors and countries is undergoing a noticeable transformation. It would be dangerous to draw any firm conclusions about the outcome of the present technological 'revolution', the basis of these now obsolete regularities. This conclusion is particularly important for employment.

Different factors now shape the level of employment. First, a comparison of pre- and post-1973 correlation matrices (Table 9.1) shows that nearly all links between growth, investment rate, productivity and external trade have changed. In the 1960s, employment had no identifiable relationship with most of the other variables. In the 1980s, all these factors combine to produce a confused picture of employment determinants. Nevertheless, output growth seems to be a more powerful variable than during the 1960s, which suggests that labour intensive industries have been playing a prominent role. Secondly, this pattern is checked by a direct graphical analysis (Figure 9.2). Before the crisis, countries whose manufacturing sector had better productivity achievements experienced higher job creation (Italy and France), while those with poor productivity experienced de-industrialisation (United Kingdom). This is coherent with the Fordist logic, complemented by a mechanism of external competitiveness à la Beckerman: the more rapid the modernisation, the greater the world market share and the greater national growth. On the contrary, after 1973, a positive differential in productivity improves the external position, but at the cost of reduced employment growth. In particular, and this is a third result (R. Boyer, P. Ralle, 1985), the degree of openness of a national economy now seems slightly detrimental to employment, whereas it was neutral during the 1960s (compare the correlation coefficients in Table 9.1). On one side industries most severely hit by the crisis, turn out to be the most international. On the other, all the sectors sheltered from external competition – in particular the services – display an employment dynamic very different from that of the traded goods sectors. Hence the contra-position between industry and services is stronger than ever (P. Petit, 1985; CEPII, 1984).

To summarise, most of the relationships between the level of

Table 9.1 The employment functions have changed: correlations matrix

	Before 1973						After 1973					
	VAB	PR	EMP	FSQ	ESQ	ISQ	VAB	PR	EMP	FSQ	ESQ	ISQ
VAB	1.00	0.85	0.27	0.42	0.21	0.22	VAB	1.00	0.26	0.73	0.17	−0.34	−0.38
PR	0.85	1.00	−0.27	0.48	0.20	0.21	PR	0.26	1.00	−0.46	−0.28	0.48	0.43
EMP	0.27	−0.27	1.00	−0.10	0.01	0.03	EMP	0.73	−0.46	1.00	0.35	−0.64	−0.65
FSQ	0.42	0.48	−0.10	1.00	−0.03	0.03	FSQ	0.17	−0.28	0.35	1.00	−0.22	−0.21
ESQ	0.21	0.20	0.01	−0.03	1.00	0.93	ESQ	−0.34	0.48	−0.64	−0.22	1.00	0.97
ISQ	0.22	0.21	0.03	0.03	0.93	1.00	ISQ	−0.38	0.43	−0.65	−0.21	0.97	1.00

Key: with VAB, value added; PR, labour productivity; EMP, employment; FSQ, investment ratio; ESQ (ISQ), share of export (import) in value added.

Figure 9.2 Differential productivity increases now seem to have negative effects on industrial employment

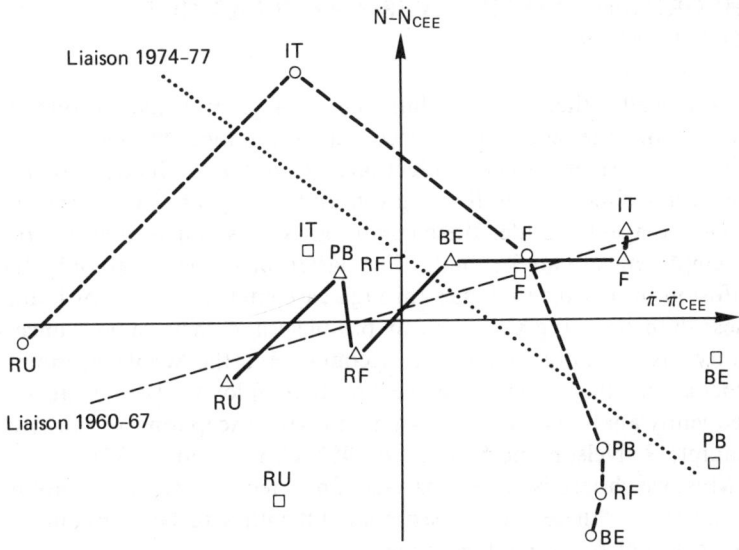

Source: 1 and 2: R. Boyer and P. Ralle (1985), pp. 11 and 40
3: R. Boyer and P. Petit (1980).

employment and technological and economic factors have probably changed. So the conclusion of more general analyses seems to be confirmed: what is true *within a given socio-technical paradigm* or system may be invalidated during a 'structural crisis', i.e. *the transition* from an old system becoming obsolete relative to the new which is unknown and hence rather uncertain (G. Dosi, L. Orsenigo, 1985). During such a period the information flows transmitted through markets are no longer sufficient to provide guidance for firm's long-term choices about technology, markets, localisation of production and so on. In fact, most of the routines, institutions and conventions have to be changed, if a new technological system has to emerge and reorganise social and economic life.

So there are marginal new technologies on one side, a series of structural changes on the other. Their effects on the macro variables, and in particular on employment, are usually far different. But what do the theoreticians say to us about this key issue?

3 NEW TECHNOLOGIES AND THE VOLUME AND DISTRIBUTION OF EMPLOYMENT: ECONOMIC THEORIES DO NOT DELIVER ANY CLEAR-CUT CONCLUSION

Paradoxically, there are few links between general macroeconomic theories on one side, and science and technology analyses on the other. The former assume production sets – or the production possibilities for technology itself – as given and totally known ex ante by economic agents. Under these conditions very sophisticated theories of employment can be built. The latter investigate carefully the diffusion of new technologies through case studies of firms or industries. Path breaking processes or products and their radical uncertainty are actually taken into account. But the whole economic process and the global outcome for the employment level are less frequently analysed, even though noteworthy exceptions do exist (for example R. Nelson and S. Winter, 1982; C. Freeman, 1982).

Must we choose between analysis of new technologies and employment? If not, there are at least four difficulties to be overcome by conventional economic theorising.

The concept of new technology has little meaning within the production function approach or even General Equilibrium Theory, since every producer knows, without cost, the whole production frontier; the technique actually used will be chosen with respect to the relative prices prevailing in equilibrium. Generally, technique selection is totally reversible and uncertainty plays only a minor role as a simple disturbance near a well defined and perceived production set in which every component is available from the beginning of time. Of course, mathematical economists sometimes do generalise the Arrow–Debreu framework along these lines, but macroeconomists usually don't. They are mainly preoccupied by choosing the production function best fitted to the historical data, under the assumption that technical progress trends are constant through time. The role of new technologies is then purely factual.

Nevertheless, at best they can be interpreted as a method for obtaining productivity increases. Even in this case, *the various theories have contradictory conclusions* (R. Boyer, P. Petit, 1981b). Let us consider some key-models of macroeconomic analysis. The implications of the *neo-classical* hypothesis that labour is always in equilibrium through wage variations are quite evident: production grows faster and *full employment always prevails*, with an unchanged labour force, but a higher growth rate of wages. The optimist may find his beliefs confirmed. But the pessimist will object that Keynesian theory leads to opposite conclusions. In the short run if a lack of effective demand leads to unemployment, increased productivity will initially reduce the employment level, as long as the nominal wage is sticky and increased profits do not spur investment. These deflationary pressures will adversely affect firms' expectations such that *in the Keynesian system*, more efficient production processes usually *worsen the unemployment problem*. But a neo-classical economist may reply that the excess of real wages with respect to productivity – due for example to downward inflexibility of nominal wage when the price level declines – is the only explanation of the inter-war or current European mass-unemployment. Under such circumstances, any improvement in productive efficiency benefits employment: more workers are demanded because their marginal productivity exceeds the prevailing wage. Then, if *classical unemployment* prevails, new technologies raise both production and employment, without requiring a wage cut.

As disequilibrium theory shows (see J. P. Benassy, 1982), these three cases do not necessarily express conflicting 'ideological' views (although they often do), they may also relate to 'objective' differences in economic mechanisms, or 'régulation'. This conclusion is still clearer when *closed economies* are opposed to *highly open* ones, or more generally when the intensity of international competition varies (R. Boyer and P. Petit, 1981d). According to the price elasticities of external trade, an identical productivity may exert opposite effects on employment: positive if the share of exports and imports in the national production is large and the economy specialises in commodities for which price competition is dominant, negative when the country is not so open or is a price leader due to its level of specialisation.

Hence, the economic theoretician cannot assess, *in abstracto* and for whatever country or period, the consequence of any new technology. But can analysis be restricted to productivity increases only? Actually, economic theory encounters two other difficulties in considering all the complexities related to technological change.

Usually, *product innovation* goes along with process innovation, but is far more difficult to integrate in any modelling of economic activity. The conventional representation of consumer's preferences and behaviour assume that the set of commodities is known once and for all, at least for simplifying the derivation of demand. Of course the distinction between the goods and their various characteristics (K. J. Lancaster, 1971) could probably help in solving the new products puzzle... but it has seldom been used in macroeconomic theories. By contrast, the interplay between new products and processes is a central topic for Science and Technology studies. A popular interpretation has been coined in order to take into account the turning point observed during the 1970s (see for example C. Freeman, J. Clark, L. Soete, 1984; G. Mensch, 1978, and many others). During some periods, product innovations outmatch process innovations, and so the growth of demand is faster than productivity: hence employment is increasing, but aside from the traditional business cycle, there is no major unemployment problem. New industries and consumers' standards spur on a twenty to thirty year-long upswing, i.e., the so-called phase A of Kondratieff's long waves. When these industries become mature, competition becomes fiercer and firms search for labour-saving production processes. Simultaneously, the impetus of new consumption goods on demand declines. Therefore, more jobs are destroyed than created. The economy now enters into a downturn with low growth. few capacity increasing investments and generally high and long-term unemployment. Here phase B of the long wave begins.

But there is a major, and to my knowledge *unsolved problem*: how does one pass from a stimulating, but merely descriptive analysis to a *theoretical explanation*? It is neither sufficient to point out a close correlation between new products and total medium-term demand growth (B. Real, 1984), nor to consider as exogenous the shift from capacity investment to rationalisation investment (G. Mensch *et al.*, 1979). Similarly, in most theoretical or econometric models of long waves, new products vanish and play no role (J. J. Van Duijn, 1982; J. W. Forrester, 1977).

Finally, this approach has a more general shortcoming: *economic theory has few analytical tools capable of accounting for the various types of technical change*. Of course, we all know the different definitions for neutrality, but they don't cope with the problem to be solved here. As far as Science and Technology analyses are concerned, every new technology may be classified according to four critiera:

1. Is the principal outcome a *new process* for manufacturing known commodities, or a *new product*, the production of which is necessarily new too? This has been discussed in the previous paragraph and will not be developed further.

2. Is the related innovation *a marginal advance* of a still existing technology and does it initiate a *radical change* as regards commodities or processes? For the former, the consequences for employment can probably be analysed through a kind of extrapolation of past technological and economic regularities. For the latter a deeper insight and more sophisticated tools are needed. Risk-taking around a known probability distribution is not the same as the choice of a major technological breakthrough. In this case, the actual implementation is the only method for checking the accuracy of shaky expectations about success or failure, more closely related to 'animal spirits' than the differential calculus.
3. A third criterion relates to the coverage of the consequences to be expected. Is the new technology *mainly, or only, local* or does it promote or allow a *transformation of the whole technological system*? In the first case, the impact on employment can be estimated by a partial equilibrium analysis, i.e. for a given macro-economic 'regulation'. In the second, the spill-over effects, the number of induced innovations and the complementarities between industrial investment and consumption patterns are such that only a general equilibrium or/and macro analysis can assess the likely effects on employment. The bunches of innovations are so powerful that they change the sectoral composition of production, the distribution and the volume of jobs, and may spur on a long term upswing. Very early, J. Schumpeter, 1911, emphasised their roles in long waves, and this idea is now rejuvenated and extended by modern neo-Schumpeterians. To sum up: is the new technology strictly micro, or is it potentially macro?
4. Finally, a fourth question has to be raised: is the *innovation basically technological* or does it relate to *social and economic changes*? Economists seem to have forgotten the comprehensive definition given by J. Schumpeter: new *markets*, original management, more efficient methods for *work organisation* or new *social relations* may be as important as purely technical devices and sophisticated machines. Actually, international comparisons show that the same equipment usually leads to very different productivity levels and competitive edges (F. Sellier, J. Sylvestre, J. Maurice, 1980). Various social and institutional patterns within the firm (relations between blue collar, foremen, white collar, and middle management) or the society (place of technical training, value attributed to manual work) usually make drastic differences in the implementation (or in some cases, the rejection) of the *same* technological change.

Unfortunately, economic theory rarely studies such issues, so essential for the present analysis. How then are we to improve our knowledge of the transformations now taking place? Perhaps by admitting that the technical system is largely integrated with almost all the components of social and economic activity. The next sections propose a very preliminary and still unsatisfactory path in this direction.

4 THE ENTIRE SOCIAL, INSTITUTIONAL AND ECONOMIC SETTING SHAPES THE DIRECTION AND DIFFUSION OF TECHNOLOGICAL CHANGE

From the previous developments (Sections 1 and 2), it is rather clear that in the 1980s, the advanced capitalist economies are groping for a new system of organisation, due to the crisis of Fordism. Simultaneously, the new technologies being introduced seem to display the following features: (a) *process innovations* (flexible automatisation of factories, informatisation of office jobs) are prevailing, even though new products are not absent (home computers, video-recorders ... and fast-foods). (b) The processes are *more than marginal improvements* of old techniques or management methods, since they all try to outcome the productivity crisis, which is typically Fordist. Radically new (or so presented) models for plant and office organisation flourish. (c) The new technologies have potentially significant impact at the *macro level*. The issue is no longer the replacement of transistors by chips, nor of huge computers by micro, but the reshaping of almost all other industries (car-making, steel, textile, banking and insurance) and consumption goods (electronisation of household durable goods, cars, phones and telecoms ...). (d) The changes are as much *managerial, human and institutional* as purely technological. In fact, the markets by geographical areas and composition shift, work rules and collective bargaining undergo major reversals, the big corporations are reorganising their departments, State interventions and economic policies are reformed ... almost as quickly as the new technologies are introduced.

Therefore, the assessment of new technologies takes place in the most difficult case: when the changes are probably radical, structural and global. Can macroeconomic theories and/or history teach us anything about such a complex and uncertain episode? *Four major conclusions* will be presented.

First, in the past technological transformations have been *different, less universal and rapid than expected* by contemporary observers, including specialists in science and technology. For example recall the hopes (and fears for others) raised in the 1950s by industrial automation: no repetitive or heavy task was supposed to be left to human labour, work duration would be greatly reduced and so on. Four decades later, this prognosis still belongs to the realms of fiction rather than every day life! Mechanisation has followed *a different* path in the various industries (the petrochemical plant has *not* been extended to the car industry), *no single principle* has been applied (craft or traditional industries still coexist with modern ones). Moreover, beyond the common belief that technical progress is faster and faster, major innovations take time to significantly alter industrial structures and employment patterns.

Secondly, *some potentially superior techniques may not spread* for, even at *the micro level*, they are dominated by more traditional ones as regards economic efficiency and profit rates, or they are stopped by social groups or existing institutions. For example, in the French building industry, the engineers can point out many innovations that could reduce very significantly the production costs of such and such component. Nevertheless some of them are never used, either because they increase other costs or they call for a know-how that the firms cannot master and raise the opposition of the craftsmen who may fear the suppression of their jobs (R. Boyer, 1985). More generally, the economic and social systems select those innovations which will spread. It would be erroneous to consider the outlook for employment based on new technologies as a mechanical and automatic implementation of scientific advances. Nevertheless, most (macro) economists do so, contrary to the conclusions taught by the Economics of Technological Change. This remark is even more important for radical and structural innovations: they can be validated (by a kind of self-fulfilling prophecy) or not according to the degree of acceptance by the socio-economic system (C. Perez, 1981).

Thirdly, efficient techniques at the micro level can indeed be retarded *by adverse macroeconomic and/or macrosocial conditions*. Let us take the example of the diffusion of Taylorism in the French car industry during the inter-war period (S. Schweitzer, 1982, partially summarised in R. Boyer, 1984). Very early after the Second World War, the French industrialist André Citroen recognised the future of the American methods of mass production and modernised and rationalised his plants. He got a competitive edge and gained market shares, increasing employment in his firm. From the point of view of micro rationality, his new methods were right. But Citroen's massive investment in assembly lines and specialised machine-tools required household incomes to increase in order to provide a growing demand for his cars. When the 1930 crisis broke out this condition could no longer be met, capacity utilisation declined, and so did productivity, even a price-war would not have been sufficient to keep Citroen's demand and production growing. It is no surprise then that he went bankrupt in 1934. Contrary to the common view, a delay in adopting new technologies is not the only method for economic collapse: *the pioneers and early innovators* may have such an advance on the rest of the economy that they also fail! They would have to wait for a more favourable macro environment (after the Second World War) in order to see their technological bets turn to success and create a lot of jobs. So the *same* technological system and management tools may first be *detrimental* to the employment and then *favourable*, once the global conditions for their diffusion are settled. Hence the striking paradox: during the crisis the sunrise industries are firing workers at the very moment where everybody hopes to be hired by them and governments attribute mass unemployment to their insufficient level of development! *Mutatis mutandis*, the same story is repeated at the end of 1984, when Silicon Valley went into crisis. There the firms in the microelectronics, software and high tech industries can hardly be blamed for being too sluggish with respect to the advances in technology or having inadequate and out-of-date skills! In fact, they know that expansion is limited first by overproduction (itself the consequence of fierce competition and too optimistic expectations) and second is the condition of the US economy (deceleration of GDP, over-valuation of the dollar, lack of structural competitiveness in mass consumption goods).

Fourthly, the diffusion of new technologies is not only a matter of competition and Darwinian process through market mechanisms. It also depends on *large corporations' strategies, institutions and social compromises and State interventions*. This huge topic has already been mentioned (G. Dosi and L. Orsenigo, 1985; C. Perez, 1981). The previous paragraph brings a logical conclusion: a minimum of macroeconomic stability has to exist if new technologies are to diffuse and create jobs. Now history as well as economic theory do show that, to be efficient, markets call for some form or another of social norms, conventions, public interventions (for a short argumentation see for example R. Boyer, J. Mistral, 1984). More precisely the innovations have often been the outcome of a kind of very risky investment which supposed a medium- long-run view. That may explain why the *large firms* – oligopolies or monopolies – played such an important role in the chemical, electrical or electronic industries. Moreover, the uncertainties, the size and the length of the research and development investments, the indivisibilities and collective aspects of major innovations call for some *State regulation* (in the English meaning), public loans, subsidies or spending. The birth, development and then crisis of nuclear power electrical plants is one example of these interventions, good (France ?) or bad (US ?)! More generally, it can be argued (M. Aglietta and R. Boyer, 1983) that the State shapes industrial structures in numerous ways: legal norms, regulation of co-operation/competition between firms working for large high tech projects (public, like armaments, or private, like new computers or superchips...), tax codes, foreign trade policy and so forth.... Japan, so often admired, exhibits a subtle but very efficient type of technological and industrial policy, which, in the long run, has proven to be very favourable to employment *and* external competitiveness.

The question first posed now takes on a new expression: 1. *Under the prevailing institutions* and economic mechanisms, what are the probable effects on jobs of the potential technological system(s) which is (are) emerging? 2. If these consequences turn out to be adverse, what are *the reforms* (if possible, minimal and of course socially accepted) which could make worthwhile these changes?

The next three sections are devoted to an investigation upon these two issues.

5 THE SAME TECHNOLOGICAL CHANGE MAY HAVE OPPOSITE EFFECTS ACCORDING TO THE SECTORS CONCERNED AND PRICE AND INCOME MECHANISMS

One way to tackle the first question, would be to take up two of the main features of the contemporary period: first, new technologies are mainly aimed at increasing productivity; second, the real wage is assumed not to benefit from these increases, at least during a transitory period (R. Boyer, ed., 1986). The rationale for these features is that relative price reductions will increase the demand addressed to the innovative sectors sufficiently to offset the initial negative impact of productivity on the level of employment. A very simple model along this line is presented in the Appendix. Its results seem to contradict commonsense – if the process innovations are mainly introduced in high tech sectors with a significant monopoly power and a small size in consumption patterns, then the impact on total employment is likely to be *negative*. On the contrary, the *same technological changes* may have *positive* effects in more traditional sectors with sharp price competition and a large share of the average consumption basket.

But even in this case, the price elasticities of demand have to be sufficiently large with respect to income elasticities, a feature which is not necessarily observed in modern economies. Then, *the diffusion through prices may not be sufficient to promote job creation*. So something has to be changed in the institutional setting in order to reverse these negative trends. The second model, developed in Appendix 9.1, suggests that a *partial indexing of average wage with productivity in key sectors* may, under some conditions, benefit total employment. As real wage increases spill over to the rest of the economy, every sector (including the mature and old ones) benefits from demand increases and hence can adapt to new technology without firing workers.

Moreover, the precise mechanism of indexation has a tremendous importance. Imagine for example that wages vary with *marginal productivity in each sector*, according to a recent proposition (Weitzman, 1984). Within the simple model (cf. Appendix 9.1) the link between productivity and employment is then unambiguously negative, the related elasticity being equal to -1. The reason is simple enough: production costs do not vary, in such a way that new technology does not improve sectoral competitiveness; only the negative effect upon the real wage bill, and hence consumption remains. Paradoxically enough, the popular mix of new technology with labour market competition is detrimental to full employment ... at least in the framework adopted here. One can find no better example of the *prominent role of economic 'regulation', social compromises and institutions*.

Thus the economist cannot avoid an economic analysis of technical change. The notion of an *accumulation regime* has been conceived to represent these links between technological, social and economical factors (Bertrand, 1983, Boyer, 1985). We will call any method for achieving and distributing productivity increases which allows a rather stable and coherent evolution in the accumulation of capital, an accumulation regime. Work organisation, the technological system, income shares for wages and profits, consumption patterns and complementarities between sectoral investments all play a role in this process. Various historical investigations have shown the succession of three regimes. The Fordist model, which is the last one, has been presented above (sections 1 and 2). Since it went into crisis, the advanced capitalist economies are now searching for a new one. Many observers think they have identified *the* future industrial model.

6 FLEXIBLE AUTOMATION AS A NEW REGIME OF ACCUMULATION AND A WAY FOR REACHING FULL-EMPLOYMENT: TWO CONTRASTING VIEWS

A review of the existing literature leads to a more balanced assessment. Moreover the concept of flexible automation needs some qualification, since it may correspond to different long-run strategies and potential effects upon employment. Let us develop briefly these ideas.

On one side, the evidences about a radical change in the Fordist model have been accumulating for several decades. The old division of work in the assembly line or in the office has been under attack by workers and unions as well as managers. Paradoxically, the *lack of technical and general knowledge* appears now as a barrier to productivity, since the shift of wage-earners from one job to another is crucial, given the new technological trends and macroeconomic instability. Hence, the *direct commitment of blue collar workers* with regard to the outcome of their work activity seems to be the aim of labour management, in sharp contrast with the previous conceptions about the Taylorian worker, assumed to be as strong, and as silly, as a cow! Simultaneously, *less control and fewer hierarchical barriers* may benefit productivity and quality, while turnover and labour conflicts decline in a better social and human environment.

The large indivisibilities of specific equipments and assembly lines are resisted and the engineers and managers now prefer to implement smaller production units and less specialised equipment that can be shifted from one line of production to another, following the consumers' preferences. *Computerised machine tools* are spreading, for they reduce the costs of quantitative and qualitative changes in production. *Customised goods* are indeed a key element for marketing purposes, as opposed to the often purely cosmetic product differentiation under Fordism. Thus, a new ideal for industrial organisation emerges: the *totally flexible automated plant*. Similarly the new wave in computers allows significant reorganisation in white collar jobs, often supposed to reduce middle management. Professional newspapers, and even economic journals, are full of these hopes or experiments. But what is the reality of the case?

Actually, the more flexible firms seem to produce better financial and economic results. A few examples are in order. In the car industry, the newly automated plants are far more efficient than older ones, as shown by a comparison of Japanese with American or European firms. Domestic industries which initiate robotisation and automation gain a competitive edge and thus suffer less de-industrialisation and may produce job creation. Within the same country, very often small or medium-sized firms expand their employment, while the huge plants usually reduce theirs or even close. One could see here a Darwinian selection process of the best entrepreneurs and pathbreaking innovators. As the Japanese model is not easily exportable to western countries and especially to Europe, Italian 'productive decentralisation' has created much interest (see for example Sabel, 1983 and his joint book with M. Piore, 1984). In fact in spite of severe macroeconomic imbalances, Italy has gained noteworthy success in foreign markets. But do all these examples produce clear evidence about the future implementation and dominance of flexible automation? Other arguments suggest a more cautious forecast about the future of the industrial systems.

On the negative side, a number of obstacles currently hinder the complete fulfilment of this model. First, a *reaction to the crisis* is not necessarily a *way out of it*. Let us recall the paradoxical evolution of the inter-war period. While the issue was the implementation of mass production and a new stage of capitalist concentration, the prevailing 'regulation' went in the opposite direction: more competitive mechanisms, relative growth of the self employed and small firms, revival of archaic production process. *Mutatis mutandis*, the same situation may occur in the 1980s: large indivisibilities in mass production still prevail (in energy supply, transportation, general infrastructures) in such a way that customisation of goods may be only a *partial* or *temporary* phenomenon. Worse, the rush toward flexibility could lower the break-even point of firms and mitigate the social pressures for an active demand management and then aggravate stagnation and the rise of unemployment (Coriat, 1984). Furthermore, even very flexible, innovative and high tech firms can experience serious trouble either because they have overestimated the growth of their markets or because they are suffering from negative macroeconomic evolutions. Recall the 1985 Silicon Valley crisis.

Secondly, *micro flexibility is not always a sufficient method for reversing adverse trends at the macro levels* and sometimes it is not even necessary. So, traditionally flexible industries are facing low productivity increases, by lack of standardisation over a large scale, as was mentioned earlier (Boyer, Petit, 1981d). Moreover ease in firing workers does not necessarily imply economic recovery: the present situation of the French (and most European) building industries is illuminating. A large rapid downwards adjustment of the workforce has not been sufficient to restore growth and productivity (Boyer, 1984). In some circumstances, labour flexibility cannot achieve what has been undone by a slackening of world demand and loss in structural competitiveness (Boyer, 1986b). More generally, the famous *fallacy of composition from micro to macro* has to be recognised: when significant resources are kept idle, a rational decision at the firm level may turn into its opposite and have negative effects for the whole economy. The paradox of saving of the 1920s could be extended to the search for flexibility in the 1980s. An adjustment more rapid than competitors is a way of preserving jobs for a given firm. But if total employment is set by macroeconomic factors quite independent of flexibility, the final outcome will be unchanged, or even deteriorate, if expectations are revised downwards. A previous paper has proposed a model of wage flexibility leading to such a fallacy of composition (Boyer (ed.), 1986b).

Thirdly, often *the technological aspects of flexibility are overemphasised* and the role of economic and institutional factors played down. Quite at odds with one of the major conclusions of labour economists and sociologists during the 1960s and 1970s, most people now consider that purely technological devices are the right medicine for returning to full employment.

Of course up to date technologies and goods are better for job preservation than obsolete ones. But equipment changeability is not the only sinews of war: the absence of any worker commitment, unskilled workers, awful industrial relations, mismanagement may transform a brand new plant from technical achievement to economic bankruptcy (see for example some failures in industrialising the Third World). So job creation is the outcome of a series of factors, flexible automation being one out of many others which may be as important: workers' information, pay system, co-operation or conflict within the firm, quality of its internal organisation, efficiency of the marketing and financial management and so on.

More basically, *there exists a wide range of flexibilities, even strictly technological, the long run and macro consequences of which are very different*. For brevity, only two will be presented here.

If flexibility is a way for adapting to a changing, more uncertain, macroeconomic environment characterised by large fluctuations and decreases in demand, then *older* principles for industrial organisation based on divisibility are again becoming efficient ... but at the cost of the loss of any law of increasing returns in the long run (cf. Figure 9.2a). Hence productivity declines less than would have been implied by the mass-production system. Similarly, faced with short-run adjustment to declining demand, the gigantic equipment (the capacity of which may satisfy the whole market when there is only a single firm left) is outclassed by smaller and more flexible ones (cf. Figure 9.2b). So, through competition (especially entries and bankruptcies), the productive structure does change. The employment in old processes declines (or even vanishes in the pure monopolist model), that of new flexible firms expands but total employment generally remains inferior to its pre-crisis level. First because the decline in productivity growth implies less favourable relative prices, hence a reduced demand and second because, by itself, this Schumpeterian process does not alter the macroeconomic determinants of total effective demand.

Very likely, *'cyclical' flexibility* limits job destruction, but does not expand *total* employment.

On the contrary, perhaps flexible automation heralds a new and superior law of increasing returns.

According to this second hypothesis, flexibility is not at all a revival of any pre-Fordist technological paradigm, but a *radical innovation* in the history of industrialisation. Production costs are lower than at any past or present level of demand (cf. Figure 9.3a). Switching to this new system would be structural, and not simply transitory. Its long- and short-run efficiency would be so marked that, even if demand went back to its initial level, the previous huge plant would continue to be replaced by a series of flexible ones. Productivity would increase, more or less according to past trends, allowing any kind of distribution (via relative prices, wages or other incomes) which would promote job creation.

Thus, *flexible automation*, considered as a new principle for cumulative technological improvement and production cost decreases, may further an upswing in productivity and competitiveness. Then, the key

I A reaction to uncertainty, fluctuations and shrinking markets

Figure 9.2a   The pure law of returns is flat

II A new law of increasing returns in the long run

Figure 9.3a   The pure law of returns is superior for current (and post) levels of production

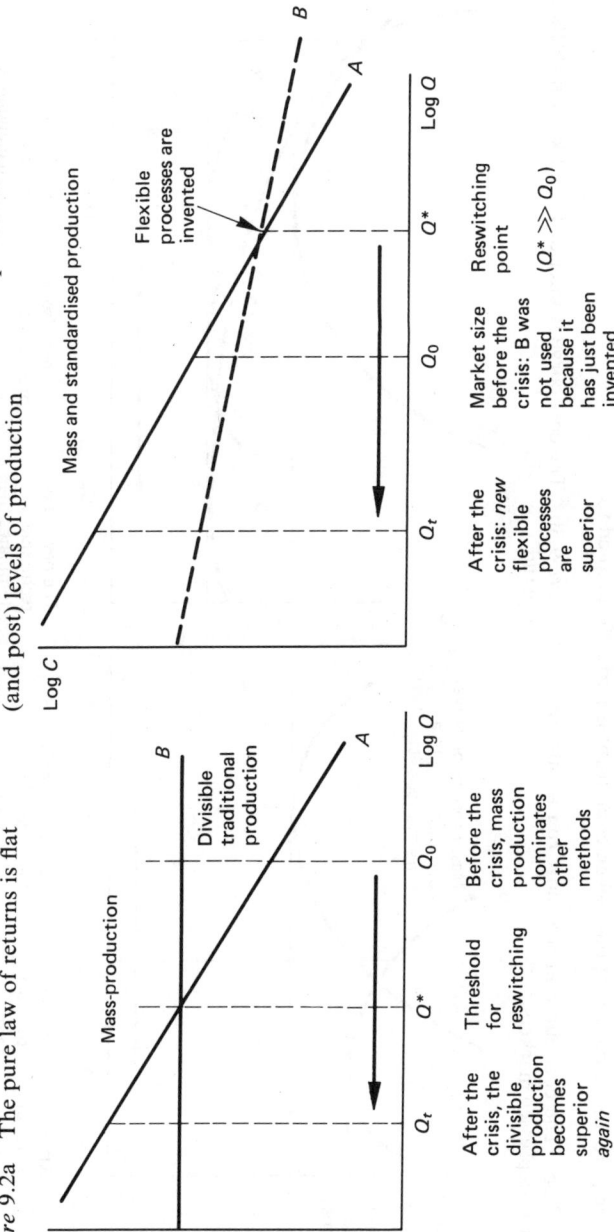

258

Note: the pure law of returns applies when equipment is perfectly adapted to

Figure 9.2b The cost curve in the short run is inferior only for depressed markets

Figure 9.3b The cost curve is inferior for all known levels of demand

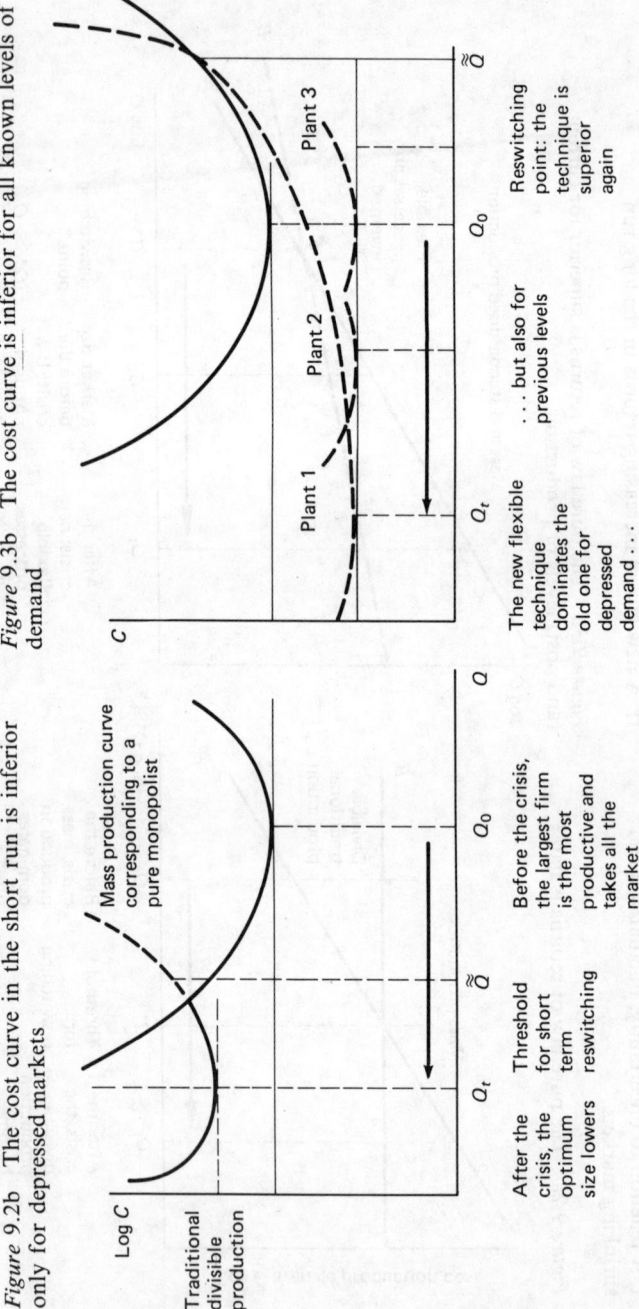

issue would be to derive the rules for sharing out these productivity increases. At one extreme, the traditional Fordist wage and price formation could be adopted again and under certain conditions of external trade balance, would benefit job creation. At another extreme, new rules can be sought, such as profit sharing (Weitzman, 1984), competitive wage formation, two-tier labour contracts and so on. It has been shown, but it must be emphasised again, that the consequences of these institutional settlements are not all minor: as regards the employment level, the outcome of this second type of flexible automation may differ greatly according to the precise mechanisms of price and wage formation (cf. Appendix 9.1).

At the present time, both types of flexibility combine one with the other, in such a way that *archaic and modernist* forms cannot easily be disentangled. For more than a decade, a mix of traditional flexibility (the underground economy, real wage decreases, heavier work) and a new flexible automation (computerisation of services and industrial equipment, robots, flexible plants) has co-existed. Moreover, for *a given* social and economic setting – especially the precise way by which productivity and *new products* are diffusing – the long-run consequences upon employment may be *opposite* if flexibility is mainly regressive or if it defines a new principle for automation.

7 CONCLUSIONS: NEW TECHNOLOGIES AND EMPLOYMENT, A COMPLEX AND (PARTIALLY) OPEN PROCESS

Six main results will be stressed.

First, much of the evidence confirms a central hypothesis: *the Fordist socio-economic system has broken down* and the OECD countries are groping for a new model for technological organisation (in manufacturing and the services sectors), industrial relations, type of competition and income distribution.

Secondly, a priori *several ways seem to be open* to replace the post-Second World War mode of development: a new deepening of the Scientific Management methods towards another stage of *traditional* automation, or a reswitching to more *archaic* flexible production or even *a brand new* 'industrial divide', based upon a cumulative process of flexible equipment and/or job requalification.

Thirdly, actually even if in the long run there is a tendency for new techniques to be more efficient than older ones, *no clear technological determinism* seems to be operating. The historical dynamics of capitalist economies and international comparison suggest that many social, institutional and economic factors shape the direction and diffusion of technological change.

Fourthly, contrary to a common view, the relation between new technologies and the level of employment *cannot be assessed on a priori grounds*. The effects of the *same* technical device are *different* whether it is local or economy-wide, if productivity increases diffuse through relative prices or wages, whether wage increases are uniform or differentiated according to firms and sectors, and finally if the economy is on a steady state or within a structural crisis.

Fifthly, *product innovation* has to be considered simultaneously with *process innovation*. In some sense, a positive or negative trend for jobs is related to the balance of these two aspects and the general 'regulation' mode. The data available for the last two decades suggest that the present trends in technological change are *employment adverse* for most European economies, the more they are open to the world economy.

Sixthly, *innovations in social and political organisation* are likely to be as important as technological change in *stricto sensu*. These transformations are mainly launched by firms' strategies, but crucially depend upon workers' individual and collective attitudes. State interventions do suppose some general knowledge about these very tricky processes. Much more research would be needed before deriving any clear assessment as regards economy policy.

Appendix 9.1 New technologies and the employment level: a negative or positive link according the structures of the economy and incomes formation

Let us consider an economy with n sectors. Each of them adjusts production to demand, which is a function of real disposable income and relative prices. A new technology is introduced in sector 1 leading to higher productivity increases, and hence (1) less employment in sector 1, and (2) a reduction in relative prices according to a mark-up coefficient. Therefore the demand for sector 1 expands and so does employment, according a movement which *may*, *or may not*, compensate the initial reduction. But there are induced effects in other sectors: lower nominal income due to the initial reduction of employment in sector 1 reduces the demands directed to them, but lower prices may check or reverse the decline in nominal income. Then the employment in sectors other than 1 may decrease or increase, according to the strength of these two effects. What is the final outcome on the total employment level? Intuition – or belief – is not satisfactory, and so we need a model. A *very simple* one will be presented here. All the variables are rates of change.

$\forall i,\ 1 \leqslant i \leqslant n$ — i: index for ith sector.

(1) $\dot{D}_i = \varepsilon_R^i \cdot (\dot{R} - \dot{p}_c) - \varepsilon_p^i \cdot (\dot{p}_i - \dot{p}_c) + \varepsilon_d^i$

The volume of demand for sector i output (D_i) varies with the real income (R = nominal disposable income, p_c = index of consumer prices) and the relative price of good i (p_i = absolute of i).

(2) $\dot{p}_i = \dot{W}_i - \dot{\pi}_i$

Prices are a function of labour costs via a constant mark-up (W_i = nominal wage in i, π_i = productivity in the same sector).

(3) $\dot{p}_c = \sum_{i=1}^{i=n} \bar{c}_i \cdot \dot{p}_i$

The consumer price is the weighted average of the price in each sector.

(4) $\dot{R} \sum_{i=1}^{i=n} \bar{r}_i \cdot (\dot{W}_i + \dot{N}_i)$

For the sake of simplicity, nominal global income is the sum of the wage bill (employment = N_i, unit wage = $_iW$) and is converted into rates of change ($\bar{r}_i$ = the share of sector i in total wage income).

(5) $\dot{\pi}_i = \bar{\varphi}_i$

Labour productivity trends are exogeneous.

(6) $\dot{Q}_i = \dot{D}_i$

Production is fixed according to the demand directed to i (no inventory variations).

(7) $\dot{N}_i \equiv \dot{Q}_i - \dot{\pi}_i$

Definitional identity for employment.

Substituting all the equations into (7), one gets the following system:

(I) $\dot{N}_i = -\varphi_i + \varepsilon_R^i \cdot \sum_{i=1}^{i=n} [\bar{r}_i \cdot (\dot{W}_i + \dot{N}_i) - \varepsilon_p^i(\dot{W}_i - \varphi_i)]$

$+ (\varepsilon_p^i - \varepsilon_R^i) \cdot \sum_{i=1}^{i=n} \bar{c}_i \cdot (\dot{W}_i - \varphi_i) + \varepsilon_d^i$

Let us define the four column vectors:

$$\dot{N} = \begin{bmatrix} \dot{N}_1 \\ \cdot \\ \cdot \\ \cdot \\ \dot{N}_n \end{bmatrix} \quad \dot{W} = \begin{bmatrix} \dot{W}_1 \\ \cdot \\ \cdot \\ \cdot \\ \dot{W}_n \end{bmatrix} \quad \dot{\varphi} = \begin{bmatrix} \dot{\varphi}_1 \\ \cdot \\ \cdot \\ \cdot \\ \varphi_n \end{bmatrix} \quad \dot{E} = \begin{bmatrix} \varepsilon_d^1 \\ \cdot \\ \cdot \\ \cdot \\ \varepsilon_d^n \end{bmatrix}$$

For every i ($1 \leq i \leq n$) and the four matrices:

$$I = \begin{bmatrix} 1 & & 0 \\ & \ddots & \\ 0 & & 1 \end{bmatrix}_{(n,n)} \quad A = \begin{bmatrix} \varepsilon_R^i \cdot \bar{r}_j \end{bmatrix}_{(n,n)} \quad B = \begin{bmatrix} \varepsilon_p^1 & & 0 \\ & \varepsilon_p^i & \\ & & \ddots \\ 0 & & \varepsilon_p^n \end{bmatrix}_{(n,n)} \quad C = \begin{bmatrix} (\varepsilon_p^i - \varepsilon_R^i) \cdot c_j \end{bmatrix}$$

The sectoral employment level is now determined, once the wage and the productivity trends are given:

(II) $\dot{N} = [I - A]^{-1} [(B - C - I)\dot{\varphi} + (A - B + C) \cdot \dot{W} + \dot{E}]$

Two general conclusions emerge:

First, a priori there exists *no general result* for the effects of greater productivity ($\Delta\varphi > 0$) on employment: depending on the values of price and income elasticities and the weight of the sectors, they may be positive and negative.

Second, this link may itself *depend on the wage formation mechanism*. On one side, imagine a constant wage – i.e. independent of productivity – and high price elasticities by comparison with income elasticities: intuitively, up to a certain threshold, more productivity will bring more employment to the sector and the whole economy (look at matrix $(B - C - I)$.

On the other hand, if for each sector the wage varies in line with productivity (i.e. $\Delta\dot{W} = \Delta\dot{\varphi}$), then the elasticity of the employment is unambiguously negative and equal to -1: as the competitive edge of each sector is cancelled out, only the accounting and negative impact remains.

To illustrate these conclusions, two extreme cases will be considered.

Case 1 The prices are sensitive to productivity increases, but wages are not
For simplicity's sake, and in order to derive some algebraïc results, the weight of each sector will be assumed to be identical (i.e. $r_i = \frac{1}{n}$). By (*I*), if productivity changes by $\Delta \varphi_i$, then employment varies according to:

$$\forall i 1 \leqslant i \leqslant n, \Delta \dot{N}_i =$$

$$-\Delta \dot{\varphi}_i + \frac{\varepsilon_R^i}{n} \sum_{i=1}^{i=n} \Delta \dot{N}_i + \varepsilon_p^i \Delta \varphi_i - (\varepsilon_p^i - \varepsilon_R^i) \cdot \sum_{i=1}^{i=n} (\bar{c}_i . \Delta \varphi_i)$$

Then, by summing these n relations, total employment ΔN_T is given by

(III) $\quad \Delta N_T = \frac{1}{1 - M \varepsilon_R} \cdot \left[-\sum_{i=1}^{i=n} \Delta \varphi_i + \sum_{i=1}^{i=n} \varepsilon_p^i . \Delta \varphi_i - \sum_{i=1}^{i=n} \varepsilon_p^i - \varepsilon_R^i \quad \sum_{i=1}^{i=n} \bar{c}_i \Delta \varphi_i \right]$

with $M \varepsilon_R = \sum_{i=1}^{i=n} \frac{\varepsilon_R^i}{n}$

Suppose that the productivity increases take place only in sector 1 ($\Delta \varphi_i = 0$ for all i except $1 \Delta \varphi_i = 1$), the different effects can be detailed:

(IV) $\quad \Delta N_T = \frac{1}{1 - M \varepsilon_R} \cdot \left[\varepsilon_p^1 - \qquad 1 + n . \bar{c}_1. \qquad M(\varepsilon_R - \varepsilon_p) \right]$

spill over from sector 1 to others due to income effects	differential competitive effect	mechanical effect	the price deceleration in 1 increases real income and demand of all goods	relative price varies inversely with the demand for other goods
	(positive)	(negative)	(positive)	(negative)
	Employment in sector 1		Employment in sectors other than 1	

Such a *simplistic* model shows that no less than five different mechanisms are at work producing the final outcome. The likelihood of a positive influence of more efficient technologies introduced into a sector on aggregate employment is larger:

— the higher the price elasticity in this sector (ε_p^I)
— the greater its weight in total consumption (c_I)
— the higher the income elasticities (ε_R) and the lower the price elasticities in all the other sectors (ε_p).

Hence the *heterogeneity of possible effects of technical progress*.

— If process innovations are introduced in sectors with high monopoly power and small size (ε_p^I and $\bar{c}_I$ small), then the effects are negative. This may correspond to *high tech* sectors.

If, on the contrary, they occur within more *traditional sectors* with significant price competition and large weight in the consumption pattern, while more modern sectors are developing (i.e. with high income elasticities), then productivity benefits job creation.

So the naïve views, either pessimistic or optimistic, do not reflect the actual complexity of the problem, especially since many other mechanisms could be built into this first model: role of non-wage incomes, investment dynamics, and so on.

Let us now extend the model in another direction. The previous one was only relying on relative prices for new technology diffusion. What happens if now wage-incomes benefit from productivity increases?

Case 2 All wages vary according to productivity in key sectors
Many studies have shown the leading role of modern oligopolistic sectors in average wage formation (see for example J. Eatwell *et al.*, 1974 and R. Boyer, J. Mistral, 1983). The model can be expanded to treat this case by adding the following wage equation:

(8) $\forall i, \ 1 \leqslant i \leqslant n \ \dot{W}_i = \dot{W} = \dot{p}_c + \lambda \varphi_I$

Where I is the index for the leading sector in wage formation. Equation (I) now simplies into:

(IV) $\dot{N}_i = (\varepsilon_R^i - \varepsilon_p^i) \cdot \lambda \varphi_I + \varepsilon_R^i \cdot \left[\sum_{i=1}^{i=n} \dot{N}_i \right] + (\varepsilon_p^i - 1) \cdot \varphi_i$

By direct summation over i, one gets the reduced form equation for total employment:

(V) $\dot{N}_T = \dfrac{n \cdot M(\varepsilon_R - \varepsilon_p)}{(1 - n \cdot M \varepsilon_R)} \cdot \lambda \varphi_I + \dfrac{\sum \varphi_i(\varepsilon_p^- - 1)}{1 - n \cdot M \varepsilon_R}$

As expected, productivity increases have *different effects depending on whether they occur in the leading sector or the others*. For every non-leading sector:

(VI) $\dfrac{\Delta N_T}{\Delta \varphi_i} = \dfrac{\varepsilon_p^i - 1}{1 - n \cdot M \varepsilon_R} \quad \forall i \neq I \quad 0 < i \leqslant n$

For probable values of ε_R (usually near 1), new technologies improve aggregate employment only if the price elasticities are inferior to 1. The conclusion is the opposite to that reached above when the nominal wage was held constant. For the key-sector I:

$$\text{(VII)} \quad \frac{\Delta N_T}{\Delta \varphi_1} = \frac{n.M(\varepsilon_R - \varepsilon_p) + \varepsilon_p^1}{1 - n.M\varepsilon_R}$$

Contrary to the effect in the 'normal' sectors, high price elasticity in sectors other than I produce a positive influence of productivity increases on total employment.

Hence a central conclusion emerges. The *same* technology may have opposite effects according to: the characteristics of demand and the size of the sector in which this change takes place; the mechanisms of productivity diffusion, the impact being quite different if the effects are transmitted through relative price, wage differentiation or average wage increases.

References

Aglietta, M. (1976) *Régulation et crises du capitalisme* (Paris: Calmann-Lévy). American edition (1981) *Regulation and Crisis of Capitalism* (New York: Monthly Review Books).
Balasko, Y. and Boyer, R. (1984) 'Employment, increasing returns and technical progress' (mimeo. CEPREMAP, Paris).
Barro, R. J., Grossman, H. I. (1971) 'A general Equilibrium Model of Income and Employment', *American Economic Review*, 61, 3, March.
Benassy, J. P. (1982) *The Economics of Market Disequilibrium* (New York: Basic Books).
Benassy, J. P., Boyer, R., Gelpi, R. M. (1979) 'Régulation des économies capitalistes et inflation', *Revue Economique*, 30, 3, mai.
Bertrand, H. (1983) 'Accumulation, régulation, crise: un modèle sectionnel théorique et appliqué', *Revue Economique*, 34, 2, mars.
Boyer, R. (1979) 'Wage formation in historical perspective: the French experience', *Cambridge Journal of Economics*, 3, March.
Boyer, R. (1984) 'Productivité et emploi dans le BTP', in *Plan construction et Habitat. Le travail en Chantiers: Actes du Colloque* (Paris: Ministère de l'Urbanisme, du Logement et des Transports).
Boyer, R. (1985a) 'Flexibilités des marchés du travail... et/ou recherche d'un nouveau rapport salarial?' (Paris: Note CEPREMAP, 8522, septembre).
Boyer, R. (1985b) 'Les approches en terme de régulation: présentation et problèmes de méthode' (Paris: Note CEPREMAP, 8523, juillet).
Boyer, R. (ed.) (1986a) *Capitalismes fin de siècle* (Paris: P.U.F.).
Boyer, R. (ed.) (1986b) *La flexibilité du travail en Europe: Une étude comparative des transformations du rapport salarial dans sept pays de 1973 à 1985* (Paris: La Découverte).
Boyer, R., Mistral, J. (1983) *Accumulation, inflation, crises*, 2nd edn (Paris: P.U.F.).

Boyer, R., Petit, P. (1980) 'Technical progress, industrial growth and employment: an essay in generalizing the Kaldor's law', (mimeo., Paris: CEPREMAP) presented at the Seminar On Policy on Choices for the European Community held in Sicily, 22–26 September.
Boyer, R., Petit, P. (1981a) 'Employment and productivity in the E.E.C.', *Cambridge Journal of Economics*, 5, 1, March.
Boyer, R., Petit, P. (1981b) 'Forecasting the impact of technical change on employment: methodological reflections and proposals for research', in *Relations between Technology Capital and Labour* (eds) Diettrich and Morley (Bruxelles: Commission of the European Communities).
Boyer, R., Petit, P. (1981c) 'Progrès technique, croissance et emploi: un modèle d'inspiration kaldorienne pour six industries européennes', *Revue Economique*, 32: 6, November.
Boyer, R., Petit, P. (1981) 'Le progrès technique dans la crise: ses déterminants, son impact sur l'emploi' (mimeo., Paris: CEPREMAP) juillet.
Boyer, R., Ralle, P. (1986) 'Croissances nationales et contrainte extérieure, avant et après 1973', *Economie et Sociétés*, Série P, 29.
Cassassuce, P., Hollard, M., Margirier, G. (1985) 'Nouveaux procès de production et implications macro-économiques. Contribution au débat sur la flexibilité', (Grenoble: Communication aux VIIIème journées des équipes d'Economie du travail CNRS, 24–25 octobre).
C.E.P.I.I. (1984) *Economie mondiale: la montée des tensions* and 1980–1990: *la fracture?* (Paris: Economica).
Coriat, B. (1982) *L'atelier et le chronomètre*, 2nd edn (Paris: Bourgois).
Coriat, B. (1983) *La robotique* (Paris: La Découverte/Maspéro).
Coriat, B. (1984) 'Crise et électronisation de la production: robotisation d'atelier et modèle fordien d'accumulation du capital', *Critiques de l'Economie Politique*, 26/27, janvier–juin.
Denison, E. F. (1979) *Accounting for slower economic growth: The United States in the 1970s* (Washington D.C.: Brookings Institution).
Denison, E. F. (1983) 'The interruption of productivity growth in the United States', *Economic Journal*, 93, March.
D'Iribarne, Ph. (1986) 'Régulation sociale, vie des entreprises et performances économiques', *Revue Economique*, forthcoming.
Dosi, G., Orsenigo, L. (1985) 'Market processes, rules and institutions in technical change and economic dynamics' (SPRU, University of Sussex), May.
Eatwell, J., Llewlyn, J. and Tarling, R. (1974) 'Money wage in industrial countries', *Review of Economic Studies*, 41(4), 128, October.
F.E.R.E. (1984) *Les transformations du rapport salarial depuis une décennie* (F.E.R.E., 1, rue Descartes, Paris).
Forrester, J. W. (1977) 'Growth Cycles', *de Economist*, 125(4).
Freeman, C. (1982) *The Economics of Industrial Innovation* (London: Frances Pinter).
Freeman, C. (1984) *Long waves in the world economy* (London: Frances Pinter).
Freeman, C., Clark, J. A. and Soete, L. C. (1982) *Unemployment and technical innovation: a study of long waves and economic development* (London: Frances Pinter).

Fuss, M., McFadden, D. (1979) 'Flexibility versus efficiency in ex ante plant design', in Fuss, M., McFadden, D. (eds) *Production Economics: A dual approach to theory and applications*, vol. 1 (Amsterdam: North Holland).
Keynes, J. M. (1919) *The Economic Consequences of the Peace, Collected Writing* (London: Macmillan, vol. IX, 1971).
Keynes, J. M. (1931) *Essays in Persuasion* (London: Macmillan).
Kondratieff, N. D. (1979) 'The long waves in economic life', reprinted in *Lloyds Bank Review* II, 4, Spring.
Lancaster, K. J. (1971) *Consumer Demand: A new approach* (New York: Columbia University Press).
Luciani, J. (1985) 'L'adaptation du système productif français de la fin du XIXème siècle aux variations périodiques de l'activité économique. Une approche historique de la flexibilité', (Grenoble: Contribution aux VIIème journées des équipes d'économie du travail CNRS, 24–25 octobre).
Malinvaud, E. (1977) *The theory of Unemployment Reconsidered* (Oxford: Basil Blackwell).
Maurice, M., Sellier, S., Sylvestre, J. J. (1982) *Politique d'éducation et organisation industrielle en France et en Allemagne* (Paris: P.U.F.).
Mensch, G. (1979) *Stalemate in technology* (Cambridge: Cambridge University Press).
Mensch, G., Kaasch, K., Kleinknecht, A., Schnopp, R. (1980) 'Innovation trends and switching between full and under employment equilibria' (discussion paper: International Institute of Management, Berlin).
Michl, T. (1985) 'International comparisons of productivity growth Verdoorn's law revisited', *Journal of Post Keynesian Economics*, 7: 4.
Nelson, R., Winter, S. (1982) *An evolutionary Theory of Economic Change* (Cambridge, Mass.: Harvard University Press).
Perez, C. (1981) 'Structural change and assimilation of new technologies in the economic and social systems', *Futures* 15: 5, October.
Petit, P. (1985) *Slow Growth and the Service Economy* (London: Frances Pinter).
Piore, M., Sabel, C. (1984) *The second industrial divide: possibilities of prosperity* (New York: Basic Books).
Pratten, C. F. (1976) *Labour productivity differentials within international companies* (Cambridge: Cambridge University Press).
Real, B. (1984) 'Progrès technique, économie et crise' (Université de Grenoble: IREP).
Sabel, C. (1983) 'From Austro-Keynesianism to flexible specialization...', Paper delivered at the Oesterreichische Nationalbank, Vienna, May 10.
Sabel, C., Piore, M. (1985) *The new Industrial divide* (New York: Basic Books).
Salter, W. E. G. (1960) *Productivity and technological change* (Cambridge: Cambridge University Press).
Schumpeter, J. A. (1912) *Theorie der wirtschaftlichen Entwicklung*, English translation *Theory of Economic Development* (Cambridge, Mass.: Harvard University Press, 1934).
Schweitzer, S. (1982) *Des engrenages à la chaîne. Les usines CITROEN 1915–1935* (Lyon: Presses Universitaires de Lyon).

Van Duijn, J. J. (1982) *The long wave in economic life* (London: G. Allen & Unwin).
Weisskopf, T., Bowles, S., Gordon, D. E. (1983) 'Hearts and Minds: a social model of US productivity growth', *Brookings Papers on Economic Activity*, 2.
Weitzman, M. (1984) *The Share Economy* (Cambridge, Mass.: Harvard University Press).

COMMENT

Arndt Sorge

I am happy to say that I am in general agreement with Robert Boyer's highly competent paper on technical change and employment. I will therefore present a number of smaller criticisms and clarifications. These will point towards a number of loop-holes in the economic theory and empirical evidence on the subject-matter. As several speakers have already noted, such questions can only be answered on the basis of research rooted in sociology and political science.

What is the barrier to full employment that is being addressed by Boyer? It may appear that it is technical change. It leads to productivity increases which, other things being equal, restrict demand for labour. On the other hand, technical change may also be linked with production increases that counter-balance the effect arising from productivity increases. The author refers to Verdoorn's Law which summarises a lot of evidence postulating a positive relationship between productivity increases and production increases. In this view, technical change would be neutral with regard to employment. Furthermore, it would have a positive employment effect if production rises faster than productivity and a negative effect if a fall in the rate of increase in production is greater than the fall in the rate of productivity increase.

Now, Boyer says that events of the 1970s have brought Verdoorn's Law into question. He conjectures that the positive relationship between productivity increase and production increase may have become more tenuous or disappeared. Let us examine the evidence presented by Boyer and others more closely.

International figures for productivity increases may be affected by changes in the number of hours worked per week and, more specifically, by changes in the share of part-time employment. Such changes are known to have taken place, above all in a country like Sweden. Depending on their extent, they may seriously disturb time-series comparisons of productivity per persons employed, such as those based on OECD-statistics which are presumably those quoted by the author. Productivity changes should be relative to hours worked in order to be meaningful in the present context.

Cross-country comparisons may yield results that are different from *sectoral* comparisons and comparisons *over time*. The question now is validity of Verdoorn's Law in comparisons across sectors and, specifically, in sectors over time. My impression is that this is not so. It still appears to be true that, by and large, sectors with faster-growing output will also have greater productivity increases. We cannot simply do away with Verdoorn's Law.

But there still seems to be a case for an increasingly tenuous relationship between productivity increases and production increases. A number of studies have investigated the ratio of the capacity effect of investment to the rationalisation effect of investment (Mensch *et al.*, 1980; Ifo, 1978). New investment has contributed more to raising productivity than to expanding productive capacity. It appears that in many countries, with the decline in rates of growth, the slow-down of output growth has been greater than the slow-down of productivity increase (Sorge, 1985, ch. 4.1). It should be noted that new technology has not brought about a rise in the rate of productivity increase but a slow-down which was, however, not large enough to compensate for the slow-down in real output growth. This description does not apply to all countries, notably not to the United States. The USA has had smaller rates of growth than before, but largely stagnant productivity at the macro-level.

In many countries of Europe, and particularly in Germany, the trend has been more clearly one of production increases slowing down more than productivity increases. The changing ratio of the rationalisation effect of investment with regard to its capacity effects can thus be offered as a well-corroborated way to define a barrier to full employment. But this barrier is not technical change as such. It appears more properly located in the economic context under which technical change occurs.

How can technical change now be related more directly to these changes in economic parameters? Without going into detail, I do not think that there is much point in reviving Kondratieff cycles and relating them to the frequency or quality of technical change at a given time. We do not have any evidence at all that the employment results we are discussing are linked with the frequency of technical innovation or some sort of quality that is necessarily inherent to new technology. Instead, I propose a more straightforward explanation.

Let us approach the problem, first, at the level of micro-economic units that develop, select, buy, install and apply new technology. A company may compete in the market by increasing its productivity, or by increasing its competitiveness through a qualitatively upgraded and more varied product range. These strategies may be congruent, but they may also conflict. In a very illuminating international comparison, Cox and Kriegbaum (1980) have suggested that the conflict between productivity and competitiveness has been over neglected in economic analyses. Productivity increase is to a large extent related to the exploitation of increasing returns to scale. This requires growing demand for a homogenous product and a concentration or specialisation in the product range. The opposite is true for the achievement of competitiveness: This requires a differentiation and qualitative upgrading, i.e. greater variation of the product range. The distinction dates back to Adam Smith who had already stressed the importance of the extent and growth of markets for economic growth. But productivity and competitiveness strategies are not only opposites but also to some extent congruent. A highly competitive firm (through product variation) may expand sales, and become more productive in due course. Also, a more productive firm may be able to invest more and become more competitive. Being neither purely conflictual nor congruent, the relationship between productivity and competitiveness may thus be characterised as dialectical.

The link of this micro view with a macro view is now the following. When the evolution of goods markets, because of reduced rates of growth and increasing problems in international trade, limits the share and extent of large and growing homogenous product markets, then strategies of companies will have to emphasise competitiveness more than in the past, in order to compensate productivity increases by real output increases that are at least as great. This seems to have been true for the past decade and more. This may be another way of defining what has become known as the strategy of flexible specialisation (Piore and Sabel, 1984).

The above analysis gives us a first idea of how to overcome the barrier of employment discussed. In simple terms, it has to be an answer to the question 'How do we get production increases to exceed productivity increases?' The simple answer is that companies have to become more able to meet existent demand which is more fragmented, quality-conscious and thus entails a more flexible production apparatus than in the past. To define the question in this way amounts to saying that demand manipulation is not the right answer to the problem. It also means that it would be silly to ask whether we need more or less technical change. Rather, we have to ask which are the organisational arrangements that permit firms to be more competitive in those kinds of markets that have recently emerged. It also means that we have to ask ourselves about the kinds of technical change that promote competitiveness rather than productivity alone. In this way, we can reverse the question about the employment 'effects' of technical change. We now inquire into the possibility of matching kinds of technical change, skills of people, education and training processes, the institutional context of company activities and forms of work organisation that are conducive to achieving a maximum competitiveness in relation to productivity.

References

Cox, J. G. and Kriegbaum, H. (1980) *Growth, Innovation and Employment: An Anglo-German Comparison* (London: Anglo-German Foundation for the Study of Industrial Society).

Ifo-Institut für Wirtschaftsforschung (1978) *Ifo-Schnelldienst*, 31/32 (München: Ifo-Institut).

Mensch, G., Kaasch, K., Kleinknecht, A. and Schnopp, R. (1980) *Innovation Trends and Switching Between Full and Underemployment Equilibria* (Berlin: International Institute of Management Discussion Paper 80–5).

Piore, M. and Sabel, C. (1985) *The New Industrial Divide* (New York: Basic Books).

Sorge, A. (1985) *Informationstechnik und Arbeit im sozialen Prozeß* (Frankfurt: Campus).

10 Environmental Problems and Employment Opportunities

Bertram Schefold

Economists offer a wide range of predictions regarding the employment effects of attempts to solve environmental problems. Assessments range from mild pessimism (restrictions to abate pollution contribute to unemployment) to dire warnings (the economic megamachine should not grow but shrink in order to avoid major calamities in the long run), and from pragmatic optimism (pollution abatement is a new industry) to promises of new life styles. There is something to be said for each of these opinions. They are to some extent conditional on theoretical considerations, but they depend much more on one's conception of environmental policy. And this, in turn, is motivated by one's perception of what might be feasible from the political, and desirable from the environmental, point of view. We therefore start with the latter question. We shall discuss the prospects for employment offered by actual environmental policies in section 2, and some more speculative ideas on future developments of environmental protection and employment will be presented in section 3.

1 ENVIRONMENTAL PROBLEMS

It is now almost generally accepted that the prosperity of the post-war period has not only led to increasing personal wealth, but also to many forms of pollution, to environmental losses and to the prospect of a possible depletion of various resources. Development involves, by its very definition, a process of creative destruction: new cultures are built on the ruins of old ones. The process of transformation has thus always affected the landscape and the environment. The neolithic replacement of virgin forests by agricultural land use and the irrigation systems of the old oriental empires remain among the largest artificial changes of eco-systems ever undertaken. Environmental change, destruction, and attempts to reverse it, are therefore not new. What is new, however, is the simultaneity and speed of a worldwide attempt at a global industrialisation with unforeseen consequences for the future availability of mineral resources, the supply of energy, the functioning of geochemical cycles, and the survival of biological species. Earlier transformations had been more limited in space and more extended in time so that traditions and legal, economic and social institutions could be found which allowed the preservation of equilibrium with nature. It usually lasted for many generations and was often only disturbed by exogenous influences.

It has repeatedly been asked whether the present mode of production could be sustained for long in view of potential environmental constraints (Malthus, Club of Rome). It is difficult to see how this question could be answered decisively in a system which is based on technological change. The prevailing opinion now is that the world economy will be able to adapt, even at some cost.

To substitute exhaustible mineral resources with other ones in adequate supply is, in a given state of technical knowledge, formally equivalent to a reversal of technical progress because the resource used for substitution would have been introduced before, if it had the same advantages as the resource it replaces. But actual technical progress may compensate this effect on the growth and distribution on income. There are reasons to believe that the exhaustibility of resources will not be a major constraint for a long time to come.

Supplies of energy are available; the question is whether their monetary costs (e.g. direct solar energy) or environmental costs (e.g. coal) are acceptable. The social costs may also be considerable. Energy will be a constraint to the extent that such costs limit its production.

It is clear that we are disrupting geochemical cycles. The climatic effects of sulphur dioxide (mainly released by coal-fired power stations) on forests, monuments, books, but also on human health, are a matter of great concern and there are moves to control them, even if slow ones, at least in some Western European countries. The disruption of another geochemical cycle, that of carbon dioxide, is much discussed; yet very little action seems to have been taken. The expected global climatic changes deriving from the release of this and other gases into the atmosphere now seem to be accepted by a number of authors as an inevitable outcome of present behaviour, with all the consequent impacts on regional weather patterns, the spatial distribution of food production, etc. In order to avoid taking major action now, the potential task of shifting population and agriculture is left to the future. I regard this attitude as alarming. The cycles are interlocked which renders both prognosis and control extremely difficult.

As a side-effect of production, particulate matter is being deposited in the soil (e.g. heavy metals); agriculture may within a few decades be endangered in much the same way as the forests now are. So far, these more complicated processes in advanced countries are still overshadowed by soil erosion which takes place mainly in less developed countries, including China.

Finally, I should like to mention the rapid loss of biological species, where the greatest destruction is probably associated with the felling of the tropical forests which are disappearing at a rate of one per cent per year.

The global consequences of all this are difficult to foresee. None of these developments is incompatible with further rises in the standard of living of at least some segments of the world population in terms of national income per head. On the other hand, it is not obvious, to say the least, that the outcome at the end of the next century, say, should be a fairly egalitarian worldwide distribution of resources at levels comparable to that of the most advanced nations today. (For more details and references see Schefold, 1985.)

The 'big' question of how mankind could survive, in the long run, was what awakened the public and the politicians to the necessity of implementing environmental policies. As Sieferle (1984) has shown, warnings against the destructive potential of the industrial system have been raised from its very beginnings, and the old criticism ranges from deploring the loss of the aesthetic qualities of a medieval world, shaped by farmers and artisans, to concrete proposals to subject technical progress to rational control. The most prominent member of the 'younger' historical school, Sombart, made an unfortunate appeal to the National Socialists to introduce what we should now call technology assessment (from the points of view of environmental and social compatibility), right at the time when they were preparing a massive mobilisation of modern technology in order to win military hegemony (Sieferle, 1984, p. 213). After the war, economists have been reminded of the side effects of industrial production by Kapp's (1950) pathbreaking work on the social costs of private enterprise. It did not at first have any practical consequences whatsoever.

But the environmental policies which have emerged lately focus on more immediate concerns. The German council of advisers on environmental issues (Sachverständigenrat für Umweltfragen) distinguished the following domains (Umweltgutachten, 1978) which may be rendered in abbreviated form as follows:

1. On the one hand, the 'basic domains' of environmental policy are to consist of:
   water management;
   the preservation of clean air;
   waste management;
   the avoidance of noise;
   food production (in particular control of the addition of artificial ingredients in food production);
   control of agricultural production, (in particular the use of fertilisers and pesticides).
2. On the other hand, three 'complex domains' are distinguished:
   the development of cities;
   the planning of traffic;
   the preservation of landscapes and of wilderness.

This list focuses on immediate practical concerns. The saving of resources is not treated as a primary target, and there is no complex domain 'energy production'.

Governments are now active in each of these domains. And this activity is popular. According to a survey (see Brunowsky and Wicke, 1984, p. 35), people are more ready to accept increases in public spending in domains related to environmental issues (including alternative energy sources) than in any other domain, with budget cuts being proposed in such domains as defence and support for the Third World. (This holds for the Federal Republic of Germany and for the United States, but not for the United Kingdom.)

The question whether the environmental policies now underway increase employment is empirical. Since it is impossible to separate all economic activities into those which are motivated, at least in part, by concern for environmental issues and those which are not, the employment effect can only be measured by asking what the effects of increased efforts to preserve the environment might be. The surveys show that there would be some readiness on the part of the public to accept increased efforts even if they are associated with higher fiscal outlays. I shall report on empirical findings concerning proposals to extend existing policies along given institutions (section 2), and I shall then discuss other forms of environmental policies, involving new institutions, which might address some of the larger issues mentioned above in relation to the problem of employment (section 3).

2 ENVIRONMENTAL POLICIES AND EMPLOYMENT

The principle of letting the polluter pay for the damage done makes sense not only according to orthodox neo-classical theory (internalisation of external effects) but (possibly within narrower limits) also according to other approaches. For the payment imposed (whether it is a tax or whatever the precise arrangement) creates an incentive to reduce the polluting activity either by abating the pollutant or, preferably, by using an alternative technology which prevents its occurrence. However, the polluter-pays principle can often not be employed because the complexity of the processes involved does not allow identification of an individual polluter or because he is situated in foreign territory. Frequently, foreign competition is such that the imposition of controls or of payments would result in a loss of market share. In the domestic sphere, the need served by the polluting industry could sometimes also be served by another, so that the former would lose part of its competitive position. The state will in such cases often be prepared to pay subsidies, and these will be justified precisely on the ground that they will allow an increase or at least preservation of employment. It has been argued that investments for environmental purposes are particularly well-suited to increase employment because the incomes they generate will have multiplier effects, without leading to important increases in productive capacity, and improve conditions for long-term growth.

Recent debates about the slow-down of productivity growth in the United States and about the sluggishness of investment in Europe have emphasised the role of environmental policy in retarding technical progress and accumulation. The attacks have focused especially on regulations; solutions making use of market instruments, such as licences, have been regarded as more acceptable. While I do not deny that the use of market instruments is often preferable (especially if they really offer a substantial saving of administrative effort), I believe that the controversy has often obscured the substantive issue: all forms of interference may retard the execution of development plans of both private and public firms. But at the same time they may provide incentives to introduce new technologies which circumvent the regulations or the cost of licences by avoiding pollution in any given industry, and such technical change may have beneficial secondary effects on technical progress in related areas and on employment. Regulations (if they are enforced) provide the clearest incentive to meet a uniform emission standard. Licences will allow a more flexible response by firms which is adequate if one starts from an overall emission standard (preferably to be reduced gradually), such that firms are allowed to share the emissions within that limit at a price to be determined in a market.

More direct links between environmental policies and employment have been established. W. Meissner and E. Hödl (1983) have proposed a programme to increase employment by means of public investment for the environment, taking due account of the possibility of financing the programme (UWIP). The plan compares UWIP with a recent programme for employment (Programm für Zukunfts-investitionen, ZIP) which was planned to have a volume of about 1800 million DM. A special concern was to propose an appropriate division of responsibilities in a State with a federal constitution such that the responsibility for the environment is not placed with the federal authorities. The programme lists seven domains in which investments are to be undertaken (waste water, air pollution, waste collection, noise protection, preservation of city centres, district heating, protection against erosion and inundations. The quality of environmental improvement to be obtained by means of the investment is uneven. Whereas, for instance, the reduction of air pollution is obviously highly desirable, the building of dams may be controversial.

It has been shown that the federal programme for the structural improvement of the economy through public investment (ZIP), used for comparison, yielded positive effects on employment. An input–output analysis showed that the direct effect on domestic production had been of the order of 1700 million DM, the indirect effect of 14 million, and that multiplier effects due to the spending of additional incomes on domestic consumption goods had been about equal to the direct effect. This yielded an increase in employment of about 450 000 man years which, given the ongoing recession, meant only in part an increase in actual employment; the other part constituted an avoidance of an increase in unemployment.

Using a comparison of the structure of the composition of the investment in the ZIP programme and the programme UWIP, Meissner and Hödl have argued that the latter would yield employment of a similar magnitude. They are careful to show that this would not be associated with bottlenecks in particular industries so that inflationary pressures could be avoided.

It is more difficult to estimate the effects on employment if one does not consider a programme involving additional investment, but the complex of existing measures to protect the environment composed of both regulations and subsidies and investment paid for by the State. The issue has been studied by Sprenger (1979) of the IFO-Institute who found positive effects on employment caused by measures to protect the environment in the Federal Republic of Germany of about 200 000 jobs per year (in 1975). Of these, a little more than one half are either created through public investment for the environment or in public administration. More than one third of the jobs are due to private investment, motivated by public legislation for environmental protection, or are permanently held by people who are directly employed by private industry to preserve the environment (Sprenger, 1979, p. 174). Later enquiries have confirmed this estimate. According to information issued in May 1985 by the Federal Ministry of the Interior there are now 410 420 people employed either directly (152 600) in administration, industry, public and private pollution abatement, waste management and research, or indirectly (257 820) through the demand for investment and goods for environmental protection both at home and abroad.

There remains the contention that there might be negative results on employment because of losses of competitive power, because investments are postponed or not executed in view of environmental regulations, or simply because of uncertainty concerning such regulations. Spokesmen of German industry have made much especially of the last argument. The measurement of the negative effects is a good deal more difficult than that of the positive ones. However, empirical estimates based on surveys indicate that the former are much smaller than the latter:

Table 10.1 Effects of Environmental Policies on Employment

Positive Effects	Negative Effects
150 000–370 000 jobs are created or at least secured for environmental protection through — investment, — permanent installations, — administration.	50 000–70 000 jobs can (at least temporarily) not be filled because investments are postponed, 50 000 jobs are declared lost to foreign investment because of more severe domestic environmental restrictions, 2000 jobs are lost yearly because environmental restrictions lead to increases in costs.

Source: Brunowsky and Wicke, 1984, p. 50.

The conclusion is therefore clear: The environmental policies which have so far been pursued, or moderate extensions which are being proposed, yield on balance positive effects on employment. The reason for this is not far to seek: investment programmes such as that by Meissner and Hödl are explicitly designed to serve both purposes – to preserve the environment and to create employment. The established environmental policy, on the other hand, always has had to take the interests of private industry and of workers into account. The result shows that a meaningful environmental policy can be pursued without drastically violating those interests.

It is easy to see that a more radical environmental policy could do damage to employment. If, for instance, the production of all known carcinogenic substances was forbidden without delay, the economic results would be catastrophic. A less trivial question is whether a more radical and intelligent environmental policy might be compatible with full employment.

To this end it would be highly desirable to be able to compare alternative strategies. The conventional procedure is to compare different situations characterised by a greater or lesser severity of regulations in terms of emission standards etc. This corresponds to the interpretation of pollution as an external effect, which is to be abated, in a general equilibrium system. But it is, from an environmental point of view, more interesting to avoid the emission of the pollutant in the first place. The main policy question then concerns investment, and the theoretical framework for such a perspective is that of the classical theory which focuses on accumulation with alternative technologies.

Alternative strategies have been discussed extensively in the case of energy. To clarify the idea it may be best first to summarise the procedure in a domain where it has already been successfully applied. 'The social compatibility of different energy systems in the development of industrialised societies' has been examined in a large research project, led by K. M. Meyer-Abich and myself, between 1980 and 1985. The desire to accelerate the substitution of oil, and exaggerated expectations of the industries concerned, had led to the publication of extremely ambitious programmes for the build-up of nuclear energy in Germany, with reprocessing and breeders as the future cornerstones of the energy system. Proposals of alternative energy sources allowed the formulation of different strategies for the substitution of oil which induced heated public debates. Apart from environmental objections, it was also argued (as it turned out, correctly) that the breeder system with its inherent dangers would make safe-guards necessary which in turn might jeopardise constitutional rights. The research project compared scenarios, worked out in great detail down to technological specifications. They showed how essentially the same level of material welfare could be reached on the one hand using a system with a growing share of nuclear power in energy production (including the expansion of the market for electricity to all forms of heating), or, on the other hand, following a scenario for the use of solar energy in all domains, especially in domestic heating. The amount of fossil fuel to be used was the same for both scenarios, only the applications differed according to the requirements of each.

The nuclear scenario (N) and the solar or savings scenario (S) were then described, with their technological characteristics, and it was asked which implications their implementation would have for the important aspects of social life, such as the economy (micro and macro, distribution, finance, degree of competition, economic policy), the legal system, and social values. Conversely, it was also asked which general developments of society regarding, for example, personal life-styles might favour the adoption of one or the other scenario.

In this way, it became possible to describe two paths for future development in one of the most important sectors of the economy, in great detail, over a period of fifty years. In a sense, this concerned the backbone of economic development, hence it was interesting to imagine and to evaluate the corresponding social evolution. Of course, it could not be said that the given technology determined the corresponding social life unilaterally. But, on the one hand, it was checked whether the likely implications of either scenario were compatible with existing values and institutions. On the other, it was also asked whether some development of the social framework, supported or wished by proponents of one of the technologies, was more plausible in the case of one of the scenarios rather than in the other.

Of the various results of the enquiry, only one will be summarised here. It had been expected that the scenario S would prove to be more expensive and that it would also create more employment than N, and that it might reduce international competitiveness. To check this, both scenarios were implemented in a large computer model with an input-output system for the non-energy sectors, with a macro-economic and government sub-model and with an activity analysis sub-model for the various technologies in the energy sectors. Choosing appropriate assumptions for the development of international trade, of limits to government expenditure and of population, further by using alternative plausible assumptions about the development of future foreign energy prices and by imposing the corresponding energy technologies according to each scenario, the economic growth rates of the scenarios and the build-ups of the energy system could be reproduced. The impact on international competitiveness could thus not be predicted, it had to be assumed equal for both scenarios. But the model showed that the total accumulated costs of both energy systems was virtually the same, and the employment generated according to each differed only by marginal amounts. There were significant differences in the distribution of investment over time, and they turned out to imply crucial differences regarding the structure, the financing and the sectoral effects on employment, which were mirrored in the investors themselves. (To simplify: big utilities as investors in the case of N versus a large number of small house owners in the case of S). The structural differences had many policy implications, but the macroeconomic effect on employment, which is alone of interest here, was the same. The scenario assumptions have thus turned out to imply a persistence of the present rates of high unemployment until the turn of the century, and a return to full employment thereafter.

The result shows that two strategies which have each – though on very different grounds – been advocated for environmental reasons, may have the same effect on employment. The similarity of the total costs and of the employment effects will appear less surprising if it is recognised that the scenario construction involved an implicit prior attempt to define efficient combinations of technologies both for N and for S. Each has its environmental characteristics. Nuclear power, though associated with high risks (especially in the case of the breeder), does, so to speak, little damage to the landscape per unit of electricity produced because it is a very concentrated form of power generation while hydro-electricity, windmills and other forms of direct solar power may diminish the aesthetic value and the agricultural use of a landscape and imply many risks which are, however, individually and even collectively smaller. (It may be remarked that our report recommends S without ruling out a limited use of light water reactors.)

The conclusion is that to look at environmental policy in terms of investment strategies is important, and that if it is done, the consequences for domestic employment will always be a relevant consideration. The coincidence of equal employment effects of rival strategies will not often be repeated. An important example in a related area where more research in terms of a comparison of different scenarios ought to be done is provided by coal-fired power stations. They should disappear according to the principle of avoiding the pollution-generating technologies in the first place. Yet, in order to maintain a domestic energy reserve, but more importantly because of social considerations, the coal-pits cannot all be closed, and State subsidies will have to be paid not only for the mining of the coal but also to introduce the appropriate abatement technologies for both sulphur and nitrogen oxides in the power plants. Elsewhere, I have proposed alternative strategies for the reduction of the pollution of the soil. Since the energy sector is here, too, the most important single polluter, this would involve, among other things, an assessment of well-known alternative energy strategies, but this time with regard to their effects on soil quality and agricultural productivity.

3 SOME WIDER CONSIDERATIONS

It has thus been established that environmental policies do not necessarily kill jobs, and that the policies actually pursued, moderate as they are, help to increase employment. As already indicated in the beginning, however, it is by no means clear that we are doing enough to prevent a bleak outcome in the long run. Let me state frankly a value judgement which is likely to be shared. I regard the impact of the modern form of industrialisation, both on cities and the countryside, as ugly and deplorable, and the destruction of historic monuments and the loss of beautiful sceneries as sad. One does not have to have seen a whale to regret their disappearance. I do mind the disappearance of butterflies. I am worried, therefore, not only about environmental catastrophes which might happen, but also about what has already happened. The aesthetic considerations which lead to this judgement are important in themselves, and, perhaps, they may even have some utilitarian value. For they are based on feelings which are more complicated expressions of the simple and plausible suggestion that what is bad for the forest might also be bad for myself.

The primary concern, then, must be to force the recognition of environmental constraints not only at the periphery of the industrial process, by abating damages or by occasionally subsidising the abandonment of harmful technologies, but by convincing the economic agents to anticipate negative outcomes by pursuing preventive strategies, and, eventually, to shape the process of production and consumption according to different standards. In our book *Work without Environmental Destruction (Arbeit ohne Umweltzerstörung*, Binswanger, *et al.*, 1983) we have proposed to extend the field of application of direct regulations, but mainly of taxes and licences for pollutants, to introduce a special tax on energy, and to measure the success not in terms of national income accounting but by means of various indicators. The price system at present is such that energy is relatively cheap, recycling is not worthwhile and the chief consideration of enterprises are wage costs. Under these circumstances, the investment is usually associated with innovations which increase the productivity of labour. The point is to create different incentives and to encourage innovations which save resources, recycle waste and reduce pollutants (Leipert and Simonis, 1985).

A number of theoretical arguments may be raised against this simplified view of induced investment, but these are not my concern here. While such measures may go some way to enlarge the impact of existing environmental policies, they are quite obviously not qualitatively different. One realises that the environment is a public good and that national accounting does not measure losses of welfare due to environmental destruction (often, destruction leads, like the building of an unnecessary motorway, to an increase of GNP). The conclusion most often advocated then is to extend the market by demanding a price (e.g. in form of a tax) for the emission of a pollutant. While this may be a useful instrument to cope with a significant, but small number of pollutants or, more generally, with some negative effects on the environment, it seems obvious to me that the list so established will not only never be complete but that it is likely to remain substantially incomplete. It may not be a good remedy to increase the associated bureaucracy accordingly, if only in proportion to the length of the list and not according to some Parkinsonian law of diminishing returns to bureaucratic efforts. Such strategies are useful only up to a point.

Past remedies like the proposals to limit the rate of growth of the economy are certainly not topical in the present situation. On the other hand, I should not regard a return to high growth rates as very desirable either. But they do not seem likely to emerge, and meanwhile it is clear that the quality of the composition of output matters more than the rate at which output grows.

Policy-minded economists do not like to be told (and perhaps they are the wrong persons to be addressed in this matter) that we shall not be able to make much progress unless the measures proposed above are accompanied by changes in social values. For if we do not want to restrict our attention to the few pollutants which actually threaten our survival, so many other effects come into view that they cannot be taken into account except at the level of decentralised decision taking. This presupposes not only personal awareness, judgement and the readiness to accept responsibility but also an institutional decentralisation of decision taking. What we need is a gradual parallel transformation of social values, technologies and of the social, legal, and economic constitution which would allow realisation of a different life style.

I have suggested elsewhere what such a different economic style might involve (Meyer-Abich and Schefold, 1981, 1985). Different economic 'styles' (as they were called by the German historical school) can be associated with the same economic system (market or planning, working for wages or slavery etc.). Though identical as economic systems, the United States and Great Britain were very different in the nineteenth century as economic styles, each with characteristic dynamic economic forces, with characteristic social values, legal and social constitutions involving specific institutions such as trade unions. There was an interplay between those aspects in the economic development of each.

The economic style is recognised best in the way in which repeated conflicts are resolved according to established traditions within any one society. The primary modern example is that of the opposition between the principle of efficiency which rules in the market and that of redistribution which governs social security. The economic styles of different European countries are similar today in this respect but the present compromise between efficiency and the distribution is quite different from that prevailing in the middle of the last century.

I suggest that the increased concern for environmental issues, forced upon society today through a necessity analogous to that of the social question in the last century, will lead to a change in economic style. One aspect of this change is a different perception of the importance of work, not in all, but in relevant segments of population. Surveys prove that attitudes to work have shifted considerably (Klipstein and Strümpel, 1985). While people still want to hold jobs, the identification with the work place is less straightforward and material aspirations have a reduced priority. At the same time, there is more interest in local communication, and the concern for the environment is more marked. People who do not find regular employment are more often ready to lead an independent existence, alone or in groups, and to accept State subsidies (including unemployment benefits) in order to pursue alternative forms of domestic production, to farm on a small plot in the countryside, to help in the healthcare system, to try some simple form of handicraft production or to pursue some other meaningful activity.

One has therefore spoken of a dual, or of an 'informal' sector of the economy which emerges and absorbs part of the unemployed labour force, for instance, some not very successful (and some of the most successful) drop outs of the university system. We have experimented with this idea in the energy project on the assumption that it gains general recognition: the dual sector is supposed to mitigate the problem of unemployment while the tasks pursued are, on the whole, rather harmless or even beneficial and creative from the environmental point of view. There is therefore some justification for giving more support to the dual sector and to letting it grow further. A likely impact for social values would be that concern for environmental questions would increase.

We have even implemented such a scenario of changing social values with a growing dual sector in the energy model. The result was very straightforward: while the effect on energy consumption was negligible, the existence of the dual sector with its subsidy worked like a Keynesian employment programme. The labour force for industrial employment was reduced while the subsidy, through multiplier effects, increased the demand for industrial labour so that a transition to full employment took place, and the dual sector in due course tended to eliminate itself.

This paradoxical result might not be reproduced in reality for many reasons which do not have to be discussed here. The aim of the exercise was not to propose a unique strategy for the solution of the environmental and employment problems, but to illustrate that there are further important fields for action which increase the number of possibilities at our disposal. Industrial employment nowadays is not always and everywhere such that it can be recommended as a primary goal in life for everybody. I still see advantages in providing some support for a dual sector both for its own sake (if the tasks pursued are meaningful) and because the variety of occupations and activities is enhanced and the understanding for different life styles is likely to grow. It is clear that authoritarian societies find it more difficult to tolerate dual sectors than democratic ones.

But however this may be, the dual sector is at most a special aspect of the more general problem of how an economic style might be generated which would resolve the environmental problem more satisfactorily than in the post-war period, in the same sense that social questions are resolved more satisfactorily today than one hundred years ago.

References

Binswanger, H. C., Frisch, H., Nutzinger, H. G., Schefold, B. Scherhorn, G., Simonis, U. E., Strümpel, B. (1983) *Arbeit ohne Umweltzerstörung* (Frankfurt am Main: Fischer).

Brunowsky, R. D., Wicke, L. (1984) *Der Öko-Plan* (München: Piper).

Kapp, K. W. (1950) *The Social Cost of Private Enterprise* (Harvard: Harvard University Press).

Klipstein, M. V., Strümpel, B. (1984) *Der Überdruß an Überfluß – Die Deutschen nach dem Wirtschaftswunder* (München: Olzog).

Leipert, C., Simonis, U. E. (1985) 'Arbeit und Umwelt', (mimeo., Int. Institut für Umwelt und Gesellschaft, Berlin).

Meissner, W., Hödl, E. (1983) 'Umweltschutz in Konjunktur- und Wachstumsprogrammen', in *Auftrag des Umweltbundesamts* (Berlin: Erich Schmidt Verlag).

Meyer-Abich, K. M., Schefold, B. (1981) *Wie möchten wir in Zukunft leben* (München: Beck Verlag).

Meyer-Abich, K. M., Schefold, B. (1985) 'Die Sozialverträglichkeit verschiedener Energiesysteme in der industriegesellschaftlichen Entwicklung', *Bericht an den Bundesminister für Forschung und Technologie*, Band 1: 'Übersicht über die Methoden und Ergebnisse des Forschungsprojekts', (mimeo.: Frankfurt).

Schefold, B. (1985) 'Ecological Problems as a Challenge to Classical and Keynesian Economics', *Metroeconomica*, 37: 1.

Sieferle, R. P. (1984) *Fortschrittsfeinde? Opposition gegen Technik und Industrie von der Romantik bis zur Gegenwart* (München: Beck Verlag).

Sprenger, R. G. (1979) *Beschäftigungseffekte der Umweltpolitik* (Berlin: Duncker and Humblot).

COMMENT

Peter Nijkamp

INTRODUCTION

The issue of employment effects of environmental policies is still an unresolved question in economics. The paper by Bertram Schefold is a welcome contribution to this old problem. On the basis of (limited) empirical evidence and a (mainly) qualitative scenario analysis, he arrives at the conclusion that pollution abatement strategies are not necessarily in contrast with employment policies. The author presents also an imaginative strategy for a different economic style, in which the dual sector plays a dominant role. But the author points also to the fact that the question whether environmental policies affect employment in a positive or a negative sense is very much an empirical one. In my reflection on this contribution, I will in particular call attention to the measurement problems of the impacts of pollution abatement strategies on the labour market.

A PARALLEL

The question whether environmental policies will affect employment conditions bears a certain similarity to the question whether new technologies have an impact on employment. At a macro level the net effect is difficult to measure, as we may have simultaneously labour-saving and labour-augmenting technological change. In addition, the employment effects of new technologies are difficult to separate, as we may have both embodied and disembodied technological progress. Consequently, many studies demonstrate that at a *macro* level a precise assessment of such effects is hard to make.

However, at a *micro* level much more can be said. First, we may observe that in specific production processes some jobs will be killed and in others new ones will be created. But a more interesting and important phenomenon is that in almost all cases – in spite of sometimes undecisive answers on the order of magnitude of the net macro effects – *qualitative* changes will occur, for instance, an increased demand for more specialised and highly trained personnel.

Apart from quantitative shifts, such qualitative structural changes are likely to take place also in the environmental sector. The most important question is perhaps not 'more or less jobs?', but 'which types of jobs?'. Unfortunately, this social distributional issue has so far received hardly any attention in empirical research.

SIZE OF THE ENVIRONMENTAL SECTOR

In most industrialised countries the environmental management sector has exhibited a steady growth in the past decade. Some figures from the Netherlands may illustrate the order of magnitude of the environmental sector. At present, the annual costs of the environmental abatement and management sector in the Netherlands amounts to approximately 4000 million Hfl. (approximately 1600 million US dollars). Per inhabitant this is over 100 dollars per year. These costs cover all areas: water, air, soil, noise, waste, etc., and are related to management costs, control costs, recycling, etc.

Of course, it is easy to predict that this large amount of financial resources has a significant impact on employment. But two questions have to be raised in this respect: (i) what would have been the employment effects if the same amount would have been used for alternative uses? and (ii) what is the impact of pollution abatement costs on the competitive position (and hence on the long-run market position and employment conditions) of firms?

There is some empirical evidence on the first question which suggests that in many cases the environmental management sector is fairly labour intensive, so that one may expect that – in terms of opportunity costs – the employment effects of the environmental sector are positive. The second question is even more difficult to answer. There is however limited empirical evidence from Japan that strict pollution standards have led to an adjusted technology which caused a comparative advantage with respect to other countries, so that after some time – when also other nations accepted more strict environmental regulations – the Japanese industry could much more efficiently compete on the international market.

A GENERAL ANALYSIS FRAMEWORK

The environmental sector is not a homogeneous sector. It is made up of various components, as it can be subdivided according to:

1. different interest groups, such as environmentalists, industrialists, etc.
2. different institutional–spatial fields, such as the central government, regional authorities with a decentralised competence, etc.
3. different economic sectors with different technologies and environmental effects, such as the primary sector, the secondary sector (subdivided into industrial branches), etc. In order to assess simultaneously the positive and negative effects of environmental policies, an integrated framework is necessary which links in a coherent and consistent way together all interest groups, national-regional decision fields, and industrial sectors, so as to be able to gauge simultaneously all employment effects (positive and negative).

This framework has formed the basis for a large-scale empirical study for the Netherlands, in which the above mentioned 3 modules were dealt with as follows:

1. the conflicting issues of interest groups were taken into account by means of a multiple objective programming framework.
2. the national-regional aspects were taken into account by means of multi-regional model reflecting the spatial subdivisions and spatial interactions of the system concerned (including pollution in the successive regions).
3. the various economic sectors were included via an input-output framework for approximately 30 sectors, at both the national and regional level.

In this way, a consistent framework for assessing the employment impacts (at a sectoral, and at both a national and regional level) could be designed and operationalised. By developing various future scenarios, the labour market effects for various alternative futures could be gauged.

AN OUTLOOK

A necessary condition for attaining more insight into the complex relationship between environment and employment is micro-based entrepreneurial research. Such disaggregate research with a more rigorous behavioural basis is of utmost importance for gaining insight into both the quantitative and qualitative employment aspects of environmental management.

Klaus Zimmermann

At the conclusion of this paper, Professor Schefold looks at the growth of the dual system, comparing its effects on the environment with the positive impacts of the social security system on the solution to the so-called social question. This comparison presents an interesting argument which deserves greater consideration. Both aspects, environment and social security, focus on securing the future. In an individualistic system, securing the future means that we save today and accumulate wealth; in the future, when we get older, we can live from this acquired wealth or, better still, on the interest payments generated from the money we saved through production processes employing the latest technical advancements.

In a collectivistic system, voluntary saving is replaced by compulsory saving. Individual provision for the future is replaced by a kind of collective apportionment. Such a system is not oriented towards the future, but rather towards the present or, more accurately, to points of time, because at every instant the actively employed must raise sufficient money to support the retired. Difficulties arise if one generation fails to support the retired and instead seeks full self-fulfilment in an age of emancipation.

A similar problem arises with employment programmes, even those with an environmental policy component. Since democratic political systems generally cannot ignore the demands of the present, there is no alternative other than acting in a protectionistic manner to cope with the unemployment problem. This means launching employment programmes to protect the standard of living and social benefits of the actively employed – i.e., guaranteeing wage level demands and social benefits which, in relation to interest rates, are obviously too high. This represents the main cause of the 'classic' problem of unemployment (Malinvaud, 1982; for recent empirical evidence see: Kirkpatrick, 1982; Sachs, 1983; Grubb *et al.*, 1983; Belassa, 1984).

Aside from the fact that this solution would be incorrect – namely, applying a Keynesian solution to a classic problem – such a strategy has some long-term disadvantages: the State would lose its financial flexibility for managing true Keynesian cases and, ultimately, it would not alter the causes of the problem. This means that the State would be acting in a distinctly short-sighted manner. This is almost certainly the problem facing every democratic system, where institutional restrictions and the selective composition of the group of politicians tend to lead to shortsighted, social decision making (Zimmermann, 1985a).

It is possible that the political-administrative system has already realised that it will not be relieved of these social pressures but that citizens actually prefer longer term thinking and acting. In the case of the environment, this would mean to do more and to pay more for environmental protection, as indicated by Schefold's suggestion that there is a high willingness to pay for the environment (p. 276). And, this is precisely why employment programmes related to the environment have come increasingly into fashion, replacing highway construction programmes as the favourites.

In the short run, however, and as all the available data indicate, environment-related employment programmes, as compared to other types, lead to relatively high employment effects (Zimmermann, 1984). Nevertheless, it does not change the fact that this sort of policy is a short-term policy related to the present, whereas ecology is more readily identified with long-term economics. The precondition for such longer-term orientation should be an individualistic approach and not a collectivistic solution. By applying the polluter-pays principle, the present generation would be preserving the environment in the interest of their own years to come as well as in the interest of succeeding generations – i.e., decreasing consumption today, conserving, and building new environmental capital.

Of course, this consideration focuses primarily on external costs – or, for the more progressive thinkers, 'expected' external costs. Further, it is clear that progressive thinkers will usually hit on the idea of prevention, that is, keeping negative external effects from occurring at all. But can one define precisely what 'preventive environmental policy' means? It seems to waver between the trivial – that emissions and environmental pollutants should be avoided as much as possible in an economically sound manner – and the utopian – that every conceivable way of polluting the environment and every unknown noxious substance can and must be controlled.

Let us limit ourselves first to one aspect on which environmental economists largely agree: that charges and market-oriented solutions generally are more likely to bring about the transition to an integrated approach to environmental protection (i.e., to process innovations) than are technology-specific standards. Again, at this point it is important to remember how the present technology-related classical unemployment has actually come about: when the relationship between wages and interest rates is distorted, showing relatively overvalued labour, the job-killers are picked out of the 'treasury of technical progress' (Giersch, 1983). This is exactly what happens on an integrated approach to environmental protection. In a narrow technological framework, preventive environmental policy would necessarily result in a second round in the discussion of the issue of jobs and the impacts of environmental policy, if the root causes of unemployment itself cannot be eliminated.

There is another interesting aspect to be noted here. There is already some information on the proportion of integrated environmental protection investment in the total figure of environmental investments – for simplicity's sake, we shall call this the prevention component of realised environmental policy (Zimmermann, 1985b). Since the prevention components during the periods analysed empirically (in Germany, 1975–81; in the USA, 1973–83) achieve nearly identical average values for both countries, only 20.7 per cent for the US and 20.5 per cent for Germany respectively, then this result must be interpreted not only as an effect of endogenous restrictions within firms, but also and primarily as results of instrumental choices and the style of regulation in environmental policy. The lack of a common institutional framework for economy and ecology, a predominance of solutions based on standards in environmental policy, constant time limits for adjustments by firms as a result of permanent crisis management, governmental regulations concerning financial assistance which force firms to apply end-of-pipe technologies, but also protectionistic employment programmes are destined to miss the goal of dynamic efficiency.

Another point must be added in analysing the relationship between the prevention component and the ratio of environmental protection investment to overall investment. For comparable environmental protection investment areas in the FRG and the US, there is an amazing degree of correspondence insofar as an increase in the proportion of environmental protection investment relative to overall investment would not lead to an increase in the share of total environmental protection investment accounted for by integrated environmental protection investments. On the contrary, if the environmental share of the aggregate total investment figure is increased by one percentage point, then there is a decrease in the prevention component of about 1.6 percentage points. The data indicate an obvious quantity–quality tradeoff. A relative increase in the quantity of environmental investment implies a relative decrease in the quality of environmental protection defined as integrated environmental investments or environmentally sound process innovations.

What in any case does not seem to help or is even counter-productive is a strengthening of standards and time restrictions for compliance as a 'stick' to beat firms into environmentally sound, long-term adjustments. In a market system based on entrepreneurial decisions, the 'big stick' strategy would definitely function counterproductively. A compulsory increase in the share of the total investment devoted to environmental investments would imply a worsening of the technological quality of environmental protection measures and entail nothing more than a long-run waste of resources, even though initially it appears as if more would be done for the environment.

What follows from these results is fairly obvious: the necessary conditions for increasing the quality of environmental protection in terms of integrated processes are more likely to stem from positive trends in overall investment, that is, from a healthy investment climate. One can also interpret this result as an empirically-based plea for an economic policy of reducing constraints on investment and opening up investment opportunities. Such a policy, as opposed to quantitative and short-sighted forms of ecological activism, would seem to be the most suitable for guaranteeing the environment.

References

Belassa, Bela (1984) 'The Economic Consequences of Social Policies in the Industrial Countries', *Weltwirtschaftliches Archiv*, 120.

Giersch, Herbert (1983) 'Arbeit, Lohn und Produktivität' (Employment, Wage and Productivity), *Weltwirtschaftliches Archiv*, 119.

Grubb, Dennis, Richard Jackmann and Richard Layard (1983) 'Wage Rigidity and Unemployment in OECD Countries', *European Economic Review*, 21.

Kirkpatrick, Grant (1982) 'Real Factor Prices and German Manufacturing Employment: A Time Series Analysis 1960I–1979IV, *Weltwirtschaftliches Archiv*, 118.

Malinvaud, Edmond (1982) 'Wages and Unemployment', *The Economic Journal*, 92.

Sachs, Jeffrey D. (1983) 'Real Wages and Unemployment in the OECD Countries', *Brookings Papers on Economic Activity, No. 1*.

Zimmermann, Klaus (1984) 'Employment and the Environment: An Analysis of Policy Relationships in West Germany', *Journal of Public and International Affairs*, 5.

Zimmermann, Klaus (1985a) 'Time Preference and Budgetary Decisions'. Paper prepared for the conference 'Time Preference', International Institute for Environment and Society, Berlin, December 16–17, 1985.

Zimmermann, Klaus (1985b) 'Präventive Umweltpolitik und technologische Anpassung' (Preventive Environmental Policy and Technological Adjustment), International Institute for Environment and Society, Science Center Berlin.

Part V
The Interplay between Economic and Institutional Factors

Part V

11 The Interplay Between Institutional and Material Factors: The Problem and its Status

N. Georgescu-Roegen*

INTRODUCTION: THE SOURCES OF DANGERS AND DIFFICULTIES

When Egon Matzner suggested the topic for my contribution, Lord Keynes's pronouncement that economics is a 'dangerous science' came to me in a flash. 'It is indeed', Joseph A. Schumpeter (1954) added his approval as he quoted it. And in the last section of his *General Theory of Employment, Interest, and Money*, Lord Keynes supported this theme by pointing out that 'practical men ... are usually the slaves of some defunct economist', so, it is the ideas of economists, not the vested interests, that 'are dangerous for good or evil'. Instructively, Robert K. Merton (1981), recently related those thoughts to President Richard Nixon's 'public confession that he was a Keynesian'. It thus seems that Lord Keynes's remark was either an implicit admission of the political ineffectiveness of any economic doctrine or a verdict about the inability of political men to understand economics rightly. Be this as it may, any economist who has ever stopped to ponder about the epistemological foundation of the economic discipline would certainly agree that economics is a dangerous discipline precisely because of the interplay between the institutional and the economic factors.

To see the source of the danger we should recall Thomas Hobbes's observation in the last sentence of *Leviathan*: 'such truth, as opposeth no man's profit, nor pleasure, is to all men welcome'. The truths of

---

*I wish to thank Nancy Latham for having to type from a hard-to-read manuscript and within a short deadline, and Ranganath Murthy for assistance in preparing the final manuscript.

geometry especially are of this kind. Yet even though Hobbes was the first to argue that everything including every human propensity is reducible to a faithful representation by geometry, he felt it necessary to explain in detail one link of his argument:

> From the principal parts of Nature, Reason and Passion, have proceeded two kinds of learning, *mathematical* and *dogmatical*: the former is free from controversy and dispute, because it consisteth in comparing figure and motion only; in which things, *truth*, and *the interest of men*, opposeth not each other: but in the other there is nothing indisputable, because it compareth men, and meddleth with their right and profit; ... And from hence it cometh, that they who have written of justice and policy in general, do all invade each other and themselves with contradictions. (*The English Works*, Vol. IV).

Economics is a dangerous science just because the relevance of any statement we may make about the economic process is not purely academic. On the contrary, any such statement is so heavy with normative political prescriptions that 'meddleth with [the people's] right and profit' and 'opposeth ... each other'. Economic life thus is a continuous struggle not only of man with nature, but also of everyone with virtually everyone else. Even though man is regularly a participant in some trade or some production, man's entire activity is not reducible to the fiction of *homo economicus*. Man is much more than a price-taker in what he sells or buys. Essentially, man is an economic agent in the fullest meaning of the term; so characteristic and vital is this human quality that nowadays we speak of man even as a geological agent. Man not only seeks to buy or sell a quantity as close as possible to the 'optimum' one – the exclusive problem considered by standard economics[1] – but man also continuously struggles to become entitled to a greater share of the general economic horn or, if one's share is already bounteous, to defend that title.

This is so simple and evident a fact that I feel like apologising for mentioning it. Yet I mention it because it brings to the surface an important point, which is that the bartering role of the individual conduced to the organisation of the market, whereas the competitive role in society has been mainly responsible for the multifarious cultural institutions which (we may well keep this in mind) emerged long before the most primitive market. The market and the cultural institutions have therefore a common taproot, from which they have grown into two essential components of the general complex usually called 'culture'.[2]

One should therefore expect a true and important interplay between cultural institutions and the phenomena in which standard economics is interested. To see that that expectation has been confirmed, we must first consider the nature of the epistemological difficulties responsible for the still controversial character of the arguments provoked thereby.

The point to which I want to draw attention first is that between the two intellectual preoccupations – that concerning the market phenomena and that interested in cultural institutions – there is an immense differential difficulty. The strictly economic phenomenal domain has submitted itself rather easily to what we usually call scientific investigation. It has even been proclaimed, certainly without much pondering, that because of the success of mathematical economics, economics 'has gone through its Newtonian revolution', while the science of culture must still await 'its Galileo, or the Pasteur' (Popper, 1964).[3]

The difficulty of the two scientific preoccupations just mentioned is not of the same nature. The phenomena governed by the relativity of time and space or by the quantum mechanics are surely complicated, but that complication is limited to their representation by mathematical artefacts. The difficulty of the investigation of culture comes from an entirely different direction: the impossibility of setting the specific cultural concepts on a precise base. Take 'culture', the fundamental concept itself. There is the so-called omnibus definition, advanced in 1871 by Edward B. Tylor:

> Culture or Civilization, taken in the wide ethnographic sense, is that complex whole which includes knowledge, belief, art, morals, law, custom, and any other capabilities and habits acquired by man as a member of a society.

Subsequent students of culture, however, have found it wanting in this or that respect. Their attempts at improving it to one's taste succeeded solely in producing an incredible number of diverse formulations. The list drawn up in 1952 by Kroeber and Kluckhohn (1963) contained not less than several hundred variants. The eminent authors had to conclude that the science of culture has 'plenty of definitions but too little theory'. So, the impression of the occasional peregrinator into that field is that controversy about definitions constitutes the weight of the local preoccupations.

The definitional dissatisfaction of which I have just spoken permeates all other concepts related to culture, that is, related to the characteristic human activities. From a more general perspective, that dissatisfaction also affects most phenomena of life, not just human life. But, we should note, the dissatisfaction grows out from the comparison with the category of analytical definitions.

The fact I wish now to bring home is that we get in mental contact with the inner or the outer reality in two and only two irreducible modes. It is this irreducible dichotomy that guided me to an epistemological configuration of two unbridgeable conceptual categories. One category consists of *arithmomorphic* concepts. Each such concept stands by itself in splendid isolation from everything else, exactly in the same way as a number, a definite geometrical figure, or any other mathematical concept. They also are wholly immutable: squeeze however little a true circle (which can exist only in your mind), the object of your thought is no longer a circle.

The other category consists of *dialectical* concepts whose distinctive characteristic is to overlap with their opposites. It is thus possible for a given dialectical entity to be both A and non-A. Dialectical concepts are not perfectly circumscribed. Instead, they are bounded by a *dialectical* penumbra, that is, by a penumbra surrounded by a penumbra surrounded by a penumbra ... in an infinite progress – which is the specific peculiarity of dialectics.[4]

The greatest contrast is provided by the ultra positivist dogma which now forms the glory of the Vienna Circle: what is not defined in 'an absolutely sharp and distinct manner' is pure nonsense. The special (albeit false) appeal of this dogma caused it to gain such an over-enthusiastic popularity that even philosophy shrank its intellectual field to just physics and chemistry, disciplines that work mainly with perfectly defined (i.e., arithmomorphic) concepts. Actually, arithmomorphism crept first into several seventeenth-century writings on economics, but was properly installed following the famous Laplacian creed appended some twenty years later by the wondrous way in which the planet Neptune was discovered on paper at the tip of a pencil. 'No science without measurement' thus became the first commandment for all who sought to know; it still is. Accordingly, the prevailing creed has been that to speak about democracy, justice, feudalism, workable competition, affluent society (even of society *pure et simple*), natural rights, and a vast number of similar concepts is to speak nonsense.

But what should one say as one reads in the statistical literature that one needs 'a sufficiently large sample'; is that of ten, of eleven, ... of forty, of forty-one, of forty-two, or of a million? It may be a potentially shocking idea, but the truth is that most of the time we talk positivist nonsense. No member of the Vienna Circle could possibly open his or her mouth if forbidden to talk so. As an eloquent illustration, consider the phrase picked up at random from the writings of a sympathiser with the Vienna Circle:

> I mean by 'historicism' an approach to the social sciences which assumes that *historical prediction* is their principal aim, and which assumes that this aim is attainable by discovering the 'rhythms' or the 'patterns', the 'laws' or the 'trends' that underlie the 'evolution of history'. (Popper, 1964)

The undeniable fact is that even though almost every word here is dialectical, the author has expressed his thoughts in a well-put way.[5]

But the ground on which dialectical notions rest is far more general than one might think offhandedly. Every thing that is inevitably subject to qualitative change – that is, to a change that does not consist of mere accretion, or its opposite, or of just locomotion – is a dialectical concept. 'Prime number' is an arithmomorphic notion because no number can be both prime and not-prime. That concept has remained absolutely unchanged ever since the time of Euclid. By contrast, 'democracy' does not have the same meaning today as in Euclid's time. A reasonable change of the voting age in a democratic polity would not change its general democratic character. Yet if other political rules keep changing, a democracy may ultimately slide into a dictatorship precisely because many polities are in the dialectical penumbra that separates those two constitutions and thus partake of both.

Species, a glaring testimony, is a dialectical concept because, as Charles Darwin (1898) put it in his piercing style, every species 'includes the unknown element of a distinct act of creation'. Anyone who would insist on an arithmomorphic definition of species would implicitly regress to the pre-Lamarckian standpoint that all species have been created immutable once and for all.[6]

Our thoughts cannot do without dialectical concepts; in fact, they cover the greatest area of what we think and communicate. Dialectical arguments have habitually been denounced as muddled-thinking. And indeed much of such thinking is interwoven with dialectical concepts used badly, however. It is inept though to blame the colours for what some untalented painter may do with them. But reasoning with dialectical notions, although not as strict and sharp as a purely arithmomorphic concatenation, can be correct (which I esteem to be the greatest gift of the human mind in comparison to the artificial one).

In what consists then the difference between the two types of reasonings, for a difference must certainly exist? Consider, first, the structures of any science – say, physics, astronomy, accounting, geometry, or computer – that deals primarily (or even exclusively) with arithmomorphic concepts. By the very nature of these concepts, their individual cases cannot only be identified by numbers but also *ordered meaningfully* thereby.[7] Numbers can be represented in an order on an axis or on a system of axes in such manner that, for instance, π is always represented between 3 and 4, and 101 between 100.999 and 102. On the scatter formed by the set of available observations (Figure 11.1a), we always try to fit some *analytical* functions, that is, functions that have the signal property of being determined over the entire range of variation by the values for an interval however small. It is because of this unique property that we can extrapolate laws beyond the range of actual observation, a procedure which constitutes the heart of scientific method. I cannot sufficiently emphasise the importance of this analytical structure which, although generally overlooked, bears not only on the services of mathematics but on other fields as well. It was on his discovery of the analytical (harmonious) structure of the organs of an animal that Baron Georges Cuvier was able to reconstruct the whole skeleton of some extinct animal starting from only one of its vertebrae.

The general use of analytical functions tacitly implies the notion that all quantitative laws are analytical functions, for which we have no solid ground of belief. The social science domain may be the strongest exception, as is suggested by the continuous failure of the analytical econometric models to predict even approximately. The usual excuse for this failure is that meanwhile some cultural coordinates have changed, which is tantamount to admitting that the evolution of culture (viz. history) does not follow an analytical trajectory, at least not one involving a manageable number of quantitative factors. The last idea bears upon any evolutionary theory of economics also. The number of relevant factors, material and nonmaterial, may perhaps exceed any technical power of ours.

In dialectics the difficulty comes from another direction. Take a

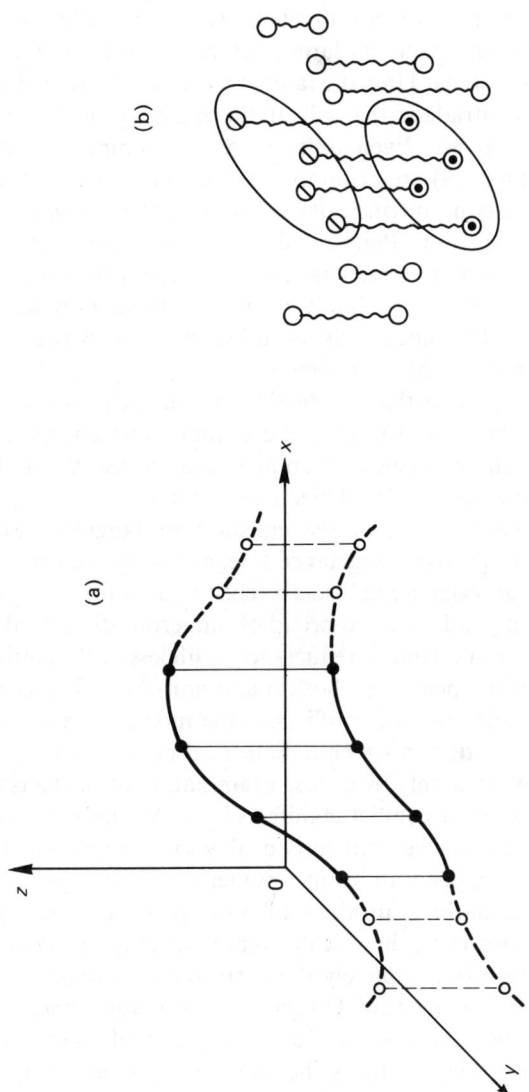

Figure 11.1a. and b. The essential difference between analytical functions and dialectical relations

dialectical condition, say democracy. Is there any intrinsic order of its possible instances to represent them on an axis? Has democracy as crystallised in the polity of Switzerland (where women do not have the same political rights as men), or of the United Kingdom (where the Parliament cannot begin legislating before it is solemnly opened by the Crown), or of the United States (where the composition of the Senate often contradicts the will of the majority of the voters) an intrinsic order at all? Even if in an actual complex some of the variables (but not all) are arithmomorphic – the most vital would be time – there exists no intrinsically ordered scatter on which to erect any functional relation. Pairs of observations of qualitative factors can, if we wish, be represented as in Figure 1b, but the order in which we represent them is absolutely arbitrary. Prediction beyond the actually observed instances, nay, even interpolation between these, is therefore entirely out of the question.

The untoward fact is that the destiny of humanity, as a whole or in its local branches, consists of endless qualitative changes, that is, changes that can be grasped, examined, and discussed only by what has, since Marx, been called dialectical materialism.

Dialectics has been under the constant onslaught of positivists primarily out of partisan reluctance to examine its import – a regrettable fact.[8] For each actual social entity – a nation, a species, a business firm, a guild – is a crossroad of numerous dialectical penumbras. Otherwise all would reduce to a lifeless self-identity. And because within any penumbra both A and non-A are true, each social entity is a complex web of conflicts, some more, some less forcible. The possible direction in which a dialectical complex may move can therefore be intuited only by a close examination of the facts through which one or another conflict manifests itself. We must not overlook that in social sciences we frequently deal with concepts that although dialectical are mapped on some numerical scales – price indices, invested capital, national product, religious tenor, political alertness, and so forth. However, these scales represent only *pseudo-measures*: they cannot identify completely the correspondent qualities because no instance of a dialectical concept has a unique linear variant. Virtually any type of average, for example, could serve the same purpose as any other: witness the average constructed by Charles Dow for the Dow Jones index. But the clearest exemplification is the arithmomorphic compression of the welfare concept into national income per capita, which has drawn adamant but legitimate protests.

THE BROADENING OF THE ECONOMIC VISION

Because dealing with dialectical structures is the more demanding task, it may then seem bizarre in retrospect that the earliest economic writers should focus their attention on the cultural elements of the economic process rather than on the market mechanism. For the first domain is intrinsically dialectical, the second, arithmomorphic. Apart from the ineffectual suggestion of Hobbes to reduce all life completely to geometry and the short-lived vogue of the arithmomorphic *Tableau économique* of the Physiocrats, the Moral Philosophers who broke the ground for modern economics considered mainly the division of society into classes of different power and interest and the moral issues pertaining to that division. The economic discipline thus grew out from moral preoccupations and genuine economists have continued to consider it in this particular light. 'Economics is essentially a moral science and not a natural science' insisted Lord Keynes in a 1938 letter (*Collected Works*, vol. XIV).

It was Adam Smith, the pupil of the great moral philosopher, Francis Hutcheson, and the author whose economic vision occupies two works of sempiternal value, who initiated the study of the market. But he remained faithful to his mentor's orientation as evidenced by the full title *An Inquiry into the Nature and Causes of the Wealth of Nations*, of the most valuable 'of all scientific books that have appeared to this day' (Schumpeter, 1954). In that work Adam Smith paid great attention to the relations of the social classes between themselves and with the government, to the associated institutions, and to situations in other societies, frequently expressing judgments concerning general welfare and justice. Highly interesting is that Adam Smith attributed a weighty role to that propensity (mentioned earlier) of the individual qua economic agent. He refers in several places to 'the universal, continual, and uninterrupted effort to better [one's] own condition' (1976).[9] But the currently recognised crown of his legacy is the tenet that a free initiative polity, with a perfectly competitive market, would at least lead to the optimum transactions between the participants *just as they are on entering it*.

A decisive turning point from Adam Smith's preoccupation with the cultural aspects came with David Ricardo who, as is well known, set up the market in the centre of the economic process and proceeded to reduce economics to a purely deductive science. But as the Classical School developed on these tracks, critics of its principles also rushed onto the stage.[10] In chronological order the first truly worthy of mention is Thomas Malthus who, without taking exception to what Adam Smith taught, pressed even deeper the truth that the welfare of mankind depends not only on how man acts in the market, but to an even greater extent on how he acts outside it. A critic of a different ideological stuff was, strangely, a formidable successful businessman turned into a socialist reformer to whom Karl Marx referred often and with gusto. In 1815 Robert Owen, undoubtedly speaking from experience, protested that because of the capitalist competition 'one man's gain is another man's loss',[11] a pronouncement which at the time could only displease the élite (to which virtually all literati belonged) and cause them to turn their back on its author.

Next was Richard Jones, a strong analytical critic of the thematic distillation of the Classical doctrine, especially of Ricardo's theory of rent (Richard Jones, 1964a). To support his dissenting position Jones investigated in detail the social relations on which rent was based in several countries with an overwhelming peasantry. But Jones's thought ran on strictly methodological lines and converged on the protest that the proper reasoning for economics is not deductive, as propagated by Ricardo, but inductive. As he declared in an 1833 lecture (1964b), 'what we call general principles will often be found to have no generality [so that] at every step of our further progress, we shall be obliged to confess are frequently false'. The point of Karl Kautsky (1936) that 'Marx designed to investigate in his *Capital* [not] the forms of production which are common to all people, as such an investigation could, for the most part, only result in commonplaces' harks back one hundred years to Jones's prescription to represent each actuality by its particular analytical description.[12]

A simple run down of the main drift of the authors just reviewed reveals that, although their criticism of the strictness of the Classical doctrine differed graphically, they all converged to the idea that the economic process is not reducible to catallactics, that is, to ordinary market transactions.[13]

But Richard Jones has two additional outstanding merits. First, from his investigations of diverse peasantries he could conclude that communities do not operate according to the same economic arrangements, that, as I have just quoted him, there is no general economic principle, no uniform economic arrangements.[14] Therefore, to attain our objective in economics we must 'look and see' instead of reasoning from a priori principles. Edgeworth (1926) was thus right in judging that Jones's role 'in political economy was like that of Bacon in physical science: to preach the importance of experience, and the danger of hasty generalisation'.

Second, it is the idea he expressed in an 1833 lecture:

> As communities change their powers of production, they necessarily change their habits too. During their progress in advance, all the different classes of the community find that they are connected with other classes by new relations, are assuming new positions, and are surrounded by new moral and social dangers, and new conditions of social and political excellence. (Jones, 1964b).

Indeed, let us consider one of Marx's formulations of that doctrine (of 1847, probably the earliest):

> In acquiring new productive forces men change their mode of production; and in changing their mode of production, in changing the way of earning their living, they change all their social relations (1963).[15]

Compared with Jones's, Marx's explication hardly differs even in style. The two minds surprisingly hit upon the same idea, with Jones preceding Marx by some fifteen years.

The strangest fact in the sociology of science is that, in spite of these momentous thoughts, Jones has received only scanty attention from economists, even from historians of economic thought.

None of the contrived excuses for the similar fate of H. H. Gossen would work in Jones's case. Modern economists, apparently dissenting from Edgeworth's extolment, usually fail to refer to him at all. The most glaring omission is that of the sixteen volumes of the *International Encyclopedia of the Social Science* where his name does not appear even once.[16] Exceptions are few. As one would have expected, Schumpeter (1954) refers to Jones on some specific points and in a long note to his ideas. Sir Eric Roll (1973), another exception among modern economists, has a whole section on him.[17] An early and very sympathetic presentation came from John K. Ingram (1888). But a highly valuable appreciation of Jones's contribution is the preface to the *Literary Remains* by William Whewell, a celebrated philosopher and scientist of wide interests known best for his works on the inductive method (Schumpeter, 1954).

Jones's oblivion by the economic profession is only a part, the smaller, of his literary destiny. The point is that none of the writers who commented on his contributions realised that it was Jones who first formulated the principle of the interplay between material and cultural factors of an economy. And even this is not the whole conundrum. Karl Marx dissected two important contributions of Jones's in ch. XXIV (one of the longest of *Theories of Surplus Value*). There he bestowed on his predecessor high praise not for having formulated first the kernel of his own doctrine, but only for Jones's criticism of Ricardo. The same is true of the numerous references to Richard Jones in other works by Marx, especially, in *Capital*.

The next approach to the interplay between the modes of production and the cultural fabric is known as institutional economics. It has become associated with the name of Thorstein Veblen, although that label is not due to him;[18] but it was he who introduced in the analysis of that interplay a specific notion of 'institution'. Yet Veblen never described his own position by an explicative statement. Fragments, many and striking, of his thoughts are scattered through all his writings. The definitions of his basic concepts are wanting even from a dialectical viewpoint. 'The institutions,' he explained in his first volume (1953, p. 132), 'are, in substance, prevalent habits of thought with respect to particular relations and particular functions of the individual and of the community.' Veblen's style is flowery, his vocabulary recherché,[19] his phrasing twirled, and his exposition devious. As his critics have complained, there is no unity in his work. Yet the bare core of his thought is truly great, as a combing (which is not easy) of his works would confirm. To be sure, he worked under the shadow of Marx, but his vision of the interplay between the purely economic activities and the cultural fabric differs from his famous exemplar in two important respects.

First, Veblen recognised the important roles for the evolution of society of some innate factors of human nature which in his characteristic style were described as 'instinctive proclivities and tropismatic aptitudes' (Veblen, 1922). He further added the instinct of workmanship, and of idle curiosity, as well as the proclivities of conspicuous leisure, conspicuous consumption, and conspicuous waste.[20]

Secondly, while declaring to be 'justly proud' of the achievements of the earlier economists, Veblen found that it was time to move away from 'the hedonistic conception of man [as] a lightning calculator of pleasures and pain [which] has neither antecedent nor consequent', as he said in an early article, of 1898. In the same article he deprecated standard theory for not being an evolutionary science (Veblen, 1919). In his conception, an evolutionary economics must be the theory of a process of cultural growth as determined by the economic interest, a theory of a cumulative sequence of economic institutions stated in terms of the process itself.

Veblen took even Karl Marx to task for not adopting an evolutionary view in his materialistic doctrine. In this, he followed Enrico Ferri, a renowned criminologist,[21] and an adherent to scientific socialism, who in a work reviewed by Veblen (1896) argued that 'everything goes to impress upon us with mathematical certainty that when this victory [of socialism] is achieved it must in turn give place to further struggles and new ideals'. Or as Veblen (1919) pinpointed it in his 1906 critique of Karl Marx's economics, 'this [social] process being essentially a cumulative sequence of causation, opaque and unteleological [could not] conceivably [end with] the classless economic structure of the socialistic final term'. Curiously, this was the very accusation Marx (*Capital*, I) thrust at the 'bourgeois' economists for believing that capitalism is the final phase of the historical process. But, to put it in a homely way, Marx's claim for socialism parallels those religious beliefs that after death there is an endless life without suffering or sorrow. The point, as I shall submit it in conclusion, is that socialism or any other social system would not bring about a New Jerusalem.

What Veblen intended by his strictures on the basic postulate of Marx's doctrine was to inject some Darwinian animation into economics just as Herbert Spencer had already suggested for the entire science of society. In view of Marx's standing on the finality of socialism it is hard to conceive why Engels at Marx's graveside eulogised him by saying that 'Just as Darwin discovered the law of development of organic nature, so Marx discovered the law of development of human history' (Engels, 1968).[22]

The institutionalist avenue attracted the interest of a good number of economists, some front line thinkers, such as John Commons, Wesley C. Mitchell, and, from Germany, Max Weber. In 1931 Homan reported that 'the institutionalists constitute one of the most active groups of economists today'. The title of Homan's article notwithstanding, institutionalism has not crystallised into a school. It has, however, induced a definite interest for the institutional factor by virtually all significant economists. Of course, Veblen's criticism of standard economics could not pass without great irritation, as witnessed by Homan's curious sally of the subsequent year (1932): 'an institutional economics, differentiated from other [the standard] economics by discoverable criteria, is largely an intellectual fiction, substantially devoid of content'.

THE TESTIMONY OF ANTHROPOLOGY

The idea that societies constantly evolve, that is, change qualitatively, is no longer subject to any doubt. As I mentioned earlier, some evidence was familiar to writers of the Greco-Roman world. But only in recent times, in the Western world new and ampler evidence was brought (some say, dragged) to light from two distant sources almost at the same time. August von Haxthausen-Abbenburg (invited, of all people, by Tsar Nicholas I), made a survey on the spot of the Russian peasant communities and published his elaborate findings in three volumes (1847–51). These aroused a general and lasting interest in the peculiar peasant institutions.[23] In the United States, Lewis H. Morgan's frequent reports from 1851 onwards revealed still another peculiar type of sociality, that of the Iroquois. They culminated in his *chef d'oeuvre Ancient Society* (1877). This work has generally been considered as the opening of a new discipline about man, the anthropology followed by palaeoanthropology, although 'it [also] was in turn ignored, belittled, and ridiculed' (Leslie A. White, *IESS*). But in the last analysis anthropology provided historical materialism with a more extensive underpinning. This time, not Darwinism, but anthropology was thought to be 'destined to revolutionise the political and the social sciences as radically as bacteriology has revolutionised the science of medicine' (Lapouge, 1897, quoted by Veblen).

After so many hopes that have kept growing about the discovery of the laws that can explain how the cultural matrix is determined in each case by the extant modes of production, it seems worthy to examine the extent to which such laws have been actually evidenced.

To begin with, Morgan's *Ancient Society* became a classic of Marxism. The title of one of Frederick Engels most celebrated works is *The Origin of the Family, Private Property and the State in the Light of the Researches of Lewis H. Morgan*. But Morgan, like some before and many after him, did not do anything more solid about the crucial problem than using known historical facts to establish three evolutionary stages: savagery, barbarism, and civilization, which Engels further divided each into lower, middle and upper substages.[24] Later, numberless anthropologists have turned to studying on the spot one 'primitive' community after another as their locations were discovered. The number of such studies staggers the imagination. The list of only those mentioned in a single article on stateless societies seems endless.[25] Some primitive societies have formed the subject of thorough studies by prominent anthropologists with the intention in each case of expounding some particular conception of social structure and organisation.[26]

One may think that the detailed observations of that great number of communities separated in space and of varying social structures would constitute a complex of data of the same sort as that derived from a laboratory experiment in which some co-ordinates are allowed to vary. One would then expect – as in fact has been the sanguine hope of the expounders of historical materialism – that from all those anthropological studies we may establish some general theorems relating material conditions to institutional structures. But this expectation has been fully thwarted. To see why, I will use what I have called a simile of a dialectical grid (Georgescu-Roegen, 1966, 1971).

Let (M_K, C_K) denote the observation of a community, such as those mentioned above, with M_K denoting the complex of the material co-ordinates, and C_K, the complex of the purely cultural structure. Even though most of these co-ordinates are truly qualitative, and hence cannot be arranged in an objective order, we may imagine them represented in an abstract space where the actual observations would form a scatter (Figure 1b). Strictly interpreted, any law of historical materialism would prohibit the existence of pairs with only one co-ordinate identical. But in the anthropological world such coincidental pairs are frequent. For example, a hostile natural environment happens to be associated with highly peaceful people (the Kung) as well as with strongly aggressive ones (the Ik). Within the same climate conditions, some people began to use pieces of clothing for adornment first and only later for the protection of the body. Of course, no society could develop agriculture in a location of very poor soil, but a good soil did not necessarily induce every community to do so. Because material conditions have not always been the sole determinants, it stands to reason that factors included in C may also have their own genetic influence. Along this line of thought, the most glaring snag is that, although the Soviet Union and the Western nations, all use virtually, and some totally, identical modes of production, their social and political institutions are fundamentally different.

What social scientists have generally struggled to do with an anthropological scatter has been to find out whether to some relevant *subset* of [*M*] – relevant in the sense that it is coalesced into a pertinent dialectical notion – there corresponds a relevant *subset* of [*C*]. Such a correspondence would indeed be a triumph for the exploration of the still enigmatic evolution of human society on multifarious tracks. Leslie White (1949) is the outstanding anthropologist that has proposed such a correspondence on which he based his own view of human evolution. Arguing that culture is 'a specific and concrete mechanism employed by a particular animal organism in adjusting to its environment' and that humans achieved this by operating technological artefacts, White suggested that the advance of human communities is determined by the amount of energy harnessed per capita.[27] But appealing though this principle may be (especially today), it met, as expected, with opposition. Franz Boas and his European disciples, for one example, argued that the evolution of the human society displays no linearity (as envisioned by White), but multiple divergence. Culture in the strictest sense, is the sole determining factor of evolution. As more than one commentator on the anthropologists' claims and counter-claims has judged, a field of inquiry so complex and colourful escapes any attempts of mirroring it in a theoretical framework.

TO PREDICT AND TO EXPLAIN

An elementary situation would suffice to pinpoint the difficulty of converting the evolutionary facts into precise laws. For if there were essentially evolutionary laws, an expert biologist could *predict* the somatic constitution of the platypus solely from the knowledge of its particular environment, inert and biotic. We know that such a feat is not possible today, and probably never. Let us turn to Marx's presumed law of the correlation of modes of production and social institutions. Would a genius great beyond imagination have been able to say *before the fact* what Marx (1963) said, namely, that 'The handmill gives you society with the feudal lord; the steam-mill, society with the industrial capitalist'? And for a real acid test, who can *predict* now what kind of 'lord' we may get after the exhaustion of the fossil fuels when either some nuclear reactor will replace the steam-mill or we will enter a new Wood Age? As I believe, absolutely no one can have now the faintest idea of what kind of society in which people will live, say, not ten thousand, but just one hundred years from now (Georgescu-Roegen, 1971). Of course, after the fact but not before, we can *explain* most of the evolutionary changes. To explain how capitalism emerged from a feudalist fabric, for example, was the aim of the institutionalist John R. Commons in his *The Legal Foundations of Capitalism*. The point, which I consider of paramount epistemological importance is that, contrary to what Hempel and Oppenheim (1948) claimed, 'prediction' and 'explanation' are not symmetrical.

The history of our species consists of a series of surprises, of novelties, that can be explained only *ex post* and only in part from the particular past. To illustrate this fact Egon Matzner once invoked very apropos a moral story of Islamic folklore, that of Nasreddin Hodja who rode backwards on his donkey so as to know at all times from where he came – as to the donkey, Nasreddin said, it knows pretty well where to go. This is not a facetious remark. For as the eminent physicist and philosopher David Bohm (1957) advised us

> to understand ... what things are, we must consider the process in which things *have become*, what they are starting out from, what they once were, and in which they continue to change and to become something else again in the future.

In strict terms, Bohm's idea boils down to saying that for predicting the future, nay, even explaining the present, one should know (in some workable sense) the entire past. But as a mathematical authority, Paul Painlevé, protested, science would then be utterly impossible. This theorem unveils the predicament of any student of evolution. If we can predict how long, say, a dog will live and, in broad lines, how he will behave, and so on, it is only because we have witnessed numberless dogs being born, growing up, getting old, and dying. But, from what we know now, I believe that mankind stands no chance of observing other 'mankinds', to know whereto ours is going (Georgescu-Roegen, 1976). Historically unique events can be only explained *ex post*; prediction requires previous observation of an analogous event.

NOVELTY IN BIOLOGY AND IN ECONOMICS

By definition, a novelty is an unpredictable event, unpredictable to the point that Thomas Edison, for example, had no idea of a phonograph before he hit upon it. Schumpeter, in particular, envisioned the economic process as a sequence of innovations, that is, as invented modes of production or institutional relations incorporated into the social matrix. But several important pillars of the Schumpeterian system have so far escaped the deserved attention of the exegetes.

As is well-known, Alfred Marshall is the economist most admired for his conviction that biology, not dynamics, is the Mecca of the economist (1949). But excepting a few remarks on the edge, Marshall only preached that principle. Schumpeter, on the other hand, never preached biologism; it just happened that in his own vision the nature of the economic process emerged as essentially evolutionary to such a depth that he anticipated by some thirty years a salient idea propounded by Richard Goldschmidt for biology (see note 6, above). Like Goldschmidt, Schumpeter (1934) found it difficult to accept the idea that any innovation whatsoever could influence the evolution of the economic process. Only large innovations, concerning either technics or institutions, he argued, can be effectual. To make this idea clear, in a subtle note (p. 81), Schumpeter adopted a thoroughly dialectical reasoning: small and large are opposing dialectical qualities, and the difference between the two results solely from the situation at hand.[28]

'Add successively as many mail coaches as you please, you will never get a railway engine thereby' is a now famous apophthegm by which Schumpeter aimed at making two fundamental facts crystal clear. First, that development (that is, evolution) is essentially distinct from growth (that is, from mere accretion). Second, that a proper innovation consists of a categorical qualitative change. In a way, what Schumpeter said boils down to looking at a railway engine as a 'successful monster' if compared to a mailcoach.

Schumpeter's explanation of the factors that punctuate economic evolution fails to note an important dissymmetry of those factors, a feature that would have bridged his view with the twin nature of institutions. There is no good explanation why this feature, important though it is, has generally not attracted interest. In recent times, Frank Knight (1951–2) observed rather casually that institutionalists 'have slurred over the contrast between ... patterns moving in predestined grooves under the influence of relatively unconscious social forces versus those embodying deliberate organization and control'. Shaking hands as in the West illustrates the former, the United Nations, the latter. Neither invention nor innovation has this double connection.

The existence of this difference for institutions was long ago underlined by Baron Charles de Montesquieu: 'Intelligent beings may have laws of their own making; but they also have some which they never made.' F. von Hayek (1973), in quoting Montesquieu, adds the important observation that a spontaneous institution ordinarily is, with the terminology used earlier, an *analytical* system (an order). As he defines it, it is a state of affairs such that knowledge of a part of it allows correct expectations concerning the rest.

The interplay of institutions and purely economic factors raises a new problem, of whether the material factors have the same strong correlation with the spontaneous and the planned institutions. Unfortunately, I do not have anything to report on this issue. I am not prepared to take it for granted, as is usually done, that we can deal with any material constrictions by some deliberate measures.

ENTER MATHEMATICS, EXIT CULTURAL VALUE

As should be clear from the foregoing considerations, the economic discipline has not lacked great minds to point to the right way. Robert Lekachman (1976), who ten years ago wrote a timely book to show that the standard emperor has no clothes, sang the praises of 'four visionaries': Adam Smith, Karl Marx, Thorstein Veblen, and John Maynard Keynes. Personally, I find it hard to see why Lekachman bypassed Marshall and Schumpeter. With the exception of Lord Keynes (whose *General Theory*, in my judgement, focuses on a transitory episode), about the others one may say what Schumpeter (1951) said about Marshall: 'His thought ran in terms of evolutionary change, in terms of an organic, irreversible process [but] his vision of the economic process, his methods, his results are no longer ours.' Both the praise and the lament applied to my chosen great are even more apposite today than ever.

But as history marched on economists began following strictly their cherished economical axiom: proceed so as to minimise effort. For, as even natural scientists have pointed out, to do mathematics is a complicated technical endeavour, but to come to grips with facts mentally is the hardest imaginable. It was not very long after the Classical doctrine acquired a broad acceptance that it became contaminated by counter-productive elements from mathematical enthusiasts and, especially, from Bentham's extreme hedonism. There can be no valid reason against the use of mathematics in economics. As W. Stanley Jevons (1924) argued in 1874, economics is by nature mathematical since its variables are quantities – an idea later used by

Schumpeter to support the Econometric Society. But Jevons also added that because the scientific method cannot be applied to human affairs, economics must retreat from reality into an abstract edifice. However, following a few spectacular tours de force during the 1930s, most young economists rely, as one admitted publicly, on cranking the mathematical engine to get a paper.

As the economists' attention thus shifted from the institutional structure to the catallactic actions, economics began to lose its prestige. Jones (1964a) reports that already by 1831 'a feeling of dislike to the whole subject has been creeping over a portion of the public mind. Political economy has been distrusted.' The continuation, even the accentuation of this situation spurred the well-known fulminations of Thomas Carlyle and John Ruskin. But what is not so well-known but more symptomatic is that in 1877 Sir Francis Galton, the celebrated biometrician, formally moved that the British Association for the Advancement of Science should close the section of the disreputable science (Dorfman et al., 1963). In our own time, recognition of the ineffectiveness of the economic theory swollen beyond proportion by empty mathematical exercises has come from the highest fringes of the profession.

As best characterised by the Oxford historian, Thomas Arnold, the main affliction of the standard economics has been and still is that of being a one-eyed exploration, the good eye seeing only what occurs on the markets. The eye capable of perceiving the actions of the people outside the market, their hopes and struggles to better themselves is blind. This is how it came that economists being unable to discern the economic value that distills from the aspirations and the idiosyncrasies of the people surrounded by a web of habitual or legal relations, have taken the position that 'economic value' is a nonconcept, that only price is a valid concept (Coats, 1963). Even James M. Buchanan, whom I would not have expected to think so, claimed that Gunnar Myrdal's view that economic truths must involve value 'removes all scientific content from the discipline and reduces discussion to a babel of voices making noise' (Krupp, 1966).

On the other hand, we should not underestimate the difficulty of an approach to the economic process so as to take proper account of institutional value. As Richard Jones argued, there are no general principles in that domain. Or to put it differently, institutions are not ruled by a general logic, although each situation has its own logic, an internal logic, that is. It is this logic that we must *discover*.

Let us recall first that the cornerstone of standard economics is that *'Each individual acts as he desires'*, as two most venerated economists – Irving Fisher and Vilfredo Pareto – proclaimed. Most obviously, the statement is a splendid tautology. It is natural that it has been replaced by some objective form – the utility function. However, the utility function reflects the standard sin in a glaring, albeit unsuspected, way. Its principle is that man's choices are determined only by the quantities of commodities at his disposal. Yet man's actual choice is also affected by the proclivity of conspicuous consumption (to recall a piece of Veblen's teachings). The determinants of choice should then be represented by a simile such as $f(X, Y)$, where X stands for a vector of the quantities of goods at the disposal of the individual and Y, for the goods possessed by some other selected individuals (Georgescu-Roegen, 1966). But even this representation is not completely satisfactory. Indeed, many choices (the most important ones for that matter) are not free in the sense that the choice is of the same nature as that, say, of choosing a card from an irrelevant deck. The important choices do not boil down to choosing just between two commodity vectors, X and Z, but between two complex pairs, (X, A) and (Y, B), where A and B stand for the actions by which X and Y can be obtained. A man may beg for a dollar, or pinch the cash register, or ask his employer to give him one for keeps, and so on. What the individual will do does not depend only upon his own proclivities but also, and to a great extent, on the cultural matrix in which he lives. The point is that whether the choice is Y or Z depends also upon the *values* of the actions A and B within that society (Georgescu-Roegen, 1971). Representing choice by such similes in actual situations would undoubtedly be a very hard (and hence unattractive) task. But it would absolve us from typical protests made by Marx and, surprisingly, by Marshall that Ricardo reasoned as if all people would behave in the same way.[29]

To leave an employer with whom one has been associated for many years just because another employer will pay more is, certainly, not compatible with every institutional structure. And whether it does or not, it will have a reflection on the price constellation as well as on the income distribution, all purely economic factors. The same consideration applies to an employer who does or does not let his workers go when the business becomes slack. Looking back at the history of the labour regimens in various countries and the problems of overwhelming importance that have continuously agitated almost all social relations would without fault cause us to recall the objectives for which John Commons militated on the basis of institutional economics.[30]

A very instructive illustration of how institutional factors influence the transactions pattern and even create new channels for them is supplied by the economies where free markets are prohibited by law and prices are fixed authoritatively. There many goods can be obtained only if a the buyer pays a supplement to the person who, as a shop clerk, a physician, a waiter, or provider of some service, enjoys some kind of quasi-rent. The planned egalitarian income distribution is thus thwarted. Schumpeter, to remember, taught that income at all times consists of wages, rent, interest, and profit. The institutional structure just described shows how a quasi-monopolistic income arises in substitution for the normal profit of the firm under the capitalist rules.

CONCLUDING THOUGHTS

The general drift of the foregoing observations is that even though there is some correlation between cultural and economic factors this correlation does not follow a general principle. Each situation has its own internal logic. Yet the human societies have shown from the dawn of history a definite trend which both supports and goes further than the main thread of historical materialism.

Man differs from other living creatures in many ways. But the most consequential is his particular conduct in dealings with 'the material means of life', as Veblen (1919) defined the economic process. The most crucial event in man's development is that at some period he transgressed the biological evolution as he began producing himself exosomatic organs instead of waiting for biological mutations to improve his somatic ability. Everywhere on the globe man thus became addicted to the extraordinary comfort provided by these detachable organs which have steadily grown more powerful and more absorbing. With them we can run faster than a cheetah and fly higher than any bird, for example. But what we seem to ignore is that this evolution is not an unadulterated blessing. Above all, it transformed *Homo* into a species dependent on finite accessible resources (an irreversible transformation about which I wrote more elsewhere, 1971).

As the *invented* exosomatic organs became increasingly complex with every day, their production could no longer be achieved only by a single family, even by a single clan. Production forcibly became a social enterprise, a novel and most fateful institution. And as such an enterprise needs to be planned, supervised, and controlled, a new division among people naturally came about, not a division of labour which had already been operating, but a division of *roles*. A new *social* class grew out containing planners, supervisors, administrators, instructors, legislators, judges, and so on down the line. These social roles (not necessarily all of them in each situation) constitute the governing class – the social élite, with another term. All other members of the community form the governed class.

This division which grew out of the material conditions that support the life of the species *Homo sapiens sapiens*, turned into a division of material status. As we know very well, the social élites are the economically privileged section of any society. Curiously, an intellect from another galaxy may, I think, expect that the governed should be treated with an ampler slice of the national pizza produced by all. The reason for this opinion would be that only what the governed ordinarily do can be measured objectively: so many bricks laid, so many acres ploughed, so many letters delivered to the addresses, etc., etc. By contrast, no result of a governor's work can be measured in some objective manner. Is there any way to attribute a relevant quantity to the content of this paper, to any verdict of a judge, or to any discussion of a bill by a parliament?

It is because of this difference that my imagined extragalactic intellect would be intrigued by the institution of élites that has been prevalent in all human societies. But all would be in order, if he or she happened to realise that only what cannot be measured can be exaggerated.

And, indeed, from a broad look at history it comes out crystal clear that the élites have always created a favourable social mythology about their indispensible role for the good of the governed. To wit, the High Priests in Egypt boasted of alerting the farmers when to start preparing for the flood; the Roman consuls and emperors vaunted their policies for expanding the realm of peace; the feudal lords extolled their efforts to defend their own people against nature and man; capitalists, in recent times, claim to be the initiators of economic growth. Nowadays, we are already moving toward the era when the technocrats of all expertises will claim that without them society, because of its increasing complexity, would be lost.

A point deserving emphasis is that neither of these claims is false. At each industrial stage, the society needs a definite governing institution. What is unfortunate is the fact, first, that élites (as Adam Smith remarked) tend to outgrow their necessary numbers by nepotism, smart-aleckism, operatorism and politicianism. There is a competition within the leisure class, as Veblen (1919) argued, to get something for nothing. Second, given the nature of our proclivities the resulting social conflict between the élites and their social platform is inevitable and will last under varying forms as long as mankind remains a species living by social production and social distribution.[31] Although this may sound like buttering up Marx's thesis of historical materialism, in fact it is a strong rebuttal as no other known to me. For it unveils the immutable root of the covariation (which is more than an interplay) of the material and the institutional conditions of our kind.

Notes

1. In a 1960 paper (reprinted in Georgescu-Roegen, 1976) I proposed the term 'standard' for the body of economic ideas that spread out, albeit without essential alteration, from the neo-classical basis. Later, I found out that the same terminological idea had already been used by Gambs (1946), among others.
2. The last remarks may sound rather materialistic, yet I do not intend thereby to deny the important role the specific human nature – with its biology, psychology, the multifarious proclivities, sentiments, and instincts, above all its power of creativity – has played in the development of human cultures. This precaution will be substantiated as I proceed.
3. On things of this sort people do not seem to agree ever. Some years later, Emile Grunberg (Krupp, 1966) asserted that in social science there had been 'not one major breakthrough' comparable to those of the natural sciences.
4. Georgescu-Roegen, 1966 and 1971. On this epistemological vision see several articles in Mendelsohn, Weingart, and Whitley (1977), and especially Richard Mattessich (1978). As I explained originally, in my conception of dialectics I follow Hegel's, but (with an admittedly great risk) in part only.
5. What positivists seem to overlook is, for example, that the attack, the driest ever, Karl Popper wrote against dialectics (*Mind*, **59**, 1940, pp. 403–26) would become truly unintelligible if purged of all dialectical terms.
6. Ernst Mayr (e.g., 1970) more than anyone else has insisted on an arithmomorphic definition: '*Species are groups of interbreeding natural populations that are reproductively isolated from other such groups.*' But this definition implies either the negation of biological evolution or the separate complement of the emergence of 'successful monsters'. This last idea, advanced by Richard Goldschmidt (1940), fared badly until recently when it drew such eminent support as that of Stephen J. Gould's (1977). But more of this later, in relation to economic evolution.

7. To be sure, the items Sears and Roebuck have for sale are identified by a catalogue number, which has no additional meaning though.
8. Cf. note 5 above.
9. 'Of course, this is nonsense,' pronounced Frank Knight (1960), who maintained that 'most people are content to live at a stationary level.' This is the reason for which John Stuart Mill (1848) praised the stationary state, but even as Knight admitted almost in the same breath, one must be certain that conditions will remain stationary. In fact, to get ahead would be the inevitable rule in a declining society.
10. The special chapter in Marx (1971, vol. III), 'Opposition to the Economists', we should note, fails to describe that episode completely.
11. For Robert Owen see the excellent and not ampler than necessary *voce* by Asa Briggs, IESS, vol. 11, pp. 351–2.
12. The study of traditional peasant villages, as undertaken by Richard Jones, is the simplest way to reach and pinpoint this fact in the case, for example, of a tithe system which prevailed in many parts of Europe until the late nineteenth century (Georgescu-Roegen, 1966, 1976).
13. As we may recall, catallactics was the unsuccessful suggestion of Bishop Richard Whately for a science of barter (Schumpeter, 1954).
14. It is hard to understand why the recognition that societies located differently in time and place have as a rule different socioeconomic arrangements came so late. The Greek and Roman historiographers – Herodotus, Strabo, Thucydides, Tacitus, and even the poet Lucretius – bore witness to that variability and even made commendable attempts to supply a reason for it.
15. Twelve years later in 1859, Marx offered another wording which though far more popular is not as smooth and explicative:

> In the social production of their existence, men inevitably enter into definite relations ... of production appropriate to a given stage in the development of their material forces of production. The totality of these relations of production constitutes the economic structure of society, the real foundation, on which arises a legal and political superstructure and to which correspond definite forms of social consciousness (Marx; 1970).

16. Jones is there in glorious company: Francis Hutcheson is not mentioned either. Perhaps this was a reflection of the arithmomania of the prevailing economic orientation.
17. One should not overlook the monograph by Nan-Tuan Chao (1930). In addition to Edgeworth's (already mentioned), other *voce* are by E. M. Burns and Gerhard Stavenhagen. The recent article by William L. Miller (1977) limits its elaborate discussion to rent.
18. According to A. B. Wolfe (1936) the label might have been suggested in a conversation with Veblen by Max S. Handman (whom I have been unable to identify).
19. For an eloquent sample, 'If we are getting restless under the taxonomy of a monocotyledonous wage doctrine and a cryptogamic theory of interest, with involute, loculicidal, tomentous and moniliform variants,

what is the cytoplasm, centrosome, or karokynetic process to which we may turn?' (Veblen, 1919).
20. Veblen leaned heavily on psychology. We must remember that he was a contemporary of William McDougall, known for his theory of instincts as 'driving forces, urges to reach some goal'. McDougall's famous *Introduction to Social Psychology* reached the 30th edition in 1950! But by now hardly any scientist would object to the notion of instinct.
21. Cf. Thorstein Sellin, 'Criminology', *IESS*, **3**, pp. 505–10.
22. Later, in the 1888 Preface to the English edition of the *Communist Manifesto*, Engels intimates that he arrived, independently of Marx, at the idea of historical materialism 'which, in my opinion, is destined to do for history what Darwin's theory has done for biology' (Marx, Engels, and Lenin, 1974). That Marx wanted to dedicate the first volume of *Capital* to Charles Darwin is only a legend. But he wrote a flattering inscription on the copy he sent to Darwin.
23. *Studien über die innern Zustände, das Volksleben und insbesondere die ländlichen Einrichtungen Russlands*, 3 vols. (Hanover: Hahn, 1847–52). The volumes were soon translated into English, 1856. Haxthausen's initiative induced some English functionaries in India to study the institutions of the Indian village communities (Georgescu-Roegen, 1976). Haxthausen is yet another startling omission of the *IESS*.
24. The division into evolutionary stages has been a popular, because usually facile, preoccupation from Aristotle to W. W. Rostow. See in particular the essay of Bert Hoselitz in Hoselitz (1960).
25. Aranda, Amba, Bwamba, Dinka, Dodoth, Gisu, Gusli, Ifuago, Jie, Kalinga, Karamojong, Lugbara, Luo, Mampurugu, Marille, Masai, Murngin, Nambikuara, Nakanai, Nandi, Nuer, Siane, Siriono, Star Mountain, Talis, Tallensi, Tiv, Tiwi, Tonga, Turkana, and Winnebago, almost all listed by Southall (*IESS*). There are also the more familiar ones, the Aztec, Inca, and Maya, as well as those mentioned in the next footnote.
26. Boas (1909) for the Kawkiutl; Malinowski (1921) for the Trobriands; Firth (1940) for the Tikopia; Elizabeth Thomas (1959) for the Kalahari Bushmen; and Turnbul (1961 and 1972) for the Pygmies and the Ik.
27. In this, White falls in with the natural scientists, some exceptional authorities, who during the last decades of the eighteenth century propagated the energetic theory of material reality. (For this see, Georgescu-Roegen, 1980.)
28. In the same vein he protested against the idea held by many that 'entrepreneur' is a false concept because no one can specify where exactly it ends and the opposite begins. It is quite amazing what a forceful grip the tenet that every useful concept must have an arithmomorphic boundary has on our minds.
29. I cannot avoid recalling in this connection Schumpeter's assertion that 'a peasant sells his calf just as cunningly and egotistically as the stock exchange member his portfolio of shares'. The implication is that standard economics is justified in adopting an ophelimity function of quantities alone. But the puzzle is resolved if we remember that Schumpeter very probably never saw a peasant, if he did at all, only in

the urban market where, indeed, all peasants behave, because they must, like every other trader (Georgescu-Roegen, 1971).
30. Homan (1932) represents a typical attack of standard economists against all approaches that are not arithmomorphic. The same temper is displayed by Homan in his favourable appraisal of Max Weber's 'ideal types' in comparison to Veblen's institutions. Talcott Parsons in his introduction to Max Weber, *The Theory of Social and Economic Organization* (The Free Press, 1964) goes so far as to describe Veblen as 'a highly unsophisticated person'. Of course, the ideal types should be praised by all who admire pure analysis, for they are only conceptual mirrors of the abstract models of standard economics (say, a market of a moment with complete knowledge), although not from an equally objective standpoint.
31. Another claim to glory of institutional economics is the realisation that within the not too old societies there exists not only that conflict alone, but several that are also responsible for social friction: buyers and sellers, lenders and borrowers, farmers and townees, etc. (Commons, 1934).

References

Boas, F. (1909) *The Kwakiutl of Vancouver Island* (New York: Stechert).
Bohm, D. (1957) *Causality and Chance in Modern Physics* (London: Routledge).
Burns, E. M. (1932) 'Jones, Richard', *Encyclopaedia of the Social Sciences*, vol. VIII (1932) pp. 415–16.
Chao, N. (1930) *Richard Jones: An Early English Institutionalist* (New York: Columbia University).
Coats, A. W. (1964) 'Value Judgments in Economics', *Yorkshire Bulletin of Economic and Social Research*, 16.
Commons, J. R. (1924) *The Legal Foundations of Capitalism* (New York: Macmillan).
—— (1934) *Institutional Economics* (New York: Macmillan).
Darwin, C. (1898) *The Origin of Species*, 6th edn (London: J. Murray, 1898).
Dorfman, J. et al. (1963) *Institutional Economics* (Berkeley: University of California Press).
Edgeworth, F. Y. (1926) 'Jones, Richard', *Palgrave's Dictionary of Political Economy* (London) pp. 490–1.
Engels, F. (1968) 'Speech at the Graveside of Karl Marx', in K. Marx and F. Engels, *Selected Works* (New York: International Publishers).
—— (1972) *The Origin of the Family, Private Property and the State in the Light of the Researches of Lewis H. Morgan*, Introduction by E. B. Leacock (New York: International Publishers). German original dates from 1884.
Firth, R. W. (1940) *The Work of the Gods in Tikopia* (London: Humphries).
Gambs, J. S. (1946) *Beyond Supply and Demand: A Reappraisal of Institutional Economics* (New York: Columbia University Press).

Georgescu-Roegen, N. (1966) *Analytical Economics: Issues and Problems* (Cambridge, Mass.: Harvard University Press).
—— (1971) *The Entropy Law and the Economic Process* (Cambridge, Mass.: Harvard University Press).
—— (1976) *Energy and Economic Myths: Institutional and Analytical Economic Essays* (New York: Pergamon).
—— (1980) 'Matter: A Resource Ignored by Thermodynamics', in L. E. St-Pierre and G. R. Brown (eds), *Future Sources of Organic Raw Materials, CHEMRAWN I* (Oxford: Pergamon Press).
Goldschmidt, R. (1940) *The Material Basis of Evolution* (New Haven: Yale University Press).
Gould, S. J. (1977) 'The Return of Hopeful Monsters', *Natural History*, 86.
von Hayek, F. A. (1973) *Rules and Order* (Chicago: University of Chicago Press).
Hempel, C. G. and Oppenheim, P. (1948) 'Studies in the Logic of Explanation', *Philosophy of Science*, 15.
Hobbes, T. (1839–45) *The English Works*, 11 vols (London: John Bohn).
Homan, P. T. (1931) 'The Institutional School', *Encyclopaedia of the Social Sciences*, vol. v, pp. 387–92.
—— (1932) 'An Appraisal of Institutional Economics', *American Economic Review*, 22.
Hoselitz, B. F. (1960) *Theories of Economic Growth* (Glencoe, Ill.: Free Press).
Ingram, J. K. (1888) *A History of Political Economy* (New York: Augustus M. Kelley, 1967).
Jevons, W. S. (1924) *The Principles of Science*, 2nd edn (London: Macmillan). Original dates from 1874.
Jones, R. (1964a) *An Essay on the Distribution of Wealth and on the Sources of Taxation: Part I, Rent* (New York: Augustus M. Kelley, reprint of the 1831 original).
—— (1964b) *Literary Remains Consisting of Lectures and Tracts on Political Economy* (New York: Augustus M. Kelley, reprint of the 1859 original).
Kautsky, K. (1936) *The Economic Doctrines of Karl Marx* (New York: Macmillan).
Knight, F. H. (1951–2) 'Economics', *Enclycopaedia Britannica*, vol. VII, pp. 925–34.
—— (1960) *Intelligence and Democratic Action* (Cambridge, Mass.: Harvard University Press).
Kroeber, A. L. and Kluckhohn, C. (1963) *Culture: A Critical Review of Concepts and Definitions* (New York: Vintage Books).
Krupp, S. R. (ed.) (1966) *The Structure of Economic Science* (Engelwood Cliffs, N.J.: Pretice-Hall).
de Lapouge, G. V. (1897) 'The Fundamental Laws of Anthropo-Sociology', *Journal of Political Economy*, 6.
Lekachman, R. (1976) *Economists at Bay* (New York: McGraw-Hill).
Malinowski, B. (1921) 'The Primitive Economics of the Trobriand Islanders', *Economic Journal*, 31.
Marshall, A. (1949) *Principles of Economics*, 8th edn (New York: Macmillan).
Marx, K. (1959) *Capital*, 3 vols (Moscow: Foreign Languages Publishing House).

—— (1963) *The Poverty of Philosophy* (New York: International Publishers). The French original dates from 1847.
—— (1970) *A Contribution to the Critique of Political Economy*, Introduction by M. Dobb (New York: International Publishers). The German original dates from 1859.
—— (1971) *Theories of Surplus-Value*, 3 vols (Moscow: Progress Publishers). The German manuscripts date from 1861–63.
Marx, K., Engels, F. and Lenin, V. (1974) *On Historical Materialism* (New York: International Publishers).
Mattessich, R. (1978) *Instrumental Reasoning and Systems Methodology: An Epistemology of the Applied and Social Sciences* (Dordrecht: Reidel).
Mayr, E. (1970) *Populations, Species, and Evolution* (Cambridge, Mass.: Belknap Press).
Mendelsohn, E., Weingart, P. and Whitley, R. (eds) (1977) *The Social Production of Scientific Knowledge, Sociology of the Sciences*, vol. I (Dordrecht: Reidel).
Merton, R. K. (1981) 'Our Sociological Vernacular', *Columbia*, November.
Mill, J. S. (1848) *Principles of Political Economy*, 2 vols (London: J. W. Parker).
Miller, W. L. (1977) 'Richard Jones Contribution to the Theory of Rent', *History of Political Economy*, 9.
Morgan, L. H. (1964) *Ancient Society* (ed.) L. A. White (Cambridge, Mass.: Harvard University Press). Original published in 1877.
Popper, K. R. (1964) *The Poverty of Historicism* (New York: Harper Torchbooks).
Roll, E. (1973) *A History of Economic Thought*, 4th edn (London: Faber and Faber).
Schumpeter, J. A. (1934) *The Theory of Economic Development* (Cambridge, Mass.: Harvard University Press). The German original dates from 1912.
—— (1951) *Ten Great Economists* (New York: Oxford University Press).
—— (1954) *History of Economic Analysis* (New York: Oxford University Press).
Smith, A. (1976) *An Inquiry into the Nature and Causes of the Wealth of Nations*, edited by E. Cannan (Chicago: University of Chicago Press).
Southall, A. (1981) 'Stateless Society', *IESS*, vol. xv, pp. 157–68.
Stavenhagen, G. (1956) 'Jones, Richard', *Handwörterbuch der Sozialwissenschaften*, v (Göttingen, 1956) pp. 422–3.
Thomas, E. M. (1959) *The Harmless People* (New York: Knopf).
Turnbull, C. M. (1961) *The Forest People: A Study of the Pygmies of the Congo* (New York: Simon and Schuster).
—— (1972) *The Mountain People* (New York: Simon and Schuster).
Tylor, E. B. (1958) *Primitive Culture: Research Into the Development of Mythology, Philosophy, Religion, Art and Custom*, 2 vols (Gloucester, Mass.: Smith). Original dates from 1871.
Veblen, T. (1896) 'Review of E. Ferri, *Socialisme et Science Positive*', *Journal of Political Economy*, 5.
—— (1919) *The Place of Science in the Modern Civilization* (New York: Huebsch).
—— (1922) *The Instinct of Workmanship* (New York: Huebsch).

—— (1953) *The Theory of the Leisure Class* (New York: Viking). Original dates from 1899.
White, L. A. (1949) *The Science of Culture: A Study of Man and Civilization* (New York: Farrar and Straus).
——, 'Morgan, Lewis Henry', *IESS*, vol. x, pp. 496–8.
Wolfe, A. B. (1936) 'Institutional Reasonableness and Value', *Philosophical Review*, 45.

COMMENT

Fritz W. Scharpf

I have read and re-read Georgescu-Roegen's paper with great fascination, admiration and almost total agreement, and I have also learned a lot from it. Thus, the comments which I have to offer are not intended as criticisms but, rather, as questions which might call forth further clarifications of Georgescu-Roegen's approach or, sometimes, as an attempt to clarify my own thinking on the issues which he has treated in such masterly fashion.

When I had first responded, at the conference, to the preliminary version of Georgescu-Roegen's paper, I had understood him to argue that there is a precise correspondence or parallelism between three dichotomies defined at the levels of epistemology, of real-world phenomena, and of academic disciplines, namely between arithmomorphic and dialectical concepts, the market and cultural institutions, and ('Standard') economics and the other social sciences.

A more precise reading of the final version has persuaded me, however, that Georgescu-Roegen is also considering the 'market' as one of the cultural institutions – but one which is different in so far as it is more amenable to being described by 'arithmomorphic concepts'. As a consequence, 'the strictly economic phenomenal domain has submitted itself rather easily to what we usually call scientific investigation' (p. 299), while the other cultural institutions have not and will not. It would seem to follow that the other social sciences are not merely lagging behind the scientific progress achieved by what he calls 'standard economics', but that they cannot ever hope to achieve the status of a true science.

It is clear from the rest of the paper that Georgescu-Roegen considers the scientific success of standard economics a pyrrhic victory and would like to see it replaced by an evolutionary approach to the study of economic phenomena which would be similar to the more modest aspirations of the other social sciences. But before I discuss this conclusion, I should like to raise some difficulties which I have with the premises.

Obviously, the 'irreducible dichotomy' between the 'two unbridgeable conceptual categories' (p. 300) – 'arithmomorphic' and 'dialectical' concepts – is fundamental to the analysis. The former are distinct and precisely defined, while the latter are bounded by a 'dialectical penumbra' and tend 'to overlap with their opposites'. That surely is a valid and useful distinction. The difficulty begins when arithmomorphic concepts are further equated with the possibility of 'measurement', by the use of numbers and, ultimately, by the application of interval scales permitting interpolation and 'prediction beyond the actually observed instances' (p. 304).

It seems to me that the argument rests upon a fusion of two logically separate distinctions. Having been trained as a lawyer, and as a good nominalist, I am very much aware of the possibility of precise definition (without dialectical penumbra, that is) even of concepts whose corresponding real-world phenomena could not be measured on an interval scale. Thus it would be entirely possible, to use Georgescu-Roegen's example, to develop completely non-ambiguous definitions of the various types of 'democracy' discussed in political theory. That they could only be 'measured' on a nominal scale would probably preclude the fitting of what Georgescu-Roegen calls 'analytical functions' which are 'determined over the entire range of variation by the values for an interval however small' (p. 302) but it would not preclude some other, less demanding forms of statistical analysis and it would certainly not preclude application of the analytical tools of symbolic logic in order to draw out the valid conclusions implicit in precisely defined nominal concepts. In other words: the distinction between 'well-defined' and 'fuzzy' (or 'dialectical') concepts seems to be logically independent from the distinction between concepts whose empirical referents allow measurement on nominal, ordinal or interval scales.

It seems to me that Georgescu-Roegen may have come to fuse these separable distinctions because he treats the possibility of prediction as the acid test of the scientific character of an academic discipline, and because he equates the possibility of prediction with the possibility of quantitative measurement and the use of interval scales. I tend to disagree on both counts.

First, the possibilities of prediction, outside of the field of astronomy and its likes, seem to be quite limited even in the natural sciences – whose 'scientific' character is assumed as a matter of course even by Georgescu-Roegen. Take earthquakes, volcanic eruptions, blizzards, droughts and floods, hurricanes, harvests, locusts or even 'Waldsterben', and it is obvious that the prediction of real-world phenomena is not one of the strong points of even the most advanced natural sciences. What they are good at is a game from which social scientists are largely excluded: the experimental isolation of causal relations, and engineering under controllable conditions. That does not mean that 'social engineering' could be as successful as 'physical' or 'chemical engineering' if only social scientists had more possibilities of controlled experimentation. But it does suggest that the difficulties of empirical prediction might be quite similar in the social sciences and in the natural sciences.

The reason, I propose, lies in the fact that most real-world processes, natural or social, partake, to a greater or lesser extent, of the conditions which Georgescu-Roegen ascribes only to 'social entities': They are, he suggests, 'a crossroad of numerous dialectical penumbras' (p. 304). And so they are. But the idea of a 'cross-road' or intersection of concepts or explanatory theories seems to be logically separable from, and more pregnant than, the notion of dialectical penumbras. All of our conceptual tools are radical simplifications of real-world phenomena, and it seems that the human mind – and certainly scientific progress under the imperative of Occam's razor – is forever striving to reduce their complexity by focusing upon ever simpler constitutive relationships. But the reduction of complexity has its price: As we escape from 'unscientific' holistic theories, real-world phenomena are progressively transformed into composite events which cannot be explained, and much less predicted, within the confines of any single scientific theory. They appear to our specialised scientific perceptions as intersections or 'crossroads' of separate chains of causation, each of which may be well-explained and predictable within its own theoretical frame of reference, but whose co-incidence must appear unexplainable and unpredictable (in other words: 'coincidental') from all theoretical points of view.

For the natural sciences, whose usual goal is physical, chemical or biological engineering, rather than the explanation and prediction of complex real-world phenomena, this 'crossroads problem' is often not very important. But when it is important, as it is in the case of 'Waldsterben', the natural sciences are not only weak in prediction but often have difficulties even with those after-the-fact explanations of 'historically unique events' which Georgescu-Roegen describes as the sole recourse of social sciences which are unable to employ arithmomorphic concepts (pp. 312–13).

Secondly, even though the natural sciences have their difficulties with prediction, it would not necessarily follow that the social sciences, employing 'dialectical' rather than 'arithmomorphic concepts', are totally incapable of predicting. Their difficulties, certainly, are much greater. But they seem to have less to do with the epistemological character of the concepts employed than with the fact that the social sciences are dealing not with the immutable laws of nature but with human action whose potential creativity is only constrained, but not fully determined, by antecedent conditions. That fact, by itself, is of immense importance for an understanding of what the social sciences can and cannot hope to achieve. Dealing with constraints, that is with capabilities and impossibilities, they could firmly predict only the consequences of the latter. Within the realm of what is not impossible, however, the best that the social sciences could hope for is stochastic explanations and predictions allowing for a good deal of unexplainable and unpredictable variance around any empirically identifiable central tendency.

But how do we identify central tendencies within the 'noise' of random variation? Georgescu-Roegen seems to suggest that there is only one possible way: statistical inference based upon quantitative data measured on interval scales. That explains his emphasis upon the epistemological distinction between dialectical and arithmomorphic concepts, and the equation of the latter with the possibility 'to fit some analytical functions ... that have the signal property of being determined over the entire range of variation by the values for an interval however small' (p. 302).

That possibility, surely, is an invaluable help to scientific explanation and prediction. But is that all we have to work with? In order to deal with this question, we need to specify more precisely what it is that we are looking for. The constraints limiting the random variability of spontaneous and idiosyncratic human action are of two kinds, natural and cultural-institutional. As the former are reduced in importance with the historical progress of science and industry, it is now almost correct to say, as Georgescu-Roegen does, that 'culture in the strictest sense, is the sole determining factor of evolution' (p. 312). So if we are searching for empirical regularities in the realm of human action and social interaction, we are primarily looking for the influence of 'cultural institutions' shaping and constraining human choices. Now it should certainly be possible to trace that influence in the quantitative data representing the quantifiable aspects of human behaviour – and much empirical social-science research (not only in 'standard economics') is doing just that. But that is not the only valid approach in the social sciences.

When discussing 'cultural institutions', Georgescu-Roegen repeatedly speaks of their 'internal logic' (e.g. p. 316) – which I interpret as referring to the circular, 'autopoetic' relationship through which an institution selects and reinforces certain patterns of human action and is, in turn, reproduced and reinforced through them. The discovery of that 'internal logic' is a process which differs fundamentally from the discovery of empirical regularities in large masses of quantitative data. Maybe we need to have witnessed, as Georgescu-Roegen suggests, 'numberless dogs being born, growing up, getting old and dying' before we can predict how long a dog will live (p. 313), but the mere observation of any number of watches would never inform us about the clockwork mechanism that makes them keep the time. For that, we would have to get inside the 'black box' and to develop, through a process of theoretical reconstruction, a model of the 'internal logic' of a watch – i.e. of how its different parts fit together and work together.

Of course, that process of theoretical reconstruction could be aided by empirical observation, but it could not be deduced from it. Its success would probably owe more to experimentation, including pencil-and-paper 'Gedankenexperimente' and, in the social sciences, to that peculiar 'operation called "Verstehen"' which the Vienna school of logical positivism found so hard to accept. Furthermore, the internal validity of the model and its 'logic' could be established or refuted even in the absence of any empirical tests (as in the case of the flying machines designed by Leonardo da Vinci, for which suitable materials or sources of power were not yet available). And, conversely, a correct model of, say, a mechanical watch would not be invalidated by the empirical finding that some – or even all – presently observable timekeeping devices are operating from batteries. At the same time, a correct model of the 'internal logic' of a watch or of a 'cultural institution' would allow us to make powerful but contingent predictions: They would be true whenever applied to phenomena governed by that particular logic – but the logic itself would not allow us to predict the occasions of its own applicability.

In his paper, Georgescu-Roegen has clearly acknowledged the predictive potential of the internal logic of cultural institutions, but he seems to limit its application to what he, quoting von Hayek quoting Montesquieu, calls 'spontaneous institutions'. But why should they be the only institutions capable of creating 'a state of affairs such that knowledge of a part of it allows correct expectations concerning the rest' (p. 315)? Apparently they are privileged, in Georgescu-Roegen's eyes, because they are thought to be universal in character, 'spontaneously' appearing whenever and wherever human beings interact. But does that mean that all other knowledge about institutions must be relegated to the ex-post discovery of the historically unique logic of paraticular 'situations' (p. 313)? I think not.

In his sweeping comparison of universalistic and particularistic explanations, Georgescu-Roegen leaves out the broad middle ground of what Michele Salvati in his comments has aptly described as 'contingently stable theories', and what I had elsewhere discussed under the label of 'theories of limited applicability' – whose discovery I regard as the true calling of the social sciences. What is meant is that institutions need to be recognised as powerful stabilisers and, hence, predictors of human behaviour and that, at the same time, institutions must also be seen as artefacts of human creation and, hence, likely to differ in time and space, and to change. The social sciences would be foolish to throw away, in a misguided effort to emulate the universalism of the natural sciences, the explanatory and predictive potential of instituional analysis, but they would be equally foolish to forget the historical contingency of all institutions, and their potential for change through purposeful or spontaneous human action. This, I suggest, is the central insight which establishes our identity as social scientists *vis-à-vis* the universalism of the natural sciences and the particularism of historiography alike. But there is yet another difficulty for the social sciences, and Georgescu-Roegen may well have had it in mind when he emphasised the need to discover the internal logic, not of institutions but of 'each situation' (p. 316).

This makes perfectly good sense if we relate it to the 'crossroads problem' discussed above. The social sciences do not usually enjoy the protective isolation of the R and D laboratory, which shields the natural and engineering sciences from premature exposure to the complexities of the real world. Instead, social scientists are generally expected to demonstrate the power of their theories in the explanation and prediction of real-world phenomena, and if there is any social-science equivalent to engineering, it is likely to take the form of policy advice to 'decision makers' operating under real-world conditions. But real-world situations, in the natural as well as in the social realm, are likely to be intersections, rather than straightforward applications, of scientifically established theories. To make matters worse, the interaction effects of several theoretically well-understood processes are less likely to be purely additive in the social realm than they are in the realm of nature. The reason seems to be quite straightforward: as the institutional logics underlying each of the intersecting theories operate as constraints upon human action, without fully determining it, additional degrees of freedom may be mobilized at the intersection. As a consequence, interaction effects cannot be completely deduced from a knowledge of all partial theories involved. To the extent that this is true, it is indeed correct to assert, as Georgescu-

Roegen does, that 'each situation has its own logic ... that we must discover' (p. 316). But in that endeavour it would still be extremely useful for us if we could draw upon validated partial theories explicating the internal logic of the particular institutions which are involved in a real-world 'situation'. If that were accepted, three conclusions would seem to follow.

First, as all scientific theories tend to provide at best partial explanations and poor predictions of complex real-world phenomena, there seems to be little reason for taking 'standard economics' to task because of its failure to account for the evolution of real-world economies. Instead, we ought to admire and profit from its power as a partial theory to reconstruct the logic of human action under the institutional conditions of near-perfect markets. That power is rooted not only, as Georgescu-Roegen suggests, in its arithmomorphic concepts and the availability of quantitative data, but also in the utter simplicity of its motivational assumptions, and in the relative stability and ubiquity of patterns of market exchange. In all of the social sciences there is nothing like it – as far as it goes.

But, secondly, standard economics does not and could not go far enough, if the goal is to explain, predict and guide real-world processes even in the economic sphere. And there is no point in asking economists to widen their horizons and to take account of all varieties of other 'cultural' influences upon the behaviour of economic agents. That would only force them to overstep the institutional logic of competitive markets – and to lose all their comparative advantages over the other social sciences. Instead, what is needed is the vigorous development of the other social sciences. Rather than submitting to, or wasting our efforts in opposition to, the manifest intellectual imperialism of standard economics, political scientists, sociologists, anthropologists and social psychologists ought to concentrate on 'doing their own thing' – that is upon discovering and reconstructing the 'internal logics' of such institutions as industrial relations systems, labour unions, interest associations, government coalitions, ministerial bureaucracies, the mass media or nuclear and extended families. Resting upon less simple motivational assumptions and dealing with more complex and more changeable institutional arrangements, our theories will perhaps never attain the elegance and stability achieved by standard economics. But they can be more than mere story telling and *ad hoc* theorising.

Yet even if we are successful, what we will achieve will be partial theories which will not be able to explain, and much less to predict or to guide, the evolution of real-world societies, polities or economies. If standard economics is to be faulted, it is for often ignoring the limitations inherent in the 'crossroads problem'. Even competitive markets (whose logic may, indeed, be nearly universal) always intersect with more parochial and more ephemeral institutions, so that the actual behaviour of economic agents will differ from one country to another and from one time to another. Behavioural regularities observed in the United States will not necessarily apply in Sweden or Germany – and neither will the policy recommendations derived from them. There is a heavy price, therefore, which smaller countries must pay if their economists begin to import their real-world knowledge from abroad.

That, of course, is begging the question of whether accurate real-world knowledge (as distinguished from specialised theoretical knowledge) can be obtained at all in the social sciences. Georgescu-Roegen seems to think that it cannot, and that the best we can hope to achieve is the ex-post explanation of historically unique events. I am somewhat more optimistic, given the relative stability of the institutional arrangements which are interacting, but the difficulties should certainly not be underestimated. They arise from the fact that accurate real-world knowledge must necessarily be 'situational', and that it must be 'intersection knowledge', linking our understanding of the internal logics of several institutions at the same time. That means, first, that we are operating under some kind of 'minimum law': Our understanding of the situation as a whole is limited by the least well-understood institutional logic involved. And it means, secondly, that there are pragmatic limitations to the degree of 'useful sophistication' in intersection analyses: if some of the important factors in an equation can be measured only very crudely, there is no sense in developing other measures to a much greater degree of precision. In that sense, we would probably profit most from a more vigorous development of institutional analyses in political science and sociology, as well as from a variety of economics which would be more interested in the interfaces of competitive markets with other institutions, and somewhat less intent upon drawing out the logical implications of ever more rarefied assumptions under hypothetical market conditions.

The difficulties of generating accurate 'intersection knowledge' should not be underestimated, but neither are they insuperable. The most convincing example that I am aware of is the 'Rehn-Meidner model' of Swedish labour market policy developed in the early 1950s.

It was based upon an analysis of the opportunities and constraints of a 'small, open economy' in competitive world markets combined with a sympathetic understanding of the institutional logic of a powerful trade union movement driven by a quasi-religious fervour for equality, and with a subtle appreciation of the developmental potential of an under-utilised labour market administration. On that basis, Gösta Rehn and Rudolf Meidner were able to design a set of interconnected policy recommendations linking union wage policy with government fiscal and labour market policy in such a fashion that the overall degree of goal achievement of all the parties involved was probably greater in Sweden than in any other country during the time that the Rehn-Meidner model was in operation. Of course, as we have been reminded at this conference, the model did not work nearly as well in other countries, and it has not worked very well for some time even in Sweden. But that only supports the theoretical point I am trying to make.

'Intersection knowledge' is not for export, and it is a perishable good – and so are the policy recommendations derived from it. Thus, what worried me when doing interviews in Sweden a year ago was not the fact that the Rehn-Meidner model was considered entirely passé by the present generation of Swedish economists. I was worried by the fact that none of them seemed even interested in replacing it with a more up-to-date but equally complex model of economic policy under present institutional conditions, and that so many of them seemed entirely content to accept the findings of American empirical studies as reasonable proxies for the workings of the Swedish economy.

To end on a more positive note: if we are able to reconstruct the logic of the 'cultural institutions' which constrain and shape human behaviour, we should also be able to develop the 'intersection knowledge' linking the logics of several institutions which are simultaneously involved in any real-world situation. They are changeable, to be sure, but institutional change tends to be difficult and slow enough for the social sciences to catch up with it. If we do, the promise is not only the broader and deeper understanding of real-world situations, but the more pertinent guidance which the social sciences might have to offer to policy makers dealing with the irreducible complexity of the real world. The success of the Rehn-Meidner model, in its time and place, should encourage us in that endeavour.

Michele Salvati

Commenting upon Georgescu-Roegen's paper is a very difficult task. First, it should not be considered a paper in the usual meaning of the word. It is an extremely condensed version of the product of many, many years of work of a subtle and passionate mind reflecting upon the epistemological foundations of our discipline. Secondly, and particularly for me, it is a very difficult task because I so much agree with the overall thrust of Georgescu-Roegen's reflections. Were I a neo-positivist belonging to some of the various persuasions prevailing in economics – a verificationist, a falsificationist, an operationalist, or whatever – it would be feasible to express a wholehearted rebuttal of Georgescu-Roegen's main points: this would be a pretty uninteresting religious clash, but at least it would be clear. Yet I am no neo-positivist. In particular, I do not have any clear-cut position in the monism *vs* dualism debate, that is, in the debate between those who believe that science has a unique methodology of the *Naturwissenschaften* and are radically different from those of the *Geisteswissenschaften*. Since it is so, much of what Georgescu-Roegen says falls on a soil which is prepared to receive it and evokes many sympathetic questions. Let me simply hint at two of them.

Am I right in thinking that Georgescu-Roegen is suggesting some kind of evolutionary paradigm? I mean, something of the sort that Herbert Simon, Richard Nelson and Sidney Winter are striving at? In this case, how would he react to the powerful criticism that Jon Elster (1979) has raised against the use of evolutionary and functionalist metaphors in social sciences? Or, how would he react against the convincing defence that Raymond Boudon (*La place du désordre*) has recently advanced of the rational action paradigm, as the proper paradigm for social sciences?

Another question I would raise, if there were time to discuss it, is the following. True, social sciences are mainly concerned with non-controllable, uniquely variable, real time sequences, whereas natural sciences usually succeed in cutting out for themselves a domain of controllable, timeless, stable, repeatable relationships. On the one side, however, natural sciences do sometime make predictions or advance explanations in the real time, historical world: there is a natural history – a geological, a biological, and astronomical history – and, besides, we have to make weather forecasts. And it turns out that such predictions and explanations are usually much better than those of the social sciences, but they do not compare with the engineering successes of the same natural sciences. On the other side, even in the messy and uniquely changing world of human history, something can be cut out which is contingently stable: can't we build up unpretentious, small scale, contingent models about that? If we can't, we are left with history alone. We all love history, but this would not be a satisfactory way out: there are very few historians today who would share Ranke's prescription to tell a story as 'es ist eigentlich gewesen'.

A careful re-reading of Georgescu-Roegen's paper, suggests an answer to my first question which was formulated after his oral presentation. The world of cultural institutions is an evolutionary world, but there is no reason why an evolutionary *theory*, à la Simon, would explain it: through dialectical concepts we can explain evolutionary change only *ex post*, by means of history. But, if this is Georgescu-Roegen's position, we are led straight to the second question. Since this question is one that cannot be answered instantly I shall instead consider some of the specific points raised by Georgescu-Roegen and apply them to a sketchy epistemological review of the discussions of the last few days. Four items can be selected for discussion: visions, theories, ideal types, historicism.

Vision is a Schumpeterian word, which is sometimes equated to the Kuhnian paradigm. It has a different meaning, however, because it underlines the broadness of the picture more than the paradigm does, and it stresses even more the pre-analytical, cultural-ideological choices which inevitably go with theory-building. We cannot do without visions, since they are powerful intellectual organisers. The initial discussions thus involved a clash of visions. Now, the problem with discussions based on alternative visions is that they are imperialistically motivated; there is a tendency to expand particular visions into areas where their organising function diminishes and their ideological residual increases. One can hardly accuse the post-Sraffian classical vision of imperialism for it is at present only seeking modest recognition in its proper ground, that of relative price determination and income distribution. May I, however, scandalise my Sraffian friends by suggesting that the modern classical vision has had little to say – up to the present, at least – about the forces that in the long run and on average have produced a sustained level of employment in capitalist economies, despite the decentralised character of decision making? Why does the bumblebee succeed in flying? That is: how do billions of individual decisions get co-ordinated and resources decently allocated?

The step from vision to theory is a perilous one. I sincerely doubt whether it can be taken in the social sciences, if by theory we mean something similar to theory in natural sciences, that is, bodies of knowledge capable of enunciating universal laws. At this point I must turn to the neo-classical vision, because it is from that vision that Popperian 'laws' have been derived in recent times: positive economics is neo-classical economics. But we must be cautious: this may have been more a product of historical contingency than of necessity. It simply happened that neo-classical paradigm was in ascendancy: Austrian purists, a branch of neo-classicists, reject positive economics and defend an unfashionable dualistic position. In any case, it is a fact that the neo-classical vision has produced a number of pseudo-laws which are frequently submitted to econometric 'verification': the most astonishing example of this intellectual attitude is, to my mind, Denison's work on the causes of differentials in economic growth. But to stick to our topic, we had a very interesting discussion on NAIRUs and Wage-gaps, which are dervied from the neo-classical paradigm by means of procedures similar to those Denison employed to derive his estimates. The result was recognition that the same statistical results may have, and probably have, an explanation that has nothing to do with production functions and all that. But, if this is the case, why do we keep using them as the basis for analysis? This is a good example of a vision with imperialistic ambitions, which is continuously extended to fields where it is logically inapplicable.

If there is such a danger in enunciating theories and Popperian laws on the basis of a vision, what can we do? Must we fall back on history? Perhaps not: there are some intermediate steps that might be preferable. A first step, of a theoretical nature, is to fight the imperialistic tendencies of the visions, to confine them in their proper field. This is easier said than done; yet it is surprising how little thought has been devoted to this problem. If we were really convinced that the neo-classical vision only has application to the problem to resource allocation, a lot of useless extension could have been avoided. A second step, more methodological in character, is the one we have already hinted at: that is, to extract from visions not so much Popperian 'theories', but less pretentious and contingent models, either in the vein of Max Weber's ideal types, or in the vein of 'statistical uniformities', as John Hicks called them, a bit improperly, I think, in his marvellous little book: *A Theory of Economic History* (1969). Something of this kind is present in David Soskice's contribution: more a *divertissement* than a model. But it can be developed into a model explaining the tensions between centralising tendencies and necessity to decentralise faced by contemporary unions.

Finally, on historicism. If our discussion did exhibit a clash of visions; and if we fell into the trap of Popperian theories; we did not fall into the trap of historicism. There is, however, the danger of falling into this trap every time we think about long-run historical developments, as we are forced to do when considering today's unemployment. Our French colleagues are fully aware of it, and there is no trace of historicism in their present theorising about *régulation*. But every time we are thinking about a succession of stages, phases or periods, as they do; when these stages are seen as complex wholes, as they are; and when the transition from one to another is thought of as being brought about by mounting internal tensions (contradictions?), as it is; the dangers of historicism and holism are right around the corner.

References

Boudon, Raymond (1984) *La Place du Désordre* (Paris: Presses Universitaires de France).

Elster, J. (1979) *Ulysses and the Sirens* (Cambridge: Cambridge University Press).

Hicks, John (1969) *A Theory of Economic History* (Oxford: Clarendon Press).

Part VI
A Summing Up and Conclusions

12 New Lines of Research on the Question of Full Employment

Josef Steindl

Our discussions over the last few days have dealt with the identification of 'Barriers to Full Employment'. But recognising them does not solve them; further research is necessary. Since the problem of unemployment involves a major part of economic theory the field is so wide that my choice of topics for future research will be of necessity subjective, but I hope not arbitrary. I shall take my cue from various contributions and try to relate them to each other.

Some papers are general and abstract, others deal directly with contemporary problems. Such a mixture is all to the good. We can't do without theory even if, as Georgescu-Roegen has reminded us, our concepts cannot possibly have the same precision as those of the physicists, whom economists have unfortunately often tried to emulate. We might rather turn to Myrdal who once defined the function of theory as 'putting questions to the empirical material'. It is like a map which tells us where to look and what to look for. Without it we are disoriented.

I refer first to Kregel's paper on wages and unemployment where, following Weintraub, he uses a sophisticated non-neo-classical equilibrium model to deal with this problem. An important feature of it is that prices and quantities are both included as endogenous variables in the system. We are immediately reminded of Roncaglia's paper, where we are told that the classics always dealt with these two variables one at a time. Now as far as I know, most applied economists dealing with concrete problems of economic policy or analysing actual events follow the strategy advocated by Roncaglia. As an example, consider input–output models. They assume prices as given and deal with some problems of quantities, say a multiplier analysis, on this basis. Or they start from a given final output, as Sraffa also does, and analyse prices and distribution. All Kaleckian economics works with given and constant prices, operating on deflated values of macro-economic variables. In this sense, Kalecki certainly was a classicist! The simultaneous treatment of quantities and prices involves non-linearities: The flex-price relations are typically non-linear (agricultural and other primary commodities) and bottle-necks generally involve non-linearities. For an abstract equilibrium theory this raises no problems. But for an applied economist such simultaneous equation systems are not very helpful. He has to start from given initial conditions and work out the process as it evolves in time, for example by means of difference equations. This is what Paul Davidson implies when he says that economic processes are not ergodic, that is, they do not lead to a steady state independent of initial conditions. (I should add that even if they are ergodic they do not converge quickly so that they never get old enough, in practice, to reach the steady state, being again and again interrupted by disturbances from outside.) Now if you try to work with difference or other functional equations, non-linearity will not be easy to deal with. I have no recipe to offer, unfortunately. In the field of microeconomics (information approach) Streissler has not given us much encouragement to pursue this line of research. Moreover, it would rather seem to carry coals to Newcastle if one entered a field in which so many people have tried their ingenuity. The chances of finding still another variant of the same ideas can only get smaller and smaller.

Let me pass now to another type of contribution. Guger and Walterskirchen have dealt directly with the post-war history of employment. They have, first of all, stressed the importance of monetary policy, both in Keynes's thinking and in the troubles of our times. (As to the latter I might mention that the abandonment of the cheap money policy practised under the influence of Keynes during the war came very early, around 1950, in Britain and in the US, helped by the experience of inflation.)

It is not irrelevant to theoretical discussions of interest rates that they depend much on institutions which are different according to place and time. In the period after the *General Theory* the prevailing view in England was that the influence of interest rates on investment was very small in general. This view was supported by interviews with businessmen (Hitch and Hall in Oxford). The economists' view on the insubstantial role of interest rates on investment decisions (excepting housing and power stations) was based on the argument that only the long-term interest rate was relevant for fixed investment, and this varied only within narrow limits in the short period. This does not contradict Keynes's hopes that over a longer period the rate might be altered substantially. The situation has never been quite the same on the continent where industrial investment has always been financed to a large extent by bank credits with practically variable interest. Today, changes in long-term interest rates are substantial and take effect more quickly than before. What matters most today is that national interest rate policy is not autonomous; the influence of outside financial powers, so much deplored by Keynes, is currently formidable. Under present conditions capital flows are very difficult to control. The one country which could control them is the US. They could turn away capital in excess of what they need to finance their balance of payments deficit, as the Swiss have done formerly.

I think that Salvati was quite right when he observed that international problems have not been given the role they deserve in the context of the problem of barriers to full employment. (Perhaps this was due to the feeling that the balance of payments constraint is not of crucial importance in Germany.) It is quite a different question however, whether one should conduct research in this direction. The competition in this field, from international organisations and personalities with long standing experience, is strong. One would enter this fray only on the basis of the very strong interest of a team of collaborators.

The Guger-Walterskirchen paper suggests that studies on the finance of industry, based on the flow of funds data and on company balance sheets, would be of very great interest. How has accumulation been financed? What did finance contribute to accumulation? We hear that banks on the European continent have contributed more than those in the US and *a fortiori* more than in Britain.[1] On the other hand, high tech entrepreneurs complain that German banks are not able, or not willing, to finance innovation. It is thus a question not only of how much but also of where and how. We also hear of funds of large industrial concerns held in the form of financial investments in preference to real investment, of the increasing role of financial and real estate business in the activities and gains of large industrial concerns. It would evidently be of great interest to go into the question of how the practice, the attitudes and aims of industrial concerns have developed over the post-war period. How much investment was induced by a given flow of retained profits (taking into account a plausible lag) in the 1950s and 1960s, and how much later, in the 1970s and 1980s? As a second priority a study of how much household saving is institutional. Though it makes no difference whether the household invests directly in bonds or whether this is done for him by pension funds, etc., but there may be effects on the rate of saving. In fact, the low saving ratio of recent years in the US has been explained by high interest rates which made lower payments into pension funds sufficient to secure given future pension rights. Consumption credits and house building are further elements influencing household saving.

The subject of saving is obviously closely connected with income distribution which is therefore very relevant for effective demand and employment. Today the personal distribution of income is no less, perhaps even more, important than the functional distribution between wages, profits, etc. But it is also even more difficult to get information about it. In fact, there are yawning gaps in our information. Even partial information in this field, bringing us a few steps further, would be, however, exceedingly valuable and worth a lot of trouble.

Something might now be said about the three post-war periods which Keynes anticipated (cf. Guger and Walterskirchen, p. 108). The second period faded out gradually in the course of the 1960s. In its earlier stages it was strongly influenced by the catching up process in Europe. The continent of Europe had been cut off from American technological development for many years; a reserve of knowledge had thus accumulated which became available after the war, aided also by Marshall Plan technical assistance; it had a strong influence on the scale of investment and growth of productivity on the European continent. Drawing on available know-how is infinitely more easy than creating new methods and the effects on investment are strong. We cannot say exactly when these effects were exhausted, but their gradual disappearance must have contributed to the ending of the second period. The flagging of animal spirits was a motive for increasing tax allowances, illustrated by the decrease in profit taxes in various countries such as Britain and the US.

The basic reason for the ending of the second period, as Keynes foresaw, was the accumulation of productive capacity and a decline in its rate of utilisation, helped also perhaps by the accumulation of excess depreciation, although this was counter-acted by inflation. These considerations suggest a fairly wide field of empirical study on investment, depreciation, capital stock, capacity and utilisation. In an interesting study of the United Nations Economic Commission for Europe[2] the available data on utilisation were used, by means of the production index, to calculate the implicit index of capacity. The results were then compared with the data on gross capital stock. This showed for some countries such as the US a lower growth of capacity which was interpreted as a shortening of the life-time of equipment. This attempt to make explicit the implications of a very shaky data base throws some light on our ignorance in this field. We know much less about capital equipment than demographers know about people. We have no statistics at all about scrapping (death) and our ideas about the length of life are rather conventional. The assumption of a constant length of life underlies all statistics of the capital stock. The concepts of capacity and utilisation as well as the empirical data need considerable study. This would also give opportunity for interdisciplinary work (co-operation with engineers to obtain technical expertise). The importance of the capacity concept has also been suggested by Roncaglia when he spoke of the distinction between classical and Keynesian unemployment. Classically unemployed are those who cannot be employed for lack of capital – for what I would call employment capacity in contrast to output capacity which is the usual meaning of 'capacity'. Roncaglia suggested that classical unemployment is being created by the policy of restricting demand because it leads to a deficiency of investment. (Perhaps the neglect of investment in 'human capital' is even more grave.)

But lack of capacity may arise also for demographic reasons: at the end of the second period there was a substantial increase in the growth rate of the labour force in the US. The reasons were higher birth and participation rates, especially for women. Thus the US would have had to increase its growth rate in order to keep unemployment from growing. In Europe the tendency was blurred by the movements of foreign workers. Here the restriction of investment played the more decisive role. As a result there is a legacy of mass unemployment which certainly could not be removed in one stroke. If there is indeed not enough employment capacity to absorb the masses of unemployed then this would offer at least a motive and a justification for building this capacity, creating in this way at the same time the necessary increase in effective demand. There is the objection that after building this employment capacity the output capacity will be so large that there will be no possibility to use it. There is some force in this argument, but I think most of the sting can be taken out of it if we manage to increase the real wage *pari passu* with the ratio of output capacity to employment capacity. The process makes economic sense but it needs some ignition, it does not start by itself. We can develop suitable policies only if we understand the reasons for the hesitation of the investor. The beginning of what Keynes designated the third period was marked by unusually great uncertainties. They came from technology, from the environment, from energy, from the dissatisfaction with the existing organisation – the bureaucratic large concerns – and from consumption. What are people going to do with further increases in real income? Here Schefold's remarks are relevant: the consumer does not have a map of indifference curves printed in his brain from which he can read off his automatic reaction to a change in circumstances. He has to learn everything, which he cannot do on the basis of habit and tradition. It should be realised how much of our economic behaviour rests on repetition and imitation. To create new forms is much less easy, it demands time and effort and therefore it implies hesitation. This is where the papers of Delorme, Boyer and Schefold come in. They have no doubt that a major change is occurring in technology and organisation – the 'regulation' as Delorme would have it. In this conviction they are following Charles Sable. Delorme reflects the uncertainty in the strongest terms: we cannot know, he maintains, what the future 'régulation' will be like. Schefold, dealing with a more special subject, takes a very positive view of the relation of environmental protection to investment and employment. Environmental policies may cost money, but on balance they create new employment.

In fact the now prevailing view that the need for material production has reached limits may seem a little one-sided if one considers the needs of the environment, the needs arising from the structural changes and the necessity to repair and modernise the infrastructure of neglected and depressed regions which in some cases seem to extend to whole countries.

But what is the proper policy for the third period, that is for a time with chronic deficiency of effective demand? In the short run public spending and support for ailing firms have served some small countries well in keeping unemployment at a lower level than in most large countries. But the measures cannot be continued indefinitely because of the burden of interest on the public debt. As a long-run policy there are the two alternatives of either reducing full employment saving by a change in income distribution or stimulating useful investment. Either of these methods would be suitable, in principle, to absorb the high levels of unemployment. With regard to the first I have already indicated the usefulness of studies of inequality of income and saving, and such studies might also throw some light on the feasibility of policy measures designed to reduce inequality.

The second alternative is linked up with the wider question of technology policy. Kalecki in his writings on the trend regarded innovations as the main stimulus to growth. This justifies looking at technology policy as a possible instrument for the stimulation of investment. Technology policy is based on the conviction that the technical development can be influenced according to the *desiderata* of public policy such as environmental aims, preference for saving of material and energy rather than saving of labour, desirable life-styles, working and social conditions, etc. The national struggle for markets need not be the prime aim, although it will be legitimate for countries with chronic balance of payments deficits.

Technology policy involves a systematic study of technical possibilities and capabilities of industrial firms. It will further the application of new technology by information and co-ordination, striving at synergy, and combination of complementary developments. This corresponds very much to Keynesian thinking: we can expect results from better information of entrepreneurs and from greater confidence resulting from co-operation and co-ordination.

In spite of the very great interest of technology policy it does not follow that research in this field could be recommended unconditionally. I have a feeling that such research in general could not very well be carried on as a sideline but only with a fairly considerable concentration of resources in personnel and money. The field is very wide and complicated. Instead I would advocate, among the numerous lines of research which might suggest themselves in connection with the major question of 'regulation', the following study: An attempt to find out about the experiences, views and attitudes of young entrepreneurs who have not so long ago set up in business. This would be interesting both from a practical and from a more general point of view. What difficulties are these people encountering? What motivates them, what attracts them and what discourages them from their career?[3]

I turn now to the topic of labour relations brilliantly dealt with by Meidner and Soskice. I am rather ignorant of the subject, but perhaps this made me a relatively unprejudiced listener. As such I have the impression that the considerable differences of opinion which emerged in the discussion do not represent hardened doctrinaire views but are amenable to be influenced by new information and experience.

Soskice pleaded for concentration of unions and of the bargaining process. In my country the conditions for income policy and consensus policy are very favourable since there is a great concentration of decision-making power on all sides. But the very conditions which make income policy and short-run policy in general so eminently successful involve great disadvantages for long-term economic policy. The required concentration and stability of power involves great conservatism and immobility. There is a lack of interest in long-term policy altogether, and the climate created by entrenched hierarchies is quite unfavourable to innovation and technology policy.

What struck me in the discussion were the doubts, partly open, partly implicit, about wage structure and the related policy. We know that in spite of professions of solidarity, wages are vastly unequal in many countries with concentrated union power. They cannot be otherwise if the weak industries and firms are to be protected. Hence Meidner's principle of brutality – let the weak firms die – is a decisive condition for equality. But can we afford it? (It may also be a regional problem.) Inequality and wage drift are also of importance for inflation and for the structural problems (the declining basic industries have high wages).

In view of the great interest of these questions it seems to me that a comparative study of trade union organisation in relation to wage formation, technology and training in a number of countries would be a very promising line of research. At the same time it will be necessary to extend such a study to the dynamical and historical aspects, that is to the changes which have happened and are happening in the field of labour relations and trade unions (we have to think, for example, of the effect of the decline of the basic and smoke stack industries, the rise of new industries and attitudes of management). Since such studies would be very topical they would be sure to find much interest, and the researchers would have a chance to work on recent experiences where there is a greater chance of 'getting in' first.

Notes

1. G. Nardozzi, 'Structural Trends of Financial Systems and Capital Accumulation: France, Germany, Italy', Economic Papers, Commission of the European Community (CEC No. 14) May 1983.
2. United Nations: Economic Commission for Europe, EC.AD/SEM.9/R.2, Geneva, 18 July 1985.
3. If anybody needs to be convinced of the great interest in interviews with managers he might look at an article on the 'New Managerial Elite' in *Business Week*, 23 January 1985.

Index

ability, and voluntary unemployment 50–1
absorption of private savings 114, 135
accumulation regimes 252–9
adjustment, rational expectations and 94–6
'After Keynesian Macroeconomics' (Lucas and Sargent) 90
aggregate analysis of wages 31–3, 45, 46
Aglietta, M. 236, 251
Akerlof, G. A. 43
Alban, C. 172
Albeda, W. 176
Albrecht, C. 172
allocation and labour market policy 165, 167–8
alternative strategies and energy 280–3
analytical functions 302, 303
Ancient Society (Morgan) 310
André, C. 182 *figs*, 183, 191, 199, 201
anthropology 310–12
anti-cyclical saving behaviour 115
'Appraisal of Institutional Economics, An' (Homan) 309–10
arithmomorphism 300, 301, 302, 327–30
Arnold, T. 316
Artus, P. *et al.* 198
assets, rational expectations theory and exchange of 94–5
astronomy 79
Austria 51, 123, 127–8
Austrian Institute for Economic Research *see* WIFO
Austro-Keynesianism 128
automation
 flexible 253–9
 prognosis for 249
 see also technology
Azariadis, C. 57, 58

Baily, M. N. 56–8
balance of payments 120–1
Belassa, B. 291
Benassy, J. P. 236, 245
benefits, social security 185–6, 189, 192, 210, 211
Bertrand, H. 236, 252

Beyond Contract: Work, Power and Trust Relations (Fox) 230
Binswanger, H. C. *et al.* 139, 284
biologism 314
Blanchard, O. 137, 198, 200
Blinder, A. S. 44
Bliss, C. J. 25
Boas, F. 312
Bohm, D. 313
borrowing, flow of funds analysis 111–15
bottlenecks, labour market policy and 159, 167
Boudon, R. 336
Boyer, R. A. 249, 348
 accumulation regimes 252, 255
 economic policy 197, 198, 199, 201
 growth and productivity 240, 241, 243 *fig*, 244, 245
 institutions 250, 251
 new technology 234, 236
Bruche, G. 174
Bruno, M. 133
Brunowsky, R. D. 276, 279 *fig*
Buchanan, J. M. 316
budget deficits *see* deficits
buffer stocks 117
building industry 255
Bureau of Labour 240
business borrowing 111–13, 114
business cycles 90

CEPII 241
capacity, utilisation of 14, 17–18, 346–7
capital
 co-operation with labour 229–30
 liquid asset prices and marginal productivity of 85–7
 Sraffa and 11–12
 see also capital–labour substitution
Capital (Marx) 308
capital–labour substitution 193, 196–7
car industry
 flexible automation and 254
 French 249–50
carbon dioxide cycle 274–5
Carlyle, T. 316
Causality and Chance in Modern Physics (Bohm) 313

351

Causality in Economics (Hicks) 79, 82–3
centralisation *see* corporation, flexible
Challenge of Unemployment, The (OECD) 190
Chan-Lee, J. H. 188
choice
  individual and value 316–17
  labour supply and 46
Citroen, A. 249–50
Clark, J. 246
Clark, K. B. 43
classical economics
  and employment levels 15–18
  and wages 27–8, 30
coal-fired power stations 283
coalitions, distributional *see* distributional coalitions
Coats, A. W. 316
Collected Writings of John Maynard Keynes, The (ed. Moggridge) 89, 105, 305
Commons, J. R. 309, 313, 317
communities, studies of 310–12
compensation, unemployment 185–6
competition
  and employment 39–40, 41
  international: Fordism 237–8; intensified 217
competitiveness
  alternative energy strategies and 281–2
  flexible automation and 256–9
  pollution abatement and 277, 289
  productivity and 271–2
  wages and 197, 224, 225
computerised machine tools 253
computers 254
conflict, social 320
consumption
  and production 236
  real wage moderation and 225
  redistribution in favour of 134–5
continuous stock equlibrium 94–5
'Contact Costs and Administered Prices: An Economic Theory of Rigid Wages' (Klein) 58
contract theories 56–60, 66, 67–8
  see also contracts, labour
contracts, labour 54–5, 56–60, 63–4
conventionality, theory of 93
co-ordination, international
  and reflation 221–2
  and unemployment 201
Coriat, B. 235, 237, 254

corporation, flexible 212–32
costs
  of employment programmes 173–4
  of labour and mark-ups 13–14
Cox, J. G. 271
creative destruction of the environment 273–4
crises
  Fordism and 236–8, 240–1, 243
  regulation approach and 194–5
crowding out 121–8, 187–9
crucialness 80–3
culture 299–300
  and economics 305–12
  see also institutions
currencies
  competition between 136
  volatility of 77–8
customised goods 253
Cuvier, *Baron* G. 302
cyclical unemployment 57–8, 61, 62–3

Darwin, C. 301, 309
Davidson, P. 79, 105, 344
decentralisation 212, 222–3
de-certification 227
decisions 80–3, 84, 94, 100, 101
deficits, budget 111, 115, 116, 118–20, 121–8, 129
deflationary policies 219–20
Delorme, R. 191, 195, 199, 200, 348
  public spending 182 *figs*, 183
demand
  aggregate: and employment 215; wage restraint and 196, 198
  effective: chronic deficiency of 348; employment and 16–17
  fiscal 138–9
  productivity and 236, 239
  supply and: goods markets 51–2; labour 27–47
  Swedish labour market and 152
demand management 103–4, 116
demand-oriented manpower measures 149, 151–2, 158, 166, 167
demand-outlay curve 30–1
democracy 301, 304
Denison, E. F. 338
de-unionisation 227
dialectics 300–4, 311–12, 327–30
disabled workers 149, 155, 157
  see also sheltered work
discipline and unemployment 68
disequilibrium theory 45–6, 193–4, 245

dissynchronisation of the Welfare
     State   209–11
distributional coalitions   227–32
   see also unions
dollar exchange rates   77–8
Dorfman, J. et al.   316
Dornbusch, R.   137
Dosi, G.   243, 250
Drèze, J.   197
'dropping out'   285–6
dualism
   economy   286–7, 291
   labour market   58, 68
Duijn, J. J. Van   246
duration of unemployment, Sweden   154

early retirement   167
Economic Doctrines of Karl Marx, The
     (Kautsky)   306
'Economic History and Economics'
     (Solow)   83
Economic Outlook (OECD)   126 fig
economic policies
   and flexibility   197–9
   and manpower policy in
     Sweden   143–4
   and the Welfare State   199–201
   see also fiscal policies; monetary
     policies
economic styles   285–7
Economic Survey of Sweden
     (OECD)   163–4
economic systems and technological
     change   249–51
'Economics' (Knight)   314
Economist, The   77–8
Economists at Bay (Lekachman)   315
Edgeworth, F. Y.   306, 307
education   190
EFA   155, 156, 157
effective demand see demand
efficiency and employment   240–3
efficiency wage model   49, 60–3, 64, 68
'Efficiency Wage Models of
     Unemployment' (Yellen)   61, 63
efficient market theory   76–7, 79
   see also rational expectations
effort and wages   61–2, 68
élite, social   319–20
Elster, J.   336
employment
   classical analysis and   15–18
   environmental policies and   277–83,
     288–90

equilibrium level of   33
full: capitalism and   104; definition
     of   39; difficulty of regaining   63;
     Kalecki's three ways to   115–17;
     Rehn/Meidner model and   163;
     Smith and   51, 55–6; Swedish
     goal   143–4, 154–5
growth and   124–7
new technologies and   238, 240–8
relationship with wages see wages
shift from private to public   187
Welfare State and   178–9, 181 figs,
     209–10
Employment Outlook (OECD)   45, 126
     fig, 185, 186
employment policies   117–30
   see also manpower policies
'Employment Promotion Law'   169
employment programmes   173, 291–2
employment services   157–8, 171
employment subsidies see subsidies
energy
   alternative strategies and   280–3
   industrialisation and supplies of   274
Engels, F.   309, 310
English Works, The (Hobbes)   298
entrepreneurs   349
environmental policies see environmental
     problems
environmental problems   139, 273–94,
     348
Epistemics and Economics
     (Shackle)   75–6, 80
equilibrium
   classical analysis and   16
   continuous stock   94–5
   theory of general   25, 26
'Equilibrium Unemployment as a
     Worker Discipline Device' (Shapiro
     and Stiglitz)   61
ergodicity   78–89, 99–100, 344
Eskilstuna, Sweden   157
*Essay on the Distribution of Wealth and
     on the Sources of Taxation: Part 1,
     Rent* (Jones)   316
Etat et l'économie, L' (Delorme and
     Andre)   191
Europe   214–6, 219–20, 346
   see also under names of individual
     countries
European Economy   182 fig, 197
Eurostat SESPROS   184 figs, 185 fig
evaluation studies of Swedish manpower
     programmes   155–8, 165

evolution 307–12, 314, 318–20, 336
'Evolution des finances publiques et sociales, Les Comparison internationale et interprétation' (André and Delorme) 182 *figs*, 183
exchange rate of dollar 77–8, 96–7
expectations *see* rational expectations
expenditure, public
  German on labour market policy 170
  on the environment 276
  Swedish on manpower programmes 148–9
  Welfare State and 180–4, 187–8
explanation and prediction 312–13, 328–30, 332–4, 336–7
exports
  and GDP growth 221
  see also trade

factor substitution 44–5
family allowances 189
Ferri, E. 309
finance
  and industry 74–6, 345
  of the Welfare State 182, 185 *fig*, 204
  see also financial markets
financial interplay of sectors 111–15
financial markets 3
  internationalisation of 213–4
  investment and employment 73–102
'Financial Markets and Macroeconomic Fluctuations' (Shiller) 77
fiscal policies
  and fear of inflation 137–9
  and growth 123–4, 129
  in a worldwide monetary economy 135–7
  Keynes and 105, 106–7
  see also economic policies; monetary policies
Fisher, I. 317
fixed wages 25, 58–9, 66
flexible automation 253–9
flexible corporation 212–32
flexible specialisation 271
flexibility and wage restraint 196–9
flow of funds analysis 111–15
Fordism 195, 199–200
  breakdown 235–9, 253, 259
foreign sector as borrower 112–13, 114
forests, tropical 275
Forrester, J. W. 246
Fox, A. 229, 230
France 120

free markets, prohibited 317–18
'free-riders' 121, 129
Freeman, C. 244, 246
Friedman, M. 228
full employment *see* employment
fully liquid assets 73–4
fundamental equation, Harrod's 109–10
funding 74–5
  see also finance
future
  determination of 78–80, 81–2, 89, 100
  securing 291

Galton, *Sir* F. 316
Garbarino, J. W. 231
GDP growth rate and unemployment 221–2
Gelpi, R. M. 236
general equilibrium theory 25, 26
General Theory of Employment, Interest and Money (Keynes)
  fiscal policy 107, 109
  involuntary unemployment 50, 67
  monetary policy 105, 106
  practical men 297
  rational expectations and 76, 80, 82, 85, 89
  sub-normal activity 48–9
  transitory episode 315
  wages 27–8, 34, 37, 39
geochemical cycles 274–5
Germany, Federal Republic of
  anachronistic laws 207
  environmental policy 279, 293
  fiscal and monetary policies 121, 123, 125, 136, 138–9
  flexible corporation 213
  labour market policy 169–71
  reducing inflation 219–20
  vocational training 232
Giersch, H. 292
Goldschmidt, R. 314
Gordon, R. J. 43
Gossen, H. H. 307
governments
  and coordinated reflation 221–2
  and environmental policies 276
  as employers 180, 181 *figs*
  debts and interest payments 118–20
  see also intervention
Great Britain *see* United Kingdom
growth
  and employment 124–7
  and labour market policy 172–3

Index

and productivity 240–1
slow in Western Europe 219–20
warranted rate of 109–10
Grubb, D. et al. 291
Guger, A. 344

Hahn, F. 16, 25
Hamermesh, D. S. 45
Hansen, A. 108, 109
Harrod, R. 109–10
Hart, O. D. 24, 59–60
Haxthausen-Abbenhausen, A. von 310
Hayek, F. von 228, 315
health insurance 206
Hempel, C. G. 313
Hicks, J. R. 79, 82–3
historicism 301, 339
history 337
Hobbes, T. 297–8, 305
Hödl, E. 278, 280
Holmstrom, B. 60
Homan, P. T. 309–10
hours worked
 and productivity changes 269
 Sweden and 159, 167
households
 savings 111–15, 135, 345–6, 348
 Welfare State and 206, 207
housing 189
Howitt, P. 63
Howson, S. 105
Hull, C. 172
human action *see* man
Hutchinson, F. 305
HWWA 121

illiquid assets 74
implicit contract theory
 see contract theories
'Implicit Contracts and Unemployment
 Equilibria' (Azariadis) 57, 58
income redistribution 116–17, 130, 134–5
increasing returns
 and real wages 38
 law of 235–6, 237, 240, 256–9
industrial development, active policy
 for 159, 171–2
industrial relations 212–32, 349–50
industrialisation and environmental
 problems 274–7
inflation
 employment policies and 117–18
 fiscal policies and fear of 137–9

Rehn/Meidner model and 144, 167
'informal' sector *see* dualism
information approach to labour market
 theory 48–69
Ingram, J. K. 307
innovations
 Schumpeter and 313–14
 see also process innovation ; product
 innovation; technology
*Inquiry into the Nature and Causes of the
 Wealth of Nations, An* (Smith) 51,
 55–6, 67, 305
Instinct of Workmanship, The
 (Veblen) 308
'Institutional School, The'
 (Homan) 309
Institutionalism of social
 expenditure 195
institutions
 centralised and
 unemployment 214–15, 222
 cultural 297–339
 employment programmes 173–4
 social integration 228–30
 technological change and 248–51, 256, 259
insurance, unemployment 205–6
 see also insurance contracts
insurance contracts 57–8, 59–60
integration, social 228–30
intensification of the employment
 service 157–8
interpendence, economic 130, 219–20
interest payments for government
 debt 118–20, 123–4
interest rates
 and investment 344–5
 Keynes and 105–6, 118
 Monetary Authority and 87–8
internal logic of cultural
 institutions 316, 330–3
*International Encyclopedia of the Social
 Science* 307
internationalisation of economics 130, 213–14, 345
intersection of disciplines 4–5
 and real-world situations 332–5
 and unemployment 48, 69
intervention by government
 economic liberty 228
 financial markets 87–8, 98–9, 101–2
 investment 106–7
 new technology 250–1
 see also governments

inventory substitution 44–5
investment
 crowding-out 121–8
 finance, funding and 74–5
 in evironmental policies 278–83, 284, 292–4
 interest rates and 344–5
 Keynes and post-war 106–7, 108–9
 stimulation of private 115–16, 129
invisible hand 55–6
involuntary overemployment 59, 68
involuntary unemployment see unemployment
Italy 254

Japan 217, 240, 289
Jefferson, T. 228
Jevons, W. S. 315–16
jobs
 Welfare State and 177–201
 see also public relief work
'Jobs for everybody' (Swedish government employment commission) 154
Johannesson, J. 170
Johnson, W. R. 58–9
Jones, R. 306–8

Kaldor, N. 117
Kaldor-Verdoorn law 240
Kalecki, M.
 as classicist 343–4
 full employment 104, 115–17
 innovation 348–9
 political business cycle 118
Kapp, K. W. 275
Kato, H. 188
Kautsky, K. 306
Kessler, D. 185
Keynes, J. M.
 crowding out 121
 economics 297, 305
 fiscal and monetary policy 104, 105–7, 116, 344
 inflation 117
 interest rates 76, 118
 labour supply and demand 27–9, 34–40 passim
 marginalism 11, 18–19
 post-war development 108–15, 346, 347
 psychological view of financial markets 76, 77, 78, 93
 rational expectations and 80, 82, 89
 short-run 52, 85
 subnormal activity 48–9
 technological change 16–17
 unemployment 50, 53–4, 67
 visionary 315
 wages 66, 137
 see also Keynesianism
Keynesianism
 and balance of payments 120
 and corporatism 213
 and expectations 93
 and unemployment 17–18
 post-war adoption of 103, 134
 see also Austro-Keynesianism; Keynes
Kirkpatrick, G. 291
Klamer, A. 99
Klein, B. 58
Klein, R. 190
Klippstein, M. V. 285
Kluckhohn, C. 299
Knight, F. 314
Kondratieff's long waves 246, 270
Kregel, J. A. 107, 135, 343
Kriegbaum, H. 271
Kroeber, A. L. 299
Krupp, S. R. 316

labour
 co-operation with capital 229–30
 demand and real wages 133–4
 disequilibrium and 193
 mobility of see mobility
 theory of demand and supply 27–47
 unemployment and 17, 220–1
 Welfare State and 185–92
 see also labour market
labour market
 aggregate analysis 34–6, 45–6
 free and trade unions 228
 government intervention in 3–4
 information approach 48–69
 New Classical Economics and 43
 Swedish policy see manpower policies
 Welfare State and 209–10
Labour Market Board
 expenditure 148 fig, 149
 manpower programmes 150, 151 fig, 155, 157, 158
 projected change 159
 Swedish Labour Force 153
 unemployed 146 fig, 147 fig
'labour standard', Keynes' 39
Lambert, J. P. et al. 198
Lapouge, G. V. de 310

Layard, R. 133
layoffs 57–8, 59–60
Le Cacheux, J. 198
Legal Foundations of Capitalism, The (Commons) 313
Leijonhufvud, A. 105
Leipert, C. 284
leisure 59
Lekachman, R. 315
lending, flow of funds analysis 111–15
Lerner, A. 118
Leviathan (Hobbes) 297
liquid assets 74, 85–7
liquidity 73–4, 75–6, 83–4, 88
Literary Remains Consisting of Lectures and Tracts on Political Economy (Jones) 306, 307
locomotive roles 120–1, 222
long-term planning, Keynes and 107
'Long-term Problem of Full Employment, The' (Keynes) 108
long-term unemployment *see* unemployment
low trust 229–30
Lucas, R. E. 81, 83, 90

machine tools, computerised 253
Maddison, A. 178
Malcolmson, J. 62
malfunctioning of the Welfare State 191–2
Malinvaud, E. 193, 291
Malthus, T. 306
man as an economic agent 298, 305–6, 308, 317–19, 330
manpower policies, Swedish 143–74
marginalism 10–11, 12, 15–16, 18–19, 25
mark-up and quantity produced 13–14
market, study of the 305–6, 327
  see also financial markets; labour market
market-clearing 24, 25, 192–3
market makers 73, 74, 86–7
Markov processes 99–100
Marshall, A. 80, 314, 315, 317
Marx, K.
  and Jones 308
  income and expenditure 52
  modes of production 306, 307, 312
  Ricardo's reasoning 317
  socialism 309
  visionary 315

material factors, institutional and 297–339
mathematics in economics 315–18
Matthews, R. C. O. 116
maturity theorem, Steindl's 109, 110
Matzner, E. 115, 313
Maurice, M. 190
Meidner, R. 162, 350
  see also Rehn/Meidner model
Meissner, W. 278, 280
Mensch, G. *et al.* 246, 270
Merton, R. K. 297
Meyer-Abich, K. M. 280, 285
Michl, T. 240
mineral resources 274
Minsky, H. 105
misery index, Okun 216, 218
Mistral, J. 250
Mitchell, W. C. 309
Miyazaki, H. 62
mobility of labour
  decreasing 152, 154
  grants 149, 150, 156, 158, 159
models from visions 338–9
Modigliani, F. 13, 197
Moggridge, D. E. 105
Monetary Authority 87–8, 98
monetary policies
  and crowding out 188–9
  Keynes and 105–6
  restrictive: and budget deficits 122, 129; and inflation 104, 117–18; and interest payments 119–20, 130
  see also economic policies; fiscal policies
money, neutrality of 90–1
Money and Inflation (Hahn) 16
money wages 19, 27–9, 33–4, 37–8, 39–40
  see also real wages; wages
monopolistic factors and unemployment 24
Montesquieu, *Baron* C. de 315
Monthly Labour Review 240
Mooslechner, P. 111
Moral Philosophers 305
Morgan, L. H. 310
Myrdal, G. 316, 343

National Central Bureau of Statistics 146 *fig*, 147 *fig*, 150, 153
Neary, J. P. 63
Nelson, R. 244, 336
neo-classicism 244–5, 338

neo-Ricardian theory 25, 26
Netherlands, The 40, 289, 290
New Classical Economics 43
new classical macroeconomics 99
new issue segment of financial
    market 74–5
Newell, A. 133
NIC's (newly industrialised
    countries) 217
Nixon, R. 297
non-ergodic systems *see* ergodicity
novelty 313–14
Nowotny, E. 111
nuclear energy 280–2

OECD
    financial balances by sectors 112–13
    governments: budgets 119, 122 *fig*,
        123 *fig*, 124 *fig*; employment 125 *fig*;
        investment 128 *fig*; public
        expenditure 182 *fig*, 184 *fig*, 185,
        186, 188
    Phillips curve 163–4
    real wages 45, 126
    savings ratios 114 *fig*
oil, substitution of 280–2
Okun misery index 216, 218
oligopoly theories 13–15
Olson, M. 227–8
Oppenheim, P. 313
order, social 229–31
Organisation for Economic Co-operation
    and Development *see* OECD
Origin of Species, The (Darwin) 301
*Origin of the Family, Private Property
    and the State in the Light of the
    Researches of Lewis H. Morgan*
    (Engels) 310
Orsenigo, L. 243, 250
output *see* production
overemployment, involuntary 59, 68
Owen, R. 306

Padoa-Schioppa, T. 13
Painlevé, P. 313
Pareto, V. 317
partial equilibrium 30
partial theories and interactions 332–3
pensions, old age 185, 205
Perez, C. 249, 250
performances, economic
    distributional coalitions and 228–9
    US and Western Europe 218–20

Petit, P. 234, 241
    productivity 243 *fig*, 244, 245, 255
Phillips curve 144, 163–4
Physiocrats 305
Piore, M. 236, 254, 271
Place du Désordre, La (Boudon) 336
*Place of Science in the Modern
    Civilization, The* (Vebeln) 308–9,
    318
'Political aspects of full employment'
    (Kalecki) 104
pollution *see* environmental problems
Popper, K. R. 301
post-war development
    employment 116–17
    Keynes vision 108–15, 346, 347
    see also Fordism
Poverty of Historicism, The
    (Popper) 301
Poverty of Philosophy, The (Marx) 307,
    312
power stations *see* energy
prediction and explanation 312–13,
    328–30, 332–4, 336–7
preventive environment policies 292–3
prices
    and capital 12
    and quantities 343–4
    and wage-employment
        relationship 13–15
    financial markets and 76–8, 84–7
    new technology and 251–2
*Primitive Culture: Research into the
    Development of Mythology,
    Philosophy, Religion, Art and
    Custom* (Taylor) 299
Principles of Economics (Marshall) 80
process innovations 245–6, 248, 260
product innovations 245–6, 260
product markets 213, 214
production
    and capacity utilisation 17–18
    and consumption 236
    and mark-ups 13–14
    and new technology 244–5
    and productivity 269–70, 271–2
    and real wages 37
    see also productivity
*Production of Commodities by Means of
    Commodities* (Sraffa) 11
production oriented services 172
productive coalitions 230
productive decentralisation 254

productivity
    Fordism: demand and   236, 239;
        employment and   240–1, 243,
        244–5; slowdown   237
    flexible automation and   256–9
    growth and corporatism   217, 218
    in the Welfare State   191
    production and   269–70, 271–2
    wage indexed with   252, 261–5
    see also production
profit sharing   134–5, 225
profit squeezes   238
profitability   193–4
Programm für Zukunfts-investitionen *see*
    ZIP
psychological view, Keynes' and financial
    markets   76, 77, 78, 93
public expenditure *see* expenditure
public relief work   150, 156, 165–6,
    171–2, 173
public sector, borrowing   112–13, 114

qualification and voluntary
    unemployment   50–1
qualitative changes and
    employment   288–9
quantities and prices   343–4

radical changes, new technologies
    and   247
Ralle, P.   240, 241, 243 *fig*
Ranke, L. von   337
rational expectations (ratex)   76–9, 81–4,
    88–90, 93–5
*Rational Expectations and Econometric
    Practice* (Lucas and Sargent)   81,
    83
real wages
    aggregate analysis and   34, 36–7
    and classical unemployment   137–8
    and employment   13–15, 27, 28–9,
        124–6, 133–4
    moderation   221, 224–5
    see also money wages; wages
real-world phenomena   328–9, 332–4
recession, world   216–17
reflation and GPD growth   221–2
régulation theory   194–6, 200–1, 339
regulations
    environmental policies and   227–8
    Welfare State   192, 207
Rehn, G.   162
    see also Rehn/Meidner model

Rehn/Meidner model   144–74, 334–5
Rein, M.   191
Reissert, B.   174
relief work *see* public relief work
re-switching phenomenon   24–5
Research Program for 1985–89
    (IIM/LMP)   9
retirement, early   167
returns
    fiscal and employment
        programmes   173
    increasing *see* increasing returns
    no new law of   241
'Review of E. Ferri, *Socialisme et Science
    Positive*' (Veblen)   309
Ricardo, D.   305, 306, 317
rigid wages *see* fixed wages
*Rise and Decline of Nations, The:
    Economic Growth, Stagflation and
    Social Rigidities* (Olson)   228
risk   55–6
risk-shifting   57–8, 59–60
Robbins, *Lord* (Lionel)   199
Robinson, J.   104
robot decision makers   83–4
roles, division within society   319
Roll, *Sir* E.   307
Roncaglia, A.   343, 347
Rueff, Jacques   199
Ruskin, J.   316

Sabel, C.   236, 254, 271, 348
Sachs, J. D.   133, 136, 291
Sachverständigenrat für
    Umweltfragen   276
Salvati, M.   332, 345
Samuelson, P. A.   80–1
Sargent, T. J.   81, 83, 90
Sargent supply equation   43
savings, household *see* households
Say's Law of Markets   51
Scharpf, F.   172
Schefold, B.   280, 285, 348
Schettkat, R.   173
Schmid, G.   170, 171, 172, 174
Schmitter, Ph. C.   227, 230
Schultze, C.   63
Schumpeter, J.   297, 305, 307, 315, 316
    innovations   247, 313–14
Schweitzer, S.   249
science
    economics as dangerous   297–9

Science–*continued*
 natural: arithmomorphism 300, 302; ergodicity 79; explanation and prediction 313, 328–30, 336–7
 see also social sciences
Science and Technology studies 246
Science of Culture, The: A Study of Man and Civilization (White) 312
selectivity in the Welfare State 211
Sellier, F. 190, 247
Semlinger, K. 171
Shackle, G. L. S. 75–6, 79, 80
Shapiro, C. 61
sheltered work 150, 157, 159
 see also disabled workers
Shiller, R. J. 77, 85–6
shirking 61–2, 63
shocks, external and corporatism 216–17
sickness benefits 186
Sieferle, R. P. 275
Silicon Valley 250, 255
Simon, H. 336
Simonis, U. E. 284
skills and training 225–6, 232
Smith, A. 64, 315
 and labour market 51–3, 54, 55–6, 66–7
 markets and growth 271
 study of market 305
Sneesens, H. 198
Social Democratic Party, Swedish 143, 144
'Social Efficiency of Fixed Wages, The' (Johnson) 58–9
Social Expenditure 1960–90. Problems of Growth and Control (OECD) 184 *fig*, 191
social order 229–31
social organisation and new technology 247–51, 260
social sciences
 arithmomorphism and dialectics 302, 304
 explanation and prediction 329–30, 332, 336
social security
 benefits *see* benefits
 contributions 169, 185 *fig*
social services as employers 190–1
social values and environmental policies 285
socialism 309

society
 and long-term unemployment 64
 evolution of 307–12, 318–20
Soete, L. 246
solar energy 281–2
solidaristic wage policy 146, 154, 165, 170
Solow, R. M. 83
Soltwedel, R. 170
Sombart, W. 275
Sorge, A. 270
Soskice, D. 338, 249
specialisation of machines 235, 271
species
 dialectical concept 301
 loss of biological 275
speculative markets 75–8, 83–91, 94–9, 101–2
speculative motive, Keynesian 54
'Speech at the Graveside of Karl Marx' (Engels) 309
Spencer, H. 309
spontaneous institutions 314–15, 331
spot financial markets 76ff
Sprenger, R. G. 279
Sraffa, P. 11–13, 15–17, 19, 24–5
stabilisation, Rehn/Meidner model and 144–5
stabilisers, automatic 121–2
stagnation 109–11, 139
state intervention *see* intervention
'State of Exchange Rate Theory, The Some Skeptical Observations' (Tobin) 95
Steindl, J.
 budget deficits 121–2
 flow of funds analysis 111, 114
 industrial policy 116
 maturity theorem 109, 110
 profit sharing 135
step function for unemployment 49–50
Stiglitz, J. E. 43, 44, 61, 63
Streeck, W. 227, 230
Streissler, R. 137, 344
Structure of Economic Science, The (ed. Krupp) 316
Strümpel, B. 285
subsidies
 environmental policies and 277
 wage 150, 157, 159, 172–3
sulphur dioxide 274
Summers, L. H. 43

supply
  and demand: in goods markets 51–2;
    of labour 27–47
  supposed and effective 138
supply-oriented manpower
  measures 149, 151–2, 158, 159–60,
  166–7
supply-side adjustment and industrial
  relations 221, 222, 223–6
Sweden 143–74, 334–5
Switzerland 127
Sylvestre, J. J. 190, 247
Symons, J. 133
Szpiro, D. 198

Tannenbaum, F. 230
taxation
  and pollution 284
  and the Welfare State 186–7, 204–5
Taylor, E. B. 299
Taylorism in the French car
  industry 249–50
technology
  alternative 280–3
  and product markets 214
  and the environment 275
  new and unemployment 16–17, 19,
  217, 233–72
  unions and 226
technology policies 348–9
Ten Great Economists (Schumpeter) 315
theories from visions 338
Theory of Economic Development, The
  (Schumpeter) 314
Theory of Economic History, A
  (Hicks) 338
Theory of Surplus Value (Marx) 308
Theory of the Leisure Class, The
  (Veblen) 308
time 78ff
Tobin, J. 95
trade, international 39–40, 120–1, 195,
  219
training
  centralisation and 225–6, 232
  labour market 150, 155–6, 158, 159
transaction costs 55
'Transaction Costs in the Theory of
  Unemployment' (Howitt) 63
Treatise on Money (Keynes) 27
trust, low 229–30
truth 297–8

uncertainty
  Keynes' and 80, 347–8
  volatility and 95–6
Uncertainty in Economics (Shackle) 80
unemployment
  economic policy and 117–18, 127–8
  industry relations and 212–32
  involuntary 50–1
  Keynesian and classical 17–18, 347
  long-term: difficulty of
    explaining 48–69; rational
    expectations and 89–91; Welfare
    State and 178–80; 185–6, 205–6,
    211
  registered in Sweden 146–8, 154
  temporary 43, 206
  voluntary 89–90
  youth 156, 159, 179–80
'Unionism without unions: The New
  Industrial Relations'
  (Garbarino) 231
unions, trade
  centralised: policies needed 224–6;
    and unemployment 222
  importance of 227, 229–31
  need to study 350
  Swedish (LO) 143, 144, 149
  see also distributional coalitions
United Kingdom 125, 169, 212, 219–20
United Nations Economic Commission
  for Europe 346
United States of America
  and capital flows 345
  and deficits 120, 136–7
  economic performance 218–19, 220
  environmental protection 293
  productivity slowdown 240
utilisation of capacity *see* capacity
UWIP programme 278

value and choice 316–17
variability and volatility 98
Veblen, T. 308–9, 315, 318, 320
Verdoorn's Law 269–70
  see also Kaldor-Verdoorn law
Vienna Circle 300–1
visions and theories 337–8
volatility of spot prices 77–8, 95–8
voluntary unemployment *see*
  unemployment

Wadensjö, E. 174

wages
  concentrated union power and 350
  fixed 25, 58–9, 66
  productivity and 238, 252, 261–5
  relationship with employment:
    classical 27–8, 30; Keynes
    and 30, 39–40; Sraffian
    view 9–26
  restrictive policies and 129–30, 196–9
  subsidies for *see* subsidies
  temporary jobs and 54–5
  see also efficiency wage model; money
    wages; real wages
'Wages and Employment under
  Uncertain Demand' (Baily) 56–7
Walrasian model 26
Walrasian spot markets 49
Walterskirchen, E. 111, 344
warranted rate of growth 109–10
waste
  avoidance of 51–2, 54
  industrial 274–5
Weber, M. 309
Weintraub, S. 29, 30–1
Weisskopf, T. 237
Weitzman, M. L. 24, 259

Welfare State 177–211
Wharton Econometrics 198
'What Classical and Neoclassical
  Monetary Theory Really Was'
  (Samuelson) 80–1
Whewell, W. 307
White, L. A. 310, 312
Wicke, L. 276, 279 *fig*
WIFO 112–13, 119 *fig*
William II, German Emperor 207
Wilson, T. 178
Winter, S. 244, 336
work
  change in perception of 285–6
  practices and unions 226
Work without Environmental Destruction
  (Binswanger *et al.*) 284
working age population 179 *fig*
Works and Correspondence (Ricardo, ed.
  Sraffa) 15

Yellen, J. L. 61, 63
youth unemployment *see* unemployment

Zimmermann, K. 291, 292, 293
ZIP programme 278